New Zealand
Filmmakers

CONTEMPORARY APPROACHES TO FILM AND TELEVISION SERIES

*A complete listing of the books in this series
can be found online at wsupress.wayne.edu*

General Editor
Barry Keith Grant
Brock University

Advisory Editors
Patricia B. Erens
School of the Art Institute of Chicago

Lucy Fischer
University of Pittsburgh

Peter Lehman
Arizona State University

Caren J. Deming
University of Arizona

Robert J. Burgoyne
Wayne State University

Tom Gunning
University of Chicago

Anna McCarthy
New York University

Peter X. Feng
University of Delaware

Lisa Parks
University of California–Santa Barbara

Jeffrey Sconce
Northwestern University

New Zealand
Filmmakers

EDITED BY Ian Conrich and Stuart Murray

WAYNE STATE UNIVERSITY PRESS   DETROIT

© 2007 by Wayne State University Press, Detroit, Michigan 48201. All rights reserved. No part of this book may be reproduced without formal permission.

11 10 09 08 07   5 4 3 2 1

Library of Congress Cataloging-in-Publication Data

New Zealand filmmakers / edited by Ian Conrich and Stuart Murray ; with a foreword by Terence Bayler.
  p. cm. — (Contemporary approaches to film and television series)
  Includes bibliographical references and index.
  ISBN-13: 978-0-8143-3017-3 (pbk. : alk. paper)
  ISBN-10: 0-8143-3017-7 (pbk. : alk. paper)
  1. Motion pictures—New Zealand. I. Conrich, Ian. II. Murray, Stuart, 1967–
  PN1993.5.N43N485 2007
  791.430993—dc22
                        2007003145

∞ The paper used in this publication meets the minimum requirements of the American National Standard for Information Sciences—Permanence of Paper for Printed Library Materials, ANSI Z39.48–1984.

Designed and typeset by Maya Rhodes
Composed in Adobe Caslon and Franklin Gothic

Contents

Foreword ix
Acknowledgments xi
Note on the Filmographies xiii

Introduction 1
   Stuart Murray and Ian Conrich

Part 1. Pioneers 15

1. Free Radical: The Life and Work of Len Lye 18
   Roger Horrocks

2. A Rough Island Story: The Film Life of Rudall Charles Hayward 35
   Sam Edwards and Stuart Murray

3. John O'Shea: A Poetics of Documentary 54
   Laurence Simmons

4. Between the Personal and the Political: Feminist Fables in the Films of Gaylene Preston 72
   Estella Tincknell

5. Images of Dignity: The Films of Barry Barclay 88
   Stuart Murray

6. Lives of Their Own: Films by Merata Mita 103
   Geraldene Peters

7. *Ricordi!* Peter Wells, Memories of a Queer Land 121
   David Gerstner

Part 2. The New Wave 135

8. Between the National and the International: The Films of Roger Donaldson 138
   James Chapman

9. Embodying the Commercial: Genre and Cultural Affect in the Films of Geoff Murphy 152
   Jonathan Rayner

10. "Kiwi as . . .": Ian Mune and Filmmaking as Cultural Expression 169
    Stan Jones

11. The Man Alone: Bruno Lawrence's Screen Performances of the Kiwi Bloke 185
    Andrew Spicer

12. Working in Close-Up: Jennifer Ward-Lealand, Performance, and Collaborative Film Production 201
    Barbara Cairns

13. Crisis and Conflict: The Films of John Laing 217
    Ian Conrich

14. "Carry Me Back": Time and Place in the Films of John Reid 236
    Bruce Babington

Part 3. Visionaries and Fantasists 253

15. Leon Narbey: Art, Politics, and the Personal 256
    Helen Martin

16. Making Strange: Journeys through the Unfamiliar in the Films of Vincent Ward 273
    Stephanie Rains

17. Dislocations of Home and Gender in the Films of Jane Campion 289
    Eva Rueschmann

18. Experiments with Desire: The Psychodynamics of
    Alison Maclean   304
       Kirsten Moana Thompson

19. Bringing It All Back Home: The Films of Peter Jackson   320
       Barry Keith Grant

20. The Nightmare within the Everyday: The Horrific Visions
    of David Blyth   336
       Stacey Abbott

    Contributors   349
    Index   355

Foreword

Now that New Zealand's unique contribution to cinema is universally recognized, I'm pleased to have the opportunity to record an early example of its international reception. It was a matinee in 1952 at the Ionic Cinema, Golders Green, London, and the film was *Broken Barrier*, made by John O'Shea and Roger Mirams. Having been refused a student concession at the box office, I persisted: "Actually—I'm in this film—that's me on the poster with Katy Ngarimu—I know it says Kay there but . . ." This was getting sad, so I paid full price for my first viewing of the film, nervously aware of what John was later to describe in his book *Don't Let It Get You* as "the weight of our own inexperience" when making it. Roger, with his wide experience as a news and documentary cameraman, was quick to see the potential of anything we happened upon—even an unusually tame bird—but he had never worked on a feature film. John's directing experience was confined to amateur theater; his passion was studying and writing about film. On location he was as shrewd as Roger. An elderly Maori woman asked me what our film was about. "A Maori and Pakeha love story," I told her. She smiled, "Ah, and you're the Maori boy." It seemed my coloring could confuse audiences, so I put this to John. Hand-rolled cigarette dangling from his lip, head thrown back, eyes narrowed, he muttered, "His name was Sullivan—Tom Sullivan—an Irish name, and he had that sort of dark Irish look." That became part of the narration of the film: there being no budget for a sound crew, no dialogue was recorded. *Broken Barrier* was released in the same year as *Singin' in the Rain*—but we weren't even talkin'.

That was a good thing because none of us had any professional acting experience. Katy, beautiful and dignified throughout the filming, had never wanted to act and never did so again. We met again in 1996 when, to celebrate New Zealand's centenary of cinema, four postage stamps were issued. One of these featured Katy and me in *Broken Barrier*. In a television interview we gave at the launch, Katy revealed that she had been persuaded to appear in the film by her father, who rightly felt she would be a worthy representative of her people. Training as a teacher, Katy was free to film on the Mahia Peninsula during her summer holiday, and in

Wellington at weekends. Whoever was to play Tom had to be available at these and other locations too, and no amateur actor was prepared to leave his steady job. I was doing temporary jobs to raise my fare to go to Britain in some months' time to study drama. Asked to play Tom for six pounds a week plus food and tobacco, I agreed.

Our entire traveling cast and crew consisted of four people crammed into Roger's Vauxhall, which towed a trailer packed with equipment. Watching the film in London, I recognized almost every camera set-up, having been needed to carry gear, hold a reflector, or push a dolly when not in front of the camera. I admired the performances of people who had appeared in the film out of pure goodwill, especially friends on our main location, the idyllic Mahia Peninsula. But surely a London audience would prefer a subject closer to home—an Ealing comedy perhaps? The final credits rolled at the Ionic Cinema—there was a murmur from the audience—then applause. Applause at a midweek matinee on a wet day in London! I felt then there would be no worries about the future of New Zealand cinema.

New Zealand cinema is now applauded worldwide for its achievements and, in this book, it is the subject of wide-ranging critical analysis. The essays here describe an incredible progression from early New Zealand films to the blockbusters of the present. They outline industrial achievements, the workings of film form, and the effect that New Zealand cinema has as part of the country's culture. Taken together, the essays are a fitting tribute to all those who have worked in the industry.

TERENCE BAYLER

Acknowledgments

The editors would like to thank the contributors for their help with the completion of this collection: Andrea Wright, Charles Eggen and Rebecca Sawyer, Kim Baker at SPADA for her crucial support, Lindsay Shelton (who gave much valuable guidance), Kathleen Drumm, and the staff of the New Zealand Film Commission for their generosity in supplying many illustrations. We would also like to thank the staff at the New Zealand Film Archive, in particular Diane Pivac, Bronwyn Taylor, and Kristen Wineera. We thank the many featured filmmakers who were always available to answer queries and provide advice on completing their filmographies. Jane Hoehner and Annie Martin at Wayne State University Press were invaluable in their commitment to seeing this book through to publication. Lastly, we would like to thank The British Academy for its assistance with travel and research funding.

Note on the Filmographies

Each article in this collection is supported by a filmography, which covers the film and television career of the featured filmmaker and includes not just feature films, shorts, documentaries, dramas, and television series but also training films, and, where possible, music videos and commercials. These filmographies have been compiled by Ian Conrich and Stuart Murray following considerable research and advice, and in consultation with the majority of the featured filmmakers. This has resulted in each filmography being the most comprehensive ever published or available from a single source.

The aim of the filmographies is to provide a detailed yet clear guide to a filmmaker's career, recording productions in strict date order. Significant productions have been emphasized in bold, other information simplified. For instance, the camera operator, lighting cameraman, or director of photography has been standardized as "cinematographer." All filmmaker roles that have occurred in collaboration are prefixed with "co-"; fiction films of twenty minutes or less are listed as "short," while films of between twenty and fifty-five minutes in length are listed as an "extended short." A production receiving both film distribution and television broadcast has been listed as "film/television," and the titles of specific television episodes have been recorded where known. We realize that in compiling such ambitious filmographies there will be a few gaps and errors and these will be addressed in future editions of this collection. Gaining all the required information has not been easy and for a filmmaker such as Rudall Hayward, the filmography is intended as an initial record.

Introduction

Stuart Murray and Ian Conrich

At the 2004 Academy Awards in Los Angeles, the moment at which Peter Jackson collected the Best Director award for his work on *The Lord of the Rings: The Return of the King* (2003) marked what might be seen to be a momentous occasion for filmmaking in New Zealand. Amid all the plaudits heaped on the film, and its record-breaking success both at the world's box offices and award ceremonies, it was the honoring of a New Zealand filmmaker that concluded proceedings. Jackson's achievement is considerable, but it is possibly even more remarkable that, some thirty years before the rewards gathered by the final installment of *The Lord of the Rings* trilogy, New Zealand barely had an industry that could sustain feature film production. A glance at the number of feature films made in New Zealand from the beginning of the twentieth century to the mid-1970s reveals a process of occasional activity, especially after the introduction of sound technology, with an average of fewer than five films made per decade in the period from 1915 to 1975. Since the latter date though, and especially with the initial support that came through the establishment of the New Zealand Film Commission (NZFC) in 1978, production has increased, with some 250 features being made since 1976.[1] In no small part, the success of the industry has been framed around the work of a number of individual filmmakers, like Jackson, whose commitment to their craft has been paralleled by a desire to express the complexities of the culture from which they come.

This collection of essays examines the role played by New Zealand's filmmakers in the development of cinema in relation to the country. We take "filmmakers" to mean not only directors but also those key figures whose talent and drive often animates film production, especially in a small industry, and particularly during its formative years. So the essays here discuss actors and figures whose work in photography, scripting, and production is as important to the films they make as their direction. Equally, though each essay title names an individual, and even as we are keen to discuss specific figures who may not be that well known outside

New Zealand, the essays in this volume often use individual filmmakers as a point of focus for the analysis of the wider forces that affect the industry within New Zealand, forces that are themselves both national and international. Given the size of New Zealand's film industry and its local market, there is always the temptation for the country's filmmakers to work abroad, and many of the figures discussed here—Roger Donaldson, Geoff Murphy, Vincent Ward, David Blyth, Jane Campion, Alison Maclean—have in different ways negotiated the move to filmmaking contexts beyond New Zealand. Even Jackson, for all his commitment to working in New Zealand, has necessarily had to develop a working relationship with the various power structures of Hollywood in order to produce his films. A "New Zealand Filmmaker" then is a figure for whom a sense of location may focus on the representation of the cultures of the national space, or include the kinds of international mobility inherent in the structures of the modern global film industry. In this sense, such a figure enacts the complex but often productive elements that characterize the position of New Zealand itself as a modern settler state, always negotiating the demands of the local and the international.

We have divided the collection into three sections—Pioneers, The New Wave, and Visionaries and Fantasists. These headings seemed to us to best suggest a broad organizational framework for the discussion of filmmakers in New Zealand. Those figures working in the early cinema of the nation were obviously pioneers and were often required to produce features under the most challenging of circumstances. But we also take the word pioneer to denote later initiatives, such as those that came with the development of Maori and women's filmmaking, or queer cinema, or those whose formal innovativeness challenged prevailing orthodoxies of what cinema in New Zealand might be. The second section of the collection focuses on the New Wave in New Zealand cinema, a period from 1977 to 1986 that saw the emergence of sustained government film funding and support, in terms of financial aid for script development, overall production and final distribution, and the rise to prominence of several key filmmakers who would shape the country's screen culture. Much of the discussion of the New Wave has been in explicitly national terms, as the fraught definition of the national space was a key motivator for many of the filmmakers seeking to put New Zealand on the screen. As with all other New Wave movements around the world, filmmakers in New Zealand had to work within the shadow of Hollywood as they searched for a cultural distinctiveness that was part of the project of establishing a national cinema.

Although the question of national legitimacy and validity is a vital one in any consideration of culture in New Zealand, it would be a mistake to think that a national nerve somehow controls all filmmakers in the country. Even as some figures sought to engage with the idea of a filmic national identity, others produced stories unconcerned with the idea of the public space. The third section of this collection, Visionaries and Fantasists, examines key filmmakers who explore personal visions or generic conventions. To some degree, filmmaking such as this has been made more possible in New Zealand by the success of the New Wave, allowing for a greater range of production, but it is also the case that the filmmakers themselves often drive such projects, and the careers of a number of the filmmakers discussed in this section overlap with production during the New Wave. Overall, the division of the collection into the three sections aims to help structure the reading of the book, without imposing a frame on the contents that is too rigid or over schematic.

Up to the 1970s and the development of institutional support, filmmakers and filmmaking in New Zealand operated within significant constraints. The silent era and transition to sound posed considerable technical challenges. Even as new technologies emerged from Hollywood and Europe, their complexity and cost often meant that local versions had to be invented to be affordable. The key figure during the pioneering efforts of the early period of New Zealand filmmaking is Rudall Hayward, whose work both laid the base and set standards for much of the production that was to follow. As the essay on Hayward by Sam Edwards and Stuart Murray demonstrates here, the technical achievements in his work were considerable, but Hayward's work was equally noteworthy for its commitment to the representation of New Zealand history and culture. In his early career, Hayward drew his inspiration from the United States, both in terms of the generic models he used for his films—historical melodramas, comedies, and narratives of racial and cultural relations—and also in that he saw New Zealand's nineteenth-century history of encounter and settlement as a source for filmic narratives in a manner similar to that used by Hollywood in its representation of American history. Hayward's feature films outline an attempt to portray the distinctiveness of a New Zealand society still in transition between the colonial and the national, with a particular concentration on associations between Pakeha (European) and Maori, and a stress upon the nature of the individual subject. Hayward's own career is notable for its productivity between 1920 and 1940, but even though his later work failed to make the impact that characterized this early phase, he was very much a center of energy in early filmmaking.

Another major pioneer during the early period of filmmaking was Len Lye. He was drawn to the kinetic arts of modernism in the early 1920s and traveled throughout Polynesia before leaving New Zealand for London in 1926, where he forged a career as an experimental and often radical filmmaker with works such as *Tusalava* (1929) and *A Colour Box* (1935). As Roger Horrocks discusses in his essay on Lye in this volume, Lye's rejection of the standard narratives of film involved the use of figurative and abstract symbols in complex evocations of myths and with extraordinary representations of movement and synchronized image and music presentation, achieved through directly drawing on the celluloid itself. His obvious modernism had clear sources in art movements in Europe in the first half of the twentieth century, and undoubtedly it was the internationalism of Lye's work that had a huge effect on visual artists in New Zealand. Yet, at the same time, and again as Horrocks notes, the direct nature of many of his films, and especially the mythic resonances in his work, can be attributed to a New Zealand and South Pacific context, and Lye remains part of a tradition of radicalism that sees the new spaces of the emerging nation not as sites of conservatism and mimicry but rather as opportunities for innovative forms and expressions.

In 1940 John Grierson, the leading figure in the British documentary movement, visited New Zealand at the invitation of the government. Asked to comment on official state filmmaking, Grierson's report led to the establishment of the National Film Unit (NFU) in 1941. For seven years, the NFU was the only production unit in New Zealand, up to the 1948 creation of Pacific Films by Roger Mirams and Alun Falconer. These two production houses became the training grounds for those filmmakers who worked through the 1950s and 1960s, and the tradition of documentary filmmaking in particular established during this period is vital in any understanding of New Zealand film production through the 1970s and even beyond. Important figures such as Barry Barclay, Gaylene Preston, and John Laing, who began their filmmaking careers with documentaries in the 1960s and 1970s, had initial associations with these production houses.

The central filmmaker during this period however, and the figure most associated with the output from Pacific Films, was John O'Shea. Other than a single documentary made by the NFU, O'Shea's *Broken Barrier* (1952), *Runaway* (1964), and *Don't Let It Get You* (1966) were the only features made in New Zealand in the thirty-one years between 1941 and 1972. As Laurence Simmons demonstrates in his essay, O'Shea's feature work developed out of his training as a documentary filmmaker and is animated by a complex documentary aesthetic. Within this, O'Shea's themes were varied: interracial relations in *Broken Barrier*, the nature of isolation and masculinity in *Runaway*, and emerging popular culture in *Don't Let It Get You*, then New Zealand's only musical. These are landmark films, but they were produced during a time when feature filmmaking was a rare occurrence in New Zealand, and the nation's landscape was more likely to be used as a backdrop by visiting filmmakers than a source of inspiration for local directors. O'Shea is especially important then as a figure who provided the thread of continuity from the immediate postwar era to the resurgence of filmmaking activity in the 1970s. His work as a producer continued on key features made by Pacific Films into the 1980s, marking him as a central figure in New Zealand filmmaking for over three decades.

Much of the work that constituted the pioneering period of film production within New Zealand was clearly concerned with the infrastructural details (financing, technical development, distribution, and exhibition) of getting a film made. But it is very much the case that these features were part of the development of a specifically visual idea of a national and cultural communal identity. The subject matters of Hayward's and O'Shea's narratives in particular took their place in the wider national story of New Zealand's cultural transitions in the twentieth century, anticipating the concerns that would come with the filmmaking of the New Wave from the 1970s onward. The ideas of environment, gender, and cultural relations in films such as Hayward's *My Lady of the Cave* (1922) and *The Te Kooti Trail* (1927) or O'Shea's *Broken Barrier* and *Runaway* are part of a search for an idea of nation and, especially for the Pakeha majority, legitimacy within the context of a history of postcolonial settlement.[2]

The methods by which such features outlined the ideas of cultural relations between Pakeha and Maori, or questioned the position of the isolated male, or of the relationship between community and landscape, all point to their place within the contested imagined space of New Zealand as it emerged in national form. Key to this sense of the national imaginary was the potentially illegitimate position of the Pakeha majority, as a dominant community with a short history of occupation and settlement, and one threatened especially by an indigenous presence. The films of the pioneering period of New Zealand filmmaking, even as they displayed technical innovation and explored generic conventions, returned frequently to such questions, often in order to attempt to preserve a notion of the happily "settled" community. For national audiences, the novelty of seeing the local culture up on the screen was accompanied by the fact that the narratives of place contained in many of the early features were those finding other forms in the culture and society at large. In this sense, there is an obvious transition between the pioneer period and the more obvious national consciousness that came later with the beginning of New Wave filmmaking.

There is no doubt that the 1970s was the pivotal decade in New Zealand filmmaking, a period in which key filmmakers such as Donaldson, Murphy, Blyth, and Ward emerged. At the start of the decade, the situation had not seemed especially propitious. Made in 1972, *To Love a Maori* was Rudall Hayward's last feature. A confused and confusing film, its poor reception marked a sad end to an illustrious career and brought to a close part of New Zealand's filmmaking history. With the concomitant rise in television production during the 1970s, the situation for feature film production might have looked bleak; yet, by 1980, the country was experiencing the initial fruits of a discernable new wave of filmmaking. The success of Murphy's *Wild Man* (1977) and Donaldson's *Sleeping Dogs* (1977) led in no small part to the 1978 establishment of the NZFC. The subsequent government-supported financial incentives for script development and production created a space for filmmaking that hitherto had not existed. Several of New Zealand's key filmmakers made their first major film in this period. Ward adapted Janet Frame's novel *A State of Siege* as a short in 1978, Blyth made *Angel Mine* also in 1978, John Reid directed *Middle Age Spread* in 1979, while Laing's *Beyond Reasonable Doubt* was released in 1980. The major popular breakthrough feature of the early New Wave—Murphy's *Goodbye Pork Pie*—was made in 1980. Its success with a national and international audience confirmed that sustainable feature filmmaking in New Zealand was possible and, as Jonathan Rayner stresses in his essay, Murphy's subsequent films in New Zealand, before he left for Hollywood, express ideas of national identity and landscape within features that have a strong commercial drive.

The terms of the NZFC's support for film production were that the films made with its help display "significant national content," and the filmmakers of the New Wave articulated national visions that explored the questions of individual and communal life in New Zealand, often with a concentration on key thematics such as geography, the nature of society, and the legacy of the pioneering male. Films such as Donaldson's *Smash Palace* (1981), Reid's *Carry Me Back* (1982), Laing's *Other Halves* (1984), and Ward's *Vigil* (1984) in their different ways outlined the seemingly fraught position of the New Zealand subject, desiring legitimacy but often constrained by family and community and left inarticulate in the face of a complex present. As the essays by Stephanie Rains on Ward, Ian Conrich on Laing, and James Chapman on Donaldson display, these filmmakers stressed narratives of alienation and discord in their 1980s work, with dysfunctional families threatened and frequently battling against the limitations imposed by social formations or the landscape. It is particularly instructive that this national context is true of Ward's work in *Vigil*, given his status as a visionary filmmaker working in a European art house tradition.

Extending this idea of the problematic subject, Bruce Babington's essay on Reid shows how, in *Middle Age Spread* and *Carry Me Back*, the centrality of the male protagonist outlined the emerging questions of the New Wave in terms that were peculiarly masculine. In this sense, New Zealand cinema's New Wave reflected an earlier literary nationalism, when during the 1930s and 1940s the concerns of putting the nation on the page equally assumed the normative nature of the male experience.[3] Filmmakers such as Reid, Laing, Murphy, and Donaldson, or Ian Mune, with their stress in certain films on the troubled male at odds with community and landscape, rehearsed the kind of settler narratives canonical in New Zealand's cultural history. If part of the project for such directors was to provide a cinematic "home in the world," they did so with images of geography, questions of location, and issues of gender that emphasized downbeat and understated unease. In particular, the focus on masculinity, and the idea of the male as the emblematic motif of New Zealand identity, is crucial here. The New Wave directors were part of a male-dominated industry, a significant part of which emerged from a counter-cultural movement that developed in the early to mid-1970s and brought to film a fixation with action and anti-authoritarian attitudes that were particularly male in their conception. For the most part, these figures constructed their sense of both narrative and community in a manner that worked to reinforce orthodoxies of masculinity. The male was still the central figure through which social and cultural stories were told, with the presumption that such centrality was a natural, rather than a constructed, position. The pioneering legacy of nineteenth-century history that established the relationship between man and environment as the crucial indicator of individual self-expression and communal worth here emerges in a new guise as part of the foundations of a specifically *national* film culture.[4]

At the same time however, it is important to see such issues of the national and the masculine in the films of the New Wave not as articulations of a realistic reflection on the questions posed by a consideration of place, but rather as the expressions of concerns particular to one sector of New Zealand's artistic and intellectual community. This is exactly how the New Wave might be seen to constitute a form of cinematic national imaginary, and one that is as provisional and contested as other forms of local cultural nationalisms. Mark Williams has written on contemporary New Zealand cinema that "the troubled and divided psyche of the nation is represented in a series of images radically at odds with the tourist vision of New Zealand as an idyllic retreat from the anxieties of modern life," and that such cinema "recasts in new images themes that have run through the literature from its beginnings. At its heart lies the disenchantment that is part of every colonizing experience, when the hopes of a new and better world at the end of the voyage confront the inevitable disappointments of the actual."[5] As with the producers of all other versions of the "actual" in New

Zealand culture, the filmmakers of the New Wave necessarily brought in limited and partial narratives when seeking its expression.

The opportunities offered following the establishment of the NZFC created other kinds of space for filmmaking than those centered on the supposed pre-eminence of the Pakeha male. Other filmmakers had different stories to tell, and in particular different ideas of culture to promote. In 1980 Merata Mita co-directed *Bastion Point Day 507*, a documentary detailing the land rights occupation of Takaparawha/Bastion Point by members of Ngati Whatua o Orakei (the Ngati Whatua tribe of Orakei, Auckland) and their supporters. As Geraldene Peters emphasizes in her essay, with a background informed by Mita's Te Arawa upbringing, an involvement in the Nga Tamatoa (warrior children) Maori activist group in the 1970s, and subsequent links to trade unions, her filmmaking emerges as one dominated by ideas of community. Such narratives as those in *Bastion Point Day 507*, and the later *Patu!* (1983)—Mita's documentary focused upon the opposition to the 1981 tour of New Zealand by the South African rugby team—are in contrast to the stress on the often isolated individual that characterizes Pakeha filmmakers of the same period.

Mita was, then, a different kind of pioneer in New Zealand filmmaking. In her emphasis on community and cultural politics, and in her recognition of the role documentary could play in the self-representation of indigenous people, her work was groundbreaking. Her peer in these processes was Barry Barclay, who had joined Pacific Films in the 1960s, and following his training there went on to make a number of hugely important documentaries in the 1970s before moving to direct feature films in the 1980s. Barclay, of Ngati Apa and European descent, and like Mita a figure politicized by his participation in Nga Tamatoa, directed the *Tangata Whenua* television series in 1974. The series, six documentaries presenting differing aspects of Maori culture, was the first major mass audience visual representation of the intricacies and complexities of Maoridom, and its impact on the nation at large was significant. As Stuart Murray shows in his essay, a number of the cultural and technical approaches to filming in indigenous communities that Barclay developed during *Tangata Whenua* became vital to his later feature filmmaking. *Ngati* (1987), Barclay's first fiction feature and the film generally credited with being the first such feature made anywhere by an indigenous filmmaker, revolves around issues of community and the right to self-determination. Barclay's later films, *Te Rua* (1991) and *The Feathers of Peace* (2000), are equally committed to notions of communal justice. With Mita, who herself moved to fiction filmmaking in the 1980s when she made *Mauri* (1988), Barclay forged a politics and aesthetics of indigenous cinema that produced a distinctive development within New Zealand filmmaking during this period. As texts in the wider debates surrounding national culture, the films of Barclay and Mita also clearly constituted a challenge to the dominant concerns of the white settler imagination. Their reminder of the force of indigenous presence brought a sharp sense of contestation to the images of the nation that the evolving film culture brought to the screen.[6]

If Maori filmmaking represented concerns that differed from the main preoccupations of many New Wave directors, then the same was true of others for whom narrative filmmaking offered opportunities for representation. Following *Angel Mine*, with its explicit focus on sexuality, Blyth explored Gothic and horror themes in *It's Lizzie to Those Close* (1983) and *Death Warmed Up* (1984) and, as Stacey Abbott reveals in her essay, continued to produce work that challenged the boundaries of the conventional and real. Peter Wells, a writer as well as a filmmaker, emerged in the 1980s with short films such as *Foolish Things* (1980) and *Little Queen* (1983). These films, as David Gerstner demonstrates in his essay, were made with a formal and narrative innovativeness, and a stress on the sensual, that provided a counter-narrative to the desired realism that lay at the heart of many New Wave films. They also challenged the heterosexuality of the New Wave's alignment of individuality with the national, and in later films such as the 1990 short *A Taste of Kiwi*, with its juxtaposition of images of the revered All Blacks national rugby team with those taken from gay pornography, Wells made such a critique incisively and playfully clear. *Desperate Remedies* (1993), the feature Wells co-directed with Stewart Main, was a breakthrough film, a camp tour de force of heightened melodrama and visual sensuality that offered a non-realist revision of settler history and proved to be a major international art-house success. In a nation where many cultural values are so wedded to notions of the homosocial, and where such connections have a long history in articulating ideas of masculinity within the very fabric of the national, Wells stands as a filmmaker continually working against orthodoxies.

Like those of Wells, Preston's films speak to a New Zealand experience not contained by much of the filmmaking that emerged during the 1980s. With initial training in documentary, Preston moved to feature filmmaking with *Mr Wrong* in 1985, and has made a number of features since, both fiction and documentary, that place women at the center of their narratives. If the women in the early films of Murphy and Donaldson are thinly sketched characters, often operating as peripheral figures to stress the centrality (in both narrative and social terms) of the male, then Preston, in films such as *Ruby and Rata* (1990) and *War Stories Our Mothers Never Told Us* (1995), creates spaces in which women's narratives are central. Estella Tincknell's essay discusses how Preston retains a critical edge in her representations of female domestic spaces, and the place of such spaces within a wider notion of New Zealand's cultural life, despite working across a range of different content and forms. Of the women filmmakers who made features during the 1980s (the others are Melanie Read, Yvonne Mackay, and Mita), Preston's subsequent career has arguably seen the most comprehensive development of the filmic portrayal of the multiple and complex nature of women's lives in New Zealand.

An integral part of the industry in New Zealand as it developed up through the 1970s and 1980s was the sense of community created by the new commitment to filmmaking. Individuals worked on a range of films, from shorts and features to documentaries, often performing likewise a range of jobs, from acting to technical support. Leon Narbey, as discussed in the essay by Helen Martin, moved from making experimental short films in the late 1960s and the 1970s to become a pioneering director of photography on New Wave documentary and fiction features (a role he has continued up to the present), briefly turning to directing with the production of *Illustrious Energy* (1988) and *The Footstep Man* (1992). In terms of performance, actors such as Bruno Lawrence and Jennifer Ward-Lealand emerged to become the faces of the New Wave output, embodying and voicing a sense of the local. Lawrence (who also worked as a scriptwriter and a musician on a number of films) in particular came to express the troubled masculinity captured in so many New Wave productions. In *Smash Palace, Heart of the Stag* (1984), and *The Quiet Earth* (1985), Lawrence created a trilogy of performances that, as Andrew Spicer notes in his essay, portrayed the new contradictory place of the Pakeha male. Lawrence's powerful yet vulnerable articulation of the male self captured perfectly the tensions inherent in New Zealand's increasingly exhausted orthodox nationalism, faced by social and cultural challenges internally and international pressures externally, as the 1980s progressed. For her part, Ward-Lealand's central performance in *Desperate Remedies*, layered in glamorous melodrama, marked a kind of coronation of her as the leading female actor of the industry up to that point. In her essay, Barbara Cairns discusses Ward-Lealand specifically in terms of a contribution to the overall community of filmmaking in New Zealand, and her presence in a variety of roles as a marker of the health of the industry.

The success of the New Wave, in terms of creating a sustainable industry and series of images of New Zealand society and culture, allowed for a proliferation of filmmaking projects and a more flexible idea of what might constitute "significant national content." The country's two most internationally recognized filmmakers, Jane Campion and Peter Jackson, emerged during the late 1980s. Campion, located in Sydney for much of the decade, made her first feature, *Sweetie*, in 1989, while Jackson's 1988 feature, *Bad Taste*, has already become legendary for the resourceful nature of its production. Eschewing overt national themes, Campion and Jackson explored different conceptions of subjectivity and belonging. As Eva Rueschmann outlines in her essay, Campion's focus on central female characters, whether in her Australian, New Zealand, or Hollywood films, is frequently one in which women find themselves in new locations or spaces that challenge orthodox notions of sexual or gendered identity. For his part, Jackson swept away the generic assumptions underpinning the New Wave. In place of the largely realist driven narratives that, somewhat narcissistically, agonized over the nature of being from New Zealand, Jackson's irreverence and concentration on fantasy in films such as *Bad Taste, Meet the Feebles* (1989), and *Braindead* (1992) changed expectations of what a New Zealand film might be. As Barry Keith Grant notes in his account, within his manipulation of genre Jackson creates films that have substantial commercial appeal, significant cinematic style, and yet also speak to his commitment to the locations of New Zealand culture. Given his success with *The Lord of the Rings* trilogy, Jackson's decision to stay in New Zealand carries considerable weight and has changed the dynamics of filmmaking within the nation.

In 1993 Campion made *The Piano*, while Jackson made *Heavenly Creatures* in 1994, two features, which along with Lee Tamahori's *Once Were Warriors* (1994), proved to be milestone productions in New Zealand filmmaking. All were films that received national and, crucially, international critical acclaim as well as achieving notable commercial success. All point to the diversification of the New Zealand film industry and its development since the beginning of the New Wave in the late 1970s. They also point to what would become a more mature relationship with contemporary Hollywood, with an increasingly flexible movement of both people and resources between New Zealand and the United States. The presence of Harvey Keitel and Holly Hunter in *The Piano* cemented the place of Hollywood A List performers into features made by New Zealand filmmakers, a process that would continue with *The Lord of the Rings* trilogy.

Since the early 1990s, other filmmakers have worked with these kinds of complexities taken as given. Alison Maclean followed the success of her 1980s short films and the 1992 feature *Crush* with television work in the United States, which ultimately led to her second feature, *Jesus' Son* (1999). As Kirsten Moana Thompson discusses here, Maclean's work follows that of Preston and Campion in stressing the ambiguous nature of sexual politics and psychological selfhood. As she also discusses however, her career—with its combination of short and feature work in New Zealand and contributions to international television and film—is by no means uncommon for the contemporary New Zealand filmmaker. Donaldson, now a regular Hollywood director with features such as *Dante's Peak* (1997) and

The Recruit (2003) nevertheless returned to New Zealand in 2004 to direct *The World's Fastest Indian* (2005), whilst Murphy did likewise to make *Spooked* (2004). Equally, Sam Neill, probably the most recognized New Zealand actor within an international frame, appears in Preston's latest film *Perfect Strangers* (2003). This kind of mobility is itself a statement of the place New Zealand filmmakers, such as director Tamahori and actors Temuera Morrison, Cliff Curtis, Rena Owen, and Karl Urban, occupy within the context of international film production.

A new generation of New Zealand filmmakers has emerged in the last few years. Directors such as Niki Caro, Christine Jeffs, Glenn Standring, Greg Page, and Harry Sinclair, and actors like Danielle Cormack, Joel Tobeck, Dean O'Gorman, and Lawrence Makoare have all made significant impressions with their first productions and performances.[7] In the work of such figures, New Zealand no longer presents itself as a series of national obsessions or questions. Rather, there is a greater variety of subject matter and irreverence of tone. At the same time, filmmakers such as Barclay, Mita, and Mune remain committed to their versions of the complexities of place and to the articulation of issues that are at heart most meaningful in the national context. Jackson has become the center of an industry that has changed the very infrastructure of filmmaking in New Zealand, while figures such as Campion and Donaldson continue with their Hollywood careers. All are filmmakers whose work, in different ways and to different degrees, intersects with the dynamics of New Zealand culture.

Notes

1. Some twenty-six New Zealand–produced feature films were made up to 1976, thirteen of which were filmed during the period of silent cinema. In addition, up to 1976 fifteen foreign-produced films were made in the country. See the filmography in *Contemporary New Zealand Cinema*, ed. Ian Conrich and Stuart Murray (Detroit: Wayne State University Press, forthcoming).
2. See Keith Sinclair, *A Destiny Apart: New Zealand's Search for National Identity* (Wellington: Allen and Unwin, 1986); and Mark Williams, "Crippled by Geography? New Zealand Nationalisms," in *Not on Any Map: Essays on Postcoloniality and Cultural Nationalism*, ed. Stuart Murray (Exeter: Exeter University Press, 1997).
3. See Stuart Murray, *Never a Soul at Home: New Zealand Literary Nationalism and the 1930s* (Wellington: Victoria University Press, 1998); and Lawrence Jones, *Picking Up the Traces: The Makings of a New Zealand Literary Culture, 1932–1945* (Wellington: Victoria University Press, 2003).
4. For more on the issues surrounding the New Zealand male pioneer, see Jock Phillips, *A Man's Country? The Image of the Pakeha Male—A History*, rev. ed. (Auckland: Penguin, 1996), 1–42; and Charlotte Macdonald, "Too Many Men and Two Few Women: Gender's 'Fatal Impact' in Nineteenth-Century Colonies," in *The Gendered Kiwi*, ed. Caroline Daley and Deborah Montgomerie (Auckland:

Auckland University Press, 1999).
5. Williams, "Crippled by Geography?" 36.
6. For further discussion of the context of Maori cultural activism, see Ranganui Walker, *Ka Whawhai Tonu Matou/Struggle without End* (Auckland: Penguin, 1990).
7. Caro has directed the features *Memory and Desire* (1998) and *Whale Rider* (2002). Jeffs directed *Rain* (2001) and *Sylvia* (2003); Standring directed *The Irrefutable Truth about Demons* (2000) and *Perfect Creature* (2005); Page, who is noted for his animation shorts and music videos, directed the feature *The Locals* (2003). Sinclair is the director of *Topless Women Talk about Their Lives* (1999), *The Price of Milk* (2000), and *Toy Love* (2003). Cormack stars in both *Topless Women Talk about Their Lives* and *The Price of Milk* as well as Christine Parker's *Channelling Baby* (1999); Tobeck stars in *Topless Women Talk about Their Lives* and *Perfect Strangers* (2003); O'Gorman stars in *Snakeskin* (2001) and *Toy Love;* Makoare stars in *What Becomes of the Broken Hearted?* (1999) and *Crooked Earth* (2001).

1 Pioneers

OVER THE COURSE OF ITS HISTORY, cinema in New Zealand has experienced a number of differing pioneering moments, and the essays collected in this section outline instances of innovation and development that change or expand the nature of local filmmaking. In its earliest formations, film production in New Zealand can be seen to be part of the wider evolution of a society moving from colony to nation, in which both the structural and technical aspects of filmmaking, and the idea of the community seen through its own images, became elements in the overall expansion of a public culture. The first Edison Kinetograph was brought to New Zealand in 1896, also the year of the first public screening of motion pictures at the Opera House in Auckland. In 1898 filmmaker and traveling showman A. H. Whitehouse began filming newsworthy events, such as *The Departure of the Second Contingent for the Boer War* (1900), which is the earliest surviving New Zealand film. Such developments bracket the beginnings of film in the country with those in other parts of the modern world, but a lack of resources available to filmmakers, coupled with difficulties in their development, meant that any subsequent growth in the industry was restricted.

For much of the twentieth century, filmmaking in New Zealand was dominated by technical and financial challenges as well as by the obvious pressure created by the hegemony of British and Hollywood features. Len Lye, Rudall Hayward, and John O'Shea emerge as the pivotal figures during this period, although their work takes quite different forms. Lye's particular avant-garde style for his short animation films was an aesthetic innovation, while Hayward and O'Shea had to each develop their features with limited finances and as distinct and discrete independent projects. The foundation of the National Film Unit in 1941 established sustained government investment for documentary filmmaking (particularly short films and news items) but, by way of contrast, there was a lack of any real structural support for fiction film production up until the 1970s, which made the work of these filmmakers genuinely that of pioneers.

But there have been other forms of pioneering filmmaking. The cultural and social practices that coalesced with the development of New Zealand society emphasized certain specific formations. The nation was the key unit of thought and representation, and it was a nation conceived of in terms that reflected the preoccupations of a dominant majority. Pakeha (European) concerns normalized themselves to become orthodoxies of community through which the central questions of nationhood were discussed. That these orthodoxies were also subject to masculine and heterosexual inflections as a consequence is perhaps no surprise, and the institutionalization of such paradigms within the emerging infrastructure of New Zealand filmmaking has to be seen as a process that paralleled such moves at a wider level of polity. From the 1970s onward, reacting to social and cultural-political changes in New Zealand and abroad, Gaylene Preston, Barry Barclay, Merata Mita, and Peter Wells challenged the various hegemonies that had built up ideas of what constituted dominant New Zealand culture, especially those constructing notions of gender, sexuality, and race. Incorporating narrative innovation with particular forms of social critique, their work established new directions for filmmakers. Their pioneering work showed New Zealanders aspects of their culture that were not part of the prevailing cultural and social consensus, and suggested new ways in which stories might be told. As such they are original *and* revisionist figures, and vital to an understanding of New Zealand's film culture.

In the current global film market, the challenges faced by countries with a relatively small production output are immense. As a small nation that can only ever make a limited number of features and shorts in any given year, New Zealand faces obvious difficulties in the competition for national and international audiences. Yet the industry at present has a substantial reputation for innovation in technical production, and in particular has developed a considerable skills base of effects expertise. Resources such as these (which should be seen as a form of pioneering in its own right) have resulted in the country becoming the location for a number of major international features in recent years, giving New Zealand a high level of visibility in the world of globalized film. Such a situation should, however, be seen in the context of a national culture that has, throughout its history, fought to establish a sense of cultural distinctiveness, and has often had to do so with limited means of production and dissemination. The history of New Zealand culture shows time and again the pressures that come with wanting to assert local narratives and to create a presence in an international frame at the same time. The current state of the New Zealand film industry is not an unproblematic one—there are clear tensions between the huge budget features of recent years and the need to continue to support small-scale productions, especially those that are more obviously about the lived experiences of New Zealand life—but the successes of the present have to be seen to emerge from the struggles of previous generations to establish the basics of a film production culture. It is in the pioneering work of the filmmakers discussed in this section that such a culture came into being, and it is in their narratives that New Zealand first began to see its own complexities in cinematic form.

1

Free Radical

The Life and Work of Len Lye

Roger Horrocks

Leonard Charles Huia Lye (or "Len Lye" as he preferred to call himself) is New Zealand's most important experimental filmmaker. He was born in Christchurch in 1901 as a third-generation New Zealander, in a country emerging from a turbulent century that had seen indigenous Maori communities fighting to preserve their land and sovereignty, while European settlers struggled to come to terms with an alien environment. One might expect such a restless history to produce radical forms of expression, and certainly there was a radical strain in New Zealand politics, but most of the mainstream culture remained slavishly colonial. Artistic production tended to be a timid, unquestioning imitation of British precedents. When a local film industry emerged, it too was largely derivative. The films were certainly impressive in technical terms because an inventive, pioneer spirit was required to build cameras, create special effects, and process the films, all on a minimal budget, but their style and content tended to be old-fashioned and secondhand. The most interesting work was that of Rudall Hayward (born a year before Lye), particularly when he began a serious involvement with Maori culture in the 1930s; stylistically, though, even Hayward continued to follow earlier British and American precedents.

Lye's distinguishing feature was his extreme commitment to experiment. A typical comment in his later life was: "I've always wanted to get out of the D. W. Griffith technique. To me all film is D. W. Griffith."[1] Lye was one of the few New Zealand artists in the early years of the twentieth century whose work was as radical as one might expect from a raw, remote country where immigrants had come to make a new start. By the time he was twenty, Lye was consumed with the idea of reinventing the very basis of art. In conventional terms, his background was an unlikely one for an artist—he grew up in poverty in a series of foster homes; he was a tough kid who lived an outdoor, physical life; and he could not afford to go to high school. Yet, from another perspective, the fact that he came from the wrong side of the tracks helps explain the vehement way he rejected the conventional, Victorian-style culture that dominated the arts in New Zealand.

In his late teens, Lye did undertake part-time art classes at the Wellington Technical College, and proved he could win prizes from the New Zealand Academy of Fine Arts for conventional drawing if he put his mind to it. His teachers focused on what they called "craftsmanship and draughtsmanship." But once he had come across information about the work of Paul Gauguin, Paul Cézanne, and the contemporary modernist movements of Europe, he threw his conventional training aside. His teachers had no interest in these developments and he obtained his own information by searching through public libraries. Besides learning about the cubists and futurists, he discovered the work of Karl Marx, Sigmund Freud, and Ezra Pound. Another passion was Maori art, along with the other forms of indigenous art he found in museums, and he became deeply committed to studying, sketching, and carving such work.

Lye's reinvention of art focused on motion, for which he attempted to create his own choreographic-style notation.[2] He started to create kinetic sculpture but was frustrated by the technical problems.[3] He was not aware of similar experiments happening at that time in Europe. During a visit to Sydney in 1923, he was suddenly seized with the idea that the medium with the greatest potential to "compose motion" was film. This was triggered off by his encounter with Frank Hurley's *Pearls and Savages* (1921),[4] a feature-length documentary about the indigenous people of Papua New Guinea whose art Lye had been studying. He was scornful of Hurley's ethnographic approach, but he was struck by the energy and immediacy of some of the footage. He obtained a filmmaking job at Filmads, one of the few Australian companies that produced animated advertisements. This introduced Lye to the basics of filmmaking ("I suddenly realised that films had cuts and sequences"). In his spare time he made flipbooks with sequences of motion involving abstract shapes. He also experimented with strips of black leader by scratching "doodles" into them and staying behind after work to project the results.[5] This would have been the first abstract or modernist film made in Australia or New Zealand, but Lye failed to complete it.

Restless, he returned to New Zealand, unsure where to go next. Excited by an avant-garde magazine with an illustration of the kinetic stage set used by the Meyerhold Theater in Moscow in 1922, and impressed by what he had heard about the Russian Revolution, he investigated the possibilities of going to Russia, but this proved too difficult. Instead, he traveled through the Pacific Islands and settled for a year in Samoa, living in a village where he studied *siapo* (tapa) designs.[6] The New Zealand administration deported him around the beginning of 1925 because he sided with the Samoans in a situation of increasing colonial conflict.

It is not clear why Lye did not involve himself in any of the films then being made in New Zealand. Admittedly they were few and far between. Rudall Hayward had gone to Australia to learn from the filmmaker Raymond Longford, and after Hayward returned to Auckland in 1922 there is no evidence that his path crossed that of Lye. By this stage the younger man had become a fierce maverick and was impatient with any form of art that he regarded as conventional. When Lye came across Robert Flaherty making *Moana* in Samoa in 1923, he assumed that such a film would be "a lot of crap." Lye summed up his attitude by the phrase: "I didn't want any part of the whites."[7] If he had come across any of the New Zealand films of the early 1920s, such as Harrington Reynolds's *The Birth of New Zealand* (1922) or Hayward's *My Lady of the Cave* (1922), he would probably have included them in his general critique of filmmaking as failing to go beyond simple storytelling and entertainment (which he described as "folklore fun").[8] In the 1920s, film was seen by artists as an invention still seeking its true path. In the course of the decade many modernists would be drawn to it as a medium not weighed down with historical baggage, one that could be claimed for the visual or fine arts and rescued from popular literature and melodrama.

In 1926, Lye bought the papers of a ship's stoker who was about to jump ship, and then worked his way to London under the assumed name. On his arrival he made contact with the London Film Society and with the city's avant-garde artists who elected him to their Seven and Five Society. At Seven and Five exhibitions he showed his paintings and sculptures alongside artists such as Henry Moore, Barbara Hepworth, and Ben Nicholson. In 1927, Lye began making a nine-minute black-and-white animated film with the Samoan title *Tusalava* (which he translated as "Everything eventually goes full cycle").[9] To develop his skills he obtained a part-time job in a London studio, Hopkins and Weir, that produced cartoon commercials for beer and toothpaste. He observed the use of the rostrum camera, and then bought his own drawing table and learned animation largely by trial and error. When he had achieved a certain level of competency, he could produce one second of film per day. His only collaborator was his musician friend Jack Ellitt who had come over from Sydney to join him. A highly innovative composer, a pioneer of electronic music, and later a film director in his own right, Ellitt would work with Lye for a decade, supervising his soundtracks.[10]

What the cubists and other modernists called "primitive art" had influenced painting and sculpture but had never appeared in the film medium, at least not in the radical manner Lye proposed. When asked to explain

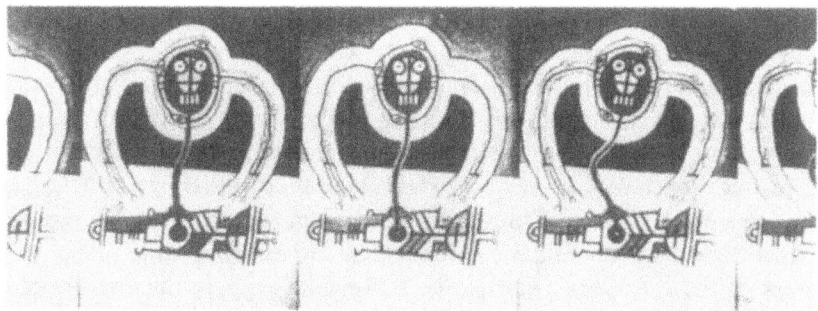

A creation myth: *Tusalava*'s radical display of evolution and movement. (Courtesy Stills Collection, New Zealand Film Archive/Nga Kaitaki O Nga Taonga Whitiahua.)

the theme of *Tusalava*, he described it as a creation myth, a story from the Dreamtime. His film showed simple circular forms—"organic life in a primary stage"—evolving into more complex forms like grubs.[11] Finally, two creatures came into conflict, the first an almost human shape described by Lye as "a totem of individuality"[12] and the second "a monstrous python shape"[13] that developed into "a cross between an octopus and a spider."[14] This ink-squirting monster attacked the human core shape, toyed with it and consumed it, but apparently destroyed itself in the process. The film ended as it began with circular patterns.

Tusalava obviously drew upon Lye's study of Australian Aboriginal art. He avoided direct imitation but his flat, linear, clear-cut shapes were certainly in the spirit of Aboriginal designs. The most dramatic moments in the film involved the making or breaking of boundaries. The split-screen layout—an idea he was using at this time in some of his batiks—produced a lively counterpoint between movements on each side of the screen, and he explored the whole area of the frame with forms dancing around its edges. *Tusalava* displayed a characteristically physical, kinetic sense of movement as creatures rose up like snakes, muscular forms pulled and pushed, and concentric circles spun this way and that. Maori art was a less obvious influence than Aboriginal art, but at times the totem of individuality was reminiscent of the tiki shape Lye had used in batiks and sculptures.

The film appeared in 1929 at a time when there were still only a few films seriously influenced by modern art. After a screening by the London Film Society (which had given Lye a grant to help him complete the film), *Tusalava* went to Paris to the Studio des Ursulines and then toured other avant-garde venues in Europe, where it made a strong impression on a few filmmakers such as Hans Richter. Reviewing it in *Film Art*, a magazine devoted to experimental work, filmmaker Oswell Blakeston described Lye as "a great artist with great ideas" and was particularly impressed by the film's rejection of Griffith-style editing in the way it evolved as a single continuous take.[15] A number of viewers were similarly intrigued by the film, but they were not sure how to talk about it or what context to place it in. Lye's involvement not only with modernism but also with Aboriginal, Maori, and Samoan cultures ensured that the film was quite unlike the work of the European avant-garde. Its organic imagery (like mysterious shapes seen in a microscope) moved very differently from the geometrical or mechanical forms favored by European modernists. Hence *Tusalava* remained isolated.

Lye said that his best return for his two years of work was receiving out of the blue a letter from Roger Fry, the well-known Bloomsbury art critic, who wrote: "When I saw the announcements of your *Tusalava* I made a point of going to Sunday's performance. I want to tell you that it seemed to me most interesting and full of promise. I thought that you had seen the essential thing as no-one had hitherto—I mean you really thought not of forms in themselves but of them as movements in time. I suspect it will need a new kind of imagination to seize this idea fully but you are the first as far as I know to make a start."[16] This was a highly prescient statement in terms of the films Lye was subsequently to make.

A collection of Lye's prose pieces, *No Trouble*, was published by Robert Graves and Laura Riding through their Seizin Press in 1930. In addition to describing his work on *Tusalava*, Lye made frequent references to his years in New Zealand. While he spoke with deep affection of his mother (who had struggled to do the best for Len and his brother Phillip through years of poverty), and while he spoke disparagingly of "the welterweight mass of London," he made it very clear that he had no intention of returning to the country of his birth with its oppressive, tradition-bound culture: "The marvel just now is to know now and yet feel good. I don't want to go home. I was dragged up among the tombstones and . . . learned that the most the monuments stand for is to be found at the foot of any lamp-post and if it's spit then there's the gutter."[17]

But the next five years in London were extremely frustrating for Lye. He had done many drawings for sequels to *Tusalava* and wanted to do "this great big film [trilogy], taking about ten years."[18] He exhibited some of the images in London galleries, but film funding became scarce as the Depression deepened. The coming of sound created problems as well as opportunities for avant-garde filmmakers as it added new costs. Sound also consolidated the victory of storytelling over the more visually oriented conceptions of the film medium championed by artists such as Lye. The potential line of development that *Tusalava* had opened up—a dialogue between indigenous imagery and modernist forms of abstract art—came to an end in film, though similar interests continued to inform the work of many painters. (This dialogue has been revived in recent years in video and multi-media forms.)

A series of unsuccessful film proposals forced Lye to move further in a commercial direction and away from his South Pacific interests. Sound was a novelty, so he proposed musical projects. The only one to be made was the 1934 *Peanut Vendor* (a.k.a. *Experimental Animation*), the three-minute black-and-white pilot for a series of puppet animations based on popular pieces of dance music. Puppets were one of the few areas of animation not dominated by Walt Disney, and imaginative work was being done by filmmakers such as George Pal. But no sponsor could be found for Lye's series, and he felt that these years added up to nothing but "experience in the art of learning to take it which is what the film packet consists of."[19] The project did, however, help to develop his interest in synchronizing images with music.

His breakthrough came with *A Colour Box* in 1935. Unable to afford to rent a camera or to get film processed, he started to collect unwanted strips of clear film from trim bins to "scratch and paint and mess around" with.[20] This harked back to his experiments in scratching film in Sydney ten years earlier. Lye's love of doodling and the increasingly free brushwork in his paintings had prepared him for a new approach to film. (He was a great admirer of the painterly style of Joan Miró, an artist he later came to know.) What had deterred filmmakers from drawing images directly onto celluloid was the jittery effect caused by the slight differences between one frame and the next. It took a special kind of artist to regard this jitter as an advantage, as a display of energy, and as a visual equivalent of musical resonance. Animators of all kinds from Walt Disney to the German abstract artists had sought smooth movement. Similarly, the long tradition of tinting film and adding hand-painted areas of color by brush and stencil had emphasized neatness and precision. Lye was well aware of these precedents, but he liked (as Malcolm LeGrice has put it) to work "with rather than against the 'imperfections.'"[21]

Lye was delighted to transform the high-tech medium of film into something handmade, like tapa cloth. The challenge was to find paint that would not crack or peel off the surface of the film but was transparent enough to produce the right colors when projected. As tools he used a camel-hair brush, various homely objects such as a fine-tooth comb that he wiggled through wet paint to make "striated wavy lines,"[22] and an airbrush to spray paint through specially made stencils such as "stars, circles, triangles, and yin-yangs."[23] He also improvised stencils, such as a fish slice that was ideal for rows of dots, and he experimented with many types of scratching tools.

A strip of film was only 35 mm in width, a tiny surface on which to paint patterns that would later be blown up to fill a huge cinema screen. To discover the best "figures of motion" (as he described them) he made and tested countless strips.[24] This process was time consuming but at least it was cheap—there was no need for a camera or film crew. It is interesting to note that handmade or direct filmmaking (as Lye came to call it) is the only form of filmmaking that literally fits the auteur theory, the approach that speaks of films as though they are the work of a single artist. The touch or signature of the artist is physically present in every frame of a direct film.

Still, even Lye needed help to synchronize his visual ideas to music. His friend Jack Ellitt had an exceptionally clear grasp of the way music could be analyzed and edited for film purposes. Ellitt had already written and performed a piano accompaniment for *Tusalava*, but unfortunately his score has since been lost. For *A Colour Box* and subsequent hand-painted films, Ellitt helped Lye to synchronize his painted strips to recordings of dance music. Lye's aim was not merely to translate the music into images but to develop visual ideas in counterpoint. He liked to have enough synchronization to keep the images in step with the music, but he felt free to pick up ideas from any aspect of the music—the rhythm, the timbre, the style of a particular player, the general mood, or the look of the printed soundtrack. He was generally inclined to associate the sound of drums with dots and circles, the piano with a shower of tiny splashes of color, and string instruments with lines that quivered and twanged, but this was not a strict code. The vertical line (drawn along many frames at a time) was a favorite motif that he would use for a variety of instruments. He learned to do many things with a line, such as make it sway, wriggle, jump, or glide.

Lye loved jazz but could not afford to purchase the rights to recordings by top bands and therefore sought out the work of groups less well known, such as Don Baretto and his Cuban Orchestra. The use of dance music turned these films into forerunners of today's music videos and helped to get them widely screened in cinemas. Lye had thus found a solution to his isolation as an experimental filmmaker. Oskar Fischinger was already using the same method in Germany to infiltrate his experimental work into the cinemas, though his taste in music was more classical. (The two filmmakers knew and admired each other's work.)

A Colour Box was controversial because it was abstract art. Public response was polarized, but the arguments among reviewers generated a huge amount of interest, and the film came to be seen (as David Curtis has pointed out) "by a larger public than any experimental film before it and most since."[25] At the end of October 1935, *A Colour Box* won a Medal of Honor at the International Cinema Festival in Brussels, whereas at the Venice Festival it was booed off the screen by Nazi sympathizers who regarded such art as degenerate.[26] The film went on to gain cult status among the avant-garde in other parts of Europe.[27] Lye's discovery had the effect of opening up filmmaking for the first time to all comers, since a direct film could be anything from a strip of celluloid covered with felt-tip-pen designs by a group of small children to a complex art film based on years of experiment.

Publicity for *A Colour Box* constantly stressed its originality, and this was a claim nobody disputed in the 1930s. Later historians have found some precedents. Around 1912 Italian futurists Arnaldo Ginna and Bruno Corra wrote an essay about the hand painting of films. Unfortunately, none of their films or reports of screenings have been found.[28] During the 1920s, Man Ray made film sequences by his photogram method, and there were filmmakers such as Hans Stoltenberg and Henri Storck who experimented with painting or scratching in one form or another.[29] When sound arrived at the end of the 1920s, several filmmakers—including Jack Ellitt—discovered that soundtracks could be painted by hand. We can acknowledge this rich body of experiment yet still see *A Colour Box* as worthy of a special place in the history books. It was a breakthrough at the time because Lye and his contemporary audiences were not aware of any precedents, and more generally, the film demonstrated the potential of the direct method in such a thorough and sophisticated way that the paintbrush had to be accepted once and for all as a viable alternative to the camera. Lye is perhaps the only New Zealand filmmaker who can be said to have pioneered not only a new style but also a new method of filmmaking.

In later years, Norman McLaren, who was strongly supported by the Canadian National Film Board, became the best-known direct filmmaker, but he always acknowledged his debt to Lye. He had made experiments but not completed a film when he saw *A Colour Box*—it "electrified" him and convinced him of the rich potential of the method. In later years he and Lye always admired each other's work, though their approaches were different, as Lye's style tended to be bolder and less elegant.[30]

Having sponsored *A Colour Box*, the GPO [General Post Office] Film Unit went on to commission three of Lye's subsequent films. John Grierson, the head of the Unit, knew enough about modern forms of art to understand the power of what Lye was doing. He also saw the possibility of using such films to liven up the Unit's packages of black-and-white documentaries. Color was still a novelty, particularly the brilliant colors produced by the direct application of paint, and a successful film made without a camera was such a striking innovation that (in Alberto

Cavalcanti's words) "Grierson, that king of showmen, wouldn't miss this opportunity."[31] Lye also received commissions from Shell Oil, Churchill Cigarettes, and Imperial Airways (later British Airways). This provided him with a modest income but required him to include slogans from his sponsors at the end of the films. He generally added such slogans in a playful, tongue-in-cheek way.[32]

Lye made a number of direct films but never repeated himself. In his words: "Every film I got . . . I tried to interest myself in it by doing . . . something not previously done in film technique."[33] In *Trade Tattoo* (1937) he manipulated the three-color-separation method (as used at that time by Technicolor) to transform black-and-white off-cuts from GPO films such as *Night Mail* into a fast-moving kaleidoscope of brilliantly colored, semi-abstract images. He added stencil effects to further enrich the texture. Technically this was Lye's most complex film, astonishingly inventive in its visual ideas and profoundly subversive in its treatment of naturalism. Technicolor experts were amazed by Lye's technical command and unorthodox use of the technology.

In the previous year he had found a different way to play with color in *Rainbow Dance*. This was not a direct film, strictly speaking, but it was highly original in its combination of live footage and animation. He had shot his own black-and-white source material on this occasion and used a modern dancer, Rupert Doone, as his actor, so that the result was a kind of film ballet with dazzling color effects.

Between 1941 and 1951, Lye directed documentary films and newsreel items. This was part of his struggle to make a living, as funding for experimental animation dried up during the war years. At the same time, his interest in politics had greatly increased, and he was eager to assist the war effort. As a member of the Realist Film Unit he directed documentaries for the Ministry of Information. The Ministry's projects were prosaic, but Lye still sought ways to make the films innovative, such as experimenting with cinema verité techniques or with stylized soundtracks. His documentaries included *When the Pie Was Opened* (1941), *Kill or Be Killed* (1942), *Newspaper Train* (1942), *Work Party* (1942), and *Cameramen at War* (1943). *Kill or Be Killed*—a demonstration of combat methods with "a slow unfolding rhythm, a rhythm that creeps into one's buttocks"[34]—was not only an effective training film but also an extraordinary study of the physical, kinetic energies of battle. Cavalcanti praised it in *Sight and Sound* as having "the weight of a classic Greek tragedy."[35]

In 1944, Lye moved to New York to become a director for the popular American current affairs series *The March of Time*. He contributed to some famous episodes but was forced to conform closely to the series style. *The March of Time* came to an end in 1951, as it was unable to compete with the novelty and immediacy of television. Although Lye struggled financially and found film jobs and sponsorship to be even scarcer in the United States than in the United Kingdom, he was excited by the emergence of New York as a center for avant-garde art. He lived a bohemian life in Greenwich Village, joined the group of artists that became the abstract expressionists, and played a significant part in the postwar upsurge in American experimental filmmaking.

Toward the late 1940s, Lye applied his camera-less approach to photography. He was well aware of Man Ray's earlier photograms but achieved his own distinctive effects through his interest in the layering of images—his photographs mixed silhouettes with objects, fabrics, drawings, and words. In *Color Cry* (1953) he created a new kind of direct film by the manipulation of a range of fabrics, colored gels, and objects. With deep colors and bold visual forms combined with a wordless, wailing blues by Sonny Terry, the film created a powerful emotional resonance despite the abstract nature of its imagery.

With *Free Radicals* (1958), Lye chose to return to the very basics of the film medium by making white scratches on black film, using a variety of scribers that ranged from dental tools to ancient Native American arrowheads. The resulting images were extremely dynamic, like flashes of lightning in the night sky. He synchronized them closely to traditional African drum music. *Free Radicals* is arguably Lye's best film and one of the most powerful experimental films ever made. The artist displays a remarkable control over his complex "figures of motion," many of which last less than a second. And he achieved this control within the tiny space of the 16 mm frame.

Although *Free Radicals* won second prize in an international competition for experimental films at the 1958 Brussels World's Fair, which attracted hundreds of entries from well-known filmmakers, Lye was still unable to find a distributor in the United States for the film, nor a sponsor for his next production. He had already had to use his and his wife's savings to make *Free Radicals* and *Color Cry*.[36] In the following year he announced he had "gone on strike" as a filmmaker.[37] Henceforth he devoted his best energies to kinetic sculpture, apart from occasional spells of direct filmmaking. To him, film and kinetic sculpture were simply two aspects of the same "art of motion."[38] He went on to establish a reputation for himself as a leading kinetic sculptor, and though he had not invented the genre his work was distinctive for its highly sophisticated sense of cyclic movement and its powerful physicality. Ironically, he encountered just as many funding problems with motorized sculpture as he had with films. He was also at a disadvantage because of the art world's tendency to compartmentalize sculpture, painting, film, and photography, associated with separate audiences, critics, curators, and museum departments. (Today there is a greater interest in seeing Lye's work as a whole because art institutions have become more accustomed to artists working in multi-media.)

Lye retained personal links with New Zealand by exchanging letters with his brother Phillip. (His other favorite correspondent, his mother, had died in 1940.) Around 1960, he explored memories of his New Zealand childhood in the vivid prose sequence, *Happy Moments* (which would be published posthumously).[39] During the 1960s, stories about his kinetic sculpture in international art magazines encouraged New Zealand artists to contact him in New York. This was a period when New Zealand was "going modern in its culture," as Lye put it.[40] As artists and curators engaged with contemporary, international trends, they were fascinated to hear about a New Zealander who had been doing the same thing for more than forty years.

Lye made his first return visit to New Zealand in 1968 for personal reasons, but while he was in Wellington he campaigned for greater public support to be given to independent filmmakers.[41] His advocacy was well timed since an important new generation of filmmakers was just emerging.[42] Lye's links with the country deepened over the next few years and he accepted an offer from the Govett-Brewster Art Gallery in New Plymouth to build some large-scale versions of his sculptures for which he was having difficulty finding sponsorship in the United States. John Matthews accepted this engineering challenge. In 1977, Lye returned to New Zealand to pass judgment on the results, and he was so impressed that he agreed to leave his work to the people of New Zealand after his death, to be administered by a non-profit trust, the Len Lye Foundation, with his collection to be based at the Govett-Brewster Art Gallery. The Foundation would have the responsibility to keep his sculptures in working condition, and would continue, as funds permitted, to realize his plans for giant versions of his sculptures.

In the final years of his life, New Zealand funding encouraged him to return to filmmaking. In 1979 the support of the newly formed New Zealand Film Commission enabled him to hire an assistant and to re-edit *Free Radicals*, reducing it to a very tight four-minute version later described by Stan Brakhage as "an almost unbelievably immense masterpiece (a brief epic)."[43] Funding from the QE2 [Queen Elizabeth II] Arts Council helped him to complete *Particles in Space*, a black-and-white film that had grown out of *Free Radicals*. Its scratched images seemed rougher in texture and more extreme than those of its predecessor—like a wild abstract expressionist painting that had sprung to life—but Lye synchronized its images to music with split-second precision. The film was highly dynamic, with its abstract patterns creating unusual effects of physical movement.

Lye died in Warwick, New York, in 1980. Since then his work has continued to command the interest and respect of experimental filmmakers and animators in many countries, as shown by a steady stream of retrospectives. Today's computers make it technically possible to do in a few minutes what would have taken Lye months, but sheer speed and complexity are no substitute for his masterly sense of kinetic energy and composition.

Ultimately, how useful is it to think of Lye as a New Zealand filmmaker? As he grew more at home in London, the South Pacific influences of *Tusalava* disappeared from his work, in painting as in film. A case can, however, be made for a *siapo* or tapa influence on his hand-painted films.[44] He continued to be fascinated by wave forms, as he had been as a young artist in New Zealand, and added animated waves to several films—most notably to the opening of *Colour Flight* (1938). The distinctively physical approach to movement in his films and sculptures could be linked with the active, outdoor life he had led as a young man. The strange biological creatures that disappeared from his films but continued to inhabit his paintings—unconnected to any known species but reflecting a lifelong fascination with nature—recalled some of the childhood experiences at Cape Campbell that he wrote about in *Happy Moments*. Lye was himself convinced that the "New Zealand imprint of nature" had given his work a particular "knotted intensity."[45] On a more superficial level, his jokes about the English climate in *Rainbow Dance* had a New Zealand resonance. Also, the strongly independent streak in his personality, with his contempt for the English class system, seemed to owe something to the fact he had grown up in a more egalitarian society.

Yet these suggestions need to be balanced by the fact that he forged his personality as much in opposition to as in sympathy with his country. Class seems as important a factor as nationality—he was a working-class intellectual with radical sympathies. There are thoughtful critics such as John Hurrell who disapprove of attempts to find traces of New Zealandness in Lye, seeing such attempts as tainted by an essentialist nationalism.[46] His internationalism is precisely what made him important for the artists of the 1960s.

Nevertheless, the Lye collection is based in New Zealand and his work continues to have a more significant place in the culture of that country than in any other, influencing local makers of music videos and experimental films as well as painters and poets. Jonathan Dennis, who established the New Zealand Film Archive, honored Lye as an ancestor and made a point of using his distinctive handwriting for the archive's original neon sign. The archive has frequent Lye exhibitions and screenings and

Len Lye, in 1968—animator and experimental filmmaker. (Courtesy of the Stills Collection, New Zealand Film Archive/Nga Kaitaki O Nga Taonga Whitiahua. Copyright John B. Turner.)

was recently involved with The Museum of Modern Art in New York in the restoration of his rediscovered film *All Soul's Carnival* (1957).

Above all, Lye's influence in New Zealand has been that of a role model—the creative thinker who demonstrated a lifetime commitment to experiment. He was still making innovative films at the age of seventy-eight. His personal example is valued because the financial difficulties of filmmaking in a small country have always created a strong incentive to compromise. His fierce spirit of independence is also important because derivative colonial attitudes have never entirely disappeared from New Zealand culture, though almost a century has passed since Lye was "dragged up among the tombstones."

Notes

1. Len Lye, "Getting Out of the Griffith Technique," in *Figures of Motion: Len Lye/ Selected Writings*, ed. Wystan Curnow and Roger Horrocks (Auckland: Auckland University Press, 1984), 55.
2. Roger Horrocks, *Len Lye: A Biography* (Auckland: Auckland University Press, 2001), 28.
3. Ibid., 52–53.
4. The first version of the film appeared in 1921. Lye appears to have seen the 1923 expanded version titled *With the Headhunters in Papua*.
5. Horrocks, *Len Lye: A Biography*, 55.
6. *Siapo*, or tapa cloth, was made by pounding the bark of the mulberry tree. Stylized patterns, sometimes bold and brightly colored, were applied by rubbing the cloth against a grooved, inked board or by a process of freehand painting.
7. Wystan Curnow, "An Interview with Len Lye," *Art New Zealand* 17 (1980): 57.
8. See Lye, "Is Film Art?" in *Figures of Motion*, ed. Curnow and Horrocks, 53.
9. Robert Del Tredici, "Len Lye Interview," *The Cinemanews* 2–4 (1979): 37.
10. Roger Horrocks, "Jack Ellitt: The Early Years," *Cantrills Filmnotes* (December 1999–January 2000): 20–26.
11. Lye, "Tusalava," in *Figures of Motion*, 105.
12. Curnow, "An Interview with Len Lye," 54.
13. Lye, "Tusalava," in *Figures of Motion*, 105.
14. Curnow, "An Interview with Len Lye," 54.
15. See *Film Art* (January 1930): 74; and (February 1930): 155–56.
16. Letter from Roger Fry to Len Lye, December 3, 1929 (Len Lye Foundation collection).
17. Lye, "Linger Longer Laura," in *Figures of Motion*, 99.
18. Horrocks, *Len Lye: A Biography*, 128.
19. Ibid., 131.
20. Joseph Kennedy, "Len Lye—Composer of Motion," *Millimeter* 5 (February 1977): 20.
21. Malcolm LeGrice, *Abstract Film and Beyond* (London: Studio Vista, 1977), 71.
22. Kennedy, "Len Lye—Composer of Motion," 20.

23. Letter from Jack Ellitt to the author, September 12, 1981.
24. On Lye's idea of "figures of motion," see "The Art That Moves," in *Figures of Motion*, 78–87.
25. David Curtis, *Experimental Cinema: A Fifty Year Evolution* (London: Studio Vista, 1971), 36.
26. See William Moritz, "Len Lye's Films in the Context of International Abstract Cinema," in *Len Lye*, ed. Jean-Michel Bouhours and Roger Horrocks (Paris: Centre Pompidou, 2000), 194.
27. See "The Len Lye Lists," *Bulletin of New Zealand Art History* 8 (1980), for documentation of European screenings of *A Colour Box* in 1936–38. The film was later "chosen as a culminating point in the cavalcade of films at the Paris Exposition" ("The First Swing Film," *Melody Maker*, September 18, 1937).
28. Bruno Carra, "Abstract Cinema—Chromatic Music," in *Futurist Manifestos*, ed. Umbro Apollonio (New York: Viking, 1973), 68.
29. Interesting discussions of the history of direct film include William Moritz, "Non-Objective Film: The Second Generation," in *Film as Film: Formal Experiment in Film, 1910–1975*, ed. Phillip Drummond (London: Hayward Gallery, 1979), 59–71, and Jean-Michel Bouhours, "La conjonction de la forme et du mouvement," in *Len Lye*, ed. Bouhours and Horrocks, 73–85.
30. See Horrocks, *Len Lye: A Biography*, 144–45 and 333–34. McLaren was thirteen years younger than Lye.
31. Alberto Cavalcanti, "Presenting Len Lye," *Sight and Sound* 16 (Winter 1947–48): 135.
32. See, for example, the end of *N. or N.W.* (1937). Incidentally, this remarkable film was Lye's most direct attempt to subvert the orthodox codes of live-action editing. His sponsor, the GPO Film Unit, decided he had gone too far and removed the most experimental sequence, which was subsequently lost. See Lye's description of the sequence in "Television: New Axes to Grind," *Sight and Sound* 8 (Summer 1939): 65–70.
33. Gretchen Weinberg, "Interview with Len Lye," *Film Culture* 29 (1963): 42.
34. Lye's description, in Horrocks, *Len Lye: A Biography*, 199.
35. Cavalcanti, "Presenting Len Lye," 134.
36. Lye had married Ann Hindle, an American, in 1948. His previous marriage (in 1934) had been to Jane Thompson, a South African living in London. Two children, Bix and Yancy, were born to his first marriage. Both wives deserve acknowledgment for the unstinting support they gave to Lye's creative work despite the severe financial pressures that were frequently involved.
37. Lye, "Is Film Art?" in *Figures of Motion*, 54.
38. See Lye, "The Art That Moves," in *Figures of Motion*, 78–87.
39. Len Lye, *Happy Moments*, ed. Roger Horrocks (Auckland: Holloway Press, 2003).
40. Horrocks, *Len Lye: A Biography*, 338.
41. Ibid., 344.
42. See Roger Horrocks, "Alternatives: Experimental Filmmaking in New Zealand," in *Film in Aotearoa New Zealand*, ed. Jonathan Dennis and Jan Bieringa (Wellington: Victoria University Press, 1992), 60–70.
43. Horrocks, *Len Lye: A Biography*, 381.

44. Lye pointed out this connection in an early newspaper interview: "Len Lye, The English Disney," *Sunday Referee*, November 10, 1935.
45. Lye, "Slow but Sure," in *Len Lye: A Personal Mythology* (Auckland: Auckland City Art Gallery, 1980), 90.
46. For an overview of the New Zealand reception of Lye, see Horrocks, *Len Lye: A Biography*, 382–88, and Roger Horrocks, "In and Out of History: A Century of Len Lye," *Art New Zealand* 101 (Summer 2001–2): 52–61.

Len Lye—Filmography

1929. *Tusalava* (UK short film: director).
1934. *Experimental Animation* a.k.a. *Peanut Vendor* (UK short film: director).
1935. *A Colour Box* (UK short film: director).
1935. *Kaleidoscope* (UK short film: director).
1935. *Full Fathom Five* (UK short film: director).
1936. *The Birth of the Robot* (UK short film: director).
1936. *Rainbow Dance* (UK short film: director).
1937. *Trade Tattoo* a.k.a. *In Tune with Industry* (UK short film: director).
1937. *N. or N.W.* (UK short film: director).
1938. *Colour Flight* (UK short film: director).
1938. *Mad about Money* (UK feature film: creative involvement for two special sequences).
1938–51. *March of Time* (U.S. newsreel: director, based in the United Kingdom from 1938 to 1944 and in the United States from 1944 to 1951, associated in particular with *The Irish Question* [1944], *Memo from Britain* [1945], *Teen-Age Girls* [1945], *Where's the Meat?* [1945], *Life with Baby* [1946], *Night Club Boom* [1946], *Atomic Powers* [1946], *T-Men in Action* [1947], *Farming Pays Off* [1949]).
1939. *Swinging the Lambeth Walk* (UK short film: director).
1940. *Musical Poster #1* (UK government information film: director).
1941. *When the Pie Was Opened* (UK government information film: director).
1942. *Newspaper Train* (UK government information film: director).
1942. *Work Party* a.k.a. *Factory Family* (UK government information film: director).
1942. *Kill or Be Killed* (UK government information film: director).
1942. *Collapsible Metal Tubes* a.k.a. *Tin Salvage* (UK government information film: director).
1942. *Planned Crops* (UK government information film: director).
1943. *Cameramen at War* (UK government information film: director).
1945. *Basic English* (US training film in six parts: co-director).
1952. *Bells of Atlantis* (US short film: special effects).
1953. *Autumn Leaves* (Canada Short film: collaborator).
1953. *Color Cry* a.k.a. **The Fox Chase** (US short film: director).
1953. *Full Fathom Five* (US short film: director).

1953. *Life's Musical Minute* (US short film: director).
1957. *All Soul's Carnival* (US short film: director).
1957. *Rhythm* (US short film: director).
1958. *Free Radicals* (US short film: director). Film subsequently recomposed in 1979 in New Zealand.
1958. *Prime Time* (US short film: director).
1958. *Percussion* (US short film: director).
1958. *Fountain of Hope* a.k.a. *Peace* a.k.a. *Fountain* (US short film: director).
1959. *The Sign of Plexiglass* (US short film: director for an animation sequence).
1968. *The Walls Came Tumbling Down* (US television documentary on Lye).
1973. *Len Who? Into an Unknown* (NZ television documentary on Lye).
1979. *Free Radicals* (NZ short film: director). Revised version of 1958 film.
1980. *Particles in Space* (NZ short film: director).
1980. *Tal Farlow* (NZ short film: director). Images initially created for the film in the 1950s. Editing completed posthumously by assistant Steven Jones, under the guidance of Ann Lye.
1980. *Kaleidoscope: Len Lye* (NZ television documentary on Lye).
1980. *Len Lye: Two Studios* (NZ documentary on Lye).
1980. *Len Lye* (US documentary on Lye).
1987. *Doodlin': Impressions of Len Lye* (UK television documentary on Lye).
1995. *Flip and Two Twisters* (NZ television documentary on Lye).

2
A Rough Island Story
THE FILM LIFE OF RUDALL CHARLES HAYWARD

Sam Edwards and Stuart Murray

> First of all you must remember that I was really fascinated by what has been called a rough island story, the history of the country. That was the thing that fascinated me. . . . When I saw all around me American films dealing with the history of their west I considered that New Zealand had material equally as fascinating because, when you look into it, you find the period of unrest in New Zealand when there was fighting going on between Maori and Pakeha [European] all through that period of pioneering—it lasted perhaps thirty years from 1840 to 1870 and during that period a vast amount of material is available in the form of historical accounts which would make fascinating films.
>
> Rudall Hayward, undated taped interview,
Australian Film and Sound Archive, Canberra

Filmmaker John O'Shea, discussing Rudall Hayward's status from the viewpoint of the 1990s, described Hayward as "the real pioneer of New Zealand film making," and there is no doubt that he stands as one of the most important figures in the development of this cinema.[1] His work is foundational not only in terms of the growth of technical and infrastructural issues relating to New Zealand cinema that developed during a period when he was a largely solitary feature filmmaker but also in the ways in which he heralded many of the key themes to which later filmmakers would return. Hayward's sense that the details of New Zealand history provided the material for narrative film, and that the society and landscape of the nation were themselves suitable subjects for feature production, anticipates the concerns the filmmakers of New Zealand's New Wave worked with in the 1970s and 1980s. Indeed, Hayward can be seen to bridge the colonial and modern periods with his consistent concern over the nature of settlement and society in New Zealand. His feature films seek to adumbrate an idea of a working and mature national society, one based on the key concept of engagement with the land, and utilizing notions of both gender and race relations. Hayward's work, even as it was inconsistent, often seems to will such a society into being, and as such it provided a series of models for local audiences that helped shape the wider feeling of being "at home" as the often-anxious community developed ideas of self-representation.

Yet Hayward's work has received very little critical commentary, and even elements of his biography are still subject to debate, a point that makes research on the films difficult. Existing documentation on Hayward is rare and his films are only occasionally screened, despite his clearly innovative role as a major pioneer in filmmaking in New Zealand. For these reasons, what we aim to achieve in this essay is to give a sense of Hayward's career as a whole, in order that those coming to his work for the first time might see the range and time span of his filmmaking, as well as provide critical commentaries on his key works. In the manner of its surveying then, and in the need to supply foundational information, this discussion will therefore be somewhat different from the other assessments of filmmakers in this volume, but it will provide a base for the future research that Hayward's filmmaking undoubtedly deserves.

Hayward was born in 1900 in Wolverhampton, Great Britain, and brought up in a tightly knit family unit in a troupe of touring musicians and performers called the Brescians. The troupe toured Australia and New Zealand shortly after Hayward was born, associating with T. J. West, an entrepreneur who eventually established himself as an Australian film distributor and exhibitor. In 1908, Hayward's father and uncle bought the Royal Albert Hall in Auckland and converted it into a cinema. Their success was immediate, and by 1910 the family had a profitable thirty-two-cinema chain with the young Hayward, aged only ten, working as a projectionist. The future feature maker began literally at the bottom of his craft, learning the trade by turning the bottom spool by hand to keep the correct tension.

After working as a theater manager for the family firm, Hayward left for Australia at age eighteen. He later claimed to have assisted in productions such as *Rudd's New Selection* (1921), with filmmakers such as Raymond Longford (who had earlier made both *A Maori Maid's Love* and *The Mutiny of the Bounty* in New Zealand in 1916), and may well have been involved at some level. Hayward returned to New Zealand, where in 1921 he worked with another Australian director, Beaumont Smith, on *The Betrayer*, work which involved, among other things, "painting the legs of an Australian actress with red ochre to keep her looking like a Maori girl."[2] Hayward's early involvement in such films was at a junior level and was very much part of his learning his trade. He worked with Harrington

Reynolds on the epic *The Birth of New Zealand* (1922), though the full nature of his participation is unclear, and it appears that he left the production after clashes with Reynolds. What is beyond doubt, however, is that the technical expertise that came to characterize Hayward's silent features was developed during this period.

Much of the popular narrative concerning Hayward has been constructed from interviews with, and the recollections of, both Hayward himself and Ramai Te Miha, his second wife. The anecdotal reports are not always supported by filmic and archival evidence, but, while he might have capitalized on this reputation to sometimes aggrandize his roles when reviewing his own past, Hayward's clear achievements should not be understated. To later generations of filmmakers in New Zealand, his status as a creative innovator in the early, difficult periods of film production endowed him with almost mythic qualities. In the 1920s and 1930s, when there was, in effect, no sustainable film industry in the country, and when the mechanics of filmmaking were often near impossible, Hayward's work was a testament to both an artistic and an organizational talent that had no peers.

Some of the films Hayward directed are lost entirely, some exist only in remnants, but there is enough material still available to give a reliable sense of his real contribution to the development of cinema in New Zealand. Hayward's importance lies not only in his development of key technical aspects of the film production process but also in the ways in which his narratives explore the often-precarious nature of settlement and cultural relations in New Zealand. A product of a late colonial culture himself, Hayward's work—especially his feature films—records and investigates the ways in which the society he found himself a part of articulated key social and cultural attitudes as it developed from a colonial to a national sensibility. Central to this are the forms of imagined community relations that emerge from Hayward's features, often as virtually utopian social spaces in which gender and racial relationships come together in an image of a benevolent population settling the new land.

Hayward's films can be divided into four categories. The first are the news items and actualities that saw him working as a photojournalist in New Zealand and later in Australia and Great Britain, reporting on anything from the 1931 Napier earthquake on New Zealand's North Island, to the arrival of the American Fleet in Auckland in 1925; or interviewing celebrities like George Bernard Shaw, and covering topical events such as strikes and horse races. These are brief items, and largely indistinguishable from the work of any other reporter using a camera, but as well as providing Hayward with an income, they allowed him to interact with significant media organizations such as the British Broadcasting Corporation (BBC), and they required of him technical skills that were essential to his later work, whether fiction or nonfiction.

The second group of productions is the short fiction films. The bulk of these are Hayward's "community comedies," more than twenty of which were made between 1928 and 1930. These are films in which, working from a stock script, Hayward would descend on a typical small town, "audition" a good-looking male or female lead, find extras from other townspeople, and shoot a comic melodrama. This normally involved a kidnapping, a chase, and a rescue in front of as many townspeople as could be mustered. The film was then developed and printed over a very short period of time, and screened to a local audience, before Hayward and his crew moved on to the next town in the series. He made other kinds of short films in addition to these comedies. In 1973, Hayward shot *The Doll's House*, beginning what was to be a series of adaptations from Katherine Mansfield stories, but the production values for the film were so poor with obviously artificial lighting, stilted dialogue, and problems adapting Mansfield's literary style, that it was not well received, and the series was dropped. In fact, writing dialogue was an enormous problem for Hayward and was one of the more obvious difficulties he faced when his films made the move to sound technology.

The third group of films is Hayward's documentaries. Many of these were aimed at the education of New Zealanders, particularly on issues of cultural relations between Maori and European cultures. The result was films such as *Eel History Was a Mystery* (1960) and *The Arts of Maori Children* (1962), which sold to schools, and some general documentaries on New Zealand life such as *The Miracle of the Pine: An Epic of Industry* (1941). None, apart from a ten-minute documentary on a Hokianga dolphin, *Opo: The Amazing Dolphin of Opononi* (1955), received significant release or sales to international distributors. Hayward also made documentaries developed from his left-wing political beliefs and connections. Invited to China and Albania with Ramai, who worked on the documentaries with him, Hayward made films like *The Young Albanians* (1972), which offered a propagandist (though Hayward claimed educative) view of socialism.

The final group of films constitutes Hayward's major achievements. These are the features, which span a period of fifty years of production between 1922 and 1972, and in which Hayward dealt continuously with the consequences of colonization and settler history, with the representation of the ordinary New Zealander, and with questions of bicultural relations. In so doing, and especially in the silent features made during the 1920s and 1930s, he both visualized and examined many of the myths that underpin New Zealand society and history. In 1921, Hayward had made his first short film, *The Bloke from Freeman's Bay*, a farce with a science fiction theme, and had seen the film become a commercial success. He followed this with his first feature, *My Lady of the Cave* (1922), with the explicit intention of dramatizing aspects of local history: "It was always in my mind, in the back of my mind, this idea of putting New Zealand history on the screen."[3]

My Lady of the Cave, a silent melodrama, was released after certification on February 17, 1922. Thematically, the film deals with the issues surrounding the need for settlers to adjust to the demands of a new environment, one quite different from the British Isles from which most had emigrated. In both its portrayal of New Zealand's landscape, and especially in its meditation on the relationship between settlers and Maori, the film is a concentrated account of a desired version of the settlement process. In the film, set in the North Island's Bay of Plenty in the 1890s, a mill clerk (Gordon Campbell) is hitching a ride on a sailing scow when he is knocked overboard. After managing to swim to a nearby island he finds a strange but beautiful young woman (Hazel West) who is mute, and who is cared for by Rau, a Maori man who is himself deaf and mute. Through a series of flashbacks it is revealed that the young woman, who it turns out is called Beryl Trite, had been the victim of a hostile raid by Maori who object to her family settling their land. With all her family murdered, the young Beryl is rescued by Rau, a family friend. This is despite his having been tortured by the raiding party—his tongue is removed—because of his sympathies with the Trite family. Rau and Beryl escape to the island, remaining in seclusion until their discovery by the mill clerk who, after adventures during which Rau is killed in a conflict with smugglers, finally returns with Beryl to the mainland where, over a two-year period, she is instructed in the ways of society until she is ready for marriage to the mill clerk.

The film is a thoroughly paternalistic and imperialist narrative of desirable settlement, accurately reflecting much of the relationship between the New Zealand of the 1920s and its connection with a perception of its Eurocentric historical legacy, a legacy seen to begin with the arrival of the first colonists. Beryl is clearly a metaphor for the complete new settler, a suitably gendered tabula rasa upon which the man who finds her can inscribe a model for appropriate social and familial behavior, and lay the foundation for subsequent generations as they become part of a maturing society. It is highly significant that the new Eve is nameless until rescued by the mill clerk; the new colonial woman, a classic beauty and model of purity, is to be formed as a consequence of his actions. Women, in Hayward's first feature, are to be designed to live with their male com-

Hayward's first feature film, the melodrama *My Lady of the Cave*, portrayed distinct gender roles. (Courtesy Hayward Collection, New Zealand Film Archive/Nga Kaitaki O Nga Taonga Whitiahua.)

panions as their guardians and support. As such the film clearly inhabits a pioneer mentality of separate gender spheres. Equally, in terms of the cultural politics of settlement, Maori are, literally, voiceless and sexless. Rau has no tongue, and we are told that he has been castrated. He thus poses no influence on and no threat to Beryl other than to act as a physical guardian, and the film's narrative can easily locate him as a benevolent native who is eased out of the story to facilitate a melodramatic conclusion that ideologically underpins the desired dynamics of the emerging Pakeha nation. In technical terms, however, the film is a considerable achievement, with some deft narrative interweaving, and is a curious hybrid of the generic conventions of early filmic melodrama and the wider account of a wished-for settler legitimacy that was specific to New Zealand in the first decades of the twentieth century.

In 1925, Hayward released *Rewi's Last Stand*, a lengthy silent feature of which only fragments (totaling some thirty-five minutes) survive, and which he was to remake with sound in 1940 under the same name. The 1925 and the 1940 films both deal with an episode of the nineteenth-century New Zealand Wars in which Gen. Duncan Cameron, commander of the British garrison, marched against a group of Maori offering armed resistance to Pakeha incursions into Maori lands at Orakau, near Te Awamutu in the North Island. The historical narrative is complemented in the 1925 feature by the story of a young settler, Ken Gordon (Edmund Finney), who joins the army in 1863, an act that forces him to leave new acquaintance Cecily Wake (Nola Casseli). After being separated from his regiment, Gordon rescues a young Maori woman, Takiri (Miss Tina), from drowning and subsequently falls in love with her. Gordon helps Takiri find her lost brother, but as the pair attempts to rejoin the British at Orakau, Takiri is shot and dies in Gordon's arms. He returns to his unit and is reunited with Cecily.

Hayward's film, in a rare departure from the denigrating representation of Maori typical of the period, shows them as heroic figures, warriors at least equal to their British opponents, and allows for the representation of the historical events at Orakau to display reciprocity in that the opposing forces are photographed from both points of view. At the same time, however, the source for the historical account of the conflict is James Cowan's study *The New Zealand Wars* (1922–23), a text Hayward was to use again in his next feature, and one that embodies the kind of paternalistic history that was an orthodoxy in describing early New Zealand.[4] Cowan wrote with imperial eyes and, despite a sympathetic view of his new home, had a British rather than a New Zealand sensibility in his interpretation of events at Orakau. Clearly such an influence affected Hayward's perception. Gordon is an obvious successor to the mill clerk from *My Lady of the Cave*, and in his relationship with Takiri there is an inevitable conflict of loyalties that is resolved only by her death from a British bullet, leaving Gordon free to marry Cecily and continue the paradigm of appropriate settlement. In narrative terms, there is a clear logic for such a result. In much of the popular thinking of the day, miscegenation was still associated in the memory with earlier practices of lowly sealers and whalers, of ruffians and degenerates, and the idea that it could lead only to the degeneration and demise of both cultures continued in certain sections of society.

The public response to, and support for, the 1925 production of *Rewi's Last Stand* was remarkable, calling up apparently unsolicited testimonials from a range of public figures, including headmasters and politicians. As advertising posters for the film put it: "The government has already recognised the importance of the undertaking from an educational point of view and have lent their help in various directions. . . . I need hardly say it should receive the support of every true New Zealander"; and: "The Strand Theater was filled to the doors with an expectant audience, and that there was no disappointment was evidenced by the applause at the conclusion of the screening. The picture was above the level of many imported films, parts of it far above that standard, and need fear no comparison with the world's best."[5] The film was thus seen to be evidence of the maturing of the industry, as well as a dramatic portrayal of the colony's history. Even as it re-worked the historical narrative in filmic terms, it was seen to point to new degrees of sophistication in the development of the nation's creative arts.

Hayward's next film continued the focus on historical and settlement concerns established in *Rewi's Last Stand*. *The Te Kooti Trail* (1927), a silent feature, deals with the physical resistance to the incursion of Pakeha into Maori territories in the nineteenth century. Set in the Bay of Plenty in 1869, and adapted from a newspaper serial written by Frank Bodle (itself based on Cowan's histories), the film dramatizes an attack on a mill settlement, Mill Farm, by Maori political, religious, and military leader Te Kooti (Te Pairi Tu Te Rangi) and his followers, in which the majority of the occupants are killed. One survivor, Monika (Tina Hunt), is later executed after refusing to divulge where some ammunition is hidden. The local military, in the shape of the Corps of Guides led by Lt. Gilbert Mair (Thomas McDermott), fails to prevent the killings, but after a year of tracking Te Kooti, Mair finally defeats him in an attack near Rotorua.

Hayward's presentation of the cultural tensions in the film is complex. Firmly immersed within Pakeha logic in all issues relating to New Zealand settlement, he nevertheless sought to represent the Maori in a positive light. Both the community at Mill Farm and the force that comes to its aid, led by Mair, are shown to be harmonious groupings of Maori and Pakeha. But, at the same time, much of the suggested barbarity in the film is shown to be the work of Baker McLean (Tipene Hotene), a lieutenant of Te Kooti, and a figure of mixed Maori/European blood (labeled "half-caste" in the film). The fear of miscegenation, as in *Rewi's Last Stand*, is palpable, even as the film contains a narrative of mutual cultural respect. The demonizing of McLean allows Hayward to negotiate Te Kooti's violence by partially sourcing it in a figure who falls between the separate definitions the film offers of Maori and European.

The Te Kooti Trail: Under attack from the forces of Te Kooti, the mixed community at Mill Farm prepares its brave defense. (Courtesy Hayward Collection, New Zealand Film Archive/ Nga Kaitaki O Nga Taonga Whitiahua.)

Again, the film was a noticeable technical achievement. *The Te Kooti Trail,* perhaps because of its deference to the traditions of the western genre, is a fast-paced, entertaining, and gripping drama. As with his previous features, some of Hayward's finest images exist in the features of his actors, and there are carefully constructed shots of Te Kooti himself that demonstrate an uneasy acceptance of a Maori leader who appears to abuse Christianity in his resistance to the processes of colonial incursion and settlement.

The Te Kooti Trail was, in a sense, entirely Hayward's film. Much of his work in the early films overall was a collaborative effort, especially with his first wife Hilda, who was virtually a full partner in some of the films made during the 1920s and 1930s.[6] But for *The Te Kooti Trail* he took responsibility for all technical areas, as director and first camera operator, and also handled all financial aspects for Whakatane Films, the production company. It seems clear that, for the key historical narratives Hayward wished to portray, he sought to establish as much control as he could. It is such a full overview of the production process that, especially during a period when filmmaking in New Zealand was a solitary activity, marks the significant nature of his contribution to the developing cinematic culture.

In August 1928, Hayward submitted a very different film to the censor. Granted a certificate for general release on August 17, the silent feature *The Bush Cinderella* is a melodrama in the mold of D. W. Griffith, a morality play set mainly in rural New Zealand beginning at the time of the Boer War. The plot is generic: a soldier, Sergeant Bennett (Tony Firth), goes to war, leaving his lover, Margaret Cameron (Dale Austen), pregnant. Bennett is then killed, and the disgraced Margaret is thrown out of her family home, to be later taken in by the Codlins, a poor farming family. Margaret gives birth to a daughter, Mary (also played as an adult by Dale Austen), but dies shortly after, leaving Mary to be cared for by her new family. The standard melodramatic plot has the adult Mary, following a number of narrative twists and turns, reclaim her birthright and marry the handsome naval officer Neil Harrison (Cecil Scott), after rejecting the farmhand Sammy (Al Mack), whose vernacular working-class status outlines an idea of settler national masculinity, but a model clearly seen to be inferior to that of the middle-class, imperial officer. *The Bush Cinderella* adumbrates an idea of family that Jock Phillips would later theorize as being emblematic of the processes of New Zealand settlement: "The ideal family was conceived to be a bourgeois family, a family of hearth and home, a private largely nuclear family sentimental in tone and ruled in maternal love by a non-earning woman."[7] The film also allowed Hayward to reprise and develop the ideas he had formulated in *My Lady of the Cave*. By having Mary grow up in a pioneering family that was unsophisticated and struggling, and out of which, Cinderella-like, her middle-class heritage could emerge when encouraged by an appropriate male, *The Bush Cinderella* again underlines a late colonial model of desirable settlement, one that is inscribed with clear boundaries of class and gender.

This fourth feature, however, was the last of Hayward's initial burst of creativity. Partly because of the financial constraints of making features, and partly because of his developing interest in the new technology of sound, Hayward moved from features to making the shorts that were to occupy him for the next three years. Beginning with *A Takapuna Scandal* in 1928, Hayward produced some twenty-three "community comedies," short films based on exploiting the desire of local audiences to see their own communities on screen. These films were extremely popular, providing a New Zealand version of Hollywood's comedy shorts, but they also affirm the values of a desired middle-class life through their focus on the individual subject and familial living in the context of a developing community. In the light of Hayward's ongoing interest in and sympathetic portrayal of Maori up to this point in his career, it is instructive to note that the comedies stress a Pakeha version of life in New Zealand. The formulaic plots outline a model of success—the attaining of a husband, the possibility of a future family—that, as with Hayward's earlier features, talk of the dynamics of settlement. In the community comedies, the mill clerk and the lady of the cave reappear in comic form, but the stress on the need for an appropriate settlement is maintained.

During the late 1920s and early 1930s, Hayward, with the assistance of Jack Baxendale and Armitage Moren, was slowly developing a sound camera. He used the new camera to make New Zealand's first talking picture comedy, *Hamilton Talks*, in 1934, and then again in the making of *On the Friendly Road* (1936). *On the Friendly Road*, at eighty-six minutes, is the first sound film made involving Hayward that is long enough to be called a feature.[8] The film is a didactic and well-meaning statement about the importance of "ordinary" New Zealanders, carrying on the theme Hayward had established in *The Bush Cinderella*, and is an extension of the popular 1930s radio sessions (titled "The Friendly Road") of the Reverend Colin Scrimgeour. Scrimgeour, who plays his radio character "Uncle Scrim" in the film, offered moralistic advice to his listeners, and *On the Friendly Road* dramatizes an incident wherein two honest, hardworking men, Mac McDermitt (John Mackie) and Old Bill (Stanley Knight), are falsely accused of a crime, but the truth is revealed following McDermitt's son Harry (Neville Goodwin) acting on Uncle Scrim's advice. The sentimental moralizing owes much to the context of the 1930s Depression, and the film contains a strong critique of capitalism and distrust of the leisured middle classes, appearing just after New Zealand's first Labour government came to power. For all of these left-wing credentials however, *On the Friendly Road* also is one of the few films Hayward was involved with in which Maori are very clearly denigrated rather than given equivalent status to Pakeha, and the first Hayward feature in which a clear tourist version of Maoridom is utilized. During the film, Maori are represented as childish and comic—wearing tattered straw hats and making jokes about Maori time, or sitting on steps smoking pipes and spitting. These are the fixed images of the nineteenth-century photographer and are in clear contrast to Hayward's earlier work.

On the Friendly Road is a weak feature overall, with particular difficulties surrounding the dialogue and acting. It marked the beginnings of a change in quality in Hayward's work, a loss of the vibrancy and raw dramatic energy that had marked his earlier major features, particularly the 1925 version of *Rewi's Last Stand* and the 1928 *The Te Kooti Trail*. In shifting focus from the features of the 1920s to his nonfiction films of

A return to the settlement myth: The 1940 sound version of *Rewi's Last Stand*. (Courtesy Ian Conrich collection of New Zealand cinema and visual culture.)

the 1940s and 1950s, Hayward's work began to express clear social concerns and left-wing sympathies that would ultimately lead to invited tours of communist China in 1957, and Albania in 1971. The shift also was marked by the beginning of a falling-off of production values, and of financial hardship that remained with him until his death.

Before this could happen fully however, Hayward made the sound version of *Rewi's Last Stand* (a.k.a. *The Last Stand*) in 1940. In the remake, Hayward altered the depiction of military events to develop the melodramatic narrative of a young settler, Robert Beaumont (Leo Pilcher), meeting and falling in love with a young Maori woman, Ariana (Ramai Te Miha). Ariana is the daughter of a sea captain who had left her mother, but who had then joined the British forces engaged with the Maori in the Waikato in the North Island. When the mission at which Ariana lives is in danger of attack, she is smuggled out, but walking with Beaumont in the bush, she is discovered and recaptured. Beaumont joins Von Tempsky's Forest Rangers and goes off on a scouting expedition in an attempt to find Ariana. He does so, but Ariana has promised to stay with her community, and they part. Following the major battle at Orakau, Ariana attempts to escape but is shot and dies in Beaumont's arms.

The sound version lost much of the tightly woven drama of the original. The romantic melodrama that was intended to provide a human face for the conflict fails to convince in narrative terms, as Hayward did not seem able to decide whether he wanted a film with a clear focus on New Zealand's history, or to stress the soft-focus sentimentality and overstated images that characterized low-budget Hollywood features of the period. A 1990 comment in the Maori periodical *Te Iwi* notes the kind of tensions this produced: "[Hayward] made an attempt at historical accuracy—but distorted the significance of the facts to suit obvious preconceived ideas about what should have been in the minds of the protagonists . . . but couldn't have been. Orakau was a bloody, almost genocidal confrontation by Maori and European with no quarter given."[9]

The 1940 version of *Rewi's Last Stand* certainly couldn't approach such a sense of history, given its position within the limitations of genre and the demands of a Pakeha-centered account of nineteenth-century conflict. It was also a troubled production, beset by organizational and financial difficulties concerning its subsequent distribution, and not a commercial success. In addition, Hayward never produced an authoritative print of the full version of the film, and he was later to take the only negatives to Britain, where the film was recut as a British Quota title and re-issued in shorter form. This is the only remaining version of what was originally a much longer film.

The years that followed the second version of *Rewi's Last Stand* show a filmmaker becoming at once more serious, more didactic, and more political, and at the same time losing the imaginative energy that had marked his early work. Hayward's films became more pedestrian and, despite the best of intentions, increasingly lacked cinematic interest. He worked progressively more as a reporter and documentary maker, in 1941 becoming a National Film Unit photographer. In 1946, he married Ramai Te Miha, and they formed a news team with Hayward on camera and Ramai as sound operator. They left for Britain the same year, taking the homemade sound camera with them, and Hayward was employed by the BBC as a news cameraman, filming, among others, Joe Louis and Eleanor Roosevelt. During 1947, he and Ramai were involved in making *The Goodwin Sands* for Warner Bros. and a documentary, *The World Is Turning (Towards the Coloured People)*. The documentary was never finished or released and was described when rediscovered by British archivist Luke McKernan as "an amateurish, rather gauche production."[10]

Following their return to New Zealand from Britain, the Haywards then moved to Australia in 1949, where they worked in early Australian television, on Colin Scrimgeour's (the "Uncle Scrim" of *On the Friendly Road*) Associated TV programs, and made cowboy films for children and documentaries for sale to American television networks. Returning to New Zealand in 1952, the Haywards continued to make documentaries, including *Opo: The Amazing Dolphin of Opononi*, which went on to sell in twenty-six countries.

Hayward's developing affiliation with left-wing politics was, in its own way, an orthodoxy in certain intellectual circles following 1945. His commitment meant that, following an invitation from the Chinese government, he and Ramai visited China to make a series of documentaries, including *Inside Red China* (1957) and *Wonders of China* (1958), and Ramai's twenty-two-minute *Children of China*. Working in China was one of a series of experiences that promoted Hayward's interest in the relationship between film and education, and in 1960, the Haywards began shooting a series of collaborative educational films, most of which were released with accompanying teaching notes that were crude and generalized but well intentioned, beginning with *The Little Shepherdesses* (1963). The films were produced at a rate of about one a year, with other titles like *Playing Safe in Small Boats* (1963) and *A French Family in New Caledonia* (1967).

In the early 1970s, however, Hayward sought to return to feature filmmaking and especially to the issues of cultural relations in New Zealand. During 1970 and 1971, he and Ramai worked together on *To Love a Maori*, writing the screenplay assisted by Diane Francis, and directing and editing, assisted by Alton Francis. The severe financial constraints under which the

Haywards were now operating meant that the production, which sought to deal with the issues of race relations and the postwar move of Maori from rural to urban locations, had to be shot in 16 mm. The consequent problems with the film's technical quality exacerbated the difficulties arising from stilted dialogue and acting from the inexperienced young lead actors. *To Love a Maori* was to be Hayward's last film, and perhaps his saddest, as the energy and sophistication that had characterized his early work had waned. In 1974 he died of pneumonia in the South Island city of Dunedin, contracted while on the road publicizing a feature that was driven by liberal politics and sought to engage again with the issues that had characterized Hayward's earlier features, but was in truth scarcely watchable.

The obituaries were, however, generous. Hayward's contribution to New Zealand cinema history is inescapable, even if his somewhat embittered final years involved his sense of a lack of recognition for what he had accomplished. The films of his last three decades are notably less accomplished than his earlier features, but in these early films he produced sustained analyses of New Zealand's social and cultural relations at a time when filmmaking was still a huge technical challenge, and he did so with a complexity unmatched by any of his peers. As such, Hayward may still claim the title of New Zealand's most significant film pioneer.

Notes

1. John O'Shea, "A Charmed Life: Fragments of Memory . . . and Extracts from Conversations," in *Film in Aotearoa New Zealand*, ed. Jonathan Dennis and Jan Bieringa (Wellington: Victoria University Press, 1992), 27.
2. Robert Sklar, "Rudall Hayward: New Zealand Film Maker," *Landfall* 98 (June 1971): 150.
3. Hayward, undated taped interview, Australian Film and Sound Archive, Canberra.
4. James Cowan, *The New Zealand Wars: A History of the Maori Campaigns and the Pioneering Period*, 2 vols. (Wellington: W. A. G. Skinner, 1922–23).
5. Quotations from posters held in the New Zealand Film Archive, Wellington.
6. This point is developed in detail in Deborah Shepard's analysis of women in New Zealand film. See *reframing Women: A History of New Zealand Film* (Auckland: HarperCollins, 2000), 12.
7. Jock Phillips, *A Man's Country? The Image of the Pakeha Male—A History* (Auckland: Penguin, 1987), 221.
8. The film production is credited to an organization called The New Zealand Film Guild, but this body was a front for a lawyer called Leonard Leary. Leary is credited with co-writing the screenplay and directing the film but was bound by the codes of legal practice then existing in New Zealand and forbidden to reveal his identity. Hayward appears on the credits as the director of photography, but although Leary claimed the copyright of the film, Hayward was the driving force behind it.

9. *Te Iwi*, February 1990, 19.
10. Letter to Sam Edwards, September 17, 1999.

Rudall Hayward—Filmography

Note: It is difficult to compile information on Hayward's career, and what is provided here is intended as an initial record. This is not a complete list, and where there are gaps it has not been possible to verify information. Also, the titles of many of the actualities are just descriptions that have been provided for ease of identification.

1921. *The Betrayer* (Australian feature film: assistant).
1921. *The Bloke from Freeman's Bay* (NZ short film: director).
1922. *The Birth of New Zealand* (NZ feature film: assistant).
1922. ***My Lady of the Cave*** (NZ feature film: director, producer, writer).
1925. *The Arrival of the American Fleet at Auckland* (NZ actuality: cinematographer).
1925. *Rewi's Last Stand* (NZ feature film: director, writer).
1926. *Hamilton Shingle & Buster Competition* (NZ actuality: cinematographer).
1926. *The Official Films of The Royal Show, Auckland, November 1926* (NZ actuality: cinematographer).
1927. *The Te Kooti Trail* (NZ feature film: director, producer, co-writer, cinematographer).
1927. *The Arrival of the Their Royal Highnesses the Duke and Duchess of York at Auckland* (NZ actuality: cinematographer).
1928. *The Bush Cinderella* (NZ feature film: director, writer, cinematographer).
1928. *Tilly of Te Aroha* (NZ short film: director).
1928. *Winifred of Wanganui* (NZ short film: director, writer, cinematographer).
1928. *Natalie of Napier* (NZ short film: director).
1928. *Natalie of Nelson* (NZ short film: director).
1928. *Patsy of Palmerston* (NZ short film: director).
1928. *A Daughter of Dunedin* (NZ short film: director, producer, cinematographer).
1928. *A Daughter of Invercargill* (NZ short film: director, producer, cinematographer).
1928. *A Daughter of Hastings* (NZ short film: director, producer, cinematographer).
1928. *A Daughter of Gisborne* (NZ short film: director, producer, cinematographer).
1928. *A Daughter of Wairoa* (NZ short film: director, producer, cinematographer).

1928. *A Daughter of Masterton* (NZ short film: director, producer, cinematographer).
1928. *Hamilton's Hectic Husbands* (NZ short film: director).
1928. *A Takapuna Scandal* (NZ short film: director).
1929. *A Daughter of Christchurch* (NZ short film: director, producer, cinematographer).
1929. *A Daughter of New Plymouth* (NZ short film: director, producer, cinematographer).
1929. *A Daughter of Thames* (NZ short film: director, producer, cinematographer).
1929. *A Daughter of Auckland* (NZ short film: director, producer, cinematographer).
1929. *A Daughter of Dannevirke* (NZ short film: director, producer, cinematographer).
1929. *A Daughter of Timaru* (NZ short film: director, producer, cinematographer).
1929. *A Daughter of Whangarei* (NZ short film: director, producer, cinematographer).
1930. *A Daughter of Te Kuiti* (NZ short film: director, producer, cinematographer).
1931. *Auckland from the Air: A Film Record of the Activities of the Auckland Aero Club, June 3rd 1933* (NZ actuality: cinematographer).
1931. *New Zealand Soundscenes: The Bigger They Are the Harder They Fall* (NZ newsreel: co-cinematographer).
1931. *The Grand Rally of Boy Scouts and Girl Guides in Honour of Lord and Lady Baden Powell* (NZ actuality: cinematographer).
1933. *King's Birthday Parade, before His Excellency the Governor-General Lord Bledisloe, Auckland* (NZ actuality: cinematographer).
1934. *New Zealand Soundscenes: Waitangi Celebrations* (NZ newsreel: co-cinematographer).
1934. *Hamilton Talks* (NZ short film: director, producer).
1936. *On the Friendly Road* (NZ feature film: story, cinematographer, editor).
1936. *Jean Batten* (NZ newsreel item for Pathe News: cinematographer).
1940. *Rewi's Last Stand* a.k.a. ***The Last Stand*** (NZ feature film: director, writer, cinematographer, editor).
1941. *New Zealand's Own News Reel* (NZ newsreel: cinematographer).
1941. *The Miracle of the Pine: An Epic of Industry* (NZ documentary: director, cinematographer).
1947. *What Am I Bid?* (NZ documentary: cinematographer).
1949. *Fighting Back* (NZ documentary: production assistant).
1950. *Song of the Wanganui* (NZ documentary: director, cinematographer).
1953. *The Challengers* (NZ documentary: director, cinematographer).
1955. *Opo: The Amazing Dolphin of Opononi* (NZ documentary: director, cinematographer).

1955. Commercial for Pherezeen Plus Sheep Drench (NZ: director).
1956. *Springbok Tour of New Zealand. 4th and Final Test, Auckland, Saturday September 1st* (NZ actuality: cinematographer).
1957. *Inside Red China* (documentary: director, cinematographer).
1958. *Wonders of China* (documentary: director, cinematographer).
1958. *New China* (documentary: director, cinematographer).
1958. *Jack Urlwin, the Human Storage Battery* (NZ documentary: cinematographer).
1960. *Eel History Was a Mystery* (NZ documentary: director, cinematographer).
1961. *Timber Loading* (NZ actuality: cinematographer).
1961. *Christchurch Airport* (NZ actuality: cinematographer).
1961. *Painting of Maori Landing in New Zealand* (NZ actuality: cinematographer).
1961. *Maori and Polynesian Faces* (NZ actuality: cinematographer).
1961. *Frozen Meat, Adelaide Star* (NZ actuality: cinematographer).
1961. *Mob of Sheep* (NZ actuality: cinematographer).
1961. *Auckland Bus, Queen Street* (NZ actuality: cinematographer).
1961. *Kauri Forest* (NZ actuality: cinematographer).
1961. *Miri's Cave Drawings* (NZ actuality: cinematographer).
1961. *Golden Shears* (NZ actuality: cinematographer).
1962. *Queen Visiting Marae* (NZ actuality: cinematographer).
1962. *Children of the Goldrush, Arrowtown Centenary* (NZ actuality: cinematographer).
1962. *The Arts of Maori Children* (NZ documentary: director, cinematographer).
1963. *The Little Shepherdesses* (NZ documentary: director, producer).
1963. *Playing Safe in Small Boats* (NZ documentary: co-producer).
1963. *A North Island Dairy Farm* (NZ documentary: cinematographer).
1963. *The Living Fossil—The Tuatara* (NZ documentary: director, cinematographer).
1964. *A Village in Samoa* (NZ documentary: director, cinematographer).
1964. *The Great Experiment in American Samoa* (NZ/US documentary: director).
1964. *Baby on Lake Forsyth* (NZ actuality: cinematographer).
1966. *Lizards and Skinks* (NZ actuality: cinematographer).
1966. *Butler Material* (NZ actuality: cinematographer).
1966. *Pine Forest, Dam, Transformers, Power House* (NZ actuality: cinematographer).
1966. *Kiwis* (NZ actuality: cinematographer).
1966. *Bush Fire* (NZ actuality: cinematographer).
1967. *Globe at Christchurch Museum* (NZ actuality: cinematographer).
1967. *Reception for Governor General* (NZ actuality: cinematographer).
1967. *A French Family in New Caledonia* (NZ documentary: director, cinema-

tographer).
1967. *Alpine Shepherds of New Zealand* (NZ documentary: director, cinematographer).
1968. *Iron and Steel Works, Beach Scenes* (NZ actuality: cinematographer).
1968. *Mt. Taranaki, Auckland Aerial Shots* (NZ actuality: cinematographer).
1968. *Motor Holidays. Mt. Eden* (NZ actuality: cinematographer).
1968. *Whitacker Wedding* (NZ actuality: cinematographer).
1968. *Anti Vietnam War March* (NZ actuality: cinematographer).
1969. *Auckland Regatta* (NZ actuality: cinematographer).
1969. *Caravan Companions—Happy Days in New Zealand* (NZ travelogue: director, cinematographer).
1971. *English Language Teaching for Maori and Island Children* (NZ informational film: producer).
1972. ***To Love a Maori*** (NZ feature film: co-director, co-producer, co-writer, co-editor).
1972. *The Young Albanians* (NZ documentary: co-director, co-producer).
1973. *The Doll's House* (NZ short film: director).
1974. *Matenga—Maori Choreographer* (NZ documentary: co-producer).

3

John O'Shea

A POETICS OF DOCUMENTARY

Laurence Simmons

Under the rubric of "blurred boundaries," documentary theorist Bill Nichols has analyzed decisive moments in the history of social representation in film, television, and video when the traditional borders of fiction/nonfiction and truth/falsehood are obscured. As Nichols says:

> We hunger for news from the world around us but desire it in the form of narratives, stories that make meaning, however tenuous, dramatic, compelling or paranoid they might be. Tales we label fiction offer imaginative answers: those we label nonfiction suggest possibly authentic ones. Inevitably, the distinction between fact and fiction blurs when claims about reality get cast as narratives. We enter a zone where the world put before us lies between one not our own and one that might well be, between a world we may recognise as a fragment of our own and one that may seem fabricated from such fragments, between indexical (authentic) signs of reality and cinematic (invented) interpretations of this reality.[1]

Not simply an instrument of demarcation, for Nichols the border is a crucial zone to negotiate received knowledge and reconstitute discursive identity, and, as such, a border is always subject to redefinition, disputation, and realignment.

It is exactly such a conception of borders and the transgression of barriers that informs the work of John O'Shea. O'Shea (1920–2001) directed three feature films—*Broken Barrier* (1952), *Runaway* (1964), and *Don't Let It Get You* (1966)—in a difficult period when there were few, if any, professional structures for film production in New Zealand. In 1953 he joined the first independent filmmaking company in New Zealand, Pacific Films (founded by Roger Mirams and Alun Falconer in 1948). By making cine-magazine items, public information films, and what are now called "corporates"—including sponsored documentaries, trade films, local news items, rugby films, and road safety films—Pacific Films kept the idea of an independent film industry alive from the 1950s through to the 1970s. It was also an important training ground for a generation of new filmmakers who would subsequently play pivotal roles in the New Zealand film industry as it developed: Tony Williams, Michael Seresin, Barry Barclay, Gaylene Preston, John Reid, and Sam Neill among others. As O'Shea has noted: "Our 'new generation'—young people—at Pacific Films were part of the sixties. Pacific became a sort of alfresco film school."[2]

O'Shea was born in 1920 in New Plymouth, where his father, who had come to New Zealand from Ireland as a small boy, worked on the Railways.[3] O'Shea's mother died of septicemia at his birth and he was taken to live with relatives in Wanganui. His father remained in New Plymouth with his four older siblings and was later to become the stationmaster at Palmerston North. As John O'Shea later remarked of his own unconventional family background: "Not only the Maori know what whanau [extended family] means—the Irish do, too."[4] He has also recounted how the animated family disagreements over politics in the evenings marked his childhood during the Depression.[5] The young O'Shea attended private Catholic schools and then completed his secondary education at the Wanganui Technical College. In 1936, O'Shea went to Victoria University, Wellington, to study law but found that his stammer hampered his progress and changed to a major in history. In 1940, he joined the army as an ambulance driver with the 3rd New Zealand Division in the Pacific and then served with the 2nd Division in Italy. Immediately after completing his war service he attended Teachers' College in Christchurch, where he married and was involved in directing stage productions. He then returned to Wellington to complete an honors degree in history at Victoria University in 1944, with a thesis on New Zealand's foreign policy from 1935 to 1939 and the implications of isolation and conformity on national identity.

O'Shea had attempted to join the National Film Unit (NFU, established in 1941) immediately after the war but found that they would hire only qualified photographers, and so after graduation he began lecturing in History at Victoria University College, where historian Peter Munz and poet Hubert Witheford were among his circle of friends. However, he retained his interest in film and became Associate Editor of the Wellington Film Society Bulletin in 1946, moving on to be Assistant Government Film Censor in 1949. He had been introduced to Roger Mirams (O'Shea's future collaborator on *Broken Barrier*) in May 1950 by Mirams's older brother Gordon, who was the founder of the Wellington Film Society and Chief Film Censor. Gordon Mirams had been posted to UNESCO to advise on the political use of film, and while in Paris fellow workers had suggested to him that a film dealing with race relations in New Zealand would be of interest in other countries.[6] Upon his return to New Zealand, Gordon floated this idea to his brother and as a consequence Roger was soon looking for a writer to help on a documentary script about Maori.[7] Mirams had already shot some footage on Maori subjects, thinking that it might end up in a twenty-minute documentary.[8] O'Shea agreed to collaborate with him but only on the condition that they produce a feature film rather than a documentary, and that O'Shea could co-direct. The film had an initial capital of seventeen pounds, and the scriptwriting took six months of 1950, going through five or six drafts. In late December 1950, the film unit went on location, and O'Shea tells the story of *Broken Barrier*'s pioneering production as follows:

> We had little money between us, but we had two mute 35 mm 200 foot load Arriflex cameras, one of them on loan from Movietone News, the other picked up from, allegedly, a dead German in the Western Desert and sold to us for two hundred pounds. Roger had a rickety camera dolly and some lights cobbled together from scrap metal. We set off in Roger's little Vauxhall car with as much of the film stock and gear as we could load into it. *Folie grandeur* was upon us! Bill Parker [who plays Wiremu in the film], whom I had known at university, arranged entree to Maoridom in his tribal area. Another university friend, Tom Ormond, welcomed us to his family's home and farm on the Mahia Peninsula. In the summer of 1950–51, we set about making the film. We did have one day's sync sound shooting—with a huge disc cutter which took three of us to lift into position on the Nuhaka marae [meeting place]. Having to hump gear across the paddocks and build trenches and little bridges for the massive dolly tracks, we were thankful we thought up the idea of "spoken thoughts" rather than dialogue recording . . . which was beyond our pockets anyway.
>
> On the Mahia Peninsula, our hosts and most of the people who helped with the gear and kai [food] were happy to appear in the film. Later, when we were shooting in Wellington, friends assisted our low budget by appearing in the film. We stuck to the storyline as best we, with all the weight of our inexperience, could.[9]

Released in 1952, *Broken Barrier* owes much to the British tradition of documentary filmmaking, despite O'Shea's later assertion that, at the time of undertaking to make the film, he "was utterly bored and disillusioned with documentaries."[10] In *Broken Barrier* we find this concern with a documentary realism in its opening shots of rolling surf and Maori gathering kaimoana (seafood) from rock pools, accompanied by an imposing, authoritative, male, Pakeha (European) voice-over, the sort of voice-over familiar to audiences from newsreel documentaries of the period:

> These people are Maoris. For them, as for all Polynesians, the boundary of their world has been the Pacific Ocean. Their ancestors voyaged across it six centuries ago to discover this rugged land far to the south. Then about 150 years ago, the white man came and called the land "New Zealand." Today many of the Maoris still lead a simple life tilling the soil, and searching for shellfish along the rocky coast. For better and worse, the white man brought with him "civilisation." Though the Maoris live in peace with the Europeans, many of them try to keep up with the pace of the modern world. They are stranded, caught like fish out of water. All of them face barriers of misunderstanding and prejudice. Whenever two races live side by side, there are problems. Here is the story of some Maoris and Europeans, and this is what they think about it all.

A concern with documentary realism appears also in the film's treatment of the vocations of nursing, sheep shearing, and forestry, which give portions of it the feel and appearance of a government training film. Indeed, Mirams and O'Shea included some footage from a 1951 documentary, *Timber for All Time*, they made on the workings of the Kaingaroa State Forest in the middle of the North Island. Scenes from the middle sequence of the film are also similar in feel to a slightly later 1954 documentary they would make together on the timber industry, *New Frontier: The Story of Kawerau*. *Broken Barrier*, as will already be apparent from these examples, consciously employs many documentary codes of filming used by earlier Italian Neorealist filmmakers: codes such as on-location shooting, the use of non-professional actors,[11] the bird's eye point-of-view shot and "objective" (i.e. non-associative) points of view, the rejection of theatrical or openly cinematic conventions, the use of standard camera angles and long shots, connecting narrative voice-overs, the repression of the signs of the apparatus of production, and a rhythm of editing that never seems to force the pace of the narrative. It is not surprising, then, to learn that Roger Mirams, behind the camera in *Broken Barrier*, was an official New Zealand camera operator in Italy during World War II and an avowed fan of the work of Roberto Rossellini.

A further obvious correlation to be made in this context concerns the ethnographic use of film. *Broken Barrier,* or at least some early sequences of the film, can be read as conforming to the mode of observational documentary that is empathetic and non-judgmental, allowing the viewer to look in on the lived experience of others, recording here being a function of social anthropology. Perhaps it is also not a coincidence that one of O'Shea and Mirams's first projects after completing *Broken Barrier* was to film *Dances of the South Pacific* (1955), an ethnographic survey of Polynesian dancing and music including the haka, poi, *siva,* Tongan stick dance, and Hawaiian hula all shot on location. Both *Broken Barrier* and *Dances of the South Pacific* undertake a double process of presenting a culture that is neglected yet attempt a recovery of that culture through re-creation of custom, where the two worlds are juxtaposed uneasily side by side. Associated with this double-bind is the, by now familiar, anthropological dilemma of the passing of cultures tinged with the inescapable bad faith of the anthropologist's intervention much anguished over by Claude Lévi-Strauss in his *Tristes tropiques* (1955).[12] In a similar state of sadness and nostalgia the opening voice-over of *Broken Barrier* laments the loss of an idealized past and the loss of authenticity found in the present state of the Maori.[13]

The fictional drama of *Broken Barrier* concerns the state of race relations between Maori and Pakeha as played out through the story of the love affair and eventual marriage between Tom Sullivan (Terence Bayler), a Pakeha journalist of Irish descent who, in order to research a series of tabloid articles on the Maori for an American magazine, becomes a casual laborer on a Mahia Peninsula farm, and Rawi (Kay Ngarimu), the farm owner's daughter, home on summer leave from her job as a nurse at Wellington Hospital. The affinities of this fiction film with forms of documentary can be conveyed by the detail of one episode of the film: the cattle mustering sequence, of narrative significance because it is where the film's two protagonists initiate their romantic relationship. It also provides evidence of what I have called elsewhere the "broken or double" structure of this filmtext and its growing unease with the British documentary tradition.[14]

The mustering sequence is shot as it occurs. It is not a staged event for the camera but an event "in reality" that the camera catches, then frames, a technique typical of O'Shea's filmmaking method. The sequence signifies itself: farmers are simply mustering the cattle. But it also signifies within the fiction the power of the natural landscape of the East Coast of the North Island, where Maori are firmly established as natural inhabitants and which defines not only their economic power and security but also their sexuality. Here Rawi is presented at one with the land, and this power is reiterated later when she decides to leave the cold alienation of urban

O'Shea's first feature, *Broken Barrier,* began the combination of documentary, drama, and cultural concerns that would characterize his filmmaking. (Courtesy Ian Conrich collection of New Zealand cinema and visual culture.)

Wellington to return home to work among her own people. Thus the real at the edges of the fictional film is absorbed by the fiction. From a real event it becomes a fictional sign, motivated within the narrative actions of the film.

Nevertheless, this sequence, like those focused on shearing and forestry, also tears the texture of fiction. Its reality is in many ways too much for the fiction to absorb completely. It reminds us, as I have suggested, of a filmic other, a government training film, or possibly one of the many documentaries on farming that Mirams and O'Shea made together about the same time, such as *Harvest of Sunshine* (1951) or *This Valley* (1952). Rather than simply serving the context in which it is inserted, a sequence like this also disrupts that context by moving away from the fiction toward reality. The film, deliberately it seems, complicates the edge between the text and what lies beyond its fringes, what is classed as real. It lies across the border between the fictive and nonfiction and blurs the boundaries between them.

It is apparent, then, that *Broken Barrier* hovers on a line between reality and fictional text. The alterity of reality is not suppressed by the fiction (as it is in classic film narratives). On the one hand, the film fictionalizes reality; on the other hand, it cites it. Reality is in the film and outside the film, a fragment of an exterior continuity brought into the fiction, but whose force, nevertheless, exceeds the film's constructed continuity of a fictional illusory real. *Broken Barrier* is constructed along a boundary that it is constantly "overrunning," to use a term Jacques Derrida has applied to all texts.[15] It is a special type of nonfictional fiction.

O'Shea's next feature, *Runaway* (1964), is the story of David Manning (Colin Broadley) who, disillusioned with his Auckland friends and their materialistic lifestyle, decides to leave Auckland and hitchhike his way around the country. On the inter-island ferry he teams up with a similarly lost young woman, Diana (Deidre McCarron), and together they flee the police who are mistakenly pursuing Manning for a suspicious death. The couple make for Westland on the west coast of the South Island, progressively withdrawing into the remoteness of the bush and the mountains. *Runaway* does not contain any actual documentary footage, but it does continue in various ways to inhabit this border between the real and the fictional. What is obvious, and was not unnoticed by early reviewers, is the staged difference between two kinds of representation in *Runaway:* the modernism of 1960s European art cinema (there are many visual citations of Michelangelo Antonioni, Jean-Luc Godard, and Alain Resnais), with its existential drama and complex camerawork, is contrasted with the rawness of a New Zealand story, with its colloquial language and popular culture elements, including the archetypal figure of the "man alone," the rural nature of a North Island Hokianga Maori community, and the participation of Barry Crump, the archetypal "good keen man" of New Zealand popular culture, as a west coast deer shooter.[16] Such a strategy of cultural confabulation is not as strange as it might have first seemed, or as untried in the visual arts, for in the late 1940s the renowned New Zealand painter Colin McCahon had already tried to blend Italian Renaissance religious painting with the popular culture of sign writing and comic strips.[17]

Runaway, as an early reviewer in *The Guardian* was quick to point out, "is an allegory about New Zealand relations with Great Britain. An allegory about New Zealand's dilemma between her prosperous past as a British dependent, and her uncertain future with lower living standards, as an extension of Asia."[18] This contemporary background is not explicitly spelled out in the film, but an awareness of its historical moment inflects its interpretation. One seminal work of Kiwi national identity, John Mulgan's prototypical novel *Man Alone* (1939), has a definite presence in *Runaway*. The novel, like the film, is set in rural New Zealand and has a lone central

European Modernism relocated: David, accompanied by Diana, reaches New Zealand's Southern Alps in *Runaway*. (Courtesy Ian Conrich collection of New Zealand cinema and visual culture.)

male character who feels ill at ease in a restrictive urban environment and "falls" into the wild landscape hoping to achieve purification through contact with it. *Runaway* is a film about facing responsibility. Other characters constantly tell its protagonist David that he cannot run away from reality: his boss Mr. Bellamy (John Atha) advises him, "I can tell you you'll have to face the music yourself"; his lover Laura (Nadja Regin) chides him, "You've never really faced up to anything have you? Not even to yourself"; his new girlfriend Diana asks, "Wouldn't it be better to face things again? You should go back and face it all." David's journey, a road movie through New Zealand, operates on one level as a kind of travelogue—a scenic naming of the nation, a physical mapping-out of the landscape—but it is also an allegory of the nation in the early 1960s. There are obvious parallels between David's break with Auckland and his family to go in search of his true identity and New Zealand's loosening of ties with Britain as the latter moved toward joining the European Common Market, with it becoming clear that Britain's status as New Zealand's primary produce consumer was no longer assured. Thus an important source and a pre-text for *Run-*

away was O'Shea's *Food for Thought*, made two years earlier in 1962. This documentary was a mixture of farm footage, including scenes of mustering, which might have been drawn from *Broken Barrier*; interviews with ordinary New Zealanders on the street about their feelings toward Britain and the European free market; and, what was novel for the time, the use of the light touch of animation to convey hard facts and statistics.[19]

In analyzing the mustering sequence of *Broken Barrier* I argue that, however relevant in narrative terms the sequence is, and however much it is therefore fictitious, the documentary images of the muster overpower the narrative to assert the grandeur of the landscape. This is also true of the final sequence of *Runaway* on the slopes of the Franz Josef glacier. Although at the end of the film we are left with an open narrative in the uncertainty of the outcome of David Manning's flight, the grandeur of the Southern Alps filmed from the air not only overpowers but also overshadows the story in which he is caught. The beauty of the event as real stands out against the narrative impetus of the event as fiction that then slides off into indecision. As with *Broken Barrier*, reality appears suddenly and inexplicably from within the heart of the fiction to the degree that the fictional is momentarily cancelled out.

O'Shea's third feature film, *Don't Let It Get You*, is a musical in which performers and spectators converge on the tourist backdrop of the North Island setting of Rotorua, where singing star Howard Morrison has undertaken to organize a summer music festival. Perhaps nothing might seem further from documentary than the genre of musical. But every musical contains two worlds, the world of its narrative and the world of its entertainment. There exists in every musical a fundamental tension between a world given as real (the world of the plot or narrative) and another realm portrayed as fictional (the world of the musical number). A musical, by its very generic conventions, is then already playing across the divide of fact and fiction, and it is another border structure that blurs boundaries.

In *Don't Let It Get You*, a form of performative documentary realism is resuscitated as the entertainers play themselves as "social actors"—for instance, Morrison as impresario; performer and local Maori celebrity, Ernie Leonard, then Rotorua's public relations officer; and future international opera star Kiri Te Kanawa—among a daily reality of motels, service stations, and local sites. This gives the film the feel of a tourist travelogue. Images of thermal activity at Whakarewarewa, which had figured negatively in *Broken Barrier* where they were the sites of the cultural misunderstandings of American tourists, are now actively promoted along with scenes of Maori boys leaping off a bridge for coins thrown by tourists. As the audience, we ride on Rotorua's model railway and explore the geothermal lunar landscape known as Hell's Gate. The long takes of the pre-concert

A form of performative documentary realism: In the musical *Don't Let It Get You*, singer Normie Rowe is one of a group of entertainers who play themselves. (Courtesy Pacific Films Collection, New Zealand Film Archive/Nga Kaitaki O Nga Taonga Whitiahua.)

sequences, for example those of performers arriving in Rotorua, provide a counterpart to the moments of farce and the energetic editing of the musical numbers.

However, it is no surprise that these two worlds of fact and fiction collide in one of the earliest songs in the film, Lew Pryme's performance of "C'mon," centered on a Caltex service station. In an exuberant performance that is pushed to become an energetic parody of "show biz" itself, Pryme uses the petrol pump nozzle as a microphone, Morrison endorses the Caltex brand Boron in Maori, Gary Wallace mimes a film camera with his ukulele, while go-go dancers strut their stuff behind a giant Caltex sign on top of the service station's roof. A similar tone of irreverent playfulness in the slippage between the real and the performed, and back again, is to be found in Gerry Merito's rendition of "Have You Ever (Seen A Letterbox)" set among the material objects of a cowshed yard to which the song constantly alludes. There also comes a point when the transitions become thematized in the diegetic storyline of the film itself, as when Gary and Judy (Carmen Duncan) approach the wharenui (meeting house) to strains of classical music. As Gary pretends to conduct, the music, whose source is not revealed, suddenly stops and we move inside to discover Kiri Te Kanawa and her tape recorder. At the request of the children seated around her, Kiri sings and the camera takes off in a sweeping movement over the painted kowhaiwhai (scroll) patterns of the meeting house interior as the notes of a Rossini aria float on the air. We thus have a revelation of reality through the theatricalization of it. By playing across the divide of fact and fiction, "high" and "low" culture, metropolitan opera and Maori carvings, O'Shea's "border work" exemplifies his stated aim for all his films that "integration [be] taken as a norm of life in New Zealand."[20]

There are, I feel, important visual links between *Don't Let It Get You*'s referencing of the car culture of the 1960s—its early shots of the bustle of multi-lane traffic in Sydney, of performers arriving in Rotorua by car, the scenes around the Caltex service station, and even the advertising poster for the film—and a number of road safety documentaries made by O'Shea and Pacific Films for the Department of Transport during the 1950s and early 1960s, documentary films such as *You Are the Jury* (1956), *Pretty Mary* (1957), *Youth at the Wheel* (1959), *Got a Moment* (1960), *Keep Them Waiting* (1963), and *Who Will Be a Statistic?* (1965). Many of these documentaries exhibit the incursions of fiction into documentary film by using fictionalized voice-overs and employing "social actors." Let me briefly examine one of them: *Keep Them Waiting* traces the separate itineraries of several couples who venture onto the road during the Labour Weekend holiday, meet at the same crossroads, and are about to collide with one another, but just before the crucial crash the film is reversed, the accident prevented, and the police, ambulance, newspaper reporter, and doctors "kept waiting." In an awareness of the fictive strategies of flashback and cinematic special effects the voice-over reiterates: "In a film you can turn back the clock; the characters can have a second chance."

Running the film backward like this re-enacts a pleasure and delight in filmic effects, a pleasure first discovered by early filmmakers; thus it invokes the cinema of attractions, the impulse to show, to put on display openly and in an exhibitionist manner rather than to experience voyeuristically.[21] But the marked presence of the film-being-made in the film also enhances the sense that the film is being made as it is being watched, that film is a process that seeks its own shape as it forms itself rather than taking up a shape imposed beforehand.

I would suggest that O'Shea's work in documentary embodies a poetics in the sense of a constructedness and an awareness of the process of producing the filmtext's meanings. I have suggested that in each of O'Shea's three feature films the fiction serves to dramatize reality by separating it out from its fiction only then to reinclude it in a tangled reciprocity where each has been defined in part through what the other is not. This is a practice that makes each feature film's inherited documentary structures and documentary elements, and vice versa O'Shea's documentaries' fictive qualities, a site of equivocation, of border work.

O'Shea's "poetics of documentary," as I have termed it, becomes all the more radical when one views it in the context of the Griersonian tradition of the NFU's *Weekly Review* that was to dominate so much documentary work in New Zealand during the period in which O'Shea was working. As is well known, English documentary filmmaker John Grierson visited New Zealand in 1940 and advised the government of the day on filmmaking policy.[22] Many of Grierson's suggestions were put into effect the subsequent year by E. Stanhope Andrews, director of the new NFU, and it was not surprising that the majority of documentaries subsequently made in New Zealand followed Grierson's documentary agenda. Grierson elaborated a tradition that maintained that documentary film served a social purpose, its intent being to mobilize viewers to act in the world with a greater sense of knowledge and a more fully elaborated sense of social structure. Among the characteristics that serve to distinguish Griersonian documentary representation from fiction are:

—a strong belief that forms of expository documentary are a reaction to fiction film and an expression of dissatisfaction with its distracting, entertainment qualities;

—an adherence to "discourses of sobriety," that is, economics, medicine, law, science, etc.—discourses that attempt to represent the state of affairs in the natural or historical world itself rather than offer imaginative representations of it;

—an emphasis on making arguments through the use of visible evidence or verbal evidence that includes the testimony of narrating authorities;

—a tendency to experience questions of style as questions of ethics;

—the impression that any resolution of the conflicts and issues posed by the documentary text requires action in the historical world itself.[23]

Recent criticism of Grierson's project has questioned the politics of the ennobling, civic-minded sense of mission in which he attempted to cloak the British documentary movement. When his work and influence is examined in terms of a politics of representation rather than the progressive, socially conscientious movement he styled himself as representing, Grierson's practice, it has been argued, can be seen as ideologically conservative.[24]

O'Shea's work, in contrast, is alert to the staging of its poetics and "artistry" in relation to the particular traditions of film language from which it speaks, and as such it has paved a way for new documentary films in New Zealand and has allowed for the revision of the documentary tradition borrowed into, or possibly imposed upon, New Zealand filmmaking. O'Shea's practice has led the way, and sometimes provided the model for, documentaries as varied as Michael King and Barry Barclay's influential *Tangata Whenua* television series in 1974, Paul Maunder's dramatized documentaries of the early 1970s, the self-reflexive feminist documentaries that emerged later in that decade, Peter Wells's documentary mix of history and desire, and more recently Annie Goldson's self-reflexive *Wake* (1994) and *Seeing Red* (1995).[25] O'Shea's has been an art of breaking barriers: the old border of documentary against drama, nonfiction against the fictive, or form against content, authenticity against style and self-reflexivity. O'Shea's work in documentaries and feature films begins by recognizing the uncertainty of these boundaries in the actual practice of filmmaking and understands them not as positions to take up, nor as lines of demarcation, but rather as sites that might be, for our benefit, explored poetically.

Notes

1. Bill Nichols, *Blurred Boundaries: Questions of Meaning in Contemporary Culture* (Bloomington: Indiana University Press, 1994), ix. For the typology of documentary modes see also his *Representing Reality* (Bloomington: Indiana University Press, 1991).
2. See John O'Shea, "A Charmed Life: Fragments of Memory . . . and Extracts from Conversations," in *Film in Aotearoa New Zealand*, ed. Jonathan Dennis and Jan Bieringa (Wellington: Victoria University Press, 1992), 26.
3. For biographical information I have relied on Brian McDonnell, "John O'Shea: The Father of New Zealand Film," *North and South* (October 1989): 86–95, as well as my conversations with O'Shea himself.
4. See John O'Shea, *Documentary and National Identity*, Working Papers No. 3 (Auckland: University of Auckland, 1997), 4.
5. See John O'Shea, *Don't Let It Get You: Memories—Documents* (Wellington: Victoria University Press, 1999), 78.
6. For a full discussion of the historical background to the treatment of racism in *Broken Barrier*, see Laurence Simmons, "Casting Aside Old Nets: John O'Shea's First Fight Against Racism," *Illusions* 33 (Autumn 2002): 12–19.
7. For biographical information on Roger Mirams, see "'Broken Barrier' as Another Chapter in the 'Mirams Story,'" *The Dominion*, April 5, 1952. In the mid-1950s

Mirams left New Zealand to work in Australia.
8. See "New Zealand–Made Films: Local Subjects and Settings Essential for Success," *Otago Daily Times*, August 12, 1952.
9. John O'Shea. Archival note accompanying video release of *Broken Barrier*.
10. See O'Shea's comments on the TVNZ "Work of Art" documentary on his work, *Breaking Barriers* (TV1, June 26, 1993).
11. Terence Bayler (Tom) had already played a number of lead roles in Wellington theatrical productions and left on a bursary to study at the Royal Academy of Dramatic Art in London after completing the film, but the other roles were filled by non-actors.
12. Claude Lévi-Strauss, *Tristes tropiques*, trans. John Russell (New York: Atheneum, 1972).
13. In 1966, O'Shea wrote a paper for UNESCO confronting these issues titled "A Report on Ethnographic Films Made on the Maori Ethnic Minority of New Zealand." This has been partially republished in *Don't Let It Get You: Memories—Documents*, 54–70.
14. Laurence Simmons, "*Broken Barrier:* Mimesis and Mimicry," *Landfall* 1, no. 1 (n.s. 1993): 131–36.
15. Jacques Derrida, "Living On: Borderlines," in *Deconstruction and Criticism*, ed. Harold Bloom et al., 75–176 (New York: Seabury, 1979).
16. For the figure of Barry Crump, see Colin Hogg, *A Life in Loose Strides: The Story of Barry Crump* (Auckland: Hodder Moa Beckett, 2000).
17. See, for example, McCahon's *The Valley of Dry Bones* (1947) where the words, as he tells us in a catalogue note, derived from a Rinso packet, or his *Angel of the Annunciation* of 1949, which is staged in front of the Nelson Golf Club building.
18. F. A. Jones, "Breakaway from Meat and Rugby," *The Guardian*, August 26, 1965.
19. Although the United Kingdom did not join the EEC (later European Union) until 1973, because France blocked the move in the 1960s, it is clear from O'Shea's interviews in 1962 that the ordinary New Zealander saw "the writing on the wall."
20. See O'Shea, *Don't Let It Get You: Memories—Documents*, 70.
21. See Tom Gunning, "An Aesthetic of Astonishment: Early Film and the (In)Credulous Spectator," in *Viewing Positions: Ways of Seeing Film*, ed. Linda Williams (New Brunswick, NJ: Rutgers University Press, 1994), 114–33.
22. For Grierson's relationship with New Zealand, see Margaret Thompson, "Grierson and New Zealand," *Journal of the Society of Film and Television Arts* 2, nos. 4–5 (1972): 15–16.
23. For a fuller discussion of these characteristics, see Nichols, *Representing Reality*, and his *Introduction to Documentary* (Bloomington: Indiana University Press, 2001).
24. See, for example, Ian Aitken, *Film and Reform: John Grierson and the Documentary Film Movement* (London and New York: Routledge, 1992), and Brian Winston, *Claiming the Real: The Griersonian Documentary and Its Legitimations* (London: British Film Institute, 1995).
25. See, for example, Paul Maunder, *Gone Up North for a While* (1972); Deirdre McCarten, *Some of My Best Friends Are Women* (1975); Stephanie Beth, *I Want to Be Joan* (1978); Peter Wells, *Napier: Newest City on the Globe* (1985) and *The Mighty Civic* (1988).

John O'Shea—Filmography

1951. *Harvest of Sunshine* (NZ documentary: additional dialogue writer).
1951. *Timber for All Time* (NZ documentary: editor).
1952. *Broken Barrier* (NZ feature film: co-director, writer).
1952. *This Valley* (NZ documentary: editor).
1952. *Sportsmen's Playground* (NZ documentary: co-producer, writer).
1953. *Buttermaking in New Zealand* (NZ documentary: editor).
1953. *The Link* (NZ documentary: co-director, co-producer).
1954. *Carpet of Grass* (NZ documentary: editor).
1954. *Royal Transport* (NZ documentary: editor).
1954. *Weapon for Prosperity* (NZ documentary: editor).
1954. *New Frontier: The Story of Kawerau* (NZ documentary: co-director, co-producer, writer, editor).
1954-58. *Pacific Magazine* (NZ newsreel: co-producer). Over thirty programs made.
1955. *The Homecoming* (NZ documentary: co-producer, writer, editor).
1955. *A Box for Christmas* (NZ documentary: co-producer).
1955. *Dances of the South Pacific* (NZ documentary: co-producer).
1956. *The Strength to Grow* (NZ documentary: writer, editor).
1956. *You Are the Jury* (NZ short film: co-director, co-producer, writer, editor).
1956. *Towards Tomorrow* (NZ documentary: co-director, co-producer, writer, editor).
1956. *Unto These Least* (NZ documentary: co-producer).
1957. *Circle of Sorrow* (NZ documentary: writer, editor).
1957. *Grand Prix Down Under* (NZ documentary: co-producer, editor).
1957. *Pretty Mary* (NZ instructional film: co-producer, writer, editor).
1957. *Progress in Pine* (NZ documentary: co-producer).
1957. *In Good Hands: A Report on New Zealand Industry* (NZ documentary: co-producer, writer, editor).
1957. *New Zealand Cheese* (NZ documentary: editor).
1957. *Sledges South!* (NZ documentary: co-director, co-producer).
1957. *The Tigers* (NZ documentary: co-director, co-producer, writer, editor).
1957. *Islands of History* (NZ documentary: co-producer).
1957. *Journeys of Romance—Tales of Tahiti* (NZ documentary: co-producer).
1958. *The World Is Fashion* (NZ documentary: co-producer, writer, editor).
1958. *Ardmore Grand Prix 1958* (NZ documentary: co-producer, editor).
1959. *New Zealand International Grand Prix 1959* (NZ documentary: producer).
1959. *Youth at the Wheel* (NZ instructional film: producer).
1959. *The Thin Line* (NZ instructional film: producer).
1958. *I Won't Be Home Tonight* (NZ instructional film: producer).
1958. *Going Places* (NZ documentary: producer).
1958. *RNZAF Coming of Age* (NZ documentary: producer).
1958. *Family Tree* (NZ documentary: director, co-producer, writer).

John O'Shea: A Poetics of Documentary

1959. *Deep Freeze Four* (NZ documentary: producer).
1959. *Earth, Fire and Water* (NZ documentary: producer).
1959. *Every Morning* (NZ documentary: producer).
1959. *For a Rainy Day* (NZ documentary: producer).
1959. *Sky Centre* (NZ documentary: producer).
1960. *A Boy and His Bicycle* (NZ instructional film: producer).
1960. *Got a Moment* (NZ instructional film: producer).
1960. *Farm Safety* (NZ documentary: producer).
1960. *L for Leather* (NZ documentary: producer, writer).
1960. *Follow the Plough* (NZ documentary: producer).
1960. *The Hare and the Tortoise* (NZ instructional film: producer, writer).
1961. *A Place Called Levin* (NZ drama-documentary: producer).
1961. *Wellington in the '60s: The Way It Seemed* (NZ documentary: producer, writer).
1961. *Parking and Manoeuvring* (NZ instructional film: producer).
1961. *Pacific Peoples—New Zealand Sheep Farmer* (NZ documentary: producer).
1961. *A World to Walk On* (NZ documentary: producer).
1961. *The Courtesy Club* (NZ documentary: producer).
1961. *Home Heating in New Zealand* (NZ documentary: producer).
1961. *Billy Crosses the Road* (NZ instructional film: producer).
1961. *Think about Tomorrow* (NZ documentary: producer, writer).
1962. *Noumea Is Noumea* (NZ documentary: producer).
1962. *The Long Campaign* (NZ documentary: producer, writer).
1962. *The Sound of Seeing* (NZ short film: producer).
1962. *Food for Thought* (NZ documentary: producer, writer).
1963. *Keep Them Waiting* (NZ instructional film: producer, writer).
1964. *The Head and the Heart* (NZ documentary: producer, writer).
1964. ***Runaway*** a.k.a. ***Runaway Killer*** (NZ feature film: director, producer, co-writer, editor).
1965. *Beware! Rabbits* (NZ documentary: producer).
1965. *Road Markings* (NZ instructional film: producer).
1965. *Who Will Be a Statistic?* (NZ instructional film: producer, writer).
1966. ***Don't Let It Get You*** (NZ feature film: director, producer, editor).
1967. *Giants of the Past* (NZ documentary: producer, writer, editor).
1967. *Mountains to Master* (NZ documentary: producer, writer).
1967. *Whom My Heart Has Chosen* (NZ documentary: producer).
1968. *All That We Need* (NZ extended short film: producer).
1968. *Cycling for Safety* (NZ instructional film: producer).
1968. *Sparkle and Speed* (NZ documentary: producer, writer).
1968. *The Glow of Gold* (NZ documentary: producer, writer).
1968. *Meat for Millions* (NZ documentary: co-producer, writer, editor).
1968. *Milk Makes a Difference* (NZ documentary: producer, writer).
1968. *Margin for Life—Macquarie Island* (NZ documentary: producer, writer).

1969. *The Sound of Spray* (NZ documentary: producer, co-cinematographer).
1969. *Union Trans-Tasman* (NZ documentary: producer, writer).
1970. *The Need for Nature* (NZ documentary: producer, writer).
1970. *The Path to Power* (NZ documentary: producer, writer).
1970. *Towards 2020: The East Coast Project* (NZ documentary: producer, writer).
1971. *A Role to Play* (NZ documentary: producer, additional commentary).
1971. *Summer and Speed* (NZ documentary: producer).
1971. *The Day We Landed on the Most Perfect Planet in the Universe* (NZ television documentary in the *Survey* series: producer).
1971. *Coming Up with the Ideas* (NZ documentary: producer).
1971. *No Accident of Nature* (NZ documentary: producer).
1971. *Gunspoof* (NZ short film: producer).
1971. *Lane and Motorway Driving* (NZ instructional film: producer).
1971. *Getting Together* (NZ television documentary in the *Survey* series: producer).
1971. *Making It Work* (NZ documentary: co-producer).
1971. *Broad Horizons* (NZ documentary: production advisor).
1972. *In the Company of Trees* (NZ documentary: producer).
1972. *Deciding* (NZ television documentary in the *Survey* series: producer).
1972. *Take Three Passions* (NZ television documentary in the *Survey* series: producer).
1972. *The Town That Lost a Miracle* (NZ television documentary in the *Survey* series: producer).
1972. *The Unbelievable Glory of the Human Voice* (NZ television documentary in the *Survey* series: producer).
1972. *A Banker in the Family* (NZ drama-documentary: producer).
1973. *Equation* (NZ documentary: director, producer).
1974. *Hemson, Carpenter, Ruming and Medcalf* (NZ documentary: producer).
1974. *Percy the Policeman* (NZ television six-part children's series: producer). Series not broadcast.
1974. *Tangata Whenua* (NZ television documentary six-part series: producer).
1974. *Rally . . . Little Boys in a Man Size Sport* (NZ documentary: producer).
1974. *The Fastest Greens in the World* (NZ documentary: producer, co-cinematographer).
1974. *Rollin' thru New Zealand with Kenny Rogers and the First Edition* (NZ documentary: producer).
1975. *Ashes* (NZ television drama: producer).
1975. *The Hum* (NZ documentary: producer).
1975. *Lost in the Garden of the World* (NZ documentary: producer).
1976. *The Right to Know* (NZ documentary, six parts: producer, co-cinematographer).
1976. *Women in Power: Indira Gandhi* (NZ television documentary: producer).
1976. *Hunting Horns* (NZ television six-part series: producer).

1977. *Autumn Fires* a.k.a. *In Search of Pakehatanga—Autumn Fires* (NZ television documentary with drama elements, in the *Scene* series: producer).
1977. *Aku Mahi Whatu Maori/My Art of Maori Weaving* (NZ documentary: producer).
1978. *From Where the Spirit Calls* (NZ documentary: producer).
1978. *Toheroamania* (NZ television documentary in the *Shoreline* series: producer).
1978. *Dat's Show Biz* (NZ television documentary in the *Shoreline* series: producer).
1978. *Water the Way You Want It* (NZ television documentary in the *Shoreline* series: producer).
1979. *To Learn... To Develop* (NZ documentary: director, producer).
1980. *Cows, Computers and Customers* (NZ documentary: producer).
1981. *Pictures* (NZ feature film: producer, co-writer).
1983. *A Mind to It* (NZ documentary: producer, writer).
1984. *Among the Cinders* (NZ feature film: producer, co-writer).
1985. *Leave All Fair* (NZ feature film: producer).
1985. *The Neglected Miracle* (NZ [multiple financed] documentary feature: co-producer).
1986. *Te Atiawa O Runga Te Rangi* (NZ documentary: consulting producer).
1987. *Ka Mate! Ka Mate!* (NZ extended short film. Training film for crew involved with *Ngati:* producer).
1987. *Ngati* (NZ feature film: producer).
1987. *Nga Tai O Makiri* (NZ documentary: consulting producer).
1989. *Whakarongo Whakaahua Maori: Listen to the Picture Maori* (NZ documentary: associate producer).
1991. *Te Rua* a.k.a. ***The Store House*** a.k.a. ***The Pit*** (NZ/Germany feature film: producer, co-cinematographer).
1993. *Breaking Barriers* (NZ documentary on O'Shea's work).
1994. *Runaway Revisited* (NZ educational documentary on the making of *Runaway*: interviewee).
1995. *Forgotten Silver* (NZ television drama: interviewee).
1996. *Te Ara Pouro o Aotearoa—A Map of New Zealand Sounds* (NZ documentary: consulting producer).
1996. *Centenary of Cinema* (NZ trailer: director).

O'Shea also made a number of commercials in the 1950s and 1960s. These include for: Crosse and Blackwell Soup, Daily Sketch, Ford, Caltex IC Plus Petrol (*Flying Saucer*), Oxo Cubes (*Home Cooking*), Persil (*Washes Whiter*), Disprin (*Dissolves Pain*), New Zealand Lamb (*Easter Parade*), Maltesers (*Puppets*), Players Weights Cigarettes (*Rugby*), Quaker Macaroni (*Marguerite Patten*), Auckland Laundry Cellopac (*New Tricks*), New Zealand Lamb (*It's Not Just Meat*), Shell ICA Petrol (*Man in MG*), New Zealand Lamb (*Mint Sauce*).

4

Between the Personal and the Political
Feminist Fables in the Films of Gaylene Preston

Estella Tincknell

Gaylene Preston directed one of the earliest fiction features by a New Zealand woman, *Mr Wrong* (1985). Both this work and her later films and documentaries are distinguished by their resolute focus on New Zealand life and by the critically acerbic eye Preston casts on the Kiwi cultural context. Yet her films have also been remarkably wide-ranging in form and content, drawing extensively on such divergent influences as the woman's film and the tradition of British "kitchen sink" realism. Showing a debt to these traditions and to feminist documentary, Preston's films foreground maternal and domestic relationships in order to revalue the everyday aspects of women's lives and experiences, combining a distinctively expressive visual surrealism with a narrative emphasis on political consciousness. This article will explore both the recurrent themes and concerns of Preston's work and the ways in which she deploys the conventions of such different cinematic influences to produce a distinctive oeuvre. It will argue that her films are significant precisely because they have been part of the development of a distinctively New Zealand cinematic style, while retaining a critical and feminist edge.

Preston was born in Greymouth in 1947. After completing her high school studies in Napier she attended Ilam School of Fine Arts at Canterbury University, where she studied painting. It was not, however, until she moved to Cambridge in the United Kingdom in 1969, that her interest in drama and the expressive possibilities of film rather than the fine arts began to be developed. Working at Fulbourn Hospital, known for its groundbreaking psychiatric work,[1] she was involved in setting up innovatory art and drama therapy at the institution. She later earned a diploma in Art Therapy at St. Albans School of Art and became the Vice President of the British Association of Art Therapists. During the early 1970s, she made three short experimental films, one with the patients at Fulbourn hospital, another with a group of severely disabled patients at Cell Barnes Hospital, St. Albans, and a third with a deaf group based in the inner city

London suburb of Brixton, at the Brixton College of Further Education, where she was teaching art and drama. These experiences led to her growing interest in professional filmmaking. On her return to New Zealand in 1977 she traveled widely, made the documentary *Whose School?* (1977) as part of the Ponsonby community struggle to retain Berresford Street Primary School, and eventually found work as an art director for John O'Shea's Pacific Films, where she also directed three episodes of *Shoreline* (a calendar program for television). Preston's real breakthrough, however, came with the documentary *All the Way up There* (1979), which she directed and co-produced. The film's account of the ascent of Mt. Ruapehu by Bruce Burgess, a twenty-four-year-old man with cerebral palsy, together with mountaineer Graeme Dingle, successfully brought one of Preston's continuing preoccupations—an interest in what might be called "small-scale heroism"—to the attention of a mainstream audience. It went on to win two international prizes and achieved widespread global distribution; in New Zealand it was screened theatrically as the short film in support of John Reid's *Middle Age Spread* (1979).

Her next two productions as director, the documentary *Learning Fast* (1980) and the short film *Hold Up* (1981), returned to questions of education, unemployment, and attitudes toward disability in an "abled" world. Subsequent work shifted between experimentalism, music video, documentary, and drama, sometimes within the same text. During the 1980s her work became more overtly concerned with politics and identity. Both the short drama *Mindout* (1984), in its use of an Orwellian "Big Brother" figure, and the documentary *Imagine* (1984), in its focus on the threat of nuclear war, represented a move toward situating the realm of the personal within an engagement with larger political questions, especially those being redefined by the Pacific Rim and South Pacific cultural politics. *Mr Wrong* (1985) marked a slightly different shift, toward an explicitly feminist model of filmmaking in which female characters were foregrounded and specifically female experiences were explored. All Preston's subsequent films have demonstrated this debt to feminist cinema, whether it is in the form of the radical documentary tradition of early second-wave feminism that shaped *War Stories Our Mothers Never Told Us* (1995) or the realist drama that informed *Bread and Roses* (1993), which told the life story of one of New Zealand's most charismatic feminist politicians, Sonja Davies. *Punitive Damage*, a documentary about Indonesia's annexation of East Timor, directed by Annie Goldson but produced by Preston in 1999, brought together some of these strands in Preston's creative history by exploring the specific experiences of one woman, Helen Todd, within the wider context of events in East Timor itself throughout the 1970s and 1980s. Furthermore, in her most recent feature film, *Perfect Strang-*

ers (2003), Preston has developed and intensified the feminist narrative viewpoint in complex ways while also offering a story that can speak to mainstream audiences.

The move in the direction of more overtly political filmmaking did not, however, mean that Preston's earlier work or, indeed, her self-identity as a film director, had not always been informed by a strong commitment to political issues. In my correspondence with her she made it clear that a number of her experiences during the 1960s shaped her attitudes and contributed to her political consciousness, especially in its emergent feminism. As she says: "For me that decade included . . . inhabiting the radical student activist 60s world of the underbelly of a conventional 'main center'—Christchurch; working in art and drama therapy in Cambridge UK; and living in an urban communal house in Stockwell, using film with my work at Brixton College of Further Education. During that time I saw only two films made by women. One was by Midge McKenzie, about her handicapped child, and another was by Gena Rowlands, *Wanda*. Both were inspirational."[2] For Preston, the relationships between political and personal identities are strongly intertwined, and her work powerfully insists on the recognition that the intimate realm of marriage, domesticity, and sexual desire is also part of a "public" political domain. In many respects this link between the personal and the political appears to be particularly characteristic of the work of feminist writers and artists who came to consciousness during the 1960s and 1970s, as Preston clearly did. She was a member of the London Women's Film Group for a short period in the early 1970s, for example, and points out that "the obvious huge, gaping gaps for me from 1965 until 1978 were in seeing any women's work at all in mainstream cinemas."[3] One of her driving motivations, it seems, has been to make space in New Zealand's still developing cinema culture for women's voices and women's perspectives.

However, Preston appears to belong more properly within a tradition of feminist humanism rather than the radical feminism of some of her filmmaking peers: her engagement with the differentials of power and their effects on lived experience encompasses an ongoing interest in issues of disability as well as gender politics, as is clear from any examination of her creative history. Perhaps it is for this reason that many of her formative cinematic influences have been male filmmakers. Preston herself is keen to assert the feminist dimensions of her project while explicitly rejecting separatist approaches: "my feminism focuses not just on prejudices about sex role definition, but on recognizing the importance of tolerating differences between the male and female principles and valuing those principles equally in a caring society."[4] By moving between genres and by refusing to be identified as only one kind of filmmaker, then, Preston has developed a remarkably diverse catalogue of work. As she argues, "the differences between documentary and drama [are] artificial boundaries anyway."[5]

Documentary, Docudrama, and the Feminine

While Preston is emphatic in her recognition of feminist influences, the films of other (male) directors, especially those working within the British documentary and social realist traditions, have been equally important in shaping her directorial approach. As she herself observes of her commitment to the social realm and her approach to film, "I am not a stylist.... The idea and content dictate the style rather than the other way round."[6] Preston identifies the films and television of Ken Loach as strong influences, particularly the controversial R. D. Laing influenced exposé of mental health treatment, *Family Life* (1971). She also cites the work of Peter Watkins, the acclaimed (but now relatively forgotten) maker of the nuclear war dystopian docudrama, *The War Game*, which was commissioned for the BBC in 1965.[7] Interestingly, she also identifies Andy Warhol's films as influential as well as the work of Donald Cammell and Nicholas Roeg, especially *Performance* (1970). The surreal qualities present in the latter, together with the focus on the threat inherent in intensive kinds of intimacy, can be traced in some of her fictional features. These two traditions, of documentary and of fantasy, represent a productive tension in Preston's work, and perhaps also suggest the political and cultural contradictions that she tries to engage with in her approach to filmmaking.

Loach's commitment to political film, as well as his ability to draw memorable performances from unknown, often non-professional and working-class players, perhaps informs Preston's commitment to interrogating the micro-level power relations of the family, state bureaucracy, and friendship. Similarly, Watkins's extraordinary and clearly politically driven evocation of the effects of nuclear war can be traced through to Preston's concerns about nuclear power in *Imagine*. The idea that films can make a difference, politically, for what she calls "the common good," is very important to her. As she says, "in the fortnight *Family Life* played in a cinema in Cambridge use of ECT dropped by 50 percent in the psychiatric hospital I worked in."[8]

Loach's influence can perhaps best be discerned in Preston's dramatic focus on the small victories and large setbacks of daily life in films such as *Married* (1992) and *Ruby and Rata* (1989), and in her desire to wed this to a critique of New Zealand's own New Right political spectrum in the latter. The searing attacks on the Thatcherite and post-Thatcherite world of non-unionized casual labor and exploitative bosses in Loach's *Riff-Raff* (1990) is echoed in some ways in *Ruby and Rata*'s critical perspective on

New Zealand's creation of a Maori underclass struggling to claim an identity and a place in the neo-liberal "free market." However, while Loach's sympathy for female victims of injustice or abuse cannot be disputed, his empathy with women and with "femininity" or a "feminine" subjectivity (however difficult that may be to define) is more problematic. The *particularity* of women's experiences as women, including their relationships with other women—especially friendships or even rivalries—is rarely addressed in Loach's films. Preston, in contrast, has an ongoing interest in the details of how women relate to and make sense of one another and of "feminine" culture more generally. She is adept, for example, at showing the nuances of voice, the inflections of feeling, which inform the social relations of femininity. She also shows how the masculine occupation and ownership of public spaces—and even some kinds of private ones—locates women in very specific ways within the social.

For example, *Getting to Our Place* (1999), the television documentary about the planning, development, and eventual completion of the new Museum of New Zealand Te Papa Tongarewa, in Wellington, which Preston made with Anna Cottrell, is particularly interesting for the ways in which it captures the vicissitudes of women's claims to the public sphere, although this is not what the film is "about" in an overt sense. The museum's Chief Executive, Cheryll Sotheran, is the main (but by no means only) focus of the film, and it is her sometimes fractious relationship with the various funding bodies, government ministers, and interest groups, all of them with an axe to grind or an agenda to fulfill, that constitutes the most memorable aspect of the film. Her difficulties in asserting her authority against that of benign patriarchs or too-clever designers, for example, is subtly underlined without also being undermining. The moment in which she has removed her shoes after a particularly grueling duel with a government minister is noticeably telling—a brief vignette that might well pass by the viewfinder of a (male) director unused to the crippling discipline of high heels on a long day. These kinds of details suggest a perspective on the world that subtly critiques the hegemony of particular kinds of gendered power in the context of a complex exploration of cultural identities. Preston's sympathy with women extends to her attitude toward her audience and their responses. As she points out, "they have paid a babysitter, found a park and bought a ticket in order to have a good time, so they go out of their way to do just that, thank God."[9]

Significantly, then, Preston identifies the documentary *War Stories Our Mothers Never Told Us* as the most satisfying of her films, both in a wider political sense and at the level of the personal, calling it "part of a nation lancing a nasty boil, in a manner of speaking."[10] The film has a deceptively simple formal technique. Featuring almost only close-ups and mid-shots of the seven New Zealand women whose experiences of World War II are recounted, and making use of only the briefest prompts from the off-camera interviewer, *War Stories Our Mothers Never Told Us* works to accentuate the tales of "everyday suffering" that are being told. Its focus is on the domestic and personal consequences of war, the broken relationships and unspoken tensions that women as the emotional baggage-carriers of marriage are required to take responsibility for. The stories themselves are remarkable precisely because they are being told by ordinary women, whose specific experiences of resilience, courage, and resistance to conventional morality or social pressures are often overlooked in public narratives of war. The direct-to-camera narratives are interspersed with archival newsreel footage and contemporary photographs that underline these accounts, pointing up their relationship to the broader picture of mass mobilization and wartime privation and to the fact that these are only seven stories among thousands. The inclusion of Preston's own mother's story in the film, and the fact that it involves the revelation of a hitherto concealed sexual affair conducted while Preston's father was missing in action believed dead (it was later learned he was a prisoner of war in Italy), makes *War Stories Our Mothers Never Told Us* even more powerful in some respects: a very public assertion that history is never simple or straightforward.

The emphasis on storytelling, on the importance of narrative structure, and on the experiential as the driving force of narrative found in *War Stories Our Mothers Never Told Us* is characteristic of Preston's approach to filmmaking more generally. She insists, for example, on the *continuities* between drama and documentary: "to me the only difference between documentary and drama is the process."[11]

Preston and the Woman's Film: Feminism and Fantasy

One of the most interesting things about Preston's work is its debt both to feminist documentary and to the mainstream "woman's film." These twin influences are traceable in the foregrounding of maternal and domestic relationships as central to narrative interest, and in the way in which women's lives and experiences are revalued. While Preston's documentaries, such as *War Stories Our Mothers Never Told Us,* seem to be underpinned by the same impulse to intervene in standard histories and retell them from a new perspective that marked earlier feminist revisionist work such as *The Life and Times of Rosie the Riveter* (1980) and *Red Skirts on Clydeside* (1984), and are relatively simple in form and style, her fiction films use elements of melodrama, social comedy, and even the Gothic thriller as their base. Moreover, in addition to these self-evident choices of genre and approach, Preston's work occasionally seems to borrow in less obvious ways from more radical influences. Her focus on gender relations and domesticity as key sites of conflict between women and men appears to mark Preston as a "feminist filmmaker" rather than a filmmaker who is also feminist. The emphasis on the repetitive, banal, and time-consuming daily chores of shopping, cooking, and cleaning in *Married, Ruby and Rata,* and *Perfect Strangers,* for example, is reminiscent at points of Chantal Ackerman's radical feminist film drama, *Jeanne Dielman, 23 Quai du Commerce, 1080 Bruxelles* (1975). In this respect, Preston's films do seem to draw on some of the conventions of 1970s feminist counter-cinema, especially in their domestic ultra-realism. This is not just about continuities with the documentary tradition, however; it is more akin to a radical break with some of its tendencies. Rather than returning her protagonists to the domestic sphere, Preston seeks to free them from it, through fantasy and desire.

Ann Hardy goes further than this, linking Preston's films not only to feminist counter-cinema but also to larger shifts in social and cultural analysis in which the practices of everyday life have become the site of representational engagement.[12] Hardy connects Preston to the cultural criticism of Michel de Certeau who, in *The Practice of Everyday Life* (1984), attempts to explore the "clandestine forms" of daily practices that resist, subvert, or reorganize power relations. The focus on suburban life in *Ruby and Rata* is, for Hardy, part of a deliberate attempt to make the marginalized central and to tell stories about those who are ignored by conventional narratives. The film was planned as a critical response to the effects the "restructuring" of New Zealand's economy in the 1980s had brought upon those already struggling to claim a place in society but was deliberately presented in terms of "a white, bright comedy about serious things," according to Preston.[13] The story focuses on an elderly and very genteel Pakeha (European) woman, Ruby (Yvonne Lawley), a young Maori welfare-scrounger posing as a businesswoman, Rata (Vanessa Rare), and a little boy—the latter's son, Willie (Lee Mete-Kingi). All of these are in their different ways marginalized figures, as the film explores. Ruby because of her age and infirmity, Rata because of her race and social class, and Willie because he is a child, either ignored or policed by the adults around him.

The film begins with Ruby failing her over-seventies driving test, an event that she believes will effectively render her a domestic prisoner, confined by the neat suburban (and shop-free) streets that had seemed to guarantee her a safe space at an earlier moment in her life. The arrival of Rata as Ruby's tenant, however, marks an opening-up rather than a closing-down of Ruby's world. Although Ruby's discovery of Rata's deception sets them at odds with each other, the two women are brought together by Willie, who is able to see the frailty and the emotional isolation beneath Ruby's reserve and hostility. Initially drawn to but afraid of Ruby because

Rata confronts her landlady Ruby on the threshold of their contested suburban space. (Courtesy New Zealand Film Commission.)

he associates her with witchcraft (something emphasized in the film by Ruby's use of a broom to hang the chocolate fish she is using as "bait" to get the boy's attention), Willie eventually acts as a mediatory figure between the women.

Spatiality is central to *Ruby and Rata*. From the opening crane shot of the suburb where Ruby lives to the way in which the house itself becomes part of the power struggle between the two women, the film never loses sight of its importance. Here, Ruby's ethnic and class "superiority" is marked by her occupation of the light and spacious upper floors and Rata's inhabitation of the less salubrious downstairs flat. Indeed, Hardy argues that "the location of Ruby and Rata in the suburbs becomes significant [because] ... what is missing, most of the time, is the center of the city, the center of power."[14] Rata's workplace, the offices where she is a cleaner, is shown and we see the networks of Auckland's highways from a pedestrian walkway, but a sense of civic space, of a city center, is entirely absent. Even Rata's appropriation of the Conspec telephone lines when she is pretending to be a wealthy businesswoman in order to secure the flat is indicative of her tactical claims to such spaces, rather than her ownership of them, as Hardy points out.[15] The person who makes most use of clandestine space, however, is Willie, who deftly transforms a washing line into a climbing frame, uses a store cupboard as a bedroom, and, in the dramatic climax to the film, goes missing only to be found hiding behind the door to a back staircase.

In addition to her exploration of these "clandestine forms," spaces, and knowledges, Preston has experimented with what she calls "genre bending," expanding, subverting, or transforming an existing and dominant film genre in order to challenge audience expectations. *Mr Wrong* was her first full-length fiction film, and was deliberately constructed as a kind of thriller with a feminist edge. The central character, Meg (Heather Bolton) is persuaded to buy what turns out to be a haunted car—haunted by the ghost of the young woman who was murdered in the vehicle. The film traces Meg's growing anxiety about the secret the car contains in parallel with her experiences with various unsuitable, predatory, or downright threatening men, "Mr. Wrongs" of all kinds. The narrative culminates in Meg's battle with Mr. X (David Letch), the sinister, quasi-supernatural murderer who has come to claim his second victim. For Preston herself, *Mr Wrong* was intended to be "a mainstream film that interrogates both film genre and gender politics."[16] Its foregrounding of the female victim, variously stalked, terrorized, and physically assaulted by men in a series of classic—and familiar—perilous situations, was intended to problematize the centrality of such conventions to dominant filmmaking practices by exaggerating their function and the figure of the abject woman, and then turning them upside down in a neat final reversal. However, while Meg is by no means a conventional, weakly desirable heroine, especially as played by Bolton, she does not really emerge as particularly powerful either. Hardy argues that the film's representation of Meg is of someone curiously unknowing about herself, her desires, and her expectations of men.[17] She appears to wander into her adventure almost blankly. Indeed, it is only when Meg is faced with her own death as a kind of erotically charged consummation that she begins to resist her tormentor. Yet by representing Meg in such passive terms the film seems to reaffirm rather than challenge the dyad of active male sexuality/passive female sexuality.

Mr Wrong was (unfairly) heavily criticized by one writer, Jane Sayle, as too simplistic in its representation of gender politics and as inhabiting a realm somewhere between the "real" and the "fairy tale" in its shifts of tone and narrative.[18] Sayle does identify some clear weaknesses with the story; the car that is central to the narrative is, as she argues, so "masculine" in its connotations (it is a Jaguar) that the viewer may well see it as a version of a heroic male rescuer when it appears to act of its own volition in Meg's defense in the absence of any human alternatives, so Meg's vulnerability as potential victim is countered by the car's strength. Furthermore, the intriguing details of Mary Carmichael's (Perry Piercy) murder by Mr. X are left untold, perhaps to avoid the sensationalization found in many mainstream thrillers, yet this particular lack of closure also leaves the viewer waiting in disappointment, as Sayle points out. Nonetheless, Sayle's critical position is itself simplistic and relatively unreflective; her article ends by asserting that the film makes the viewer feel "superficially and unsatisfactorily manipulated"—as if this were not also a familiar response

The foregrounding of a conventional subject position: Meg as a cornered victim in *Mr Wrong*. (Courtesy New Zealand Film Commission.)

to a standard blockbuster.[19] Even more importantly, I would argue that the generic shifts between realism and fantasy found in *Mr Wrong* are part of the film's strengths; they are what makes it more than a conventional feminist fable. They also prefigure Preston's later, more sophisticated, incorporation of surreal elements into her other films.

The Kiwi Surreal

Mr Wrong's (and, as will be seen, *Perfect Strangers*') blend of the banal and the terrifying, perhaps especially its anti-realist figuring of certain male characters as wolfish and predatory, is reminiscent of Angela Carter's feminist re-working of the fairy tales of Perrault, Grimm, and de Sade in her collection of short stories, *The Bloody Chamber* (1979). In this respect at least, Preston seems to be working within a specifically feminist tradition, in which mythical and fairy-tale elements are incorporated into contemporary narratives for a political rather than a purely narrative purpose. For Preston herself, the fairy-tale elements to her films (and to her approach to cinema more generally) are central: "my interest in a more mythological tale telling springs from the fact that I come from a generation of feminist women who felt a strong need for some new fairy tales (Cinderella has a lot to answer for)."[20] Sally Potter's *Orlando* (1992) does this very well, but its milieu is somewhat too obviously that of the English aristocracy rather than the suburbs. A better comparison may be with the films of another New Zealander, Jane Campion. Both *Sweetie* (1989) and *The Piano* (1993) explore the destabilization of cultural norms by powerful "natural" forces and make the experience of femininity central to narrative. Campion's work is also marked by its focus on the strangeness of domestic life and the power struggles that structure it, an emphasis that is articulated in her use of visual motifs that underline the possibilities of the "ordinary" becoming unfamiliar. Noel King and Toby Miller call this a "quirky counter-realism" but do not identify continuities between Campion's work and that of other New Zealand directors.[21]

It appears to me, however, that the surreal edges to Gaylene Preston's films bear more than a passing resemblance to those found in Campion's work and that both have a distinctively Kiwi flavor to them. The eruption into domestic quietude and gentility of violent, supernatural, or inexplicable events in her films resembles Campion's emphasis on the uneasy relationship between the natural and human spheres and seem also to express something of New Zealand's hybrid culture, and perhaps its landscape. Peter Jackson's *Heavenly Creatures* (1994), too, is remarkable for the way in which it sets up an explosion of violence—in this case murder—into the rigidly conformist and suburban (in every sense) social context of 1950s Christchurch through the use of image and color. His *Lord of the Rings* trilogy (2001–3) has made even more dramatic visual use of the landscape in an overtly lyrical fantasy. Preston, like Jackson and Campion, is part of an emergent cinematic model that positions the mundane and everyday against the fantastical and the magical. Her sly subversion of New Zealand life thus works to point up both the banality and the magic of ordinary experiences and the peculiar combination of repressive respectability and common-sense multiculturalism that is a feature of this Kiwi culture. Her films seem to suggest not only that the familiar can be "made strange," as in her domestic focus, but also that the strange can become familiar.

This exploration of the uncanny, the relationship between the strange and the familiar, and a feminist concern with the power relations of gender is brought to fruition in what is undoubtedly Preston's most accomplished and mature feature film, *Perfect Strangers*. Here, she offers a beautifully shot and staged modern fairy tale saturated with Carteresque paradox. The romantically disillusioned yet hopeful Melanie (Rachael Blake), an assistant in a South Island fish and chip restaurant, encounters what appears to be the "perfect stranger" (Sam Neill) in a dreary pub and consents to go back to "his place" (a moored boat) for the night, not quite realizing where this will lead. She awakes the next morning and begins to discover that she has been effectively kidnapped and is being taken to a remote shack situated on an offshore and bush-covered islet. The stranger, repeatedly professing that he has fallen deeply in love with her, offers attentions that are marked by a conventionally familiar romanticism—the candle-surrounded bath, the satin dress laid out on the bed, and the dinner for two—together with a silkily threatening menace. He prevents her from leaving in a series of scenes in which the complex relationship between male sexuality and the desire for possession is carefully played out. Rather than becoming a familiar narrative of male power and female subjection, however, the film twists into melodrama when, in an attempt to escape, Melanie fatally wounds her psychotic captor with a kitchen knife but does not immediately succeed in killing him. The reversal of power this engenders temporarily produces a new kind of intimacy between them as she attempts to nurse him, an intimacy that apparently concludes with his death. This is rapidly followed by a sequence of scenes that contrive to be blackly comic yet also stylistically reminiscent of Campion's visualization of landscape in *The Piano,* in which we see Melanie trundling her captor in a wheelbarrow around the lyrically evoked scenery of the island's bush and shore in an attempt to remove the body.

This neat reversal of the long history of the cultural fetishization of the dead female body, while marking a further turning point in the film that presents an emotional and moral epiphany that will inform both the development of the narrative and the story's wider thematic concerns, does not lead unproblematically to Melanie's triumphant empowerment, however. Instead, the removal of the real, living man induces a state of psychosis in which Melanie attempts to conjure up the ideal lover she wants, partly by talking to his corpse (which she stores in the shack's outside freezer), partly by imagining his ghost as a constant companion. In this altered state she begins to settle into a self-sufficient new life in the shack, apparently reconciled to the possibility of never returning to the city by the presence of a phantom lover who offers practical advice, reassurance, and nurture rather than predatory desire. Yet this twist is not the conclusion to the story. Bill (Joel Tobeck), whom we have seen at the beginning of the film in the pub where Melanie meets the stranger and who is the real owner of the shack, returns home and discovers the body. Rather than being a figure of retribution, and despite the fact that she attempts to kill him too, though, Bill seems curiously forgiving, helping her dispose of the body and eventually marrying Melanie (who is pregnant with the stranger's child) in the closing scenes of the film. Even this resolution does not offer a conventional "happy ending," however. As Bill begins his optimistic bridegroom's speech at the wedding reception (against the murmurs of female guests who are apparently baffled by their friend's decision to marry him), we are offered a series of shots of Melanie's deluded point of view, in which her "real lover," the dead stranger, enters the room. He looks lovingly at her, from close up, as Bill speaks and then envelops Melanie in a romantic embrace on the dance floor. While Melanie's marriage to Bill offers a practical solution to the problem of her pregnancy, her emotions remain attached to the phantom lover she has conjured out of the real stranger.

For Preston, *Perfect Strangers* "is about the power of interpersonal projection in romantic love being close to madness. . . . I am taking the audience on a journey where the overwhelming . . . emotional requirement, what they want regarding the happy ending, defies logic. They don't get to watch someone go mad, they get to go a little bit crazy themselves."[22]

This "craziness" is central to the film's various reversals and to its refusal of generic tradition. City girl Melanie not only takes to her remote life with apparent relish, she learns how to handle a rifle and uses it to assert herself against Bill. Having started her story dressed in a flimsy skirt and strappy sandals and expressing her hatred of the bush, she dons the thick walking boots, sweaters, and raincoat of her would-be lover to take control of the land once he is dead. What begins as an apparently familiar cautionary tale of male sexual violence is thus turned into a feminist affirmation of resistance to such violence. Indeed, the scene in which, having kidnapped her, the stranger cooks roast chicken while Melanie soaks in the bath is suffused with the audible strains of the aria from *Madama Butterfly*, thereby both invoking and eventually reversing the meanings attached to Puccini's music by the virulently anti-feminist fable *Fatal Attraction* (1987). This reversal is mischievously affirmed in the penultimate sequence in which Melanie prepares what seems to be an identical bath and meal for Bill, also to the strains of *Madama Butterfly* but with a very different conclusion. Yet all of this is offered through a sensibility filled with an awareness of the powerfully uncanny nature of New Zealand's landscape, so that such dramatic plot reversals seem to be a consequence of the land's contradictory character. *Perfect Strangers* thus brings a number of Preston's recurrent concerns together with the lyrical and nightmarish way in which New Zealand's topography has been used by her and by other Kiwi filmmakers. It is a powerfully cumulative text.

Conclusion

Preston is fully aware of this element of the uncanny, both in her own films and New Zealand culture more generally. In an interview published in 1992 she observes, "I think that there's something about the literature, the painting, the film, that's coming out of this country, that's spiritually important. There's something that comes out of the land here which is bloody spooky."[23] She goes on to make a more overtly feminist point, saying, "There's something Australasian going on among women's films, probably since *Sweetie*," identifying Campion's work and that of Alison Maclean as operating within a similar register to her own.[24] It is this self-awareness about her work and about its relationship to the antipodean in a more general sense, combined with her commitment to feminism, that marks out Preston as a filmmaker who is unusually reflective and open to discussion about her work's relationship to cultural changes.

Finally, it is important not to lose sight of the specific ways in which Preston's is very much a film project that is not only *about* New Zealand but is *for* it. As she points out, her original motivation for returning to her home country and for establishing herself as a filmmaker there, rather than in the United Kingdom, was driven by a self-consciousness about her Kiwi identity: "the most powerful film related experience was going to New Zealand House [London] and seeing a three projector promotion by the National Film Unit, *This Is New Zealand*, and another NZNFU film about pollution of New Zealand rivers which screened at the NFT [London's National Film Theatre]. When I saw these I realized it was possible to contemplate going home to contribute to my own country as a filmmaker."[25] Preston's work is an important contribution to New Zealand's still emergent film industry precisely because it draws together those elements that constitute a distinctively New Zealand voice while retaining a critical and feminist dimension. As Preston states: "this is why I make films. To make a difference in a medium which lasts."[26]

Notes

1. See David H. Clark, *The Story of a Mental Hospital: Fulbourn, 1858–1983* (London: Process Press, 1996).
2. Gaylene Preston, e-mail to author, March 3, 2003.
3. Ibid.
4. Ibid.
5. Ibid.
6. Ibid.
7. The film was originally prevented from being shown on British television because it was deemed too politically controversial.

8. Preston, e-mail to author, March 3, 2003.
9. Ibid.
10. Ibid.
11. Ibid.
12. Ann Hardy, "Wordwars in Suburbia: A Reconsideration of *Ruby and Rata*," *Illusions* 20 (Summer 1992): 6.
13. Preston, e-mail to author, March 3, 2003.
14. Hardy, "Wordwars in Suburbia," 6.
15. Ibid., 7.
16. Preston, e-mail to author, March 3, 2003.
17. Ann Hardy, "Tales of Ordinary Goodness," *Illusions* 12 (November 1989): 18.
18. Jane Sayle, "Innocence and Evil: Feminine Fear and Masculine Menace in *Mr. Wrong*," *Illusions* 12 (November 1989): 22–24.
19. Ibid., 24.
20. Preston, e-mail to author, March 3, 2003.
21. Noel King and Toby Miller, "Auteurism in the 1990s," in *The Cinema Book, 2nd Edition*, ed. Pam Cook and Mieke Bernink (London: BFI, 1999), 315.
22. Preston, e-mail to author, March 3, 2003.
23. Jonathan Dennis, "Reflecting Reality: Gaylene Preston, an Interview," in *Film in Aotearoa New Zealand*, ed. Jonathan Dennis and Jan Bieringa (Wellington: Victoria University Press, 1992), 171.
24. Ibid.
25. Preston, e-mail to author, March 3, 2003.
26. Ibid.

Gaylene Preston—Filmography

1972. *The Animals and the Lawn Mower* (UK short film: director, editor)
1973. *Draw Me a Circle* (UK documentary: director, cinematographer, editor, sound operator, narrator).
1975. *Mojak Kojak* (UK short film: director, editor).
1976. *Creeps on the Crescent* (UK short film: co-director, co-producer).
1977. *Whose School?* (NZ documentary: director).
1978. *Toheroamania* (NZ television documentary in the *Shoreline* series: director).
1978. *Dat's Show Biz* (NZ television documentary in the *Shoreline* series: director).
1978. *Water the Way You Want It* (NZ television documentary in the *Shoreline* series: director).
1978. *Aku Mahi Whatu Maori/My Art of Maori Weaving* (NZ documentary: graphics).
1979. *All the Way up There* (NZ documentary: director, co-producer).
1979. *Yesterday & Tomorrow Today* (NZ short film: stills photographer).
1979. *Middle Age Spread* (NZ feature film: production designer).
1980. *Learning Fast* (NZ documentary: director, producer).
1981. *The Monster's Christmas* (NZ children's drama: art director).

1981. *Hold Up* (NZ short film: director, co-producer, co-writer, story).
1981. *How I Threw Art out the Window* (NZ short film: director, producer, writer). Unfinished experimental video.
1982. *Taking Over* (NZ documentary: co-director, co-producer).
1983. *Patu!* (NZ documentary: production coordinator).
1983. *The Neighbours. The Only One You Need/First Love/Don't Stop* (NZ short film: director, producer). Three music videos for the band The Neighbours linked up as a short film.
1983. Music video for Tribe (director for "Angel of the Junk Heap").
1983. *Making Utu* (NZ documentary: director, producer).
1983. *Aspects of Utu* (NZ pilot for an intended six-part documentary series: director, interviewer).
1984. *Mindout* (NZ short film: director, producer).
1984. *Imagine* (NZ documentary: co-director, co-producer). Film cut into a twenty-minute video but never screened.
1985. Mr Wrong a.k.a. **Dark of the Night** (NZ feature film: director, co-producer, co-writer).
1987. *Kai Purakau* a.k.a. *The Story Teller* (NZ/UK television documentary: director, producer).
1988. *O'Reilly's Luck* (NZ extended short film: co-writer).
1990. Ruby and Rata (NZ feature film: director, co-producer, co-writer).
1991. *The Mouth and the Truth* (NZ short film: project consultant).
1992. *Sweetness* (NZ short film: consultant producer).
1992. Married (NZ extended short film: director).
1993. Bread and Roses (NZ television four-part mini-series, also screened theatrically: director, associate producer, co-writer).
1995. War Stories Our Mothers Never Told Us (NZ documentary: director, producer).
1995. *Absent Friends* (NZ television commercial for the Land Transport Safety Authority: director).
1996. *Hone Tuwhare* a.k.a. *No Other Lips* (NZ documentary: director, co-producer).
1997. *Parallel Paths* (NZ television commercial for the Land Transport Safety Authority: director).
1998. *Survivor Stories* (NZ exhibition artwork film: director).
1999. Punitive Damage (NZ documentary: co-producer, executive producer).
1999. Getting to Our Place (NZ television documentary: co-director, producer).
1999. *Campaign* (NZ documentary: co-consultant).
2001. *Wahine Requiem* (NZ exhibition artwork film: director).
2001. Titless Wonders (NZ documentary: director, producer).
2002. *Coffee, Tea or Me?* (NZ documentary: co-producer).
2003. Perfect Strangers (NZ feature film: director, producer, writer).
2006. *Earthquake!* (NZ television documentary: director, producer).

5

Images of Dignity

THE FILMS OF BARRY BARCLAY

Stuart Murray

> How can we take that maverick yet fond friend of ours—the camera—into the Maori community and be confident it will act with dignity?
>
> Barry Barclay, Our Own Image

In the February 2003 issue of *Onfilm*, the trade newspaper for the New Zealand film industry, Barry Barclay wrote an open letter to John Barnett, the head of South Pacific Pictures, and therefore the chief production executive behind the international success of Niki Caro's 2002 feature *Whale Rider*. Critical of the manner in which Barnett had, in interviews, stressed that *Whale Rider* managed to express a fidelity to the cultural narratives of Ngati Porou (the people of the area in which the story is set and filmed) and yet told an "international story" at the same time, Barclay responded with a critique that asserted the rights of Maori cultural practitioners and audiences alike in the telling and reception of Maori narratives:

> [D]on't badger us that this is the glorious path which we must all go along, head to tail; don't put us down when we raise our concerns about how non-Indigenous artists handle this type of material; and don't go hyper-promoting, in any triumphalist way, "universal story" to the detriment of genuine Indigenous efforts. Above all, don't tell us that we, as Maori, must *like* this film. It is every People's right to make their minds up on that, particularly when it is their own world being shown up there on the screen.[1]

Barclay's concerns here go to the heart of his career as a filmmaker. The director of documentaries and shorts for both television and cinematic release, and the maker of two feature films, *Ngati* (1987) and *Te Rua* (1991), and the documentary features *The Neglected Miracle* (1985) and *The Feath-*

ers of Peace (2000), Barclay's idea of cinema is one wedded to the notions of tikanga (Maori custom/law) and an appropriate sense of mana tuturu (spiritual guardianship) as well as a notion of justice that is both secular and religious in a communal sense. In the ongoing and ever-shifting debate about who has what rights in relation to the representation of Maori culture (and indigenous cultures more widely), Barclay's films present a consistent body of work that stresses the ideas of community inclusion and a reciprocity between the filmmaker and the filmed as well as the necessary modification of classical film techniques in the telling of Maori stories. In reacting to Barnett's conviction that the specificities of any Maori narrative can also include the smooth edges that make such representation palatable for an international audience, Barclay's argument articulates the complexity of an indigenous worldview that is sourced in historical legacy and contemporary cultural politics. Equally his films address the often-vexed questions of cultural and social self-determination, the arguments surrounding tradition both within and beyond the indigenous community, and the lingering presence of historical event. Ultimately, Barclay is an advocate of cultural strengths, and of the necessity to understand any social multiplicity in its full nature. As such, he is one of New Zealand's most important filmmakers.

Barclay's feature film career begins with the making of *Ngati* in the mid-1980s, but it is advantageous to see *Ngati* as the culmination of work that began in television over a decade before. Initially trained as a cameraman, Barclay joined John O'Shea's Pacific Films in the late 1960s and directed a number of documentaries, trade films, and television commercials. In the early 1970s he also became increasingly involved in Wellington with Nga Tamatoa (warrior children), the Maori activist movement, a process he has described as a "grounding on many levels" in the key debates within Maori society and culture.[2] What Barclay himself has described as "my first full experience in the Maori world"[3] came with his directorial work on the *Tangata Whenua* television series in 1974. The six-part documentary series, in which Barclay worked with Pakeha (European) cultural historian Michael King and a crew that included many Maori contributors, was a landmark event in the history of representing Maori culture. It brought before a national audience key aspects of Maori history as well as political and cultural practice, of which the bulk of New Zealand was completely ignorant. In presenting activities and issues such as carving, or the importance of rangitiratanga (Maori leadership), or the legacy of the King Movement in the Waikato region of the North Island, *Tangata Whenua* allowed for Maori expression in its own terms. In so doing, Barclay developed ways of filming that he carried through to later features, especially *Ngati* and *Te Rua*. *Tangata Whenua* is the earliest example in Barclay's career of the necessity for what he has termed "a tapestry of people" to inform the filmmaking process, an attempt "to achieve on screen that sense of community participation in important talk that is the heart of the culture."⁴ Crucial to this is a sense that the camera is not an intrusive presence in the community, that the film (be it a documentary or fiction feature) is made with communal backing, but also that the images themselves are understood to be "given" and not "taken." In Barclay's documentary filmmaking, this has a technical aspect, with the use of long zoom lenses, and 300 mm and 600 mm lenses as well as similarly modified sound rigs, which allow for the camera to be situated farther away than is usual from the talking subject.⁵

Such details, both in the technicalities of filmmaking practice and in the wider approach to the cultural narrative being disseminated, are at the heart of what Barclay has theorized as "Fourth Cinema," an organizational term and an ideological approach that links the work of indigenous filmmakers around the world. For Barclay, indigenous cultures lie outside all structures of nationalist orthodoxies, be they socioeconomic indexes used to assess material status or the critical approaches used to discuss film cultures. In fact, he asserts, indigenous cultures "are outside the national outlook *by definition*."⁶ Faced with such a politics of exclusion, Fourth Cinema presents indigenous cultural practice as vital to the social well-being of the communities it represents as well as to those wider communities it encounters. With specific reference to Maori and filmmaking, Barclay notes, "if we as Maori look closely enough and through the right pair of spectacles, we will find examples at every turn of how the old principles have been re-worked to give vitality and richness to the way we conceive, develop, manufacture and present our films."⁷ Central to such a conception is that the idea of culture and tradition represented is respected but not static. As with fellow filmmaker Merata Mita, or novelist Patricia Grace, for Barclay it is precisely the idea of "re-working" that gives power to the stories and methods of the past as they inform the present. Barclay's documentary work of the 1970s and 1980s, including post–*Tangata Whenua* productions such as *Aku Mahi Whatu Maori/My Art of Maori Weaving* (1977) and *Te Urewera* (1987), exemplifies such ideas, always locating both the camera and narrative *within* the community, never seeing either place or people as objects that need to be spoken for.

In *The Neglected Miracle*, this method was expanded beyond New Zealand, with a focus on the complexities surrounding the stewardship of genetic plant resources in Europe, South and Central America, and Australia. As with his New Zealand documentaries, Barclay characterizes his work here by a focus on the people who are the subjects of wider forces, in this case local farmers excluded and exploited by multinationals developing protectionist policies for the marketing of agricultural produce. The film

Barry Barclay, the first director of an indigenous fiction feature film. (Courtesy New Zealand Film Commission.)

is a complex account of the ways in which the "ownership" of genetic resources functions to underscore the power and financial discrepancies that exist between developed and developing nations. In a series of examples that provide an intriguing analogy with ideas of cultural power, *The Neglected Miracle* makes it clear that Europe and North America need plant types from the developing world because they are resistant to the diseases that have eroded the gene pool of European and American agriculture. The "wild" plants offer the opportunity to develop commercial cultivations, such as Dutch maize/corn and potatoes (developed from Bolivian and Peruvian sources respectively). For Barclay, the European practice of patenting plant types and genes, and thereby depriving those farmers in developing countries from access to the wealth generated by the use of such plants, carries analogies with debates surrounding cultural artifacts and narratives. When, in *The Neglected Miracle*, the camera focuses on maize farmers in Nicaragua, or Aboriginal Australians harvesting natural sweet potatoes, it is the complexities of the production and guardianship of natural resources that animates the communities involved, and these are questions that are key to Barclay's conception of indigenous cultural rights worldwide. As with his work in *Tangata Whenua* and the other documentaries detailing Maori society and culture, Barclay's method in *The Neglected Miracle* is always to allow the communities involved to speak for themselves, and the film is a powerful record of the traditions, responsibilities, and struggles that come from within such communal life.[8]

Ngati emerged out of this documentary work on communal ties and values, specifically following the making of *Te Urewera* in the mid-1980s.

Set in the late 1940s in and around the small fictional town of Kapua on the east coast of the North Island, the film revolves around central aspects of tikanga: inclusiveness, dialogue, self-determination. At the time of its making, both Barclay and screenwriter Tama Poata realized the strengths of having as many Maori members of the film crew as was possible, since—as Barclay stated in interviews—the film itself was "about being Maori. . . . It's a determined attempt to say what it's like being Maori."[9] *Ngati* is a communally made film about community, in which the narrative and thematic dimensions match the organizational and technical aspects of filmmaking Barclay had developed in his documentary work.[10] The film elaborates three separate narrative strands that fuse in its overall presentation of society and culture in Kapua. It opens with the community gathering around the bedside of terminally ill Ropata (Oliver Jones), who is dying of leukemia and whose illness is the context for a discussion of Maori and Pakeha approaches to medicine. At the same time, young doctor Greg Shaw (Ross Girven) arrives in Kapua from Australia, sent by his father who had previously worked as a doctor in the community. Initially Greg is brash and insensitive to those he visits, but the film reveals that, born in Kapua to a mother who died shortly after his birth, Greg is in fact Maori although unaware of the fact until his visit. The third narrative strand, which arches over the whole community to provide a more obviously social theme, concerns the threatened closure of the local freezing works, the major employer in the region, due to the lack of business caused by some Maori farmers sending livestock to other abattoirs. In this narrative, Ropata's father Iwi (Wi Kuki Kaa) agrees at the film's conclusion to take over the management of the local livestock station, and thus ensure the supply of stock to the freezing works.

The issues of control central to Iwi's employment as station manager have parallels with the various statements Barclay has made about the necessity for Maori to be in control of the ways in which images of Maori are produced, disseminated, and stored.[11] This is only the most obvious way in which *Ngati*, for all the tranquil, rural nature of its setting, is a political film. At the hui (community gathering) called to discuss the threat to the freezing works, the key speech by Iwi's daughter Sally (Connie Pewhairangi) stresses the capability of the community to manage its own affairs: "Our people stick together when times are hard. We've done it in the past—we'll do it again. Let us run our own freezing works, our own farms, our own fisheries. Let us run them ourselves." Sally, only recently returned to Kapua from an unnamed city, is at first frustrated by her perception of the restrictions of the community. Her ultimate decision to stay, like that of Greg who agrees to work in the local medical practice, is a sign of the final strength of communal bonds.

The community gathered in Kapua: The heart of *Ngati*. (Courtesy New Zealand Film Commission.)

At an obvious level *Ngati* is a celebration of Maori community. The scenes set amid core communal activities—sheep shearing, shellfish gathering, food preparation at the wharenui (meeting house), evenings in the pub—are filmed with sunlit colors and warm indoor tones, and are edited and accompanied by the score to achieve a narrative pace that signifies a quality of ease and comfort. The landscape as it is figured in *Ngati* is a world away from that of a film such as Vincent Ward's *Vigil* (1984), where the overt focus on the trauma of Pakeha settlement is conveyed through harsh images of fracture and dislocation, and where the farm that is the film's focus is lashed by wind and rain.[12] At the level of image, *Ngati* conveys a rural communality that might seem to suggest a pastoral nostalgia, but, within the cultural politics of the time of the film's making, the details of the community represented actually make a series of points about self-determination.[13] For a Maori audience (and Barclay has stressed that *Ngati* has a primal relationship with the Ngati Porou tribe of the film's North Island's east coast setting, and then with other tribal communities[14]), the figuring of children and elders, of the land and sea, and of the day-to-day activities of social life constitute a politics of image that stresses the contemporaneity of tribal culture. At the heart of this sense of the film is a refusal to present indigenous issues only for non-indigenous audiences. In part, the codes of *Ngati* require the viewer to appreciate tikanga to grasp its full complexities.

Yet even as *Ngati* makes a direct case for the validity and legitimacy of Maori culture, conceived on its own terms, the film's narrative strands focused on Ropata and Greg articulate an idea of integration between

Maori and Pakeha. Suspicious of the Pakeha medicine of local doctor Paul Bennett (Norman Fletcher), Iwi attributes Ropata's illness to mate Maori (Maori sickness) and prefers to use the local tohunga (spiritual elder) Eru (Tuta Ngarimu Tamati). Yet neither method can save Ropata, and both Bennett and Eru come together at his tangi (funeral) as equals whose knowledge and expertise can benefit the community as a whole. In a similar vein, Eru identifies Ropata's friend Tione (Michael Tibble) as the young figure who will potentially inherit the knowledge and narratives carried within the tribal sense of community, and it is Tione who at the film's close begins the process of instructing Greg in taha Maori (Maori practices). As Greg says to Tione when offering himself as a subject who needs to be taught, "I'm only a new Maori," and the phrase is deeply significant in a 1980s context of increasing biculturalism and a Pakeha desire to identify with Maori as a mechanism for dealing with the heritage of the guilt associated with a colonial history. Indeed, through Greg, *Ngati* offers the Pakeha majority within New Zealand the opportunity to connect to the processes of tikanga. The bigot who discovers his indigenous roots is, perhaps, a utopian gesture toward a greater sense of national inclusion.

Ngati was a major critical success. Winning awards for best film, best script, best actor, and best actress at the 1988 national Film and Television Awards, the film was also selected for Critics Week at Cannes in 1987. But, in keeping with Barclay's ideas of communal inclusiveness, *Ngati* was premiered at a special screening for Ngati Porou at Iritekura marae in Waipiro Bay in 1987.[15] The notion that, having given the images to the filmmakers, the community should be the first recipients of it as a finished product, completed the cycle of production and reciprocity that Barclay would later outline as a key strength of Fourth Cinema. As Barclay contemplated work after the success of *Ngati*, the totality of filmmaking—all aspects of production, distribution, and reception—became for him an example of Maori cultural activity more widely.

His second feature, *Te Rua*, addresses the issues of rights, ownership, and guardianship directly, with a focus on the claim made by a group of Maori on a collection of tribal carvings held in a German museum. For Barclay, *Te Rua* was explicitly bound up with the negotiations he and other filmmakers conducted with the New Zealand Film Archive in the late 1980s and early 1990s with regard to the issues of the kaitiaki (guardianship) status of any Maori images offered to the Archive for long-term holding.[16] When, shortly after work on *Te Rua* was finished, the Archive agreed to introduce a protocol based on the principle of mana tuturu, Barclay felt that a significant achievement had been made. In a fictional vein, *Te Rua* is both a meditation on such issues of guardianship and an account of a confrontation with the historical legacy of colonial possession and its consequences.

The film itself revolves around the quest for the return of three carvings taken by a member of the fictional Uritoto tribe, sold to a German in the late nineteenth century and subsequently kept in the basement holdings of a Berlin museum, and is framed overall by a series of marae scenes shot in a self-consciously theatrical manner. Peter Huaka (Peter Kaa), a performance poet working in Berlin, is drawn into a political movement to campaign for the return of the carvings and, in an increasingly militant mode, returns to the Uritoto to organize a group of young Maori to visit Berlin with a view to reclaiming the carvings by force. Peter's uncle Rewi (Wi Kuki Kaa), a successful patent lawyer in Europe, but a figure who is seen to be divorced from his Uritoto origins, becomes engaged in the struggle as well, clearly for both familial and cultural reasons (as a return trip he makes to New Zealand demonstrates). The attempt to reclaim the carvings fails, but Peter's group instead takes three valuable busts from the museum. Following a standoff with the police involving Peter and Rewi, both are arrested (Peter having been shot), but the public response to the incident forces the museum director, Professor Biederstedt (Gunter Meisner), to publicly sign a document releasing the spiritual guardianship of the carvings back to the Uritoto.

Te Rua is first and foremost an angry film, and one that is as concerned with ideas of responsibility as it is with issues of justice. The fact that the carvings are held in Berlin is the source of an immediate anger, and one that the film expresses fully, but the principles of mana tuturu involve more than only the physical possession of Maori taonga (treasures). Key to the film is that it was one of the Uritoto who originally aided in the theft of the carvings, and it is revealed that everyone living in the region is related in some way to that one man. The family narrative of the tensions between Peter and Rewi (the young activist and the older lawyer) thus becomes part of a wider thematic in which the claim for the return of the carvings is contextualized within the presentation of an appropriate understanding of the cultural logic of that claim. For Barclay, the idea of any return of taonga based purely upon a conception of its material value is an anathema, and the national context for *Te Rua* is best seen to be the increasing corporatization of elements of Maori culture in the early 1990s as negotiations with the government concerning the return of land became embedded in materialist concerns and the language of the market. The Uritoto scenes in *Te Rua* show that the issues of spiritual guardianship must not be motivated by a sense of material justice alone; that the knowledge needed to house the carvings is itself the responsibility of the people, and that it needs to be learned if it has been forgotten.[17] Rewi's trajectory in the film, as a figure forced to confront elements of a culture he has left behind, makes this clear.

Barclay has commented that "for many people" *Te Rua* is "not accessible."[18] In part, this is undoubtedly (as with the details of tikanga in *Ngati*) because the primary frame of reference for the film is within cultural models intrinsic to Maori communities within New Zealand, and thus possibly the ideas of value contained within the film are not apprehended by those unwilling or unable to work to comprehend them. To this degree, the film is not as "international" as it might appear, with a focus on the reclamation of artifacts that seemingly could include any culture in which such theft has taken place. For Barclay, while this wider context does exist in relation to the narrative, it is clear that the issues at work are fundamentally questions for Maori. At the same time, a number of the technical aspects of *Te Rua* contributed to the question of the film's "accessibility" and reception. There is much cross-cutting that attempts to keep the various narratives in play, and certain key plot details lack a degree of depth in their development. The theatrical nature of the Uritoto marae scenes is extremely powerful but does not always sit easily with the more conventional narrative contained in those segments shot in Berlin. To a large degree *Ngati* is a deceptive film in terms of its technical aspects—many of the revolutionary techniques prompted by considerations of tikanga are not automatically obvious on viewing. By way of contrast, *Te Rua* carries its narrative and technical difference in an up front and obvious manner. It consistently refuses the narrative orthodoxies of feature filmmaking, but there is no doubt that aspects of its plot in particular suffer as a result.

The modification of classic film techniques key to *Te Rua*, and the consequent cultural statements that result from this, were to become more pronounced in Barclay's fourth film, the documentary feature (the term is his own description) *The Feathers of Peace*. The film recounts the historical events that obliterated the Moriori people of Rekohu/the Chatham Islands (an island group some 870 kilometers [540 miles] east of mainland New Zealand) from the 1790s to the 1870s, and was a topic Barclay came to in the early 1990s after reading Michael King's book *Moriori: A People Rediscovered* (1989). The islands were first visited by a Royal Navy brig, the *Chatham*, blown off course en route to Tahiti from New Zealand in 1791, but the key contact that determined the history of the Moriori was not the arrival of the British but rather the invasion of the islands by the Maori Ngati Tama and Ngati Mutunga tribes in 1835, pushed out from mainland New Zealand following a succession of conflicts in the Taranaki region of the North Island. Upon arrival, the tribes asserted their right to "walk the land" and claim the island as conquerors, enslaving and killing the Moriori and leaving the original inhabitants to live on small areas of poor land. Following an appeal to George Grey, the Governor-General of New Zealand, a survey was carried out of the islands and a Native Land Court established to adjudicate on the claims of land ownership. Despite the fact that many of the Maori returned to Taranaki in the 1860s, the court ruled in 1870 that Ngati Tama and Ngati Mutunga were the rightful owners of the land, by virtue of conquest, and awarded them 97.3 percent of the islands. The Moriori were given the remaining 2.7 percent, largely rugged forest or wetlands.

The film captures all these historical events as news. Barclay's key intervention in the telling of Moriori history is the presence of cameras and an interviewer (Alan de Malmanche) that render the past as viewing for the present. Using detail from historical records, participants from Moriori, Maori, and British communities involved either talk to the camera, are interviewed, or are filmed engaged in the specifics of arrival and conquest. In the light of the historical record that is the Land Court's decision, *The Feathers of Peace* offers its own cinematic narrative as a counter-history, a space for Moriori in particular to articulate their version of events, to lay a claim for an idea of justice.[19]

For Barclay, the project of *The Feathers of Peace* articulated a number of key unsettling conundrums. Passionately concerned with the effect on Maori society and culture of white settlement and colonial history in mainland New Zealand, he was only too aware of the complexities that come with an analogous narrative of invasion in which it is the Maori who are the aggressor. In part the film is a product of Barclay's unease at the rise in the 1990s of a re-worked, and largely constructed, idea of "warriordom" within Maori culture. The careful cultural intricacies of knowledge and responsibility vital to *Ngati* and *Te Rua* outline a full and complex idea of Maori society, but the success of Lee Tamahori's *Once Were Warriors* (1994), with its emphasis on urban deprivation and competing versions of masculine behavior, promoted to both a national and international audience a vastly different portrayal of Maori life. Keenly aware that both Tamahori's film and the 1990 novel by Alan Duff on which it was based were being discussed as social documents that purported to depict the reality of contemporary Maori existence, Barclay creates in *The Feathers of Peace* a portrayal of what "warrior" activity might be. As he commented in an interview following the first screenings of the film: "Our tolerance of violence is that we have Jake the Muss [the central character of *Once Were Warriors*] hanging in rugby league clubrooms as a hero. We have a whole generation of Maori that have accepted *Once Were Warriors* as part of their culture and very few have spoken out about whether it's accurate or the effect it might have."[20] Within *The Feathers of Peace*, the idea of the

Ritual greetings before the violence of invasion: Moriori in *The Feathers of Peace*. (Courtesy New Zealand Film Commission.)

"tolerance of violence" is explicit in Moriori responses to outside contact. Following an initial landfall conflict with the British in 1791 in which one of the Moriori was killed, the people of the Chatham Islands resolved never again to greet visitors with any activity that could be deemed as provocation. It is this law, Nunuku's law (named after Nunuku Whenua, the elder who argued most powerfully for its adoption), that proscribed any Moriori attempt to resist the Maori invasion, with the result that both Ngati Tama and Ngati Mutunga violence went unopposed. Warrior status, Barclay shows here, led to the slaughter of innocents.

The film conveys this consequence of conflict most powerfully through the interviews with Moriori. In an opening scene, Riwai (Sonny Kirikiri), a Moriori spokesman, stresses the people's philosophy of peace—"Killing is not our way. It is forbidden." The feathers he wears in his beard are the symbols of the society's commitment to non-conflict. Following the first visit by the British, the early nineteenth-century development of trading and sealing brought more Europeans to the islands. Waiteka (Star Gossage) is a local woman who married trader Richard Freeman (John Callen). For her, this initial development of intercultural relations is profitable and non-problematic: "We're well off really. We have our shellfish, eels, we have our berries, and the ships are coming in more and more." But following the Ngati Tama and Ngati Mutunga invasions, the film returns again to interview Waiteka, now finding her a slave following Freeman's pragmatic re-marriage to Moemoe (Herena Wood), a Ngati Tama woman. Physically broken by her new life of servitude and typical of the effect on Moriori following the arrival of the Maori tribes, Waiteka remembers the Ngati Tama landfall: "They just appeared with their muskets and tomahawks. They did not speak. Their eyes were fixed ahead of them and they rode straight through. And these were the people we directed to food, water and clearings to plant." Moemoe, herself interviewed, is asked whether she took part in any of the Ngati Tama killing of the Moriori. Initially reticent, she ultimately replies: "Yes, what would you expect? It's part of our custom."

The power of the interviews is the way in which they offer what Stephen Turner has termed "a sense of justice or truth-to-history that the positive facts, considered alone, denied the Moriori in courts of law."[21] Thus it is actually within its cinematic qualities, its "visceral visual affect," that *The Feathers of Peace* articulates "historical truth" and demands a reconsideration of events in terms of a wider idea of justice.[22] The irony is that it is precisely because the Moriori were prepared to share the island with the Maori tribes that the Land Court, using the protocol of occupation at work on the New Zealand mainland, decided in favor of the Maori. This is one thing in the historical record, but as seen in the dramatized submissions to the Land Court of Te Wetini (Piripi Daniels) and Hiriwanu Tapu (Calvin Tuteao), two of the last surviving Moriori, it displays a power that is entirely the product of cinematic construction. The traumatized nature of Hiriwanu Tapu's account in particular is haunting in its presentation of loss. There is a logical connection here to the technical aspects of interviewing that characterized Barclay's work on the *Tangata Whenua* series, and the extension of these techniques in *Ngati*. For all the obvious "fiction," the willful suspension of belief in the empirical nature of historical accountability, in *The Feathers of Peace*, the concerns of the cultural community are still paramount. Discussing the acting in the film, Barclay's comments could have been true of his work on *Ngati*: "That type of drama is deeply religious but it's also secular in the sense that it's dealing with the here and now. I think that the communal dramatic process, which has some religious overtones, is what's going on in the making of something like *Feathers*. So when I'm trying to figure out why those performances feel apt I think it's somewhere in that area."[23]

At the same time as such issues of community stress the continuity of *The Feathers of Peace* with Barclay's previous work, the film's commentary on the issues of conquest and peace continue the analysis of Maori/Pakeha relations inherent in his filmmaking. It is precisely because the Land Court ruling against the Moriori borrowed the working law of mainland New Zealand that, for all the specifics of the Maori invasion dealt with in the film, its deliberation on the nature of conquest and occupation refracts back on to the dynamics of the European settlement of New Zealand. As Turner notes, the legal arguments in the film are "inevitably understood in terms of the conflict of white settler and Maori."[24] This parallel narrative is a constant shadow throughout the film, especially in the nuanced accounts of how elements of the Church and trading communities colluded with the exploitation of the Moriori. For Barclay, the violence in the film is the violence of the invader, because invasion and violence become synonymous. In contrast, the decision of the Moriori to stress their pacifism is a point about dignity. Even as it uses the historical record to point to a too-easily forgotten moment of near cultural erasure, and even as it gathers together the material that demands a reconsideration of justice, *The Feathers of Peace* is a film that pays testament to that dignity.

At heart, Barclay's films are a refutation of the logic that European, or indeed Hollywood's, modernity asserts a claim to a singular legitimacy, one that other cultures and other narratives can only, for all their sophistication, ever be "outside." His primary point of reference as a filmmaker is to the complexities of the community that is his subject. Within such terms, the necessary fidelity required of the camera to the truths of those it views is seen as part of the responsibility of the filmmaker. At the same time, Barclay's films are far more than simply texts that record the intricacies of society and culture. Key to all his work is the sense of indigenous culture as a base from which to make statements and arguments, and—for all their sense of history—his films are resolutely contemporary in their demand that certain stories need to be told and certain voices require to be heard. Barclay is aware that Maori filmmaking is only an extension of being Maori within New Zealand. The complexities of film production—of funding, script development, crewing, promotion, and more—enact the wider questions of prejudice and belonging that characterize participation in the national culture as a whole. But within such a world, Barclay's work from the 1970s onward has been remarkably consistent. At all times, his films return to the importance of community, dialogue, participation, self-knowledge, and tradition—the key concepts of tikanga—and then extend from this to ask that the products of such engagements are given a fair hearing. Without Barclay, New Zealanders would be that bit more incapable of the most important conversation they can ever have, namely the process of articulating themselves to the multiple communities that make up the islands.

Notes

1. Barry Barclay, "An open letter to John Barnett from Barry Barclay," *Onfilm* 20, no. 2 (2003): 14 (the letter actually says: "It is every People's right to make up their minds up on that," but I have corrected what seems to be an obvious printing error). Barclay's letter was, in part, a response to an interview Barnett gave in *Onfilm* 19, no. 12 (2002): 2–3, and there was a subsequent correspondence involving filmmakers Alan Brasch and Carey Carter about the issues raised by the letter.

See *Onfilm* 20, no. 3 (2003): 11; 20, no. 4 (2003): 11; 20, no. 5 (2003):11.
2. Barry Barclay, e-mail to author, June 24, 2004. For more on the Nga Tamatoa context, see also Barclay, "Amongst Landscapes," in *Film in Aotearoa New Zealand*, ed. Jonathan Dennis and Jan Bieringa (Wellington: Victoria University Press, 1992), 123–24.
3. Lynette Read (interview with Barry Barclay), "*The Feathers of Peace,*" *Illusions* 31 (Summer 2000–2001): 3.
4. Barry Barclay, *Our Own Image* (Auckland: Longman Paul, 1990), 10 and 11.
5. Ibid., 15–16.
6. Barry Barclay, "Celebrating Fourth Cinema," *Illusions* 35 (Winter 2003): 9.
7. Ibid., 11.
8. For more on *The Neglected Miracle*, see Barclay "Amongst Landscapes," 117–21.
9. Barry Barclay, quoted in Rongotai Lomas, "A First for the Maori: Ngati," *Illusions* 5 (1987): 4. In the same interview Barclay notes that, at the time of the film's making, it was difficult to find qualified Maori to work as producers or directors of photography, so the ideal of "100 percent Maori crew" was still some way off (ibid., 4).
10. Helen Martin notes: "Many of the young Maori who crewed on the film were part of a collective, Te Awa Marama, recruited from a training course." Helen Martin and Sam Edwards, *New Zealand Film, 1912–1996* (Auckland: Oxford University Press, 1997), 128. Barclay ran the training course in Hawkes Bay, and the crew went on to make the short *Ka Mate! Ka Mate!* (1987) before commencing full work on *Ngati*.
11. See Barclay, *Our Own Image*, 63–64.
12. Barclay has commented that he finds *Vigil* "a disturbing film . . . it's disturbing to see the depth of alienation in the invader and to know that having undergone many hardships, the invader is so lost in the country of his new-found possession." Read, "*The Feathers of Peace,*" 6.
13. For more on ideas of history and nostalgia in *Ngati*, see Martin Blythe, *Naming the Other: Images of the Maori in New Zealand Film and Television* (Metuchen, NJ: Scarecrow, 1994), 276–77.
14. Barry Barclay, e-mail to author, January 17, 2002.
15. See Ann Simpson, "Haere Mai Homecoming," *Onfilm* 4, no. 4 (1987): 3–4.
16. See Barry Barclay, "Housing Our Image Destiny," *Illusions* 7 (November 1991): 39–42.
17. The idea of "housing" the carvings is vital to the film. "Te Rua" means "the storehouse" and is the location for the carvings in the Uritoto following their original theft. What *Te Rua* reveals is that such a location is as inappropriate for the works as the basement of the Berlin museum, and that—to be living, working elements of culture—the carvings require to be placed in a social context where they are understood. A similar idea of how images of Maori should be treated is undoubtedly behind Barclay's argument in "Housing Our Image Destiny."
18. Read, "*The Feathers of Peace,*" 6.
19. See Stephen Turner, "Cinema of Justice: *The Feathers of Peace,*" *Illusions* 33 (Autumn 2002): 9–11.
20. Read, "*The Feathers of Peace,*" 5.
21. Turner, "Cinema of Justice," 9.
22. Ibid., 9.

23. Read, "*The Feathers of Peace,*" 5–6.
24. Turner, "Cinema of Justice," 10.

Barry Barclay—Filmography

1968. *A Matter of Taste* (NZ documentary: cinematographer).
1971. *Spinning a Yarn* (NZ documentary: cinematographer).
1972. *All That We Need* (NZ extended short film: director, writer).
1972. *There's a Problem Here* (NZ documentary: director).
1972. *The Town That Lost a Miracle* (NZ television documentary in the *Survey* series: director).
1972. *In the Company of Trees* (NZ documentary: director).
1974. ***Tangata Whenua*** (NZ television six-part series: director, co-writer).
1975. *Ashes* (NZ television documentary: director, writer).
1976. *Hunting Horns* (NZ television six-part series: director).
1976. *Women in Power: Indira Gandhi* (NZ television documentary: director).
1977. *Autumn Fires* a.k.a. *In Search of Pakehatanga: Autumn Fires* (NZ television documentary with drama elements, in the *Scene* series: director).
1977. ***Aku Mahi Whatu Maori/My Art of Maori Weaving*** (NZ documentary: director, writer).
1979. *Mahaweli* (unfinished feature film: director, writer).
1985. ***The Neglected Miracle*** (NZ [multiple financed] documentary: director, writer).
1987. *Ka Mate! Ka Mate!* (NZ extended short film. Training film for crew involved with *Ngati*: director).
1987. ***Ngati*** (NZ feature film: director).
1987. ***Te Urewera*** (NZ television documentary: director).
1991. ***Te Rua*** a.k.a. ***The Store House*** a.k.a. ***The Pit*** (NZ/Germany feature film: director, writer).
2000. ***The Feathers of Peace*** (NZ documentary: director, writer).
2005. ***The Kaipara Affair*** (NZ documentary: director).

6

Lives of Their Own
Films by Merata Mita

Geraldene Peters

For Merata Mita,[1] whakapapa (genealogy) is more than a linear genealogy; it is about "the name of a person, the associations of that name over her history, the area she worked in, the area she walked in, the battles she fought."[2] The personal pronoun here can be read as an allusion to Mita herself, whose whakapapa embraces the lived experiences of whai korero (oration), mana wahine (the power of women), and whose work includes documentary as well as feature filmmaking. In a wider cultural context, it also includes struggles for turangawaewae (a place to stand) in Aotearoa/New Zealand and the Pacific going hand in hand with an assertion of the place of tikanga Maori (Maori custom) within New Zealand. The first indigenous woman to have solely directed a feature film (and the first woman in New Zealand to have solely directed a feature-length film[3]), Mita continues to be regarded as a source of inspiration for indigenous filmmakers around the world.

A filmmaker for twenty-five years, Mita's first documentary, *Karanga Hokianga*, was finished in 1979 and her most recent film *Hotere*, premiered at the Auckland Film Festival in July 2001. In particular, this essay discusses four films made between 1978 and 1990: *Bastion Point Day 507* (1980), *Patu!* (a club; to assault) (1983), *Mauri* (life force) (1988), and *Mana Waka* (the power of the canoe[4]) (1990). Each of these films has a distinctive place in Mita's filmmaking oeuvre, and taken together they reveal a consistent revisiting of her preoccupations with history, land, labor (both creative and industrial), language, resistance, and the genealogy of women. After the 1990 premiere of *Mana Waka* in Auckland, Mita left to work in the United States, and has continued working and living in Hawai'i since then. She has never lost sight of Aotearoa/New Zealand as turangawaewae however, constantly returning for film projects, teaching commitments, and family.

The period 1979 to 1990 can be seen to represent something of a first evolution in Mita's filmmaking practice, a process of definition where it is possible to trace the move from what Mita has described as a period of internship on documentary films about community and struggle within Maoritanga (Maori culture) and trade union movements, to work that integrates the perspective of cultural resistance in these documentaries within the forms of feature and archival film. Overall, Mita's films are characterized by the dialogue between modern change and cultural tradition: a dialogue informed by lived experience, and one most clearly articulated through the films of this period. Taking this dialogue into account, alongside the point that documentary is the generic term most often used to describe Mita's work, this essay will map connections between *Mauri* as a feature film, *Mana Waka* as a re-working of archival film, and a documentary impulse recognizable in *Bastion Point Day 507* and *Patu!* through approaches to camerawork, editing, narrative structure, and the treatment of subjects. Although my focus is on this first evolution of Mita's work, many of the themes and concerns discussed above also surface in more recent documentaries such as *Te Pahu* (1996) and *Hotere,* made during the times of returning to New Zealand.

Kite (to See), Korero (to Speak)

This first evolution of Mita's filmmaking was informed by the context of Maori cultural and political renaissance—or, Taha Maori—growing through the 1970s and 1980s, giving renewed life to an earlier period of struggle that owed much to the prewar efforts and inspiration of Maori leaders such as Apirana Ngata (1874–1950), Te Rangi Hiroa (1877–1951), and Princess Te Puea Herangi (1883–1952).[5] In Mita's films, history is invoked so that the past is apparent in a context of the present, a characteristic that Mita has referred to as film's power to make the present eternal. One way in which her films achieve this is through a layering of cultural references within each narrative, a process that has its basis in the manner by which experiences and stories give shape to the oral tradition of whakapapa. Customarily, whakapapa is formally and publicly articulated on the marae-atea (forecourt of a Maori meeting place) through the oratorical practice of whai korero. Mita has noted that the experience of watching a film within a marae (meeting place) context is not unlike the attention given to speech makers where "what the screen communicates is absorbed in a sitting and so carries on the oral tradition with a heightened visual aspect."[6] Given this association, it is relevant to think further about the role of the person who oversees the shaping of these visual stories.

With the exception of some iwi (tribe/s) such as Ngati Porou, whai korero is a male preserve, although in special circumstances it is not unknown for women who have accrued sufficient mana (prestige) to take on the role of kaikorero (speaker, narrator).[7] During the 1970s and 1980s, prominent Maori women called for more marae to accord speaking rights to women. Pakeha (European) feminists have in the past interpreted this call as a statement about the extent to which sexism is embedded in marae protocol when, as commentators such as Kathie Irwin have suggested, it has been rather more a question of redistributing traditionally assigned roles along gender lines.[8] From Mita's perspective, traditional practices do often cloak the kind of sexism that informed the criticism she received from older Maori men for fronting the first Maori television news program, *Koha* (gift) in 1980.[9] Ostensibly, the program was seen to function as if within a marae environment and as such it was considered a breach of protocol to have a woman as a front person. It can be said that the televisual constraints of setting and time contribute to there being little ground for assuming a literal transposition of marae protocol to *Koha*. Nevertheless, whether from egotistical or traditionalist perspectives, men were affronted that a woman had the role of speaking for Maori within such a powerful public forum as television. Looking back, Mita has made the wry observation that she was brought up to respect Te Arawa traditions in Maketu (Mita's birthplace), where even if women who spoke out did not have speaking rights on the marae-atea, men of stature would never disparage them.[10]

This is a point of view that has led contemporary Maori women to affirm mana wahine Maori (the power of Maori women) as a way of understanding the strength of Maori women within Maoritanga, as well as a means of asserting a cultural difference from Pakeha feminism—a difference that is largely predicated on race.[11] As Mita has said, "I am Maori, I am woman, I am family, I am tribe, and only one of the facets of who I am, fits comfortably under the label of feminism."[12] Certainly in the present day, it could be said that she has accrued enough mana as a filmmaker, teacher, and mentor to sustain if not a literal transposition, then at least an analogy between her work and that of the kaikorero.

Mita's body of work can be considered to have a life of its own in an authorial sense. That said, whakapapa demarcates the genealogical character of authorship, so that the individual author is considered less important than the way in which she or he functions as a conduit for ancestral and community knowledge. Mita has stated that her films are about communities in the first instance and that her experiences growing up in Maketu, and then becoming involved with the Maori activist group Nga Tamatoa (warrior children), informed a perspective about the place for gender equality. "More than movements, I've gotten strength from communities, and Nga Tamatoa was a community."[13] Syd Jackson, a Maori trade unionist and founder member of Nga Tamatoa, has commented that Mita's films were an extension of her involvement with the group during the 1970s and early 1980s.[14] This is a perspective Mita concurs with, and one that is consistent with an earlier comment she made in discussion with Bruce Jesson: "it's more truthful to say that I'm not a political filmmaker but that my films make politics . . . my interest in social issues is a consequence of the fact that . . . I've actually been on a collision course with political and social reality in this country."[15]

Mita is more interested in her films being understood in the first instance as motivated by cultural rather than political concerns. This is not to say that she feels culture is not political, but that Maoritanga and its articulation through both visual and oral storytelling as well as the deployment of te reo (the language) has a specificity that needs to be marked out in relation to, rather than subsumed by, the broad category of "political." Such a perspective led Karl Mutch, writing about the development of a diverse "alternative tradition" in New Zealand filmmaking, to make a connection between Mita's perspective and Peter Wells's thoughts on politics as comprising "a point of view which sees people banding together as something valuable—emphasizing community and activity toward a purpose."[16] Certainly, communities in action, often mobilizing around an event, have figured prominently in Mita's work: "I can unite the technical complexity of film with a traditional Maori philosophy that gives me a sense of certainty, an unfragmented view of society, and an orientation toward people rather than institutions."[17] Mita's first film as director, *Karanga Hokianga* (a welcome to the Hokianga) (1979), was about the New Zealand visit of a papal delegation to the Northland community of Pangaru, in order to celebrate the presence of the Catholic Church in the Pacific. She interpreted the brief to also go behind the scenes and document the efforts of the Maori community to host the event. The strands of narrative that focus on local communities in the trade union films of Mita's internship period—*Kinleith 1981* (1981), and *The Bridge: A Story of Men in Dispute* (1982)—can in part be attributed to her eye for the way in which communities, often at the initiative of women, pull together in times of need. And in *Keskidee—Aroha* (Keskidee—Universal Love) (1981), an array of Maori and Pacific Island community structures from rural marae, to gangs, to urban work scheme projects, set in relief the rather more individualized concepts of community interaction exhibited by a visiting theater troupe from London.[18] This is a point of view that also enables Mita to locate her later work, *Mana Waka*, as a film that has been produced from within the Tainui community in New Zealand's North Island.[19]

Mita has noted that the rise of Maori nationalism can be traced through documentary, more so than any other form of visual media.[20] Commenting on her work of the early 1990s, Roger Horrocks makes the point that the New Zealand of Mita's documentaries is very different from the dominant images of New Zealand most often seen on television and film screens.[21] Writing about *Patu!*, Karl Mutch also observed that "for Merata Mita, part of this 'alternative' is to re-write, or rather to re-see, New Zealand's social history."[22] Writing and speaking about indigenous cinema in the present day, Mita sees it differently:

> It was my intention to reflect a Maori point of view of our changing society. To see it as a Maori sees it, to write visually as a Maori would write it. To re-write and re-see negates our place as being a legitimate one from which to view social change within Aotearoa.
> [*Bastion Point*] . . . is a Maori film because . . . it crosses from the most valuable piece of real estate in the middle of Auckland, into this piece of tribal land that belongs to *Ngati Whatua*—and that's a huge distance to travel in telling the story.
> It's exactly the same technique that speakers on the marae use—they take you from one point of origin to the other. From the modern to the ancient and the ancient to the modern—that's their job, their function—to translate space and time, to perceive them in different ways to what Pakeha are used to—[conveying] a sense of history, spirituality and the vast distance that you take your audience through.[23]

Bastion Point Day 507 documented the eighteen-month land rights occupation of Takaparawha/Bastion Point by members of Ngati Whatua o Orakei (the Ngati Whatua tribe of Orakei, Auckland) and their supporters.[24] In 1992, Mita made a connection between this documentary and her subsequent films by stating, "it is a style of documentary that I have never deviated from because it best expresses a Maori approach to film making."[25] Certainly *Patu!* shares many of the formal characteristics of *Bastion Point Day 507*—observational-style handheld camera, expressively textured soundtracks, ironic or associative juxtaposition in editing (sound against image/image against image), borrowed and resurrected (reversal, or negative) film stock, sequences of photographic montage, inclusion of broadcast radio commentary, and the occasional use of Mita's voice-over narration. To draw from Bill Nichols's schema of documentary modes, a mixture of observational, expositional, reflexive, and even performative characteristics here inform rhetorical approaches to argument.[26] Consequently, although a point of view is clearly discernible, a belief in the critical capacity of audiences to work toward understanding layers and associations also gives shape to the story told. Despite local and overseas commentators critiquing *Patu!* for a lack of structure and inadequate contextualization, the formal characteristics of *Patu!* (as with Mita's other films) provide as much a clue to a context for indigenous filmmaking as any expositional narrative.[27]

A crucial difference between the two documentaries does however lie in *Bastion Point Day 507* focusing on the struggle to retain sovereignty of te whenua (the land), and *Patu!* needing to accommodate the representation of a range of community interests involved in national and indigenous struggles over identity. In the case of the former, Roger Rameka, a leader of the occupation, approached Mita in the first instance about filming the events and community at Takaparawha. In this respect, although the documentary was made collectively with her then partner Gerd Pohlmann, and cameraman Leon Narbey, Mita could readily locate herself as a Maori woman making a documentary about Maori issues. *Patu!* in contrast, focused on the anti–Springbok Rugby Tour protests of 1981, and was necessarily an account of the participation of a broad cross section of community and political groups across New Zealand.[28]

More so than *Bastion Point Day 507, Mauri,* and *Mana Waka, Patu!* was made with the intention of holding a mirror up to race relations and state governance in New Zealand society. One overriding irony apparent in the documentary was that it took protest against apartheid in South Africa to act as a catalyst for anti-racist protest in New Zealand. Mita faced different challenges in wanting to make the film representative, while at the same time locating her perspective as that of a Maori woman: "It seemed to me to be a genuine people's movement. It was astounding the number of people who could have a say.... The film has been criticized for not having enough of the leadership, and for lacking a "peg." ... I didn't see the tour like that. This is not a film about a leadership, it's more about the dynamics of our society."[29]

Collaborative activity toward a purpose has been typical of Mita's approach to documentary making. *Bastion Point Day 507* was simply credited as a Mita, Narbey, Pohlmann production. Until 1982, under the name "MerGer Productions," Mita continued to produce documentaries together with Gerd Pohlmann. For Mita, it was a relationship founded on exchange, among other things valuable for learning and experimenting with filmmaking skills. Leon Narbey's name appears on the credits of other MerGer documentaries, as does the names of filmmakers involved with the left-wing Wellington film collective, Vanguard Films. In a similar way, the footage for *Patu!,* although shaped by the point of view of the director, can also be thought of as an assemblage of material filmed by different camera people from around the country who contributed their footage

A people's movement stands prepared in protest in *Patu!* (Courtesy Ian Conrich collection of New Zealand cinema and visual culture.)

to the documentary. Importantly for *Patu!* and her subsequent films, Mita considers she learned the most about the craft of filmmaking through her creative partnership with film editor Annie Collins: "[I] developed a strong philosophy because of my association with her—Annie'd probably say that I came with one, but . . . she strengthened my approach to filmmaking . . . from a sense of community, rather than from a hierarchical way."[30] Given the emphases on collaboration and community, it is not surprising that training initiatives for young Maori have also been a part of the kaupapa (organizing ideas) of Mita's films.

Documentary narration in *Patu!* consciously articulates an argument alongside a story about the journey of a movement. The activities of Pakeha grassroots and liberal activists give initial focus to the narrative, which then shifts to gradually reveal Pakeha traveling alongside the separate paths of rangatahi (young people), kuia (matron/s), and kaumatua (elder/s) within the Maori community. The actions of tangata whenua (people of the land) are propelled by desires for Maori self-determination. The documentary begins with three articulations of national identity coming together through the sound/image juxtapositions of South Africa (Steve Biko, Sharpeville, Soweto, Springboks, "Amandla" chants), Aotearoa (the title, *Patu!*), and New Zealand (the national anthem, "God Defend New Zealand"). *Patu!*'s final scene is of a march to Mount Eden jail in solidarity with imprisoned protestors. It is an open ending that suggests that the struggle for Maori sovereignty and national identity that *Patu!* identifies will manifest itself in the future. The story told by *Patu!* has its antecedents in Maori struggles for justice against colonial powers—just as the Bastion Point occupation can lay claim to the pacifist protests of Maori leaders Te Ua (?–1866), Te Kooti (?–1893), and Te Whiti (?–1907) as part of its legacy. Certainly, both films have a point of view that draws from themes of history and colonization significant for tangata whenua. Accordingly, the underlying significance of their narrative structure pertains to whai korero "which can pull these themes together and present them as one,"[31] and the story is one that is able to articulate the past and future within the events of the (filmic) present.

As with the practice of whai korero, in each of the films discussed here there is a place of respect marked out for "those that have gone before"—be they elders, the recently deceased, or more distant ancestors. Such a space constitutes a tracing back akin to the recalling of whakapapa. In *Bastion Point Day 507*, the faces of Auntie Hope (Tumanako Rewiti) and Piupiu Hawke—the matriarchs of the occupation—are both points of departure and return for the camera and edit. In one powerful sequence after the eviction, Joe Hawke and supporters return with a request to speak a karakia (prayer/chant) over the grave of his niece, Joanne.[32] They are denied entry, further undermining the land's significance as a place of return for Maori. Similarly, the film as a historical document can be seen to act as a repository for the "life" of people who participated in the occupation and passed away during that time, or in subsequent years.

Although *Patu!* focuses more on the activist energies of rangatahi, the wisdom of those kuia and kaumatua "that go before" is asserted at strategic places in the narrative. Two-thirds of the way through the film, a kuia interviewed outside her marae in Christchurch begins by stating simply, but resolutely, "I'm not afraid of danger, Maoris are not afraid of danger," and then recounts the story of how Waihirere Maori welcomed the South African rugby team on to Te Poho o Rawiri marae in Gisborne, "and then wero'd (challenged) them, told them never to come back." Her commentary is extended a few scenes later by rangatahi present at marae hui (gatherings) and political meetings, calling on the anti-apartheid movement to recognize that racism exists in New Zealand. Their position is backed up by an interview with kaumatua Canon Hone Kaa, who reasserts a need for the anti-apartheid movement to take account of the racism at home. His presence fills the frame through a direct address to camera, denoting stature, and underscoring a shift in tenor of the documentary's argument.

The rhetorical force of a kaumatua endorsing the sentiments expressed by rangatahi cannot be underestimated. This shot, like the one of the kuia, is framed according to the conventions of the "talking head" interview. However, set within the overall style of Mita's documentary, where such shot set-ups are rare, it takes on a different significance—one more orientated toward the framing of an orator than of an interviewee. The sequence constitutes a powerful rhetorical/oratorical turn in the narrative. It functions as a key point, where a Maori perspective takes on a stronger role, and the thematic preoccupation of the documentary's argument becomes most apparent.

Wairua Ora (Life)

In an interview shortly after the making of *Patu!*, Mita foreshadowed *Mauri* when talking about her plans for a fictional feature film based on "a Maori story about the philosophy of life . . . a kid's odyssey through life and death and through the grandmother's life and death."[33] At the time of scripting, it was conceived of as a low-budget film, shot over a year to accommodate the role of the seasons in the child's process of learning. Similar to the making of an observational documentary, there were to be two actors, and a crew consisting of the director and a cameraperson. By 1986, it had evolved into Mita's first fictional film, *Mauri*. Mita was now working with more crew and better post-production resources, yet she was conscious of retaining elements of documentary style, most evidently in terms of the casting of untrained actors in pivotal roles. Anzac Wallace, a Maori trade unionist, had been involved in the Bastion Point and Mangere Bridge struggles articulated through the documentaries *Bastion Point Day 507* and *The Bridge: A Story of Men in Dispute*. Subsequent to those documentaries, he acted in a number of feature films including *The Protestors* (1982), *Utu* (Reciprocity) (1983), *The Silent One* (1984), and *The Quiet Earth* (1985), before his casting as Paki/Rewi Rapana in *Mauri*.

Mauri begins urgently, with an opening sequence built around the birth of a child. A Pakeha doctor stands by, out of place in the wake of Kara's (Eva Rickard) purpose. Kara delivers the baby, severing the umbilical cord with a generations-old paua shell, taking the placenta back to the land to bury it as "part of us." Structurally, the event acts as a catalyst for bringing together key narrative elements and characters. As a précis of the film's thematic concerns with the rhythms of birth, death, relationship to the land, and destiny, meanings are interwoven and laid down as an introduction, much like the traditional takapau horanui (birth mat).[34]

The existential dilemma of Paki/Rewi, as an escaped convict impersonating a dead man's identity who comes into a small 1950s commu-

Personifying community leadership: Eva Rickard as Kara in *Mauri*. (Courtesy New Zealand Film Commission.)

nity, is crucial for the film's dramatic direction. Paki's appropriation of the identity of the dead Rewi violates tapu (taboo), and mauri, understood here as both life force and the power of the gods to bind body and spirit, assumes an awesome energy. For Mita, the relationship between death and destiny is played out through the character of Paki/Rewi, whose "story is really a parable about the schizophrenic existence of so many Maori in Pakeha society. Our psychological prisons are sometimes worse than jail, and only by breaking free of colonial repression and asserting our true Maori identity can we ever gain real freedom."[35] The cross-cultural marriage between Steve (James Heyward) and Ramiri (Susan Ramiri Paul) functions importantly as an antidote to the racist ravings of Mr. Semmens (Geoff Murphy), exemplifying the productive potential of Maori-Pakeha relations. Nevertheless, it is Paki/Rewi's child that Ramiri bears, and implicitly the healing of alienated identity lies in this union.

Like Wallace, Eva Rickard was an untrained actor, although she had some experience in amateur theater. A veteran Maori cultural leader and land rights activist, the mana accrued by Rickard as a social role model invests the character of Kara with an aura that reaches beyond the life of the film to the record of her achievements within a "real historical world," conventionally the domain associated with documentary reality. As Mita states: "a woman like her in real life was the woman that the character was meant to represent."[36]

For Mita, Eva Rickard embodied a similar kind of leadership role to the one that her paternal grandmother assumed in her own life. Although intertwined with the Paki/Rewi Rapana plot strand, it could be said that the relationship between kuia Kara and her mokopuna (grandchild) Awatea (Rangimarie Delamere), is at the heart of *Mauri* where mana wahine Maori gives direction to the assertion of a Maori identity in the film. Their relationship alludes to the creative presence of mauri as "life force." In a sequential motif stated at the beginning of the film and reiterated after the death of Kara, there is a symbolism to the camera tracing the path of a departing kotuku (white heron) in an extreme long shot, which segues to a mobile aerial shot of ancestral land, with the hill as its locus. After Kara's death, the camera circles around the tiny figure of Awatea running along the hill after the heron, and descends to frame her in a medium close up. It then assumes the role of partner to the child in a continuous swinging circular movement. Maori proverbs, sayings, and funeral oratory make an analogy between the flight of the kotuku and the soul of the departed soaring to heaven. This sequence quite clearly alludes to the spiritual bond between Kara and Awatea being part of a continuum that exists beyond material life.

Women of strong standing accrued through age, leadership, and activism provide a focus in many of Mita's films. She has made a connection between her focus on the stories of women, and the sense of destiny associated with Hine Nui I Te Po, the goddess of death. In *Te Pahu*, Hirini Melbourne talks about the processes of assembling tribal knowledges to gain insight into the history of Maori instruments, and pays tribute to the role of women as transmitters of that history through such means as waiata (song). Hema Temara for instance, carries the living memory of her grandfather's lore. This is a connection that is particularly salient for the way in which the restoration of archival footage in *Mana Waka* brings to life the presence of Princess Te Puea Herangi—a cultural and spiritual leader of the Tainui people. Princess Te Puea had commissioned the footage, shot between 1937 and 1940 by R. G. H. (Jim) Manley, as a record of the building of the waka taua (war canoe) fleet—Ngatokimatawhaorua, Takitimu, and Aotea—which was part of the Tainui contribution to the 1940 centennial celebrations of the signing of the Treaty of Waitangi. A lack of government support meant there was insufficient funding to finish the fleet in time, or to finish the film, most of which lay unprinted and unedited in a shed until Jonathan Dennis of the New Zealand Film Archive was given permission by Maori Queen Te Arikinui Te Atairangikaahu to restore the footage. Mita noted: "The restoration of the nitrate film stock was to make a film out of the neglected footage in order to make it an accessible whole to the public, and to revitalise the work and vision of Princess Te Puea Herangi in her efforts to uplift and uphold the people in the wake of the depression era. As well, it is a tribute to the work and tenacity of R. G. H. Manley."[37]

The film interweaves images of Te Puea at work on the land, teaching children, presiding at hui and ceremonial gatherings, with the process of carving canoes—whether or not she is visible, her presence is a constant in the film. As Mita states, "I had been told it was about the building of the waka but as I watched it . . . I became aware of something intangible but real, a spiritual element. . . . I realised it wasn't about constructing canoes. It was actually about a great woman and her vision for her people."[38] As director, Mita, with the assistance of Annie Collins as film editor, was commissioned to edit the material in time for the 1990 sesquicentennial of the Waitangi Treaty: "The film has a wairua [spirit, soul] of its own. The film's mana is inherent in its subject matter. My job as a director was to make sure that that mana manifested itself in the final cut. The film was mute, shot without sound, so I designed a soundtrack which would endorse the hard physical work that was done, that would evoke past memory, culture and identity, and enhance the film's spirituality."[39]

The film is brought to life through the soundtrack, with wood chipping and native birdsong contextualizing the bush location. The orchestrated sound effects of tools meeting wood, heightened through amplified sound and minimalist tracks, confer rhythm upon the labor, evoking something of the sense of ritual and vocation for those men who worked voluntarily through twelve-hour days that began each morning with prayer.

Mana Waka was edited in a room close to the dining room of Turangawaewae marae in Ngaruawahia, the place of the film's inception, storage, and rediscovery. Mita has spoken of her role in terms of participating in the history of *Mana Waka,* and taking inspiration from Te Puea as a woman and as a cultural leader. Importantly, three of the builders were still living at Turangawaewae when Mita began editing. Their memories and experiences of "what it felt like to be there" were crucial to the process of giving life to the film. In interviews, Mita has observed:

> It is the first film ever made in Aotearoa which was established on a true foundation of kaupapa Maori . . .[40]
>
> It has refused to be defined either as a documentary, or as a drama, [but] there is an in-built drama—it's like sculpting away at something and uncovering what the essence is. *Mana Waka* is very much made like that—it's about peeling away the layers to find the canoe in the tree, rather than taking away the extraneous wood and [finding] the waka in the middle.[41]

Te Puea's commission to Manley was an implicit recognition of the power of film to communicate the significance of the waka taua project. Although not completed until fifty years after filming, as a repository of history *Mana Waka* reasserted the continuing relevance of Te Puea's project for the 1990 sesquicentennial. Mita once described Te Puea's vision of self-determination and cultural renaissance as a "cornerstone for nation building in Aotearoa."[42] This recalls a point noted earlier about the place of documentary in tracing the rise of Maori nationalism. *Mana Waka* though, needs also to be thought of in terms of its specificity as an assemblage of archival film, shaped in accordance with indigenous filmmaking practices. At first sight, the film can be seen to share in the desires of much ethnographic film to observe and preserve culture. To be sure, Manley also had a vision that helped determine decisions made about camera work and the material filmed. However, the context of the production qualifies this interpretation, given that fifty years later the completion of the work was commissioned by Tainui, for Maori and the rest of the people in Aotearoa/New Zealand.[43] In this sense, the film was principally motivated by an investment in self- (as distinct from "other") preservation. This is reinforced by the intimate response of iwi and hapu groups to screenings of *Mana Waka* around the country. In the Waikato region of New Zealand's North Island, Mita experienced older members of the audience responding with a karanga (call of welcome) to the faces of people on screen: "The images of those people, and the images of the building of the canoes were very tangible to them. It was a very deeply spiritual and emotional feeling on a level that people don't normally associate with film."[44] Such responses underscore a preferred purpose of archival film as a conduit of active, rather than passive, history. Again, Mita's work demonstrates the power of film to make the present eternal. Not only was the film brought back to life through the edit, but the fragility of deteriorating and highly flammable nitrate stock also necessitated a process of material restoration and preservation. Mita's own comments on *Mana Waka* suggest that there is a way in which the life of the film resides within the images captured: "They [kaikorero] conjure up this imagery so that it's very visual—they make connections with land . . . and genealogies that are critical to the journey, and that's what I like to try and do with images."[45]

Hotere can be understood as an extension of this process. Instead of archival film, it is rather Ralph Hotere's paintings and sculptures that here encapsulate life. The appropriateness of rendering this via film is alluded to through visual motifs of light playing on surfaces, referencing of the camera lens, and analogies between the film frame, mirrors, and windows. The play of light has a rhythm, and these associations are extended by the insertion of fragments of film leader as well as mesmerizing sequences of quick montage with Hirini Melbourne's soundtrack emanating breath and pulse. Just as *Mana Waka* is invested with the presence of Te Puea, *Hotere* is the portrait of a living taonga (treasure). Famously reticent about being interviewed, the film captures glimpses of Hotere at work and at home. It is telling that the one time he speaks at length during the film is to talk about the land and environment where he lives and works. Early in the documentary, a written quote from Hotere contextualizes his reserve: "There are very few things I can say about my art that are better than saying nothing." The resonance of his silence through the film is made palpable when a time-textured sound recording of Hotere's voice relating his whakapapa breaks through as a last spoken coda to the documentary.

The "life" strand of whakapapa travels through each of Merata Mita's films, existing both within and outside of the temporal and spatial limits of filmic narrative. Similarly, her ability to talk in pictures enables a mode of communication that more readily navigates inevitable translation failures occurring in the shift from Te Reo Maori to English. The mobility of editing, camerawork, and projection enables a form of communication that conveys meaning beyond what is immediately seen or spoken on screen, making the moving image an apposite medium for conveying that sense of "extra" life. Accordingly, Mita has often spoken about her later documentaries in terms of "negotiating space."[46] Although her immediate meaning relates to using the medium of film to make a place for that extra "life," the idea of "negotiating space" is also relevant to Mita's ways of working with subjects. The practice of negotiating space and carving out a place for indigenous cinema has also been about maintaining a dialogue between tradition and modern change, as well as engaging with the opportunities and struggling against the constraints provided by funding bodies and broadcasters. Although frequently in negotiation with hegemonic institutions, in the spirit of mauri, Mita's work can be seen to take on a life of its own.

Notes

1. Mita's tribal affiliations are with Te Arawa (an iwi [tribe] of the Bay of Plenty region), and the hapu (sub-tribe), Ngati Pikiao. Much of the written commentary on Merata Mita's film work has emerged from dialogue between herself and various interviewers. It is a characteristic that resonates with the formative presence of Maori oral tradition in Mita's films—and one that I have attempted to build into the discursive structure of this essay. Many thanks to Merata Mita for discussing her work with me, and to Barry Barclay and Roger Horrocks for commenting on drafts.
2. Bruce Jesson with Merata Mita, "Film and the Making of Politics," *The Republican* (February 1983): 15.

3. Notwithstanding Ramai Te Miha Hayward's co-direction of *To Love A Maori* (1972).
4. As well as the object, *waka* refers to the tribal groups associated with each canoe that, according to Maori tribal history, brought Maori from a land named Hawaiiki to settle in Aotearoa.
5. For an overview of these periods of renaissance, see Ranginui Walker, *Ka Whawhai Tonu Matou: Struggle without End* (Auckland: Penguin, 1990).
6. Merata Mita, "The Soul and the Image," in *Film in Aotearoa New Zealand*, ed. Jonathan Dennis and Jan Bieringa (Wellington: Victoria University Press, 1992), 39.
7. See Hiwi Tauroa and Pat Tauroa, *Te Marae: A Guide to Customs and Protocol* (Auckland: Reed Methuen, 1986), 59–62.
8. Kathie Irwin, "Towards Theories of Maori Feminism," in *Feminist Voices: Women's Studies Texts for Aotearoa/New Zealand*, ed. Rosemary Du Plessis (Auckland: Oxford University Press, 1992).
9. From 1980 to 1981, Mita worked for *Koha* as a researcher and reporter, later assuming the role of front person.
10. Merata Mita, interview with author, January 30, 2002.
11. See Linda Tuhiwai Smith, "Discourses, Projects, and Mana Wahine," in *Women and Education in Aotearoa*, vol. 2, ed. Sue Middleton and Alison Jones (Wellington: Bridget Williams, 1992); "Getting Out from Down Under: Maori Women, Education, and the Struggles for Mana Wahine," in *Feminism and Social Justice in Education: International Perspective*, ed. Madeleine Arnot and Kathleen Weiler (London: Falmer Press, 1993).
12. Merata Mita, "Trick or Treat: Issues of Feminism and Post-Colonialism in Relation to the Arts." *Te Pua* 3, no. 1 (1994): 37.
13. Mita, interview with author, January 30, 2002.
14. *Merata Mita: Making Waves*, television documentary, directed by Richard Rautjoki, 1998.
15. Jesson and Mita, "Film and the Making of Politics," 8.
16. Karl Mutch, "The Alternative Tradition," *Alternative Cinema* 11, nos. 2–3 (1983): 4.
17. Jesson and Mita, "Film and the Making of Politics," 15.
18. A keskidee is a bird common to the West Indies and was the name of the visiting theater troupe.
19. Tainui is a confederation of six tribes and sub-tribes, all of which descended from the Tainui canoe (see note 4). The Tainui area embraces the Waikato region of the North Island from the west to the east coasts.
20. Mita, "The Soul and the Image," 50.
21. Roger Horrocks, "New Zealand Film Makers at the Auckland City Art Gallery: Merata Mita," program notes, August 2, 1984, 1.
22. Mutch, "The Alternative Tradition," 4.
23. Mita, e-mail to author, April 27, 2002.
24. The Maori name for Bastion Point is Takaparawha. See preface to *Takaparawhau: The People's Story*, ed. Sharon Hawke (Orakei: Moko Productions, 1998). Ngati Whatua is the Auckland iwi, with a regional reach as far north as Dargaville.
25. Mita, "The Soul and the Image," 46.
26. See Bill Nichols, *Representing Reality* (Bloomington: Indiana University Press,

1991), and his *Blurred Boundaries: Questions of Meaning in Contemporary Culture* (Bloomington: Indiana University Press, 1994).

27. See Pascale Lamche with Merata Mita, "Interview with Merata Mita." *Framework* 25 (1984): 6. During the discussion with Lamche, Mita responds to a criticism from *New Musical Express* that *Patu!* failed to contextualize the anti-apartheid movement. She iterates that the documentary was made "about New Zealand, for New Zealand" to address a neo-colonialist lack of critical perspective about the history of race relations and the place of tangata whenua.

28. See Tom Newnham, *By Batons and Barbed Wire: A Response to the 1981 Springbok Tour of New Zealand* (Auckland: Real Pictures, 1981).

29. Roger Horrocks and Merata Mita, "Patu!" *Alternative Cinema* 11, nos. 2–3 (1983): 14.

30. Mita, interview with author, January 30, 2002.

31. Mita, e-mail to author, April 27, 2002.

32. Joanne Hawke was a child of the family who died on site when a fire broke out on the marae.

33. Julie Benjamin and Helen Todd with Merata Mita, "Meshes of an Afternoon: An Interview with Merata Mita." *Alternative Cinema* 11, no. 4 (1983/84): 40.

34. Hirini Melbourne and Richard Nunns, sleeve notes, *Te Ku Te Whe* (Auckland: Rattle Records, 1994), Rat D004–CD. Melbourne and Nunns introduce their recording of traditional instruments by unrolling the takapau horanui. The analogies between birth, the introductory track to *Te Ku Te Whe*, and the opening of *Mauri* seem particularly apposite given the integral role of Melbourne's soundtrack in the film.

35. Mita, "The Soul and the Image," 49.

36. Eva Rickard's performance in the film bears traces of her appearance as herself in the documentary *The Spirits and the Times Will Teach*, from the *Tangata Whenua* television series directed by Barry Barclay in 1974. See Harriet Margolis, "Indigenous Star: Can Mana and Authentic Community Survive International Coproductions?" *Quarterly Review of Film and Video* 19, no. 1 (2002).

37. Mita, e-mail to author, April 27, 2002.

38. Merata Mita, cited in Cushla Parekowhai, "Puea o te Ao: Rise to the surface of the world. Merata Mita and *Mana waka*," in *alter/image: Feminism and Representation in New Zealand Art, 1973–1993*, ed. Christina Barton and Deborah Lawler-Dormer (Wellington, NZ: City Gallery; Wellington, Wellington City Council; Auckland, NZ: Auckland City Art Gallery Auckland City Council, 1993), 22.

39. Mita, e-mail to author, April 27, 2002.

40. Ella Henry with Merata Mita, "*Mana Waka*," *Onfilm* (February/March 1990): 21.

41. Mita, interview with author, January 30, 2002.

42. Merata Mita, "Nga Waka," *NZ Film Archive Newsletter* 23 (September 1989): 3.

43. Mita, e-mail to author, April 27, 2002.

44. Mita, interview with author, January 30, 2002.

45. Ibid.

46. Ibid.

Merata Mita—Filmography

1977. *Waitangi. The Story of a Treaty and Its Inheritors* (NZ/Germany documentary: interviews and production liaison).
1979. *Karanga Hokianga* (NZ documentary: director, co-producer, co-editor).
1980. ***Bastion Point Day 507*** (NZ documentary: co-director, co-producer, co-editor).
1980. *The Hammer and the Anvil* (NZ documentary: co-director, co-producer).
1980/81. ***Koha*** (NZ television current affairs/magazine program: researcher, reporter, and later presenter).
1981. *Keskidee—Aroha* (NZ documentary: co-director, co-producer).
1981. *Kinleith 1981* (NZ documentary: research, production liaison).
1982. *The Protestors* (NZ television drama in the *Loose Enz* series: actor).
1982. ***The Bridge: A Story of Men in Dispute*** (NZ documentary: co-director, co-producer).
1982. *South Auckland: Two Cities* (NZ television documentary in the *Lookout: New Streets* series: researcher).
1982. *Auckland Fa'a-Samoa* (NZ television documentary in the *Lookout: New Streets* series: researcher).
1982. *One of Those Blighters* (NZ television drama: actor, production manager).
1983. ***Utu*** (NZ feature film: actor, casting director, production liaison).
1983. ***Patu!*** (NZ documentary: director, producer).
1983. Music video for Diatribe (director for "Dangerous Games").
1984. *Te Hikoi Ki Waitangi* (NZ documentary: director, producer, co-editor).
1985. *The Quiet Earth* (NZ feature film: script collaborator).
1985. *Tonga—For God and King* (UK television documentary in *The World about US* series: director, writer).
1988. ***Mauri*** (NZ feature film: director, producer, writer).
1990. ***Mana Waka*** (NZ documentary: director, designer).
1992. *Freejack* (US feature film: assistant to the director).
1993. *The Shooting of Dominick Kaiwhata* (NZ documentary: director, producer, writer).
1993. *From Spirit to Spirit* (NZ/Canada documentary series: narrator on thirteen episodes).
1994. *The Last Outlaw* (US television film: second unit director).
1995. *Under Siege 2: Dark Territory* a.k.a. *Under Siege 2* (US feature film: consultant to the director).
1996. *Te Pahu: The Maori Drum* (NZ television documentary: director, writer).
1996. *The Dread* (NZ television documentary: director, writer).
1997. *Witi Ihimaera* (NZ documentary: consultant producer, interviewer).
1998. *The Magnificent Seven* (US television series pilot: second unit director).
1998. *Merata Mita: Making Waves* (NZ television documentary in the *Rangatira* series).

1999. Music video for Che Fu (director for "Waka").
2000. *Te Pito O Te Henua: Rapanui* (Hawai'i documentary: director, producer, writer).
2001. *Hotere* (NZ documentary: director, co-producer, writer).
2004. *Spooked* (NZ feature film: co-producer, actor).
2004. *Pear Ta Ma 'On Maf* a.k.a. *The Land Has Eyes* (US/Fiji feature film: executive producer).

7

Ricordi!

PETER WELLS, MEMORIES OF A QUEER LAND

David Gerstner

Peter Wells is prolific.[1] He reads voraciously and writes consistently for film, magazines, books, and theater. He is also openly gay and decidedly queer in his aesthetic sensibilities. Although New Zealand in recent years has passed legislation legalizing homosexual partnerships and elected the world's first transgender member of Parliament, Georgina Beyer (the subject of a recent film co-directed by Wells), the national popular culture remains soundly masculinist and heterosexual.[2] Wells's films and writings directly confront this masculine terrain through an aesthetic that derails the more linear models of form and content generally associated with his (mostly heterosexual) New Zealand contemporaries.

Born in the Auckland suburb of Point Chevalier in 1950, Wells was of that generation situated between the end of World War II and the introduction of television to New Zealand.[3] It was, to be sure, a queer moment to be born. As Wells's memoirs indicate, his family straddled the generational tensions of postwar globalization framed by British cultural and social tradition on the one hand and the enthusiastic American-Hollywood version of new Empire on the other.[4] His 1983 short film, *Little Queen*, for example—a title rife with pun—parodies the absurdity of nostalgia in an incipient longing for the British "mother country." The little boy in the film, dressed like a queen, parades himself in front of a mirror. This "little New Zealand queen" undoubtedly replaces (yet keeps all the glamorous accessories of) the privileged station of Elizabeth II, the Queen of England. Indeed, while obeisance to the Queen in New Zealand remained significant until recently, one might argue that its slow erosion ensued when American television began transmitting a new set of images directly into the nation's homes. The country's image of itself became more uncertain as it straddled the ideologies of both the old and new empire.

How was New Zealand to represent itself during this transitional period? What histories, myths, and works of art would put New Zealand on the international map as well as sustain a collective national identity? Although many artists and entrepreneurs have historically made claims for a "pure" sense of New Zealand identity to shape the country's zeitgeist, Wells consistently challenges such over-determined and hubristic rhetoric.[5] The forces of national destiny are not so neat and tidy, particularly when these memories are filtered through what Wells refers to as "mindspaces."[6] For Wells, "mindspaces" are manufactured through an assorted use of visual, aural, and literary media to portray the intricate connections between national and individual memory. Wellsian "mindspaces" have much to do with the artist's love of camp and its aesthetic of excess, multi-media, and cultural debris.[7] Festooned by the fanfare and operatics of Oedipal drama, Wells's films juxtapose and confront familial memory and his homosexuality with the country's angst attending its self-identity.[8] Rather than consecrating national memory, Wells fragments the desired narrative cohesiveness of cultural nationalist myth and renders it a perverse sensual experience. This is perhaps why several critics decry what they see as Wells's "lack of plot" in his storytelling.[9] Critical discomfort is also provoked through what is perceived as Wells's decadent narcissism and "overblown prose"—his work is really *all about himself*.[10] Such autoerotic pleasure sits uneasily in a national culture that habitually frowns upon self-aggrandizement.

There is always something queer in whatever Wells recalls or conjures up about his homeland and the people. "I wanted to say," writes Wells in his 1994 collection of short stories, *The Duration of a Kiss*, "I only wished to match his face with my memory, to confirm its dimensions. Yet already it was hopeless, as if by removing his physical form he left me with only one thing: memory."[11] Positioned toward the face of another man in an erotic pose announces Wells's pleasure to record, to (hopelessly) remake memory at the intersection of the fictions that write biography (or *memoir* as Wells would prefer) and nation. "Haunted sensibility," "trauma," "detritus," and "interior landscapes" are the Wellsian tropes of historical memory that sensually unravel the insistence of a New Zealand cultural memory that has been marshaled through the various associations of the heterosexual Kiwi bloke.[12] Wells's blokes are instead sexual partners who have met discretely in backrooms, public toilets, and other urban environs not usually associated with many of the narratives central to orthodox depictions of New Zealand cultural nationalism.

Memory, for Wells, is not an ethereal aura that transcends history and its material effects. His work embodies memory as well. This is to say, his wide and varied use of media that explores national memory is more than a facilitating tool for, to put it banally, capturing memory and *re*-presenting yet another version of history.[13] Such history occurs through the mediated experience of here and now where the pleasures of history reside in the process of its writing, scripting, and filming; it is not writing that claims or reclaims the historical. Michel de Certeau argues that history is the "space" where the "dancing lady" performs history.[14] For de Certeau, the writing of history is marked by the dancer's "foreign footprints" where a perpetual rewriting (certainly a re-choreographing) of fact, truth, and memory is always taking place. The same might be said of Wells. He dances through the memory and material debris of history, performing it through various media that serve as his imaginative writing tools. Significantly, these media forge memory and corporeality together in his work. The "intoxication of the cinema," Wells writes, blurred the line between "reality" and the experience of going to the movies: "[It] was if we were trapped in a movie. ... This was why ... I relived the texture of the film we had just seen until we wore thin the fabric of gesture and remembered word, at which point, like an expended garment, the film would drop us, and we would await, with unsated hunger, the movie next week."[15] Memory, body, and work of art are sensually, if not decadently, "relived through the texture of the film" so as to elicit something more than the machinations of a pure national history.

The Not-So Straight and Narrow

Early New Wave features from New Zealand (such as *Sleeping Dogs* [1977], *Goodbye Pork Pie* [1980], and *Smash Palace* [1981]) often revel in the rubbled remains of the bush where heterosexual men reign supreme. The narrative structures of these films are assembled, for the most part, as linear constructions. Aside from their independent "quirkiness," early New Zealand Film Commission films have been easy on the critic's digestion precisely because their stories are legible within a nationalist and often realist tradition. Because Wells emphasizes the sensual corporeality of memory—a jouissance in the fragmentation of the here and now—his work sits strangely next to that of his peers.

Wells's earlier short films were experiments for his aesthetic of memory using traditional modernist avant-garde editing and voice-over techniques. During the 1980s, Wells spearheaded New Zealand's polemical views on the importance of short-film production.[16] *Foolish Things* (1980) is a short experiential film erotically charged by snapshots of lost loves, snippets of notes on loose pieces of paper, postcards, and visits to favorite public toilets where momentary acts of love took place. The film begins with the silhouette of a boy undressing, then masturbating. It is as if the act of masturbation serves a Proustian moment of pleasure that triggers the images that unfold before us. Lost love is presented in the film through the collection of memorabilia that often accrues during a relationship. But, as with many of Wells's films, the material world is fleeting and of the moment. Ultimately, the images and detritus of the film that give memory its ephemeral shape are set alight and are reduced to ashes.

Films such as *Good Intentions* (a.k.a. *Postcard from New Zealand*) (1989) and *A Taste of Kiwi* (1990) cinematically (and scandalously) caress the hard bodies of New Zealand men (third-place winner of Mr. Gay Auckland in the former and the All Blacks national rugby team in the latter). *Good Intentions* is made with what Wells (as the narrator) tells us was indeed "good intentions" for viewers in England. The film begins as a tour by Wells of the gardens at his Auckland home. The film of "good intentions," however, transforms into something quite different. The very-British view of gardens gives way to the view of the muscular talent-contest winner who, after displaying his "talent," parades his Sydney Mardi Gras costume (crowned with a papier-mâché version of the Sydney bridge) for the camera. Wells's most radical short film (and, to date, least seen because of censorship issues), *A Taste of Kiwi,* brilliantly juxtaposes All Blacks' locker room scenes with gay pornography. The film is less than two minutes long, but contains some of the most erotic images to emerge out of New Zealand.[17] The defensive and strong-willed performative dimension to the New Zealand male pose (especially by those who play sports) is not simply critiqued and dismissed in the film. What makes *A Taste of Kiwi* so egregiously erotic is that it is precisely these representations of masculinity that are (homo)sexualized and displayed as sexually pleasurable for gay men. The All Blacks are easily made into and exchanged with gay porn stars for the purposes of eliciting homosexual desire and excitement.

Whether working in the short-story/film form or full-length narrative, Wells's immersion in reading, watching, and participating in all the arts bespeak a long-standing queer-modernist sensibility. His wide-ranging allusions to painting, film, literature, and theater as well as their effects on the body and culture are a key component of a queer art that revels in the debris of commodity culture. Wells, a white middle-class colonial queer boy of British Empire, sits squarely along this aesthetic and experiential line that echoes those queer bodies of Western civilization: René Crével, Marcel Proust, Andy Warhol, Derek Jarman, and certainly Oscar Wilde. Wells repeats the queer-modernist tradition but never in quite the same way given his own particular history with New Zealand and its cultural distinctiveness. Wells's multi-layered collages of Giuseppi Verdi, Luchino Visconti, Thomas Hardy, Rainer Werner Fassbinder, Ken Russell, Lana Turner, *Middlemarch,* trashy biographies, television, scrapbooks, and the Queen of England deconstruct New Zealand as Empire's ideal aide-mémoire.

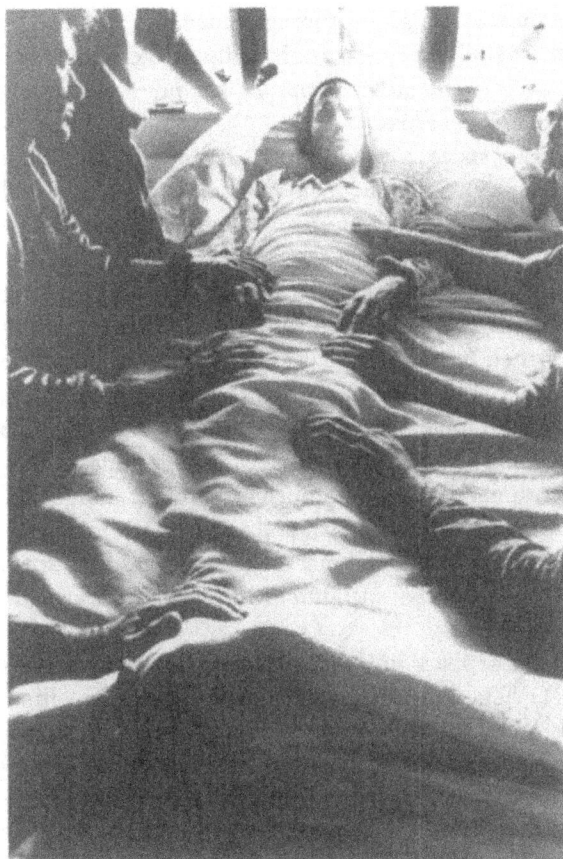

The family reconstituted: The hands of many embrace the dying friend in *A Death in the Family*. (Courtesy Ian Conrich collection of New Zealand cinema and visual culture.)

Tactility, Space, and Queer Memory

The sites of memory in Wells's films are extremely rich and central to the filmmaker's exploration of "mindspaces." Houses, Wells writes, "are a national obsession."[18] In films such as *Little Queen, Jewel's Darl* (1985), and *A Death in the Family* (1987), the family home is reconfigured through images that are both risible and painful. Bodies pass through the portals and ambiguous domestic surroundings while they struggle for a secure and grounded sense of family that proves to be nothing more than myth. In *A Death in the Family*, the biological family of the character who has AIDS cannot surmount its homophobia and embrace the son/brother on his deathbed. The family is reconstituted instead with gay men whose friendship-bonds create the home space and redefine the site of family.[19]

Loss calls forth both sadness and pleasure through cinematic memory. In all these films, there are only celluloid images of the filmmaker's imagination—history evaporating at twenty-four frames per second—to offer any sort of succor for the experience of loss.

Wells's documentaries of space, *Napier: Newest City on the Globe* (1985) and *The Mighty Civic* (1988), envisage the memory and history of physical sites as something more than fantastic. *Newest City* is about the rebuilding of Napier, the North Island city (destroyed after the 1931 earthquake). As it is presented here, the city is a dream-place built on the images of Hollywood, Santa Barbara, and the Art Deco architectural movement of the era. The city is presented "not as it is, but as it seems to be." If there is anything "New Zealand" about Napier, it is that it is an internationally, amalgamated multi-mediated imagined space. *The Mighty Civic* (a guide through Auckland's orientalist Picture Palace) takes us on a tour of New Zealand's speculative venture into the glamorous Hollywoodization of the world. Reenactments in the film of orientalist and exotic performances at the theater recall Jack Smith's erotic embrace of libertine lasciviousness and perverse pleasure of Hollywood in such films as *Flaming Creatures* and *Normal Love* (both 1963).

The most dramatic use of space in Wells's oeuvre is certainly the feature *Desperate Remedies* (1993, co-directed with Stewart Main). The film's mise-en-scène is rightly identified as operatic, melodramatic, and camp.[20] *Desperate Remedies* has been recognized as a sort of "revision" of history during the period of the nineteenth-century New Zealand Wars that reveals the less-than-perfect version of Pakeha (European) settlement. The trouble with a revisionist reading of *Desperate Remedies* is that it simply privileges one version of history over another. But Wells, the "dancer" who choreographs history with his "foreign [queer] footprints" through his rewriting of the historical, rehearses national memory through the sensualness of the materialist debris of the past. The film's mise-en-scène is texturally rich with thick curtains, saturated color, gilded mirrors, flocked wallpaper, and bodily flesh. *Desperate Remedies*, *Foolish Things*, and the more recent *Naughty Little Peeptoe* (2000, co-directed with Garth Maxwell) revisit the erotic (if not fetishistic), materialist, and corporeal remains of time and space. When Wells writes of the memory of, say, the "ideal or notional city [of Auckland]," he evokes the sensuality of the city and its "special quality, at once seedy and slightly run down, yet also sexual, physical, tactile." Like Merleau-Ponty's "flesh of the world" Wells corporealizes the city's landscape with the "flesh (Grafton Gully, torn through by the motorway) [that] never quite grows back to repair the damage of the slash."[21]

When Wells and Main created the visual "mindspace" of *Desperate Remedies*, they began with what Wells called a "marvelous [big] book" in which scraps of images from Hollywood and magazine advertisements were pieced together and then left for the crew to rummage through.[22] This use of collage and watching old Hollywood movies so that the cast might mimic the quick patter of American movie-star speak served to create the artificialized lived space of the film. In Wells's world, the "mindspace" is sexualized, made messy, excessive, fragmented, and uncertain.

Queer pleasures are made possible by the confusion that ensues when the neat and tidy order of things goes aesthetically and narratively not so straight. Under imperialist culture, the tradition associated with the organization of the lived world for the colonial heterosexual white settler is founded on a clear and efficient delineation of space. In nineteenth-century New Zealand, such desexualized spaces housed missionary forums where the indigenous Maori were "straightened" out.[23] The functional spaces of Empire for such ideological inculcation—from missionary practices to white settler domestication—are disturbingly unsettled in *Desperate Remedies*.

Historical Overload

Desperate Remedies opens with "At a distant point of Empire . . . In a town called Hope." The imperialist optimism of naming the town as such is quickly dispelled when the Fassbinderish and Russellesque docks of Hope, with their promiscuity and other bawdy activities, are revealed. In the traditions of opera and high melodrama, *Desperate Remedies* tells the story about "how to get what you want without destroying what you set out to get."[24] It is a world of self-indulgence and narcissistic decadence. Those who critique the ambiguity of plot and sexuality in the film appear to miss an essential point: this is not human liberalism where "good" people get what they want because they are entitled. The world is somewhat messier than humanism might suggest. The plot is messy, yet legible, because the melodramatics of history are just as messy. Add to this human desire and the narrative plot is sure to thicken. The world of *Desperate Remedies* houses characters that desperately desire to fulfill their own selfish wishes. The brilliance of the film is that it is unapologetic for such individualistic drives, and it refuses to cursorily align spectator sympathy with any one character. There is more at stake than mere pleasantries.

At the heart of the narrative are two women who love each other and simultaneously see their relationship as one that offers both sexual satisfaction and useful companionship. Dorothea Brooke (Jennifer Ward-

Lealand) and Anne (Lisa Chappell) live as closeted lovers (in the decorative surroundings of Dorothea's textile business; she is a "Draper of Distinction"). Anne's relationship with Dorothea now affords her an escape from the domestic servitude under which she had previously lived with Dorothea. Dorothea's sister, Rose (Kiri Mills), has an opium addiction and is pregnant with her Maori drug dealer's, Fraser (Cliff Curtis), child (as it turns out, Dorothea once carried his child as well but not to full term). Rose is yet another skeleton in Dorothea's closet, as is the haunting of her own terminated pregnancy (there appear closets within closets in the film, and Dorothea is their draper). Dorothea's attempts to keep Rose's addiction a secret are expensive since she pays Fraser for his silence. This is, it is clear, an explicit financial drain particularly in a film that dramatizes the early colony's often-precarious materialist interests.

To rescue her sister as well as her business, Dorothea (often hidden behind a translucent red veil in public) seeks to remedy the situation by finding a strong and virile immigrant man on the docks of Hope. Recalling Lana Turner's promenade on the docks of Wellington in MGM's New Zealand–set *Green Dolphin Street* (1947), Dorothea spots the man she seeks to purchase for her scheme, Lawrence Hayes (Kevin Smith). The casting of their gaze upon each other is sensually framed through extreme close-ups that strengthen the intensity—the sensuality—of the look and, later, the touch. Sexuality slides from body to body and from place to place throughout the film. Desire is met, fulfilled (or not), at the moment of an encounter between woman and woman, man and man, man and woman.

If Hayes promises to dispose of her sibling's lover, the service will require a fee. Yet the fee that men in this film demand is more than Dorothea is willing to pay—marriage to Hayes or, indeed, to any man is too high a price. Dorothea's precarious financial situation, however, must necessarily be resolved. Enter William Poyser (Michael Hurst) whose own good name threatens to be sullied by bankruptcy but can be rescued through a marriage of convenience to Dorothea. One does what one must do against the forces of destiny (as the film's soundtrack from Verdi's *La forza del destino* reiterates). The exchange of bodies for purposes of survival is more than necessary in *Desperate Remedies*. The film provocatively offers the possibility that the very gestures of exchange (the look, the business arrangement, the body) are precisely the sites of pleasure. As in a Verdi opera, closure through the salvation of romantic coupling is not where the thrill and drama occur. Dorothea's claim to happiness and bliss as she walks arm in arm with Anne at the end of the film is not a fait accompli. In a world where it is "necessary to survive," Dorothea's announcement, "I am free now from always having to act," is more tongue in cheek, since the parody

Bodies inhabiting a queerly rendered history in *Desperate Remedies*. (Courtesy New Zealand Film Commission.)

of Hollywood dialogue and conventional happy ending is nothing more than a detail of the film's style. To trust Dorothea's final proclamation as one of liberation is to disregard the film's queer pleasures in games, deceits, and intrigues.

Wells's film style is one of compromise and desperate remedies.[25] Struggling against homophobia, the often-doctrinaire principles of national interests, and censorship, Wells revels in the impurities of the transgressive body and the detailing of the historical mise-en-scène that those bodies inhabit. Wells has said, "each film has its own sort of territory and landscape. *Desperate Remedies* was part of a very high surface world."[26] Rather than, perhaps *unable to*, continue with the entrenched tradition that bundled together puritanical evangelicalism and romanticized visions of history, Wells and Main manufactured a queer rendering of New Zealand memory shot through with a rich and velvety color that drowns the spectator in spectacle.

Ironically, the dictates of a small budget led Wells and Main to conclude that they could do nothing but be excessive in their approach: "We didn't have a budget to do a kind of grand naturalistic sort of *Picnic at Hanging Rock*–type film or a Merchant Ivory period-type film."[27] The expense of the naturalistic was seen as too great by Wells and Main. This can be read literally but figuratively as well. To remain an accomplice with the institutionalization of (historical) space that claims the landscape as "natural" and pure, yet authorized under the cultural terms of masculine heterosexuality, rejects the queer pleasures of dancing through the not-so-pure historical ruins (mise-en-scène) that Wells explores in his cinematic "mindspaces." His films, short stories, and memoirs open the possibility to dance sensually through all the impurities that create the memory of New Zealand.

──────────── *In Memory of George Custen* ────────────

Notes

I would like to thank Sally Milner for her thorough research assistance and Peter Wells for making his films available to me to view for the writing of this essay.

1. Peter Wells worked on what he termed a "theatrical piece," titled *Ricordi!*, in 1996. "Ricordi" is Italian for memory or, more provocatively, as Wells tells us, "redemption." For a discussion of the production, see Judith Dale, "Performing Identity: Engendering Post-Coloniality on Stage," *Illusions* 25 (Winter 1996): 38–39.
2. The documentary film based on Georgina Beyer's life is called *Georgie Girl* (2001) and is co-directed with Annie Goldson.
3. Television was introduced to New Zealand as a domestic appliance and began transmission on June 1, 1960. See Paul Smith, *Revolution in the Air!* (Auckland: Longman, 1996).
4. Peter Wells, *Long Loop Home* (Auckland: Vintage, 2001), 53–54.
5. A visit to the Web site http://www.purenz.co.nz strikingly indicates the cultural current that capitalizes on the myth of New Zealand as an enchanted land divorced from the historical conditions of late imperial economies. This government-backed tourism-campaign Web site is part of an international advertising campaign that packaged New Zealand as "100 percent Pure." As of October 2006, the Web site is undergoing redevelopment. For a selection of queer histories and not-so-pure gossip from New Zealand, see http://gaynz.net.nz/.
6. For Wells's discussion of his messy "mindspace" aesthetics see David Gerstner, "Interview with Peter Wells," *Interdisciplinary Literary Studies: A Journal of Criticism and Theory* 2, no. 2 (Spring 2001): 106.
7. See Wells's essay, "Frock Attack! Wig Wars!: Strategic Camp in *Desperate Remedies*," Working Papers No. 1 (Auckland: University of Auckland, 1997).
8. Operatic is perhaps more accurate than Oedipal when describing Wells's relationship with his mother. Mother–gay son diva-like operatics, such as Wells's, are portrayed by Wayne Kostenbaum in *The Queen's Throat: Opera, Homosexuality, and the Mystery of Desire* (New York: Vintage, 1993), 97.
9. Misha Kavka, for example, is frustrated by *Desperate Remedies*' ambiguity. She states, "Wells seems to misunderstand his own plot at this point," and later that: "The 'negotiations of sexual identity' which *Desperate Remedies* takes as its main thematic, then, prove ultimately to be unnegotiable in this 'distant point of empire'; they are sites of narrative distortion" ("In Search of New Zealand Camp: Locating Desperate Remedies," *Illusions* 30 [Winter 2000]: 13). But it was not only New Zealand that produced such comments about the film's supposed narratalogical incoherence. In a review titled "Offbeat Saga 'Remedies' Is Desperate for a Plot," American critic James Vemiere wrote that the film is simply an "ex-

ercise in style" (*Boston Herald,* June 17, 1994, S4). In addition, Stephen Holden (who surprisingly assigns the Verdi soundtrack to Donizetti) claimed that "the story unfolds so choppily that it amounts to little more than an art director's pastiche of glamorous images, a series of beautifully photographed storyboards" ("Spoofing Movies with Arty Style," *New York Times,* May 23, 1994, C14). As Wells sees it, however, "I disliked . . . [films such as the New Zealand gay feature *Squeeze* (1980)] intensely: because, in part, it was done in such a straight linear fashion—which to me means straight in the most pejorative sense of the word" ("Glamour on the Slopes. Or: The Films We Wanted to Live," in *Film in Aotearoa New Zealand,* ed. Jonathan Dennis and Jan Bieringa [Wellington: Victoria University Press, 1992], 176).

10. New Zealander Helen Robinson finds distasteful Wells's (although she is wary to use the term) "pretentious" writing style. In a country besotted by puritanical prose and masculinist dreams of efficiency it is no wonder that self-consciously aestheticized writing makes some readers feel uneasy. See Helen Robinson, *Express,* June 7–20, 2001, 12.

11. Peter Wells, "The Duration of a Kiss," in *The Duration of a Kiss* (Auckland: Secker and Warburg, 1994), 25.

12. In *Long Loop Home,* Wells meanders through the labyrinth of what he calls the "long ride into madness" (257) of his family where "we could never arrive anywhere" (230). Wells's short stories, plays, and films invariably turn toward the affect of memory and its cultural effect. For additional autobiographical accounts and their relationship to New Zealand cultural identity, see Peter Wells, "my home town," *Metro* (May 2001): 58–61. The filmmaker's *Pansy* (2001) is a companion piece to *Long Loop Home.* For a discussion of the Kiwi-bloke film, see Russell Campbell, "The Kiwi Bloke: The Representation of Pakeha Masculinity in New Zealand Film," in *Contemporary New Zealand Cinema,* ed. Ian Conrich and Stuart Murray (Detroit: Wayne State University Press, forthcoming).

13. This is the mistake that some Wells readers have suggested. Upon seeing *Desperate Remedies,* Patrick Smith claimed that "strangely enough, and to the surprise of many of us, the New Zealand to which our Pakeha forebears escaped was, if not quite the scarlet sin city [*sic*] of the movie, certainly not the stern and tedious Christian paradise we've been led to believe" ("Unleashed! Impassioned! Hellbent!" *Southern Skies* [September 1993]: 25). Claire Monk proffers, "[*Desperate Remedies*'] ironic achievement is to end up looking more authentic than the real thing: Hope's sweaty, dirty docks with their slaves and rough sex make Hitchcock's recreation of Sydney Harbour in the recently restored *Under Capricorn* look like the tacky toy-town model it probably was" (*Sight and Sound* 4, no. 2 [1994]: 52).

14. Michel de Certeau, "The Fiction of History: The Writing of Moses and Monotheism," in *The Writing of History,* trans. Tom Conley (New York: Columbia University Press, 1988), 347.

15. Wells, *Long Loop Home,* 132–33.

16. See, for example, "Glamour on the Slopes"; also, Peter Wells, "Four Recent Small Films," *Art New Zealand* 28 (Autumn 1982): 28–31.

17. Wells tells the tale of screening the film for the School of Physical Education in Dunedin. The film sped by so fast and fascinated its viewers so much that they asked to see it again. See Gerstner, "Interview with Peter Wells," 112.

18. Peter Wells, "Home and Housed," *Listener*, January 20, 2001, 59. The site of home as a Proustian stage is a consistent theme in Wells's work. His grandmother's home in Napier plays a vital role in the rich fabric of imagery in his work.
19. AIDS hit close to home for Wells when his older brother, Russell, died from AIDS in 1989. The film was made two years prior to his death.
20. In a letter addressed to Sophie Gluck, the film's publicist, Wells and Main state that "the style of the film, its cartoon richness, its saturation with quotation, the outrageousness of its camp, is as offensive (or a turn-off) to conservative and unhip audiences as anal sex on the screen. But these people are not the film's audience" (letter located at "Peter Wells" clippings file, The Museum of Modern Art, New York). Indeed, "*Desperate Remedies,*" writes Peter Calder, "isn't for everyone," *New Zealand Herald*, September 10, 1993, section 2: 4. See also Wells, "Frock Attack! Wig Wars!: Strategic Camp in *Desperate Remedies.*"
21. Wells, "My Home Town," 60–61.
22. Gerstner, "Interview with Peter Wells," 105.
23. In his analysis of New Zealand architecture, writer William Toomath emphasizes the early and long-standing tradition of "mission houses" that "speak with some clarity and grace" or what he terms "straightforward." See Toomath, *Built in New Zealand: The Houses We Live In* (Auckland: HarperCollins, 1996), 14. In addition, see Justine Clark and Paul Walker, *Looking for the Local: Architecture and the New Zealand Modern* (Wellington: Victoria University Press, 2000), 35. Clark and Walker discuss how the "New Pioneer" modernist architects, or, I would add, New Zealand modern mythmakers (novelists, historians, filmmakers), followed a "theory" of space that was ideologically manufactured: "simplicity, honesty, realism," and, therefore, "straightforward" (30–31).
24. Wells, quoted in Lawrence Chua, "Desperate Hours," *Village Voice*, June 14, 1994, 56.
25. For a discussion of issues of compromise in the making of *Desperate Remedies* and Wells's campaign to prevent the censoring of the two women kissing, see Gerstner, "Interview with Peter Wells," 114.
26. Ibid., 105.
27. Ibid.

Peter Wells—Filmography

1980. *Foolish Things* (NZ short film: director, writer).
1983. *Little Queen* a.k.a. *Sticks and Stones* a.k.a. *The Visitation* (NZ short film: director, writer, art director).
1985. *My First Suit* (NZ film/television drama for the *About Face* series: writer).
1985. *Jewel's Darl* (NZ film/television drama for the *About Face* series: director).
1985. *Napier: Newest City on the Globe* a.k.a. *Newest City on the Globe: Art Deco Napier* (NZ film/television documentary: director, writer).
1987. *A Death in the Family* (NZ film/television documentary: co-director, co-writer).
1988. *The Mighty Civic* (NZ film/television documentary: director, writer).

1989. *Good Intentions* a.k.a. *Postcard from New Zealand* (NZ short film: director, writer).
1990. *A Taste of Kiwi* (NZ short film: director).
1993. *Desperate Remedies* (NZ feature film: co-director, co-writer).
1997. *One of Them* (NZ television drama: writer, original story).
1997. *Memory and Desire* (NZ feature film: original story).
1998. *When Love Comes* a.k.a. *When Loves Comes Along* (NZ feature film: co-writer).
2000. *Naughty Little Peeptoe* (NZ documentary: co-director).
2001. *Pansy* (NZ television documentary: director, co-cinematographer).
2001. *Rain* (NZ feature film: script advisor).
2001. *Georgie Girl* (NZ film/television documentary: co-director).
2001. *Behind the Scenes* (NZ documentary: director, writer).
2004. *Friendship Is the Harbour of Joy* (NZ documentary: director, producer).

2 The New Wave

NEW ZEALAND'S NEW WAVE OF FILMMAKING between 1977 and 1986 (between the establishment of a national film commission and the release of the last films to benefit from tax concessions) effectively laid the base for the complexities of the industry as it exists today. In so doing, it enacted a version of the process common to many of the film New Waves of the 1960s and 1970s that emerged on a global scale during this period, with the Australian example of the 1970s being an important precursor. The need to develop specific images and narratives of the local, to find a visual home in the world, was balanced by the economic arguments for the creation of a sustainable industry that would grow to benefit the nation in fiscal terms. As was sometimes the experience of other New Waves, in New Zealand these two demands were not always harmoniously juxtaposed, but what is beyond question is that the New Wave saw the emergence of several key directors and actors who established their filmmaking careers at this time and brought the intricacies of full feature film production to an industry that had hitherto lacked such specialization. The key figures of the New Wave period—such as Roger Donaldson, Geoff Murphy, and Bruno Lawrence—developed the art of filmmaking in New Zealand even as they produced highly personal narratives and performances.

The arguments for a national film industry can be traced back to the New Zealand Arts Council's 1970 symposium titled "The Role of Film and Television in Establishing a Nation's Identity." From this meeting came a series of working parties and groups that refined and developed the parameters of what something called "New Zealand Film" might be. In 1975, the Film Industry Working Party called for the creation of an interim New Zealand Motion Picture Council. The Interim Film Commission was ultimately created in 1977, and led to the passing of the New Zealand Film Commission Bill through parliament in 1978 and the subsequent establishment of the New Zealand Film Commission (NZFC) immediately afterward. As the title of the Arts Council's 1970 symposium displays, the development of a government-supported film industry in New Zealand was a process seen to be bound up with questions of the nation and communal identity. Film production was seen to be a complex artistic endeavor, one that signaled a cultural sophistication both in the technical and imaginative talents of its participants, and in the ways in which it brought local narratives to the screen. As such, a national film industry could convey images of self to those within the country, and a sense of the maturity and progress of the nation to those outside New Zealand. It would be able to combine stories of local relevance, made for both local and international consumption, with the development of industrial and commercial expertise. In the 1970s, it was noticeable that none of the bodies involved in drawing up the infrastructure of the NZFC saw these above ambitions as being in any way problematic or a cause of conflict, yet by the 1980s the economic arguments had come to dominate the production process.

The films of the New Wave emerge as often curiously hybrid texts. Many are local narratives in one form or another, either taking issues of society or, less frequently, history as their focus, but they are also driven by a commercial aesthetic that always kept the idea of the international market in mind. A high percentage of features made during the period are genre based and action driven, reflecting an idea of the kind of film that would appeal to audiences beyond New Zealand and also the fact that the New Wave itself was a movement by and large dominated by men. There is a quality about the New Wave—an idea of filmmaking as a sense of adventure—that is produced by the centrality of male figures throughout the industry at this time, for whom an enterprizing approach to production seemed to combine issues of artistic and personal expression. A consequence of this is that the national content in many New Wave features emerges as particularly masculine, an issue that was to prompt some revisionist trends in New Zealand filmmaking from the mid-1980s onward. Possibly as a result of such partiality, in many of the New Wave films the issues of national identity seem strangely provisional, as if the filmmakers in question could raise questions and issues—including those surrounding masculinity—but seemed challenged as to how to answer or conclude them.

If the project of the New Wave was to provide New Zealand with a cinematic sense of itself, then there is no doubt that a version of such a requirement was produced. But one possibly unintended consequence was that the very success of a number of New Wave filmmakers led them to leave New Zealand. In particular, the impact made by the 1980s features of Roger Donaldson and Geoff Murphy resulted in their move to Hollywood, where both became directors entrusted with significant budgets and major stars. To some degree, this meant the loss of two powerful personal visions to New Zealand filmmaking (though it is noticeable that Donaldson's fixation with the male figure in crisis has continued to be a major theme through his Hollywood features), and set a trend for later New Zealand filmmakers who would also take the route to the United States. It also paralleled the experience of the Australian New Wave, where key directors such as Peter Weir, Bruce Beresford, and Phillip Noyce followed success in the Australian industry during the 1970s and 1980s with work in Hollywood. In a global film market in which filmmakers are as much commodities as films, such processes are perhaps inevitable, given the cultural power of the Hollywood system. But the loss of certain figures should not detract from any full assessment of the New Wave's impact. What is without dispute is that, for all its rough edges and consequences, the period generated a viable feature film industry in New Zealand, and it proved to national and international audiences alike that such an industry was possible.

8

Between the National and the International
THE FILMS OF ROGER DONALDSON

James Chapman

When is a New Zealand filmmaker not a New Zealand filmmaker? Roger Donaldson's career problematizes the relationship between the oeuvre of an individual director and the wider cultural and industrial contexts of a national cinema. On the one hand, as director of the first New Zealand feature film to secure a wide release in the United States and, along with Geoff Murphy, one of the two key filmmakers in the emergence of New Zealand's New Wave in the late 1970s, Donaldson's place in New Zealand film history is assured. On the other hand, however, Donaldson is not a native of New Zealand (he was born in Ballarat, Australia, in 1945 and moved to New Zealand at the age of nineteen) and has made the majority of his films in Hollywood. These caveats notwithstanding, Donaldson clearly is regarded as a New Zealand filmmaker both by film critics and within the New Zealand film establishment. In his account of the work of "Australian Directors Overseas," for example, Scott Murray observes that Donaldson "apparently prefers to be known as a New Zealander."[1] As far as Lindsay Shelton, Managing Director of the New Zealand Film Commission, was concerned, moreover, the fact that directors like Donaldson worked elsewhere was largely irrelevant: "A New Zealand film maker working in another country is not lost to the New Zealand industry because he or she will always be identified as the New Zealand film maker."[2]

Donaldson's critical reputation rests mostly upon the two major features he made in New Zealand at the start of his career—*Sleeping Dogs* (1977) and *Smash Palace* (1981)—and on *The Bounty* (1984), an international co-production shot partly on location in and around New Zealand.[3] In 1981 he had proclaimed that he had no intention of leaving his adopted country to work in Hollywood: "For myself, I'm quite committed to the New Zealand film industry. Well, I'm committed to my own movies, really: There are real advantages here, though: *Smash Palace* is my movie, and I couldn't have made it anywhere else. I definitely have more chance to make *my* movies here: in Los Angeles, I'd be just another hack director."[4] It would seem that at this time Donaldson saw himself as an auteur filmmaker—the emphasis on personal films is a characteristic of most New Wave cinemas—and that he felt working conditions in New Zealand cinema were more likely to allow him the creative freedom he desired. Yet his words were prophetic for all the wrong reasons: not only did he go to work in Hollywood but the majority of his Hollywood work, comprising genre films and star vehicles for the likes of Kevin Costner, Tom Cruise, Alec Baldwin, Kim Basinger, and Pierce Brosnan, would lend credence to the view that Donaldson did become "just another hack director." The critical reception of his American films has rarely been poor, though Donaldson's reputation seems to have become that of a competent and workmanlike director, rather than the talented and visionary filmmaker that some critics had detected on the evidence of his New Zealand production. This essay, therefore, will focus on the critical reception of Donaldson's films, considering the extent to which his reputation rests upon his New Zealand features.

It has become an accepted orthodoxy to see Donaldson's first feature, *Sleeping Dogs*, as marking the breakthrough for New Zealand cinema into the complexities of a full national industry. Nick Roddick boldly asserts that "there was nothing that could remotely be described as a film industry before an expatriate Australian called Roger Donaldson, who had gone to NZ to avoid the Vietnam draft, made *Sleeping Dogs* in 1976–77," and avers that this film marked "the start of the New Zealand film industry."[5] Ian Conrich and Sarah Davy suggest more cautiously that *Sleeping Dogs* was "arguably the most important film of the New Zealand New Wave."[6] Even without the benefit of hindsight, the Hollywood trade bible *Variety*, at the time of the film's release in New Zealand in 1977, called *Sleeping Dogs* "the most ambitious entry in the country's current film renaissance."[7] It was not until 1982, however, that Donaldson really came to the attention of the international critics when both *Sleeping Dogs* and *Smash Palace* were shown in America. In particular it was *Smash Palace*, unveiled at the eleventh annual New Directors/New Films Festival sponsored by The Museum of Modern Art, which made U.S. critics take note. Roger Ebert described it as "the first really great film from New Zealand"; Barry Brennan considered that "*Smash Palace* is as close to perfect as a motion picture can be."[8] Vincent Canby, senior film critic of the *New York Times*, proclaimed the arrival of a major new talent: "I have not seen *Sleeping Dogs*, an earlier Donaldson film shown in New York recently, but on the basis of *Smash Palace* it's clear that this New Zealand writer-director is a filmmaker of potentially worldwide importance, a man of original visions with the technical ability to realize them."[9] Tom Allen, writing in *Films in Review*, declared that "Roger Donaldson's gifts are bountiful" and felt that, along with Australia's Peter Weir, the director was ready to take the film world by storm: "His options are wide open, he has a slight edge on Peter Weir, and both could end up beating the hell out of the costumed, well-mounted, period dramas that have traveled best so far from the Pacific side of the Southern Hemisphere."[10]

In order to appreciate the impact that Donaldson's early films made, and why *Smash Palace* in particular was so lavishly acclaimed by American critics, it is necessary to place them in the context of American as well as New Zealand film culture. American cinema in the 1970s had been witness to the emergence of a large number of auteur directors who were able, due to structural changes in the film industry and increased media interest in individual filmmakers, to make the sort of bold, unconventional, challenging films that critics admire. The 1970s was the time when the likes of Robert Altman, Hal Ashby, Peter Bogdanovich, Francis Ford Coppola, Paul Mazursky, Alan Pakula, Bob Rafelson, Paul Schrader, and Martin Scorsese enjoyed their greatest artistic and critical success.[11] While these directors did not represent a cohesive group any more than did other New Wave movements, their films attracted such journalistic labels as "the New Hollywood" and "the Hollywood renaissance." The 1970s, in hindsight, seems a decade of relative artistic freedom and concomitant stylistic innovation for American cinema, sandwiched between the break-up of the old studio system in the 1960s and the increasing dominance of the corporate blockbuster from the 1980s onward. Numerous commentators have pointed to the increasingly loose and open-ended narratives of American films of the 1970s as evidence of New Hollywood's stylistic departure from the classical model of filmmaking. Thomas Elsaesser, for example, argued that in contrast to the tightly structured and goal-oriented narratives of classical Hollywood, New Hollywood was characterized by "the almost physical sense of inconsequential action, of pointlessness and uselessness, a radical scepticism, in short, about the American virtues of ambition, vision [and] drive."[12] He also detected "a kind of malaise already frequently alluded to in relation to the European cinema—the fading confidence in being able to tell a story."[13] This fading confidence was most apparent in the emergence of the road movie, quite literally the most open-ended type of narrative, in films such as Dennis Hopper's *Easy Rider* (1969) and Bob Rafelson's *Five Easy Pieces* (1970). David Thomson similarly noted a "disdain for tidy or cheerful endings" and "the absurdity of such notions as villainy or heroism" in films such as Robert Altman's *McCabe and Mrs. Miller* (1971) and *The Long Goodbye* (1973).[14]

There is a case to argue that Donaldson's films represented the sort of intelligent, thoughtful, auteur cinema that was admired in American films of the 1970s but which, by the early 1980s, appeared to have disappeared

The dystopian vision of a police state in Donaldson's debut feature, *Sleeping Dogs*. (Courtesy New Zealand Film Commission.)

beneath the relative narrative simplicity and visual spectacle of the George Lucas–Steven Spielberg special-effects blockbusters exemplified by the likes of *Star Wars* (1977), *Raiders of the Lost Ark* (1981), and *E.T.: The Extra-Terrestrial* (1982). The Lucas-Spielberg films showed no disdain for tidy endings and presented villainy and heroism in straightforward terms. Donaldson's films—and those of other New Zealand and Australian directors such as Geoff Murphy (*Goodbye Pork Pie*, 1980) and George Miller (*Mad Max*, 1979)—share many stylistic affinities with the "new" American films of the 1970s. Such films being less obvious in Hollywood by the early 1980s, American critics were looking for new directors to champion. In this context it was a happy accident that *Sleeping Dogs* and *Smash Palace* were both released in the United States in 1982. Both films were sufficiently different from the norm—thematically and stylistically—to attract notice.

Sleeping Dogs, for example, is a characteristic 1970s film in the way in which it offers a distinctly jaundiced view of society and state. The film posits the breakdown of social order in New Zealand in the wake of a general strike and increasing tension between the unions and the government. A state of emergency is declared and, despite the promise of a national referendum to endorse the Prime Minister's new authoritarian powers, the country becomes effectively a police state in which imprisonment without trial and attacks on protesters occur with impunity. The film bears some comparison with the first two *Mad Max* films—*Mad Max II* (1981) was also released in America in 1982, under the title *The Road Warrior*—insofar as the immediate cause of the emergency is a petrol shortage (a far from fanciful scenario in the wake of the oil crisis of 1973–74 when OPEC, the Organization of Petroleum Exporting Countries, cut exports in response to the Arab-Israeli War). Whereas Miller's films assert the necessity of the rule of law, however—represented in the form of Mel Gibson's avenging cop, a sort of Dirty Harry of the outback—in Donaldson's film the law is shown to be corrupt and brutal. The main protagonist of Donaldson's film, Smith (Sam Neill), has chosen to live as a virtual hermit on a Maori-owned island in order to isolate himself from the turmoil. He is arrested by the Special Police for possession of a radio transmitter and is accused of being a revolutionary. Escaping from custody, he seeks refuge with a group of rebels led by Colonel Willoughby (Warren Oates) but finds himself alienated by their bloodlust and brutality.

Donaldson's style, with its use of long takes and long shots, and the absence of close-ups, maintains a sense of distance from the events; the spectator is an observer rather than a participant. This rather detached style is a characteristic of many New Wave movements, with their emphasis on objective realism, and represents one of the techniques that filmmakers use to differentiate themselves from the classical norm. The camera's distance helps to convey the sense of alienation felt by the film's protagonist, who is caught up in events over which he has no control. Donaldson makes effective use of landscape (a characteristic of much New Zealand cinema) and composes his shots so that his actors are shown in relation to the physical environment around them. This is especially apparent in the last quarter of the film, in which the military attacks Willoughby's camp in the mountains and hunts down the survivors, including Smith. The film ends with Smith, alone and surrounded following the death of his friend Bullen (Ian Mune), shot dead in a long shot reminiscent of the ending of films such as Mike Hodges's *Get Carter* (1971) and Liliana Cavani's *The Night Porter* (1973). It is an untidy ending that offers no real resolution and that suggests the futility of either individual or group resistance to a fascistic regime.

Smash Palace similarly refuses to offer easy solutions to real social problems. While the film is a different genre from *Sleeping Dogs* (a domestic drama in contrast to a dystopian action film) there are evident thematic similarities, foremost of which is the sense of alienation felt by the male protagonist, in this case Al Shaw (Bruno Lawrence), a part-time racing-car driver who also runs a car-wrecking yard (the "Smash Palace" of the title). The film charts Al's response to the break-up of his marriage to Jacqui (Anna Jemison) and his desperate attempts to see their daughter Georgie (Greer Robson), which lead him into conflict with the law. Focusing as

Facing the breakup of his marriage, Al (Bruno Lawrence, right), continues to work in his small town car salvage yard. (Courtesy New Zealand Film Commission.)

it does on the break-up of a marriage and in particular on the father's mental anguish at the prospect of losing access to his child, *Smash Palace* was widely compared to the Oscar-winning *Kramer vs. Kramer* (1979). In Donaldson's film, however, there is no tidy resolution; the film ends on a note of uncertainty. Critics admired the film's refusal to provide a conventional happy ending. British critic Sheila Johnston felt that the "sourly downbeat ending avoids the strained resolution of a *Kramer vs. Kramer*," and Nick Roddick described it as "*Kramer vs. Kramer* with balls." "With *Smash Palace*," he asserted, "the New Zealand cinema has decisively come of age."[15]

All critics regarded Bruno Lawrence's powerful performance as Al one of the main strengths of *Smash Palace*.[16] Al, like Smith of *Sleeping Dogs*, is a loner who is alienated from others and is unable to maintain normal social relationships (Smith also has a divorced wife and children). Al's emotional inhibition leaves him inarticulate and repressed. He is more able to speak to his best friend Ray (Keith Aberdein) about his marital difficulties than to his wife; later he discovers Jacqui and Ray are having an affair. Al is the archetypal "Kiwi bloke" who cannot reconcile his affection for his daughter with his macho self-image. Unlike Dustin Hoffman's sympathetic father in *Kramer vs. Kramer*, Al is not presented as an ideal father and Jacqui, despite her affair, is not portrayed as the villain of the piece. It is here that the film is at its most ambiguous. Noting Al's "series of dramatic and increasingly pathological *actes gratuits*"—including roughing up his wife during a violent love-making session, kidnapping a drug store assistant to provide medicine for Georgie, and putting a noose around Ray's neck—Sheila

Johnston felt that "despite—or perhaps precisely because of—Donaldson's success in eliciting sympathy for what, by any standards, is pretty unpleasant behavior, one finally wonders just how much of a variant this is on the recent 'wronged father' theme." "What needs to be considered, however," she concluded, "against the novelty of *Smash Palace*'s setting and treatment, and the chorus of praise for Donaldson's skill as a filmmaker, is whether divorce New Zealand–style is really all that different from divorce in New Hollywood."[17]

Johnston's corrective note is a useful reminder that, for all the affinity of these films with the American auteur cinema of the 1970s, they were conceived as commercial pictures intended for a wide audience. *Sleeping Dogs* was "an out-and-out commercial venture"; its budget of NZ$350,000 represented a substantial investment for a New Zealand feature and was raised through a combination of private investment, loans (the merchant bank Broadbank provided NZ$150,000 of which NZ$100,000 was underwritten by the Arts Council of New Zealand and NZ$50,000 was an interest-free loan) and television pre-sales.[18] *Smash Palace*, similarly, was seen as one of a pair (along with *The Road Warrior*) of "rousing commercial ventures that had prearranged distribution deals that may very well make a dent in the American box office."[19] Donaldson was only too aware of the commercial imperative of film production in New Zealand whereby foreign markets, most especially the American, were essential: "The American market is extremely important to a foreign filmmaker. In a country of only three million people (New Zealand) that can give you back at best a tenth or a fifth of the budget, you've got to look to an international market. Anybody who's spending large amounts making films and doesn't look abroad is totally irresponsible, being dishonest with himself and his investors."[20] There is a sense in which New Zealand cinema has had to be, simultaneously, both a cultural mode of production and an economic mode of production. A cultural mode of production is one that "distinguishes itself from economic modes of film production in so far as its logic is not determined by the profit motive (at least not directly)."[21] Donaldson's films, it might be argued, succeeded in straddling both cultural and economic modes of production. This in itself is one reason why they are so central to discourse around the "birth" of New Zealand cinema. It was the success of *Sleeping Dogs*, in particular, that "finally drew the [New Zealand] Government to the need for official support for the production of feature films."[22]

Donaldson's next assignment was unequivocally a commercial venture made with the international market in mind. *The Bounty* was a U.S. $25 million costume film, produced by Dino de Laurentiis. Donaldson explained what attracted him to the project: "It's a project I would never have initiated, but I was in the right place and it was perfect for me. I was looking for a film that would stretch me after *Smash Palace*. I'd proved I could handle the film making side of it but I wanted to go beyond that. I wanted my films to be seen by a lot of people. The problem with New Zealand is that they can sink very quickly without trace."[23] In retrospect *The Bounty* was to be a key moment in Donaldson's career, representing his move from budding auteur to director-for-hire. *The Bounty* had a long and illustrious pedigree. David Lean had been interested in making a film of Richard Hough's book *Captain Bligh and Mr. Christian*, a "revisionist" history of the famous South Seas mutiny of 1789, and a script had been commissioned from his occasional collaborator Robert Bolt.[24] Although Lean was to withdraw from the project due to difficulties in working with de Laurentiis, Bolt remained on board and it was his script that was used for the film Donaldson directed. It is fascinating (if ultimately futile) to imagine what *The Bounty* might have been like had Lean directed it. Its ingredients of an epic story featuring psychologically complex protagonists against a spectacular scenic background might have merited comparison with *Lawrence of Arabia* (1962). These qualities are all evident in Donaldson's film, though there are *longueurs* in the narrative that Lean might have been able to overcome better than the relatively inexperienced Donaldson.

The Bounty had a mixed reception from the critics and was far from being the box-office blockbuster that de Laurentiis had intended. It was compared unfavorably with the two previous versions of the story, both titled *The Mutiny on the Bounty* and both produced by MGM, in 1935 and 1962. Yet the comparisons are unfair. The 1935 film, directed by Frank Lloyd, was an old-fashioned Hollywood adventure film that cast Fletcher Christian (Clark Gable) as a courageous gentleman hero and Captain Bligh (Charles Laughton) as a tyrannical and sadistic despot. The 1962 film, directed by Lewis Milestone, suffered from its excessive length (over three hours) and from the disastrous miscasting of Marlon Brando as Christian, though Trevor Howard, always a good actor in antagonists' roles, made an effective Bligh. The 1984 version, however, was a conscious attempt to provide a more balanced account of the events before and after the mutiny that did not present Bligh as the stereotypical ogre or Christian as an out-and-out hero. Rather than presenting them as outright antagonists, *The Bounty* focuses on the friendship between Bligh (Anthony Hopkins) and Christian (Mel Gibson) and presents them as different archetypes of masculinity. Bligh is characterized as a decent family man, resistant to the sexual allure of the Tahitian women and appalled at the "sexual excess" displayed by his crew; Christian is a younger, less mature man who falls in love with the king's daughter and sulks when he has to leave her behind in the knowledge that she is pregnant. It would probably be mistaken to attribute the "revisionist" narrative of *The Bounty* to Donaldson, who appears to have filmed Bolt's script much as it was, though one feature of the film that did differentiate it from the previous versions is that it offers a greater insight into Tahitian culture, with scenes depicting island life as well as, for the first time, dwelling on the sexual appeal of the native women to the white European crew.[25]

Rather than comparing *The Bounty* to previous versions of the mutiny, however, it is perhaps more appropriate, as Jim Schembri suggested in a perceptive if largely negative review, "to view *The Bounty* as straight commercial entertainment in the adventure-romance genre, and how it seems to be part of a growing trend among recent films to adopt a traditional, cinematic formula to fill theaters."[26] There was a vogue in the mid-1980s for such sumptuously mounted costume films either based on real historical events and people—the pre-eminent example was Richard Attenborough's *Gandhi* (1983), coincidentally another project that David Lean had once wanted to film—or based on popular literary figures, such as Hugh Hudson's retelling of the Tarzan myth in *Greystoke: The Legend of Tarzan, Lord of the Apes* (1984). Perhaps the reason for the relative commercial disappointment of *The Bounty*, rather like *Greystoke*, was that it was neither an out-and-out adventure film, nor did it have the political and cultural resonances that made *Gandhi* such a success. Nevertheless, for all that *The Bounty* was a less personal project than his previous films, Donaldson's handling of the production logistics and large budget—he claimed that the film "came in considerably under budget"[27]—brought him to the attention of Hollywood.

Donaldson was ambivalent about the lure of Hollywood. Before the U.S. release of *Smash Palace* he had said he did not want to become "just another hack director"; afterward he conceded that "[the] quality of the scripts and so many aspects of the American film business is a lure. Look at all the talent involved there! To miss out on being involved in that environment is crazy."[28] On the one hand Hollywood offered more opportunities actually to make films than in New Zealand; on the other hand there has been less scope for Donaldson to develop the sort of personal projects he might have preferred. His first American film, again produced by de Laurentiis, was *Marie* (1985), a biopic of a battered wife who becomes chairperson of the Tennessee Parole Board. It failed to excite much interest, possibly because films like Martin Ritt's *Norma Rae* (1979) and Mike Nichols's *Silkwood* (1983) had already explored similar themes. Donaldson then enjoyed commercial success with star vehicles for Kevin Costner (*No Way Out*, 1987) and Tom Cruise (*Cocktail*, 1988). Yet there were signs that his critical reputation was now becoming that of a journeyman director rather than as an auteur. His style had also become more or less indistinguishable from other directors. Thus Scott Murray writes of *No Way Out*, a partial remake of the 1947 film noir *The Big Clock:* "Competently directed in the standard Hollywood manner, it suggests Donaldson as a worthy director-for-hire."[29] *Variety* praised "Roger Donaldson's impeccably slick direction" of *Cocktail*.[30] The adjectives now being used to describe his work (competent, worthy, slick), while positive, stopped some way short of the fulsome praise forthcoming in the wake of *Smash Palace*.

Cadillac Man (1990) is probably the closest of Donaldson's American movies to his New Zealand films, both because it was a more personal project (Donaldson was co-producer of the film) and because its narrative of a jealous husband (Tim Robbins) who takes hostage a car salesman (Robin Williams) might be seen as a comedic re-working of certain elements of *Smash Palace*. Critics felt that the film was unable to contain Williams's over-the-top style of performance, however, and attributed this failing to the director: "Since director Roger Donaldson developed this project from scratch, he must take the lion's share of the blame for what proves to be an unroadworthy star vehicle."[31]

The thriller *White Sands* (1992), with Willem Dafoe, failed to match the commercial success of *No Way Out*. Murray feels that "the very limpness suggests Donaldson was ill-at-ease with this genre offering."[32] He regained his commercial touch with *The Getaway* (1994), a remake of the 1972 Sam Peckinpah film with then husband-and-wife stars Alec Baldwin and Kim Basinger assuming the roles played in the original by Steve McQueen and Ali McGraw. Critics, however, felt there was nothing distinctive about Donaldson's version: "The big question is, why remake *The Getaway*? When Martin Scorsese remade *Cape Fear*, he stood it on its head for the 90s, desanctifying the good and pathologizing the bad. This version of *The Getaway* fails to make any such contemporary statement. If you think you've seen it before, that has probably more to do with the fact that this is just another routine heist movie than the fact that you've seen the original."[33]

The perception that Donaldson has become a hired hand who takes on but does not initiate projects is further demonstrated by two films he made in succession in the mid-1990s. *Species* (1995) was a horror/science-fiction hybrid and marked the first occasion on which Donaldson had turned his hand to an entirely fantastical film. Donaldson admitted that he had been an unlikely choice and explained his reasons thus: "I probably would not have been on the short list for most films in this genre, but it goes along with what I've always tried to do with my career. I've always attempted to avoid being pigeonholed as a director who does only one thing and keeps repeating himself."[34] He added, "I don't know what I'm going to be doing next, but I can tell you one thing I won't be doing next, and that's anything with special effects. That's the last thing I want to see."³⁵ Yet Donaldson's next film was the disaster movie *Dante's Peak* (1997), replete with all the requisite pyrotechnics and thrills of the genre. Again it was a star vehicle, on this occasion teaming new James Bond Pierce Brosnan with Linda Hamilton, star of *The Terminator* (1984). Donaldson successfully maintains the balance between personal story (the familiar device of the separated couple) and public events (the volcanic eruption) that is a characteristic of the genre.

Donaldson again demonstrated his versatility with *Thirteen Days* (2000), a factually based political drama set inside the White House during the Cuban Missile Crisis of 1962. It reunited Donaldson with Kevin Costner who plays Kenny O'Donnell, special assistant to the President. The obvious comparison is to Oliver Stone's *JFK* (1991), which had also starred Costner as District Attorney Jim Garrison investigating Kennedy's assassination. *Thirteen Days* shares with *JFK* the suggestion that the U.S. military-industrial complex was at odds with the Kennedy administration and in a sense might be seen as a "prequel" to that film's representation of a deep-rooted political conspiracy against the President. *Thirteen Days* is perhaps a more pedestrian film than *JFK*, but it also demonstrates greater historical integrity in sticking to the facts as they are known rather than embellishing them with speculation. *Sight and Sound* felt that "Self [writer David Self] and Donaldson have coped well in hewing a manageable drama out of a historical monolith."³⁶

For all that the latter part of Donaldson's career might not have fulfilled the early expectations, the diversity of his genre offerings suggests that he has successfully avoided becoming pigeonholed. A consequence of this diversity, however, is that the label "A Roger Donaldson Film" does not carry a great deal of meaning for either critics or cinemagoers. Donaldson probably deserves to be seen as more than "just another hack director," but as something less than an auteur. He is, to apply the old term of the French critics, a *metteur-en-scène*, for the most part a director of other people's scripts, technically skilled and adept at different genres. He was, throughout the 1990s, the most commercially successful of all antipodean directors working in Hollywood. Moreover, as one of the filmmakers who first brought New Zealand cinema to the attention of the world, Donaldson will always hold a uniquely privileged place in its history.

Notes

Since this essay was written, the critical and popular success of *The World's Fastest Indian* (2005) has seen Donaldson return to his roots as a New Zealand filmmaker. Whether this represents a significant change in his career trajectory, or whether it will be a one-off personal project remains to be seen.

1. Scott Murray, "Australian Directors Overseas, 1970–1992," in *Australian Cinema*, ed. Scott Murray (St. Leonards, NSW: Allen and Unwin/Australian Film Commission, 1994), 161.
2. Quoted in Ian Conrich and Sarah Davy, *Views from the Edge of the World: New Zealand Film* (London: Kakapo Books, 1997), 8.
3. In between *Sleeping Dogs* and *Smash Palace* Donaldson also directed the forty-nine-minute children's film *Nutcase* (1980) for Family Fare Productions. The film is perhaps best described as an adventure caper. Flamboyant villainess "Evil Eva" attempts to extort NZ$6 million by threatening to trigger the volcanoes around Auckland with an atomic bomb, but her plans are thwarted by the police chief's children who have invented a "time-space warp control machine." *Nutcase* was co-written by Ian Mune, the co-writer of *Sleeping Dogs*, and Geoff Murphy was special-effects supervisor on both films. Several cast members are common to both (Nevan Rowe, Ian Watkin, Ian Mune, and Melissa Donaldson). *Nutcase* appears to have been largely forgotten—it rarely appears in filmographies.
4. Roger Donaldson, interview, *Screen International*, May 2, 1981, 16. The same interview is quoted in *Cinema Papers* 53 (September 1985): 25.
5. Nick Roddick, "Long White Cloud Cover: New Zealand Film in the Eighties," *Cinema Papers* 53 (September 1985): 25.
6. Conrich and Davy, *Views from the Edge of the World*, 8.
7. *Variety's Film Reviews, Volume 14: 1975–1977* (New York: R. R. Bowker, 1983), October 26, 1977, n.p.
8. Ebert was speaking on his television show *Sneak Previews*, Barry Brennan was writing in the *Los Angeles Evening Outlook*. Extracts from these and other reviews can be found in *NZfilm* 18 (September/December 1982): 6–7.
9. Vincent Canby, "'Smash Palace' Plumbs the Ruins," *New York Times*, May 9, 1982, II, 15.
10. Tom Allen, "New Directors/New Films: Smashed, Broken or Missing," *Film Comment* 18, no. 4 (1982): 2.
11. On American cinema of the 1970s, see Peter Biskind, *Easy Riders, Raging Bulls: How the Sex'n'Drugs'n'Rock'n'Roll Generation Saved Hollywood* (London: Bloomsbury, 1998), and David A. Cook, *Lost Illusions: American Cinema in the Shadow of Watergate and Vietnam, 1970–1979* (New York: Charles Scribner's, 2000).
12. Thomas Elsaesser, "The Pathos of Failure: Notes on the Unmotivated Hero," *Monogram* 6 (October 1975): 15.
13. Ibid., 13.
14. David Thomson, "Why Dirty Harry Beats Harry Potter," *Observer Review* 13 (January 2002): 8.
15. Sheila Johnston, "Smash Palace," *Monthly Film Bulletin* 50, no. 593 (1983): 166; Nick Roddick, "New Zealand: Taking Off?" *Films and Filming* 333 (June 1982): 12.
16. See Andrew Spicer, *An Ambivalent Archetype: Masculinity, Performance and the New Zealand Films of Bruno Lawrence* (Nottingham: Kakapo Books, 2000), 14–18.
17. Johnston, "Smash Palace," 166.
18. Howard Willis, "New Zealand Report," *Cinema Papers* 14 (October 1977): 182.
19. Allen, "New Directors/New Films," 2.

20. Charles Sawyer, "Foreign Correspondence" (interview with Donaldson), *Films in Review* 33, no. 8 (1982): 496.
21. Thomas Elsaesser, *New German Cinema: A History* (New Brunswick, NJ: Rutgers University Press, 1989), 3.
22. Conrich and Davy, *Views from the Edge of the World*, 2.
23. Colleen Hodge, "Bountyful Prospects" (interview with Donaldson), *Onfilm* 1, no. 6 (1984): 7.
24. Kevin Brownlow, *David Lean* (London: Richard Cohen, 1996), 600–641.
25. For a comparison of the films, focusing especially on their representation of gender and sexuality, see Michael Sturma, "Women, the *Bounty*, the Movies," *Journal of Popular Film and Television* 23, no. 2 (1995): 88–93.
26. Jim Schembri, "*The Bounty*," *Cinema Papers* 47 (August 1984): 267.
27. Hodge, "Bountyful Prospects," 7.
28. Sawyer, "Foreign Correspondence," 495.
29. Murray, "Australian Directors Overseas, 1970–1992," 161.
30. *Variety's Film Reviews, Volume 20: 1987–1988* (New Providence: R. R. Bowker, 1991), July 27, 1988, n.p.
31. Nigel Floyd, "Cadillac Man," *Monthly Film Bulletin* 57, no. 681 (1990): 291.
32. Murray, "Australian Directors Overseas, 1970–1992," 164.
33. Jill McGreal, "The Getaway," *Sight and Sound* 4, no. 7 (1994): 41.
34. Donaldson, quoted in Marc Shapiro, "An Alien to the Genre," *Fangoria* 145 (August 1995): 26.
35. Ibid., 80.
36. Xan Brooks, "Thirteen Days," *Sight and Sound* 11, no. 3 (2001): 60.

Roger Donaldson—Filmography

1969. *Te Henga* (NZ short film: cinematographer, editor).
1969. *Start Again* (NZ television documentary: director, producer, cinematographer).
1971. *Geoff Perry* (NZ documentary: co-director, co-writer, editor, cinematographer).
1973. *Burt Munro—Offerings to the God of Speed* (NZ television documentary: producer, director, co-cinematographer).
1973. *The Kaipo Wall* (NZ television documentary: director, cinematographer).
1973. *Cape Horn* (NZ television documentary: director, cinematographer).
1974. *Everest* (NZ television documentary: director, cinematographer).
1974. *Rally . . . Little Boys in a Man Size Sport* (NZ documentary: cinematographer).
1974. *Derek* (NZ television drama: co-director, co–story writer).
1975/76. *Winners and Losers* (NZ television single drama "The Woman at the Store," later followed by a further six dramas and packaged as a seven-part series: co-director, co-producer, co-writer, co-cinematographer).
1977. *Sleeping Dogs* (NZ feature film: director, producer, co–art director).
1980. *Nutcase* (NZ extended short children's film: director).

1981. *Jocko* (NZ television series: occasional director).
1981. Smash Palace (NZ feature film: director, producer, co-writer, story).
1983. *Patu!* (NZ documentary feature: co-cinematographer).
1984. *Conan the Destroyer* (US feature film: co-writer for an early version of the screenplay).
1984. The Bounty (US/Australia/NZ/UK/Italy feature film: director).
1985. *Marie* a.k.a. *Marie: A True Story* (US feature film: director).
1987. No Way Out (US feature film: director).
1988. Cocktail (US feature film: director).
1990. *Cadillac Man* (US feature film: director, co-producer).
1992. *White Sands* (US feature film: director).
1994. The Getaway (US feature film: director).
1995. Species (US feature film: director).
1997. Dante's Peak (US feature film: director).
1999. *Fearless* (NZ television film: executive producer).
2000. Thirteen Days a.k.a. **Thirteen Days Which Shook the World** (US feature film: director).
2001. *Numero Bruno* (NZ documentary: interviewee).
2003. *The Recruit* (US feature film: director).
2004. *The Making of Sleeping Dogs* (NZ documentary: executive producer, interviewee).
2004. *The Making of Smash Palace* (NZ documentary: executive producer, interviewee).
2005. The World's Fastest Indian (US/NZ feature film: director, writer).

9

Embodying the Commercial
Genre and Cultural Affect in the Films of Geoff Murphy

Jonathan Rayner

With his landmark films *Goodbye Pork Pie* (1980) and *Utu* (1983), which were the first- and second-highest-grossing locally produced features at the time of their release, Geoff Murphy occupied a pivotal position in the New Wave of New Zealand film as a writer, director, and producer.[1] Against the backdrop of a previously moribund film industry, Murphy's films (which also included *The Quiet Earth* [1985] and *Never Say Die* [1988]) were distinguished as both commercially driven and nationally specific in their examination of New Zealand masculinity, landscape, and identity. The impact of these films led Murphy to pursue, along with several other contemporary Australian and New Zealand filmmakers, a career in the American film industry.

Murphy's path into filmmaking was particularly long and circuitous. After dropping out of college and forgoing a science degree he embarked on a career in teaching but later became involved in Blerta (the Bruno Lawrence Electric Revelation and Travelling Apparition), a traveling show mixing music and performance for which he wrote songs, played trumpet, and made short black-and-white films. With insufficient employment to ensure subsistence, let alone finance for more ambitious filmmaking, Murphy, Alun Bollinger, Martyn Sanderson, and Bruno Lawrence created a commune at Waimarama. This community represented a significant proportion of those involved in the renewed filmmaking activity and produced one of the New Wave's first expressions in *Wild Man* (1977). The association between Murphy and Lawrence represented the most important creative pairing, as Lawrence subsequently became one of the

---

This is a shortened and revised version of the booklet *Cinema Journeys of the Man Alone: The New Zealand and American Films of Geoff Murphy* (Nottingham: Kakapo Books, 1999).

most famous and prolific of New Zealand actors, not least because of his contributions to four of Murphy's films.

While Murphy's American films (which include *Young Guns II* [1990], *Freejack* [1992], *Blind Side* [1993], and *Under Siege 2* [1995]) continue to embody elements of the visual style that characterized his early work, it is the New Zealand films that distinguish him as a director of national and critical significance. The signature established in the first features delineates a series of thematic and stylistic emphases, which connect them with the later, superficially disparate (in generic as well as geographic terms) American films. In their treatment of violent conflict, gender and national identity, allusive landscape, and black humor, Murphy's films encapsulate the innovativeness, iconoclasm, and ironic tendency of the re-emergent New Zealand cinema. The interplay of these thematic and stylistic aspects of Murphy's films articulates their significance in auteurist and cultural terms, in affirming a directorial and national idiom that both recruits and parodies the characteristics of American cinema.

Male Landscapes

Murphy's cinema foregrounds the activities and proclivities of males. While his treatment of female characters is not immune to charges of sexism, it is noteworthy that the male behavior that drives the director's narratives is seldom free from criticism and irony. The narratives of his New Zealand films *Wild Man, Goodbye Pork Pie, Utu, The Quiet Earth,* and *Never Say Die* incorporate male journeys, some picaresque and others purposeful in nature, that leave their mark on the environment and that in turn are framed and influenced by the national landscape. Undertaking each journey is a group marked by ethnic as well as gender diversity (two con artists in *Wild Man,* two delinquent men and a woman in *Goodbye Pork Pie,* three males who straddle the ethnic and national definitions of nineteenth-century colonial identity in *Utu,* adversarial Maori and Pakeha [European] males and a white woman in *The Quiet Earth,* and a Maori man and American woman in *Never Say Die*). However, every tour of the social and natural geography of New Zealand is experienced primarily by a male core (arranged in affectionate as well as antagonistic couples or trios) whose success or failure, cohesion or fragmentation, is determined by the journey's outcome.

The journeys in Murphy's New Zealand films are precipitated by personal crises, and the active nature of the traveling often masks or comes to stand in place of more concerted investigations of the characters' commitments, opinions, and principles. The nonchalant odyssey on which

John (Tony Barry) and Gerry (Kelly Johnson) embark in *Goodbye Pork Pie*, and the lengthening list of crimes they commit to perpetuate it, distracts from their failure to conform to social demands (of employment and marriage). The venality of their ostensibly victimless crimes (stealing a rental car, shoplifting, drug taking, and stowing away on a ferry) suggests that a cheerful and attractive anarchism lies behind the excursion, rather than an empty and uncommitted immaturity that the trip may (in John's case at least) be able to cure. The car in which they travel is reduced to the bare minimum, as parts are sold or bartered for food and fuel, and the trip itself is continued in spite of and perhaps because of mounting opposition. In this respect, *Goodbye Pork Pie* sets the pattern for several of Murphy's later films, both in New Zealand and America. Frenetic and almost uninterrupted movement, car chases, and shoot-outs at roadblocks recur in Murphy's narratives and appear as much as the inevitable consequences of male non-conformity as the conventions of formulaic commercial cinema. In place of the landscape of authoritarian oppression seen in the near-contemporary *Sleeping Dogs* (Roger Donaldson, 1977), which provokes a similar, violent but self-defensive withdrawal from society, the rural and urban landscapes Murphy's males traverse facilitate and define their nationality and rebelliousness, and their nationality *as* rebelliousness: "In each of these films we are made conscious of a gap that exists between the central characters and the rest of the world, a gap that delineates them as beyond those social boundaries which enclose others. . . . *Goodbye Pork Pie* seems not especially interested in providing a social critique or in backgrounding [*sic*] its characters' alienation; it prefers instead to simply delight in the act of rebellion itself."[2]

Ironically, the distance and difference from conventional society John and Gerry appear to seek is rendered unattainable because of their unacknowledged connection to women. The males' mobility and independence are compromised both in transit (by the picking up of their female accomplice Shirl [Claire Oberman]) and in conclusion (by the recognition of the trip's real objective in the reunion of John with his girlfriend Sue [Shirley Graur]). In relation to the male couple, the principal female characters function paradoxically as both the mouthpieces for a perception of conventional society and the rewards for the males' anti-social behavior. Shirl, who joins the gang and sleeps with Gerry, is seen to share the men's rootlessness and promiscuity but still looks forward to a "real" wedding in due course. Similarly, the apparently quixotic mission to drive the length of the country actually belies John's desire to be reconciled with his estranged partner in Invercargill. The besieging of Sue's home by armed police after John's arrival emphasizes the shrinking of the entire journey (and country) to one house. Sue's sexual welcome and reward for John disarms and ridi-

The odyssey begins: Te Wheke swears vengeance after the slaughter of his community in the western-style *Utu*. (Courtesy Ian Conrich collection of New Zealand cinema and visual culture.)

cules this authoritarian backlash. Arguably and again ironically, however, the "hostage situation" the police fear is a reality, albeit with the male as the victim.

The new land wars that began in 1860 and that are portrayed in *Utu* also are conceived of in the form of a male odyssey, as different incarnations of New Zealand masculinity assess their values and allegiances in the light of violent conflict, movement across the landscape, and loss of loved ones. As in *Goodbye Pork Pie*, the initial motivation for the declaration of war is registered as a loss in a close personal relationship. Te Wheke (Anzac Wallace) vows to kill white men after he discovers that the colonial militia, of which he is a member, has massacred his community, and Williamson (Bruno Lawrence) sets out to avenge the death of his wife following Te Wheke's attack on his homestead. Later, Lieutenant Scott's (Kelly Johnson) desire for vengeance following Te Wheke's murder of Kura (Tania Bristowe), the Maori girl he loves, augments these primary revenge motives.

Scott seeks to subsume a personal vendetta in colonial justice when he orders the execution of Te Wheke once the renegade has been captured, and he is not alone among the characters in *Utu* in attempting to obfuscate a personal, emotional motive within a national, authoritarian one. Such contradictions arise frequently, the film suggests, because of the divided loyalties produced by the conflict, but the racial and ethnic diversity incarnated by the characters also represents the potential for multicultural unity. Characters who bridge the divide (Williamson in speaking several languages, Scott in loving Kura, and Wiremu [Wi Kuki Kaa] in understanding and serving both communities) embody hope for cohabitation in compromise.

The guerrilla war prosecuted by Te Wheke is reliant on movement across the changing landscape. Like the journey and pursuit in *Goodbye Pork Pie*, the male endeavors of rebellion and containment encompass a flight from and to women as symbols of loss and recuperation (Emily Williamson [Ilona Rodgers], Kura, and Matu [Merata Mita]). However, the importance of the women to male motivation is disputed or dismissed to a greater extent than in the earlier film. Kura's mischievous independence, in swapping male partners and sides as she sees fit, is as frustrating to Scott as Emily's prescriptive Britishness is to her husband. Notably, both characters are eventually removed from the narrative by their deaths at the hands of Te Wheke. Although the deaths of the women provide the motives for revenge, Colonel Eliott (Tim Elliot), Te Wheke, and even Williamson prosecute the war without acknowledgment of the female influence. Wiremu discounts Matu's right for revenge for Te Wheke's murder of her cousin Kura, and Te Wheke is similarly dismissive of Britain's sovereign, the "fat German woman on distant shores" supposedly represented at the court-martial. The decisions to end the struggle in male acts of violence (specifically Wiremu's intervention to kill Eliott, save Williamson, and execute Te Wheke) belie the disruptive and influential role of the women in the conflict. Paradoxically, the war of revenge that is supposedly fought in the name of women marks them as the victims as well as the justification for male violence. The conclusive and unifying "fraternal relationship between Maori and Pakeha which is sealed in blood, mana [integrity] and utu [revenge]" specifically excludes the females who have disrupted and mocked as well as motivated the heroic male activity.[3]

National Landscapes

From the treatment of landscape and masculinity grows the recognition, in Murphy's films, of the landscape's significance in the formation and articulation of national character. In inhabiting and negotiating the multifaceted New Zealand landscape, Murphy's protagonists exhibit resourcefulness and resignation in the face of the authoritarian structures (whether represented by conventional society, colonial authority, or a conspiratorial establishment) that seek to oppress them. Within these conflicts the human and natural landscape is part of the problem and also part of the solution. The unique landscape of the islands, on view and recognized within Murphy's narratives as a shared obstacle, is a communal formative experience and a common frame of reference for the New Zealand protagonists, antagonists, and audience.

In *Wild Man*, the pseudo-western trappings of the frontier town and mountebank travelers are indigenized by the broad accents and broader comedy. The parochial nature of existence produces the humor and the character types who fall prey to the con men's tricks. The portrait of the pioneering community in *Wild Man* stresses the national qualities of improvisation, irreverence, and idiosyncrasy, in place of the American westerns' myths of manifest destiny. The boundaries between itinerant and settled communities, and interior and exterior spaces, are challenged and contravened repeatedly in the course of the narrative, as the mountebank salesman escapes from his skeptical customers, the townsfolk assemble on the beach for the Wild Man's bout (Bruno Lawrence), and a drunken mob in pursuit of chickens crashes into a lady's bathroom.

By comparison, the heroes' journey in *Goodbye Pork Pie* takes in specific cities and landmarks over both islands, from the departure in Kaitaia at the top of the North Island to the arrival in Invercargill at the bottom of the South Island. Local scenery and chauvinism mesh when John and Gerry have a bet on who can have sex with Shirl before they reach Wanganui. Similarly, the scenes of their rain-soaked arrival in Wellington, "a city whose weather is a national joke," rely on the specific humor and recognition of the indigenous audience.[4] Subsequently, the film's advertising campaign in the major cities mirrored its action in the same locations, with convoys of Minis promoting competitions for merchandising and (in another echo of the narrative) car parts.[5] The use of the Mini as the outlaw's car was in itself an indigenizing as well as pragmatic choice. In interviews Murphy identified the car as the incarnation of the incorrigibility of the characters, while through its ubiquity as the "people's car" in New Zealand it also imparted "an underdog quality."[6]

The specificity of landscape plays a fuller and more metaphorical role in *Utu*, as civil conflict spreads across and connects varying environments and diverse communities. The narrative of war and vengeance, across the ethnic and cultural divisions within the population, produces uncertainty and ambivalence in the allegiances and principles that underpin national identity. Revenge is sought by all the major characters and justified on a

The iconic Mini in *Goodbye Pork Pie*: Stripped of parts but functioning, it signifies the persistent anarchy and defiance of the road movie. (Courtesy New Zealand Film Commission.)

variety of levels, and this moral ambiguity extends to the numerous translations of the film's title: "In a publicity release for the film, Murphy has translated utu variously as 'reciprocation,' 'balance,' 'revenge,' 'compensation,' 'payment,' to which reviewers have added 'retribution,' 'atonement,' 'honour' and 'justice.' The blizzard of terminology is as potent a symptom of present-day intercultural ambiguities as the concept itself."[7] This emphasis on a non-judgmental stance, and on the film's relevance to racial discord within New Zealand at the time of its production, is strengthened by the integration of the landscape in the portrayal of the conflict. The film's depiction of the Land War begins with the colonial militia's attack on Te Wheke's village. The siting of this atrocity in an area of habitation is answered by Te Wheke's attacks on a church and the Williamson homestead. Subsequently, settings of impenetrable vegetation, open and barren plains, and high mountainous terrain are used to varying effect in key sequences, as the war assumes a national as well as personal significance. The dialogue between Wiremu and Henare (Faenza Reuben), which immediately precedes the latter's death, takes place by a quickly flowing stream under a canopy of trees. Both men are filmed from a low angle and appear hemmed in by the vegetation that nearly obscures the sky. Such claustrophobic locations during the pursuit of Te Wheke's warriors through the forests are suggestive of the ambiguities of morality and allegiance felt by characters on both sides. This uncertainty is exaggerated by Scott's nonviolent confrontation with Te Wheke at Henare's tangi (funeral).

By contrast, the clearest evocation of the American western, and the wars between Native Americans and the U.S. Cavalry, is seen in the attack on the town of Te Puna. On the plains with little cover, Te Wheke loses his advantages of concealment and loyalty. However, the conflict does not become more clear-cut in the open space of the plains. The town may be defended successfully, but the sight of the dead in daylight convinces Williamson to abjure revenge and advise Colonel Elliot to make peace. The British commander's insistence on continuing the fight into the mountains distances him from the New Zealanders under his command, and leads to his own death. The pursuit into the mountains removes the conflict again from populated areas, and reduces the combatants to the committed, vengeful few. In these terms Te Wheke is seen to be the strongest of the antagonists, and the dubiety of the sides drawn in the conflict is most pointed in these scenes of close-quarter combat. Poignantly, the final battle, which results in the capture of Te Wheke, takes place in thick forest. In the confusion and smother of vegetation, Wiremu is able to shoot Elliot, his own commanding officer, in order to prevent him from killing a wounded man, and to save Williamson from Te Wheke's last bullet. Once Te Wheke is in custody, the conclusion of the conflict takes place in the court-martial around a campfire at night. This unspecific, neutral non-space becomes the fitting location for the extraordinary, sacrificial compromise—the execution of Te Wheke by his brother Wiremu—that is necessary to end the bloodshed.

The nationality of the landscape is implicit but crucial to the allegorical science-fiction narrative of *The Quiet Earth*. Zac (Bruno Lawrence), a New Zealand scientist working on a secret energy project in collaboration with the United States, commits suicide when he learns that a dangerous experiment is to be undertaken against his advice. The resultant "Effect" shifts the planet out of balance and wipes out the human population, except for three survivors (Zac, Joanne [Alison Routledge], and a Maori man named Api [Peter Smith]). All three had died at the exact moment of the Effect taking place: Joanne had died by accident, Zac had committed suicide, and Api had been murdered by a friend whose wife's affections he refused to return.

At first, Zac indulges the insane liberty that the total removal of conventional society permits, but subsequently he attempts to understand and halt the damage of the "Effect." Superficially, in the three survivors the previous, flawed society is recreated with its racial and sexual tensions intact. However, the male-female and Maori-Pakeha divisions are recuperated by the global crisis. Api compares the betrayal of the New Zealand scientists working within the American project with the Maori loss of authority within their own land. Acknowledging his responsibility, Zac plans to destroy the New Zealand substation that is still linked to the ongoing "Effect" in the United States. As in *Utu*, a sacrifice (in this case of a Pakeha, not Maori, male) is necessary to create a new world rather than save the old. The explosion of the station severs the link with the North-

Peter Smith and Geoff Murphy (*right*) on the set of *The Quiet Earth*. (Courtesy New Zealand Film Commission.)

ern Hemisphere, and resurrects Zac again, this time on what appears as a distant and apparently uninhabited planet.

While the characters embody the institutionalized conflicts contained within New Zealand during the 1980s (and indeed in Murphy's films more widely), they also come to represent a unified nation opposing a malign overseas influence. The specific identification of U.S. authority as a national and global threat links the film to the contemporary ANZUS (Australia, New Zealand, United States Security Treaty) crisis, which was precipitated by the enforcement of the Treaty of Rarotonga in 1985 and the declaration of New Zealand as a nuclear-free zone during 1986. *The Quiet Earth* can be read as an allegory of these events, and as a metaphorical treatment of the country's disempowerment and alienation. The nature of an alliance with a nuclear-armed country, prepared to use its weapons on its allies' territory, is reflected in Zac's helplessness and suicide. Conversely, the destructive nature of the "Effect" belies the positive change it engenders. The schism between Northern and Southern Hemispheres stimulates a political and cultural reappraisal. The destruction of the last link with the North removes Zac to an entirely new universe, in which prevailing political conditions no longer apply. In place of his earlier freedom and solitude in depopulated cities (which, in an ironic reflection on the desire of Murphy's characters to escape from society's restraints, finally drives him mad), this conclusion manifests the perfect (if fantastic) solution to the problem of external authority: the desire for a genuinely uncontested space that underpins colonial experience.

Violence and Humor

The comedic content of Murphy's films represents a substantial part of their commercial appeal and can be linked directly to the director's self-conscious approach to generic filmmaking. Examples of broad visual humor and imagistic puns can be found in both the New Zealand and American phases of his work. A jump-cut from Gerry vomiting at a party to John pouring ketchup over a breakfast of fried eggs in *Goodbye Pork Pie*, is echoed by a plate of tagliatelle and tomatoes being pushed away untouched in a restaurant as the graphic details of a road accident are discussed in *Blind Side*. At other moments, Murphy's male characters engage in droll double-acts of quick-fire dialogue. The fullest expression of this is seen in the exchanges between John and Gerry in *Goodbye Pork Pie*, but Tony Barry, who plays John, has similar lines in *Wild Man* and *Never Say Die*. This feature can also be seen to persist into the American films. In *Blind Side*, the Kaines are blackmailed for leaving the scene of an accident in which a policeman is killed. When his wife speculates that the blackmailer might have seen a different accident, Doug Kaines (Ron Silver) replies, "he probably saw the jeep behind us hit another cop." The most extreme examples of this gallows humor (such as in *Utu* when Te Wheke places the severed head of the Reverend Johns on the lectern before he delivers his alternative sermon) emphasize the integration of this disconcerting comedic material within the moral, political, or cultural meanings of Murphy's work.

Violence and the threat of death are ever present in Murphy's films but are seldom presented in terms of clear heroic potential or gravity. In *The Quiet Earth*, as the rivalry between the males boils over, Joanne exclaims that she would not go with Api even if he was "the last man on earth," to which his sardonic reply is that he is "working on it." Even the sobering events depicted in *Utu* are undercut constantly by a pervasive, mordant sense of humor. Scott shows Wiremu his Spencer repeating rifle, and assures him: "With this, one man could defeat ten." Wiremu replies drily, "That depends on how far away those ten men are," emphasizing that in this conflict the potential adversary is likely to be physically as well as metaphorically close. Other instances undercut the heroic action further. Te Wheke ponders aloud how Williamson has survived when he has shot him three times. When he fails to repel the attack on his farm, Williamson mistakenly seeks shelter in a shed full of explosives. Prior to an ambush on a supply wagon bound for Te Puna (driven by a militiaman played by Murphy himself), the raiders ask if the soldiers have seen Te Wheke, before pointing out that actually he is right behind them. Coincidentally,

Murphy's appearances in his own films constitute a significant contribution to their reflexive comedy. The director appears in *Goodbye Pork Pie* (as a garage proprietor) and has extended cameos in *Wild Man* (in a silent comedy routine as a put-upon drunk) and in *Never Say Die* as Alf's and Melissa's [Temuera Morrison and Lisa Eilbacher] lackadaisical protector, Jack. During the attack on Te Puna, Te Wheke chats with the corpse of a guard he has killed. Scott asks a soldier how he can tell which Maori have defected to join Te Wheke and is told "They're the brown ones lying on the ground, not moving with flies around them." This nationalistic slant to the humor culminates in the exchange (in Maori, and thus misunderstood by Scott) between Wiremu and Williamson when Eliott is shot:

> **Williamson** (in Maori): Has fate decided his time has come?
> **Wiremu** (in Maori): Yes, exactly.
> **Scott** (in English): What's that?
> **Williamson** (in English): I said they just got Eliott.

Such a tongue-in-cheek stance to mortal combat is unsurprising given the irony associated with the film's representation of weapons. Scott's Spencer rifle, after being mocked by Wiremu, is stolen and used against its owner by Kura. It proves a singularly ineffective weapon until it is chosen for the execution of Te Wheke at point-blank range. Williamson also brandishes a "specialty weapon" that evokes comic parallels with the heroes of spaghetti westerns: a quadruple-barreled shotgun that knocks its inventor to the floor when fired.[8] The creation and testing of the gun is detailed in a sequence of comic concentration as Williamson experiments with discharging some or all of the barrels at once, and eventually succeeds in blowing himself backward while utterly destroying his target: an outside toilet.

In *The Quiet Earth*, Zac's utilization of a gun is equally eccentric. As his madness in solitude grows, he attacks a church with a shotgun, and threatens to "shoot the kid" (Jesus's crucified image) if God does not reveal himself in person. God does not respond, and the image is duly destroyed. As another example of a deranged "hostage situation," this moment harks back to *Goodbye Pork Pie* and also anticipates the crisis of faith experienced by the gun-toting nun in Murphy's later American production *Freejack*. One constant in this ironic treatment of weapons is their subversion as symbols of male potency, which reinforces the dubious characterization of masculinity throughout Murphy's films. The forces of law and order (the police and the military) amass weapons in their attempts to stop the incorrigible drivers and their cars in *Goodbye Pork Pie* and *Never Say Die*, but to no avail. However, Murphy's heroes are similarly ineffective and rendered ridiculous by their inexpert use of weapons. They take up weapons and turn to violence as a last option, in desperation or under extreme provocation. The circumstances of personal crisis and disempowerment under which Zac and Williamson (both played by Bruno Lawrence) take up arms parallel those of Lawrence's character Al Shaw in *Smash Palace* (1981). Despite the attendant humor in this ironic treatment of violence, a pertinent observation on cultural mores lies behind these consistencies: "In American films the man of action—the *man*—carries a gun. Westerner, gangster, vigilante, war hero, rebel cop, he is a man of violence, finger on the trigger. The Kiwi bloke is not such a man. Despite the ubiquity of hunting rifles and the string of wars New Zealanders have fought in, no cult has grown up here of weaponry and its deployment."[9] It is noticeable that the American hero of *Blind Side* is also incapable of using a gun at the crucial moment, while in *Freejack* the numerous chases and gun battles do not (and must not, within the narrative's own logic) result in any physical injury to the hero.

Caren Wilton criticizes the suggestions of chauvinism and sexual violence implicit in the juxtaposition of a sex scene involving Alf and Melissa and the unzipping of an assassin's rifle from a bag in *Never Say Die*.[10] However, any assertion of potency conferred by the weapon is undone by the interruption of the coupling by the sniper. This is quickly followed by Alf's killing of the assassin with a lucky shot (watching his inept attempts to find the sniper, Melissa murmurs "Rambo . . ."). The humor and derision associated with the ineptitude of Murphy's males when they assume the stereotype of action heroes is reinforced by a comparable female capability in similar circumstances. Emily Williamson is far more effective than her husband in defending her home against Te Wheke's men but is let down by his misplacing of the extra ammunition. In *Never Say Die*, Melissa's driving skills allow the couple to evade capture. By contrast, Alf's incompetence in driving a near-derelict car almost ends in disaster.

The inclusion of intertextual reference (such as to *Rambo* in one instance and to the whole range of conventions associated with James Bond thrillers throughout *Never Say Die*) helps to illustrate Murphy's approach to scenes of violence within commercial films. Where they exist in the New Zealand films as poignant and destabilizing moments within narratives concerned with national history, character, and identity (as in Gerry's death in *Goodbye Pork Pie*, the choice of suicide in *The Quiet Earth*, and the internecine conflict in *Utu*), similar scenes in his American films, invested with a comparable self-consciousness and black humor (in *Freejack*, *Blind Side*, and *Under Siege II*), both epitomize and ironize the contemporary commercial cinema. They serve their purposes in both instances, but the disconcerting mixture of violence and humor in the New Zealand films also allows these examples to transcend them.

Conclusion: Mid-Pacific Movies?

Since moving to America, Murphy has worked on numerous movies and sequels for cable television and for theatrical release. While this employment as a journeyman director may have diminished his input in the writing of these films, it has also played to his strengths in other areas, such as working on action sequences, stunts, and special effects. An outstanding example of this is his contribution as producer and second unit director on *Dante's Peak* (1997; directed by fellow New Zealander, Roger Donaldson).

What might be termed the Murphy "method," consisting of a deliberate remodeling of accepted generic film formats, with a tongue-in-cheek adherence to timeworn formulae and the delivery of spectacle, action, and humor, has proved well attuned to (or conversely, can be seen to impose itself upon) the director's American commercial productions. The profound and ironic revision of the western in *Utu* is continued to a lesser extent in the reflexive nature of narrative and characterization of *Young Guns II*, the amalgamation of western and film noir in the Mexican settings of *Blind Side*, and the wry self-consciousness of the 1988 pilot for *The Magnificent Seven* television series (the bar where the itinerant, laconic gunfighters and outlaws first assemble is named "Murphy's"). The generic bases of the director's New Zealand films (road movie, western, science fiction) underline the ubiquity of American models for entertainment cinema. Their ironic and hybridized treatment in *Goodbye Pork Pie*, *Utu*, and *The Quiet Earth* is central to the cultural distinctiveness of these films as cinematic products of New Zealand. The discussions of Kiwi masculinity, colonial history, and contemporary geopolitics respectively in these films are constructed on intertextual conceptualizations of film genres, because the generic organization of film production and reading can be equated with the conservative, conformist, authoritarian, and hegemonic forces their protagonists are forced to confront. The frequent crossing and consequent re-drawing of generic boundaries within Murphy's films provides an analogy to their protagonists' challenges to establishment authority. However, the same ironic and self-conscious tendencies in mainstream cinema, and particularly in popular action movies from the end of the 1980s onward, have assured the integration and replication of this architextual approach in contemporary Hollywood filmmaking.

It remains to be seen how far the popular centering of Murphy's national or individual extremes (and those of his contemporaries Donaldson, Peter Jackson, and Jane Campion) represents a refinement or diminution of their skills and ambitions. Arguably, in achieving a place within the film industry of greatest popular appeal, Geoff Murphy has realized his potential as a commercial filmmaker. His stated commitment is to the making of compelling and provoking entertainment films that recognize and reward the audience's attendance, engagement, and spectatorship: "The big Hollywood film tends to be straight entertainment, with the accent on audience manipulation and technique, rather than art for art's sake. I think that's what I try for, too. . . . People go to a film for some sort of release and entertainment, and I feel an obligation to give them what they go for. The sort of films I most admire are the ones that succeed in doing that without short-changing the other side of things."[11] Murphy's filmmaking has always embodied a strong commercial sense and appeal. In his New Zealand films this awareness was closely associated with a cultural and historical specificity and a distinctive personal approach. The persistence of certain textual and stylistic features (the frequent deployment of the conventions of the western, the inclusion of action sequences and stunts and the problematization of masculinity entailed by the ironic treatment of violence) forms the basis for an auteurist appraisal that unifies a superficially varied canon and acknowledges the importance of Murphy within his generation of New Zealand filmmakers. However, his gradual submergence within the new American realm of cable and home entertainment movie releases, and his molding by Hollywood into an unidentifiable *metteur-en-scène*, must be considered a loss in terms of the emergent national cinema to which he first contributed, with acclaimed, vibrant, and pertinent feature productions.

Notes

1. Helen Martin and Sam Edwards, *New Zealand Film, 1912–1996* (Auckland: Oxford University Press, 1997), 88.
2. Reid Perkins, "Fun and Games: The Influence of the Counterculture in the Films of Geoff Murphy," *Illusions* 2 (1986): 16–17.
3. Martin Blythe, *Naming the Other: Images of the Maori in New Zealand Film and Television* (Metuchen, NJ: Scarecrow, 1994), 248.
4. Robin Bromby, "*Goodbye Pork Pie*," *Sight and Sound* 50, no. 3 (1981): 152.
5. Geoff Murphy, "The End of the Beginning," in *Film in Aotearoa New Zealand*, ed. Jonathan Dennis and Jan Bieringa (Wellington: Victoria University Press, 1992), 142. See also Ian Conrich, "In God's Own Country: Open Spaces and the New Zealand Road Movie," in *New Zealand—A Pastoral Paradise?* ed. Ian Conrich and David Woods (Nottingham: Kakapo Books, 2000), 33–34.

6. Peter Beilby, "*Goodbye Pork Pie:* Geoff Murphy: Director," *Cinema Papers* 27 (June–July 1980) (New Zealand Supplement): 19.
7. Blythe, *Naming the Other,* 235.
8. Kenneth Marc Harris, "American Genres and Non-American Films: A Case Study of *Utu,*" *Cinema Journal* 29, no. 2 (1990): 45–47.
9. Russell Campbell, "Smith and Co.: The Cinematic Redefinition of Pakeha Male Identity," *Illusions* 7 (1987): 21. Article revised and reprinted as "The Kiwi Bloke: The Representation of Pakeha Masculinity in New Zealand Film," in *Contemporary New Zealand Cinema,* ed. Ian Conrich and Stuart Murray (Detroit: Wayne State University Press, forthcoming).
10. Caren Wilton, "007, Down She Goes: *Never Say Die,*" *Illusions* 10 (1989): 8.
11. Nick Roddick, "Long White Cloud Cover: New Zealand Film in the Eighties," *Cinema Papers* 53 (September 1985): 28. Murphy makes similar comments in an interview in *Aspects of Utu* (1983), a documentary on the production of *Utu* produced by Geoff Murphy and directed by Gaylene Preston.

Geoff Murphy—Filmography

1966. *The Magic Hammer* (NZ extended short: writer, musician, set design).
1966. *Dr Brunovski* (NZ short film: director).
1967. *Hurry Hurry Faster Faster* (NZ short film: co-director, writer, actor).
1969. *Ink, Pink, Pen & Ink: A Question of Values* (NZ documentary: editor).
1970. *Tank Busters* (NZ extended short film: director, actor, musician).
1970. *Time Out* (NZ television drama in the *Survey* series: actor).
1970. *Fire* (NZ television drama in the *Survey* series: co-director).
1971. *Children's Playground* (NZ short film: editor).
1971. *Pukemanu* (NZ television series: actor in the episode "Pukemanu Welcomes You").
1973. *Uenuku* (NZ television drama: director).
1974. *Rally . . . Like Little Boys in a Man Sized Sport* (NZ documentary: camera rigger).
1974. *Percy the Policeman* (NZ television six-part children's series: director, writer). Series not broadcast.
1974. *The Longest Winter* (NZ television drama: actor).
1975. *The Games Affair* (NZ television six-part children's series: special-effects coordinator, set construction).
1976. *A Stitch in Time* (NZ short film: co-editor).
1976. *Epidemic* (NZ television series: special-effects coordinator).
1976. *Blerta* (NZ television six-part series: director, co-writer, co-editor, musician).
1975/76. *Winners and Losers* (NZ television single drama "The Woman at the Store," later followed by a further six dramas and packaged as a seven-part series: set designer).
1977. *Wild Man* (NZ feature film: director, co-producer, co-writer).
1977. *Dagg Day Afternoon* (NZ extended short film: co-director, co-writer).

1977. *Sleeping Dogs* (NZ feature film: special-effects coordinator).
1978. *A State of Siege* (NZ extended short film: assistant director).
1978. *Charlie Horse* (NZ documentary: co–assistant editor, co–sound recorder).
1978. *The Aunty Natal Show* (NZ short film: assistant director, actor).
1979. *Middle Age Spread* (NZ feature film: assistant director).
1980. *Nutcase* (NZ extended short children's film: special-effects coordinator).
1980. *The Last Outlaw* (Australia television four-part mini-series: special-effects coordinator).
1980. *Goodbye Pork Pie* (NZ feature film: director, co-producer, co-writer, actor).
1983. *Hooks and Feelers* (NZ extended short: first assistant director).
1983. *The Amazing Story of How the Corner Grocery Became the A O.K. Even Faster Fast Fast Futuremart* (NZ short film: assistant director).
1983. *Utu* (NZ feature film: director, producer, co-writer, actor).
1983. *Aspects of Utu* (NZ pilot for an intended six-part documentary series: producer, interviewee).
1983. *Wild Horses* (NZ feature film: co–stunt coordinator).
1984. *Te Hikoi Ki Waitangi* (NZ documentary: associate producer, co-editor).
1985. *The Quiet Earth* (NZ feature film: director).
1985. *Mr Wrong* a.k.a. *Dark of the Night* (NZ feature film: co-writer).
1987. *Predator* (US feature film: co-writer for an early version of the screenplay).
1987. *Rent a Cop* (US feature film: co-writer for an early version of the screenplay).
1988. *Mauri* (NZ feature film: associate producer, first assistant director, actor).
1988. *Never Say Die* (NZ feature film: director, co-producer, writer, actor).
1989. *Finders Keepers* (NZ extended short film: director, writer, actor).
1989. *Red King, White Knight* (US television film for HBO: director).
1990. *Blood Oath* a.k.a. *Prisoners of the Sun* (Australia feature film: co-writer for an early version of the screenplay).
1990. *Young Guns II* (US feature film: director).
1992. *Freejack* (US feature film: director).
1993. *Blind Side* (US television film for HBO: director).
1994. *The Last Outlaw* (US television film for HBO: director).
1995. *Under Siege 2: Dark Territory* a.k.a. ***Under Siege 2*** (US feature film: director).
1996. *Don't Look Back* (US television film for HBO: director).
1997. *Dante's Peak* (US feature film: associate producer, second unit director).
1998. *The Magnificent Seven* (US television series pilot: director).
1999. *Fortress 2* a.k.a. ***Fortress 2: Re-Entry*** (US/Luxembourg feature film: director).
2000. *Race against Time* a.k.a. *Gabriel's Run* (US cable television film: director).

2001. *Blerta Revisited* (NZ documentary: director, co-producer).
2001. *Hotere* (NZ documentary: composer for one song, musician).
2001. *The Lord of the Rings: The Fellowship of the Ring* (US/NZ feature film: second unit director).
2002. *The Lord of the Rings: The Two Towers* (US/NZ feature film: second unit director).
2003. *The Lord of the Rings: The Return of the King* (US/NZ feature film: second unit director).
2004. *Spooked* (NZ feature film: director, producer, writer, actor).
2004. *The Making of Sleeping Dogs* (NZ documentary: interviewee).
2004. *The Making of Smash Palace* (NZ documentary: interviewee).
2005. *xXx: State of the Union* a.k.a. *xXx2: The Next Level* (US feature film: second unit director).

10

"Kiwi as..."

Ian Mune and Filmmaking as Cultural Expression

Stan Jones

In 1977, Ian Mune's talents as co-writer and his nuggety screen presence as second male lead marked the breakthrough film for New Zealand cinema, *Sleeping Dogs*, a political thriller set in the near future. Twenty-five years later, Mune enjoyed his cameo in *The Lord of the Rings: The Fellowship of the Ring* (2001): "I knew he couldn't lose that scene," he says of his character's decapitation by a Ringwraith.[1] Mune figures too among the latter film's roll call of local luminaries as second unit director, and he considers the whole phenomenon a "watershed" for filmmaking in New Zealand, parallel to that of *Sleeping Dogs*. Between that early collaboration with director Roger Donaldson on *Sleeping Dogs* and his few seconds of gory glory in *The Lord of the Rings*, Mune has sought to represent New Zealand's creative identity as director, actor, scriptwriter, teacher, painter, and commentator.

Mune says of himself: "I'm still trying to tell a story that's true to its origins and comprehensible to everyone."[2] He is a storyteller, a dealer in fictions especially adept at literary adaptations, who has always aimed to popularize authentic stories of New Zealand. Very much a working artist, Mune is acutely aware of a film's potential ability to create an impact. In 1977 he told the audience assembled for the premiere of *Sleeping Dogs* to tell all their friends if they liked it, but to keep their mouths shut if they didn't![3] Of the film's success he has said, "I believe *Sleeping Dogs* was the final factor in convincing politicians that we needed a film commission."[4] Mune's films are not the art-house expression of a director such as Vincent Ward, maker of *Vigil* (1984) or *The Navigator: A Mediaeval Odyssey* (1988). With characteristic bluntness, he dismisses Christine Jeffs's stylish *Rain* (2001) for its self-consciousness as a "90 minute commercial."[5] His own style is much closer to the storytelling realism of Roger Donaldson and Geoff Murphy.

Mune began his career in the early 1960s with the Downstage Theatre Company in Wellington. The "Great OE" (overseas experience/travel) followed with an invitation from the Welsh Theatre Company, but he turned down a job with the Royal Shakespeare Company because "they were so often pretentious, and they had a condescending attitude to colonials."[6] He returned to New Zealand determined to erase such prejudice by promoting Kiwi accents, idiom, and imagery in the local media. He chose a hard road, that of an indigenous Pakeha (European) filmmaker, a local auteur who creates films for a New Zealand audience but also for overseas distributors.

Mune has always been employed in regular television work, although he has strong views on the quality of New Zealand programming. In 1971 and 1972, the series *Pukemanu* pioneered local television drama, with Mune as a scriptwriter and an actor. There followed projects such as the television drama *Derek* in 1974, in which Mune appeared as a daydreaming office worker who seeks revenge on his employer on the day he is fired. There was another lead acting role in the 1975–76 *Moynihan* series about a New Zealand unionist, a prize-winning television movie adaptation of Ian Cross's novel *The God Boy* (1976), about an eleven-year-old Catholic boy's difficult relationship with his parents, writing and directing commercials for the Labour Party in 1981, and the role of Air New Zealand's Chief Executive Officer in *Fallout* (1994), a television drama based on a national trauma, the 1979 plane crash on Mt. Erebus in the Antarctic.

The New Zealand Broadcasting Corporation provided the immediate run-up to the making of *Sleeping Dogs* when Mune and Donaldson worked together on the *Winners and Losers* television series (1975–76) of half-hour social dramas. Introducing the scripts for teachers issued by the then Department of Education, Mune and Donaldson declare, "Their strength is that they [the different dramas in the series] are very much from this country—their style, pace, subject matter, the settings. They are not like copies of programs you have seen before."[7] Both stressed the need to understand how fictions carry and generate national identity and also included brief comments by the original writers. Most writers approved, although Frank Sargeson distances himself from the version of his *A Great Day:* "I do not see TV . . . TV is here today and gone tomorrow, while the printed word, if the good printed word, lasts for ever (if history can be believed)."[8] By contrast, the novelist and cultural commentator Barry Crump was delighted: "This performance informs us that New Zealand productions need no longer embarrass us, either here or overseas. In short, we can do it!"[9] Ironically, it is Crump, the New Zealander self-styled as the "good, keen man," who here conjectures if foreigners would approve of a homegrown product.

When, in 1997, Mune looked back at these beginnings and his subsequent development, he declared that, to be successful, a film ought to have three different 30 percent factors: "a film script is only about 30 percent.

Ian Mune on the set of *The End of the Golden Weather*. (Courtesy New Zealand Film Commission.)

To me, narrative simply comes out of the interaction of characters and the forces operating on them.... That's the next 30 percent ... a great cast and crew.... A director has one job—to know what he wants, to have some idea what it should look like, at least in spirit, up there on the screen.... But he must be able to communicate it. That's the last 30 percent."[10] What makes the final 10 percent he does not say. To date, the twin reference points in Mune's filmmaking are *The End of the Golden Weather* (1991) and *What Becomes of the Broken Hearted?* (1999). They exemplify his production model but contrast markedly. *The End of the Golden Weather* is a personal project derived from close friendship with the playwright Bruce Mason (author of the play on which the film is based) and took Mune over a decade to realize. *What Becomes of the Broken Hearted?* is the sequel to *Once Were Warriors* (1994), and Mune moved from script consultant to director when a producers' squabble forced out the original incumbent, Ian Gilmour.

Mune's commitment to the New Zealand–set period drama *The End of the Golden Weather* cost him a deal of frustration and a possible springboard to international recognition. In the early 1980s he shaped the very male road adventure *Goodbye Pork Pie* (1980) with Geoff Murphy but then moved on to pursue his "souvenir sentimentale."[11] His work on *The God Boy* had already proved his skill in providing the first "30 percent," scripting from a story of Kiwi childhood, and *The End of the Golden Weather* then shows a further "30 percent" in the performances, particularly from Stephen Papps as Firpo, the cognitively impaired supporting character. The play's subjective point of view and solo performance could not be maintained on screen, so Mune shifted to an ensemble piece centered on a family in the mid-1930s. He also disposed of half the narrative, avoided the play's awkward time-shift by making its last episode, "Firpo as the Made Man," drive the narrative, and most significantly removed any references to the 1936 unemployment riots. As a local policeman says: "This is a respectable country."

Respectability is the defining social context within which young Geoff (Stephen Fulford), the central character, has to control his imagination and his sympathy with Firpo. The film constantly balances its period reconstruction with the boy's visions. Its range of eccentric beach characters suggests that Geoff's inclinations are innate to his world, as does his father's hidden talent for slapstick.[12] Thus, as Philip Kemp wrote from a UK perspective: "Rather than singling Firpo out for mockery, a place like this would have welcomed him as a further enrichment of the communal wackiness."[13] Kemp reduces *The End of the Golden Weather* to a soap opera trading on a series of overwrought characters. He also misses the irony of Firpo embodying a local dream of success through sporting prowess, and the related significance of the visiting English teacher who lectures Geoff's class on the inferiority of their culture. The ways in which Mune's filmic adaptation of the play registers but rejects elements of received culture in New Zealand becomes patent where he depicts Geoff's visions of knights and of the antlered Firpo as Herne the Hunter. At this last sight Geoff blows out his cheeks in disbelief at his own imagination because it does not fit his environment.

How Geoff responds to where he lives opens the film, when he thumps his pillow, scattering dust into a shaft of sunlight, he tracks to a handwritten notice fixed to his wall that instructs him to open his blind at the right moment onto the golden light. By contrast, the lighting of interiors frequently produces soft illumination and shadowing, reflecting Geoff's imagination and his social reality. *The End of the Golden Weather*'s look emphasizes a conflict between inner and outer environments. The beach is visible, even at night, but the familiarity of the domestic interiors also suggests an oppressive culture, one in which difference is not tolerated.

Throughout the film Mune's camera is often calm or static and is only significantly mobile in Firpo's final rage at Geoff, as it whirls through the hut and races through the undergrowth. Subsequently, *The End of the Golden Weather* reverts to tight and controlled framing and editing for the closing sequence at the family dinner table and then at the beach. Here, Geoff turns away from where Firpo resides and walks, and then jogs, in the other direction along the shoreline, and in doing so responds to his father's exasperated question: "Why can't you just be normal?" *The End of the Golden Weather* warns against challenging social expectations; that way is where madness lies. It also illustrates Mune's abiding concern with finding authentic expression for his native culture, albeit here in a purely Pakeha historical context. The film gained recognition in New Zealand although it did not succeed internationally, something Mune anticipated in his remarks on overseas reactions: "*Goodbye Pork Pie* and *Smash Palace* were mainstream, but films like *Illustrious Energy* and, I suspect, *The End of the Golden Weather*, will always be marginalized. One reason is because they [some New Zealand film and television producers] don't believe we are talking to a mainstream audience, mainly because we don't have the voices a mainstream audience listens to, that is, established actors."[14]

By contrast, *What Becomes of the Broken Hearted?* as a sequel to the enormously successful *Once Were Warriors* was viewed as a mainstream production from the start. Mune had to follow director Lee Tamahori's success with *Once Were Warriors;* he inherited the film's star, Temuera Morrison, who reprised his role as Jake Heke, and saw a distribution push that resulted in the film being released in New Zealand to more screens than the long-awaited *Star Wars* prequel, *The Phantom Menace*, exhibited the same year. His "30 percent" on script meant collaborating with author Alan Duff as script consultant on the difficult project of a sequel. Mune stressed: "It is not a sequel in the way we've come to regard sequels, as being kind of the same story."[15] Instead, he intended a second but different installment of the Heke story. Where *The End of the Golden Weather* closes by suggesting that Geoff can grow up into a world with a social system apparently secure enough at least to contain imagination and cultural difference, the final sequence of *What Becomes of the Broken Hearted?* has Jake taking his rescued son "home." The film ignores the novel's closing trial, which, in its invocation of the law, had indicated Jake's assent to the New Zealand State, and only hints at social, political, and cultural possibilities by showing him acquiring mates, who find him a job, and a girlfriend he respects. As director of the feature, Mune found himself working on sensitive issues surrounding the depiction of Maori society and culture.[16] He had previously been involved with such topics when directing *Big Brother, Little Sister* in 1976, an addition to the *Winners and Losers* television series. This adaptation of a Witi Ihimaera story about Maori children facing neglect due to adult alcoholism was almost a prequel for many of the concerns that would later be raised in *Once Were Warriors*.

As *What Becomes of the Broken Hearted?* opens it immediately establishes the impact of a narrative built on moments of action and melodrama. Jake is re-established with the ritual fight in a pub as Nig (Julian Arahanga), his son, dies elsewhere during a gang conflict. Despite being in different spatial realms, a piece of slow-motion eyeline matching shows Jake turn his head in apprehension and look across the frame as if connecting with gang boss Grunt's (Lawrence Makoare) opposing look in the shot that follows. From there the film's narrative accelerates rapidly with the multiple plots of the novel reduced down to essentially three: Jake's story, the tragic love of Sonny (Clint Eruera) and Tania (Nancy Brown) as they seek revenge for Nig's death, and the story of the enigmatic Mulla (Rawiri Paratene). Jake's viewpoint dominates as another version of the "man alone" in popular New Zealand imagining, here sited in the Maori urban working class and opposed to the communality of the gangs. In *Once Were Warriors,* Jake's pride in standing alone as "the Muss" brought tragedy on his family. He remained a one-dimensional embodiment of violence, such that the film is arguably Beth's story. *What Becomes of the Broken Hearted?*, in contrast, depicts a passion for masculinity, which it resolves through the sacrifice of another woman in Tania. To motivate her death, the script deviates significantly from the novel. Tania protects her man, Sonny, and kills Grunt in a form of utu (revenge). In the ensuing gang war, however, Sonny cannot protect her, even when aided by his father. Mune draws on melodramatic devices for the killing of Tania, who is standing in the window of a disused railway carriage as the pistol of her off-screen executioner (Pete Smith) is raised to her head.

A dark side permeates *What Becomes of the Broken Hearted?*, especially seen in the context of Nig's death. Jake attends his son's tangi (funeral) but is clearly isolated from his family. Back home, he retreats into a space of semi-darkness and, as his social environment collapses, he is increasingly shown in seclusion and in shadowy or sunless surroundings. A broken man, he attacks his own left hand (his weapon of choice in his repeated fights) and falls to the ground weeping. This is in contrast to the scenes that follow of daylight and the work outdoors, which Jake shares with his mates Kohi (Anaru Grant) and Gary (Warwick Morehu). They not only teach him a version of masculinity without the need for blind violence but also how a wry, self-ironic humor can be the mark of a secure identity. Most

The embodiment of inarticulate violence: Jake the Muss in *What Becomes of the Broken Hearted?* (Courtesy New Zealand Film Commission.)

memorable is the bush pig hunt where Jake crashes about comically after the quarry and avoids severe injury only when Gary shoots the beast dead at his feet. There follows an iconic moment as Jake the Muss struggles out of the bush with his dead alter ego on his back. And later that evening, as the men gather around the campfire where they sing Maori songs under the night sky, Mune succeeds in establishing stability in mateship, in a form of the mythic concept of Kiwi masculinity.

For the opposing Maori gangs, the film designed another series of contrasts. The gang Kaipatu Kaahu is presented with a distinctly aggressive urban Maori appearance, while the production designer Brett Schwieters says of their enemies, the Black Snakes: "I looked at Mexican gangs, Korean gangs, how they live, dress, their guns and their jewellery. We gave the Black Snakes this 'international' look."[17] With the figures of Apeman and Mulla, Mune got performances, from Pete Smith and Rawiri Paratene respectively, that rival that of Morrison in the lead. And the effect of their tattooed faces certainly bears out Mune's somewhat unfortunate remark that, "The faces are the guts of the film."[18] His fascination with dramatically lit close-ups was already evident in much earlier productions such as *Big Brother, Little Sister*. For *What Becomes of the Broken Hearted?* Mune required his designers to reflect an unsettling tone into the mise-en-scène for the gangs, though in the film's conflict of Maori on Maori, the urban industrial style of the gangs is noticeably marked by the need to secure overseas theatrical distribution through a depiction of "cool violence."

Perhaps the most fascinating Maori figure is Mulla, the gang veteran whose hatred of himself and everyone else is tattooed across his entire body as a series of elaborate Maori markings, a visual equivalent to the inner voice he is given in the novel. As he suddenly fells his boss in the film's final scene, he turns into the savior of Jake and Sonny. The film motivates this resolution by showing Mulla parallel Jake's own development. Morrison certainly gives a complex and demanding performance and carries the entire film, but the enigmatic Paratene (later to appear as the grandfather Koro in *Whale Rider* [2002]), though featured much less, threatens to steal the honors. Mune himself declared that *What Becomes of the Broken Hearted?* has a "broken back" caused by a weakness in his concept of Jake: he does not traverse sufficient suffering to allow for his redemption.[19] Hence the character can be partially eclipsed by Mulla, who is left sitting passively at the film's end in the gang's headquarters. If this character is rising to the light, then he is coming from a deeper hell than Jake ever knew.

This last scene in the film gives Jake another brutal fight, but this time his violence would appear justified. Brian McDonnell speculates that, "Perhaps the quietest conclusion of the novel was deemed too undramatic by the adaptors, perhaps it was felt that Jake the Muss deserved one last hurrah."[20] He quotes Nicholas Reid in *North and South* who sees Jake learning not much more than who are the right people to hit.[21] In creating such a conclusion, the film sticks with mainstream melodrama for the widest audience possible in a style associated with Hollywood productions.

Mune had in fact earlier in his career worked for a while as a Hollywood scriptwriter. But he returned to New Zealand in 1984 to direct his first feature film, *Came a Hot Friday* (1985). Mune produced a script with Dean Parker from Ronald Hugh Morrieson's novel, which erased the book's cynical attitude toward rural life. The action starts with Mune's voice-over: "It is 1949. The privations of war are behind us. There is money to be made." The film's central location of Tainuia Junction is presented with enough realist style to support a comic drama playing on a nostalgia for small town New Zealand where the locals are larger than life.

In *Came a Hot Friday*'s fantasy, the two leads, con men Wes (Peter Bland) and Cyril (Phillip Gordon) are outsiders whom Mune had rehearsed as figures while co-director and actor in the *Winners and Losers* television drama, *Shining with the Shiner* (1975). Here Mune played "Hon McKay," a trickster with the shabby gentility of the English "remittance man." For *Came a Hot Friday*, Peter Bland elevates the pseudo gentility of Wes the con man beyond caricature into a yardstick performance for comic acting in New Zealand film. He is as devoted as the other characters to good times and easy money, but he performs this with a seedy charisma that hints at an upper-class sophistication derived from somewhere else. Cyril is, in contrast, the lower-class version, all moves and gestures from movies, a copy who even transforms momentarily into a slapstick parody of the snappy dresser as he repeatedly shoots his cuffs to the accompaniment of a one-note whistle. Wes and Cyril integrate immediately with the locals who are played by an ensemble cast. They recruit the guileless Don (Michael Lawrence) as accomplice, make moves on the town beauties, and inevitably engage with the villains. Car-dealer Dick (Philip Holder) and his wife Dinah (Erna Larsen) provide glamour, a bit of slapstick, and the heartwarming reconciliation of two good-livers meant for each other. Norm the pub bookie (Don Selwyn) and Sel Bishop (Marshall Napier) in his shearing-shed casino add violence and malice to produce the nervous frisson to the running gags and chases. And then there is the Tainuia Kid, a Maori who thinks he is a Mexican, played by comedian Billy T. James. Although appearing mainly in the film's last third, James's inspired performance led David Robinson of *The Times* to describe him as a "purely indigenous eccentric,"[22] while the American trade paper *Variety* celebrated "this Zorro-with-a-difference, who emits a schizo blend of Western cowboy hero and Mexican patriot, with Monty Pythonesque overtones," adding "this Kid says more about cultural cross-breeding in small countries like New Zealand than any learned academic."[23] If Wes and Cyril seek to impress the locals by mimicking the ways of the Big World, the Kid lives by what he has seen in westerns and is an eccentric nuisance. Like Firpo, he lives the dream at odds with social conventions and thus makes himself appear a buffoon. Unlike Firpo's, his buffoonery is favored by the genius loci. He can outsmart the local villain precisely because he believes so completely in the role he has derived from foreign influences. He finally pays for his preservation by sacrificing a stash of money to his belief in the taniwha (mythological Maori water monster). In the film's epilogue at the cenotaph the Kid is shown gathered with the community to salute the country's fallen soldiers. The local product of American fiction thus integrates with his Pakeha compatriots into a founding myth of nationhood.

Came a Hot Friday's frenetic blend: Farce and fear as the Mexican Maori the Tainuia Kid unwittingly restrains Sel Bishop. (Courtesy Ian Conrich collection of New Zealand cinema and visual culture.)

Mune's three other features as director—*Bridge to Nowhere* (1986), *The Grasscutter* (1988), and *The Whole of the Moon* (1996)—have been less successful. With *Bridge to Nowhere* and *The Whole of the Moon*, Mune was working with a mixture of novice actors and professionals on melodramas. Of *Bridge to Nowhere* he said: "I suspect my style is essentially melodramatic. It's highly expressive, I can tell you that melodrama is an often-abused term. For me, melodrama is a strongly expressed feeling, rather than bullshit. I suppose in that sense my style is fairly barometric... living where it's hot. That's where I want people to be."[24] Mune co-wrote the script for this thriller, which has the viable notion of urban kids becoming lost in the bush, but the production is hindered by a weak plot and characterization. It attempts to motivate its story through a conflict between the aggressive city-kid neurotic, Leon (Phillip Gordon), wound up by adolescent hormones, and the bushman, Mac (Bruno Lawrence), whose contempt provokes him to deadly violence. The film tries to deploy the mysterious bridge of its title and the surrounding thick bush as key narrative motifs, but it only succeeds in tracing a hectic confrontation of mainly psychotic males. After much chasing around through difficult terrain, the film resolves itself by a melodramatic trick when the most "ordinary" of the kids, Carl (Matthew Hunter), suddenly executes a piece of skilled knife throwing that kills Mac. *Bridge to Nowhere* is perhaps only interesting for the New Zealand bush's potential as location and for Lawrence's performance, which partially rescues the film.

For *The Grasscutter*, Mune was engaged as a local director for a New Zealand/UK co-production. A television feature made primarily for broadcast in the UK market, the film was released only on video in New Zealand. Mune's one feature never to have a local theatrical release, it is a competent action/thriller for its market with a plot deriving from a father/son conflict set against the political and historical background of the "troubles" in Northern Ireland. As the terrorists from Belfast surface in New Zealand to punish the informer who has been given a new identity by the British government, the past reaches out from the other side of the world and violently disturbs the local serene way of life. For the film Mune made effective use of the South Island locations, especially in the closing sequences where the production captures spectacular views, some through helicopter shots of Queenstown, Lake Wakatipu, and the Southern Alps.

The Whole of the Moon was also a co-production—between New Zealand and Canada. But despite the film being subsidized by, amongst others, the New Zealand Film Commission (NZFC) and the Government of Quebec, Mune had no illusions about the film as product: "It's a very tough movie to sell. We know once we've got them in there, we're a winner. The problem is getting them in the door: nobody wants to go and pay ten bucks to go and see a movie about someone who's dying of cancer, especially if it hasn't got Julia Roberts."[25] Mune came into the production at the suggestion of the New Zealand producer Murray Newey to co-develop the original idea from Richard Lymposs's story.[26] Unlike the political thriller *The Grasscutter*, Mune's tackling of this film's theme was quite courageous because it meant engaging with what *Metro*'s critic, Rick Bryant, called "that degraded genre, the disease movie."[27] The film follows the unlikely pairing of a rich Pakeha kid, Kirk (Toby Fisher), and Marty (Nikki Si'ulepa), a Polynesian girl from the streets, who meet in the cancer ward of an Auckland children's hospital. To tell a story "true to its origins and comprehensible to everyone," Mune again foregrounded the elements of melodrama. His beloved shadowy lighting dominates the hospital interiors, and is used at dramatic moments. For instance, when the doctor who tells Kirk that the amputation of his leg is likely, lightning flashes accompanied by streaming rain create shadows across the image; the same techniques that are used for Marty's death scene.

The New Zealand setting is secondary to the interaction between the two leads, but one particular scene does stand out for its use of location.

Evading the police, Kirk and Marty appear cross-dressed as an unlikely couple on the town. When they reach an island in the Hauraki Gulf, Kirk, in wig and ball gown beneath the flawless blue of a New Zealand summer sky, waves a crutch at the view trying to explain its emptiness as glorious Nature. Here, late in its action, *The Whole of the Moon* acquires a harder edge by setting Kirk and Marty as small, bizarre figures against a picturesque backdrop, which, magnificent though it may be, is completely indifferent to their fates. The co-production went on to win awards both in New Zealand and overseas.[28] It went to Cannes, and the NZFC promoted it vigorously offshore, but the audience response to a brave attempt on a difficult topic never materialized.

When Mune won the prestigious Rudall Hayward Award in 2000, for special contributions to the New Zealand film industry, he warned fellow filmmakers about losing: "Not just the money—but the whole cultural history that has been so many years in the building. It will all be wasted, unless we re-structure our industry to tell the stories we, New Zealanders, are passionate about, and find ways to make the deal fit the movie, rather than the other way round."[29] He also called an open meeting on the topic for the next morning. This is a filmmaker who persists in his ambitions for a national industry on the fringes of the global market. In a sense, those ambitions have been borne out by the latest phase of New Zealand's filmmaking history. The phenomenon of *The Lord of the Rings* has certainly eclipsed Mune's work. But Jo Smith's definition of this country's filmmaking demonstrates the limits of the Jackson trilogy's relevance for New Zealand's cultural identity. Drawing an analogy with Hamid Naficy's thesis in his *An Accented Cinema*, she maintains that, "A similar attention to place and displacement can be achieved in the research surrounding Aotearoa/New Zealand cinematic productions. In terms of this postcolonial context, attention can be paid to the settler status of the nation, the indigenous Maori population and the perhaps triangulated currents of cultural influence stemming from the British Empire, American popular culture and most recently, Asia-Pacifica."[30] The style and technique of Ian Mune's films demonstrate all of these elements through his love of melodramatic narrative supported by his use of local landscape and the spoken idiom. In his commitment to filmmaking in New Zealand he was already seeking to be "glocal"[31] thirty years ago, but not solely in the sense that his ambitions identified New Zealand to overseas interests as a good location to realize your own images or have them realized for you. Mune has sought instead a cinematic heritage for New Zealand that is not sanctioned by imaginings from elsewhere but by those truly indigenous to what he claims as his own place. The consequence has been a career seeking to square the circle by negotiating the demands of the international market while preserving his vision of cultural identity and integrity. Other filmmakers working in and about New Zealand may have achieved wider recognition. However, few can match Mune's gift for a multiplicity of roles and for constantly reinventing himself, which makes him one of the most accomplished representatives of the constantly regenerating film industry of New Zealand.

Notes

1. Ian Mune, interview with author, January 21, 2002.
2. Ibid.
3. Mark McLauchlan, "Over the Mune," *North and South* 115 (October 1995): 67.
4. Ibid.
5. Mune, interview with author, January 21, 2002.
6. McLauchlan. "Over the Mune," 67
7. Ian Mune and Roger Donaldson, "Notes from the Film Directors," in *Winners and Losers: Films Adapted from New Zealand Short Stories* (Wellington: Department of Education, 1977), iii.
8. Frank Sargeson, "Author's Comment on Film," in *Winners and Losers: A Great Day* (Wellington: Department of Education, 1977), iv. Underlined in original.
9. Barry Crump, "Author's Comment on Film," in *Winners and Losers: A Lawful Excuse* (Wellington: Department of Education, 1977), iv. Underlined in original.
10. Matt Johnson, "Changed by the Journey," *Onfilm* 13, no. 1 (1997): 12.
11. John O'Shea, "Adaptation Strives to Match Original," *Onfilm* 9, no. 2 (1992): 10.
12. David Dowling, "War and Peace: On the Beach with Bruce and Maurice," *Illusions* 20 (Summer 1992): 18.
13. Philip Kemp, "The End of the Golden Weather," *Sight and Sound* 3, no. 2 (1993): 45.
14. Philip Wakefield, "Kiwi to the Core," *Onfilm* 9, no. 3 (1992): 8.
15. Anamika Vasil, "Success Is in the Lap of the Audience, says Mune," *The Dominion* May 25, 1999, 9. For a wider account of the convoluted production history, see Bill Gavin, "Look Back in Candour," *Onfilm* 16, no. 6 (1999): 15–20.
16. In the "making of" section of the DVD, Temuera Morrison declares: "Mune has our total respect" (*What Becomes of the Broken Hearted?* Universal Pictures [Australasia], DVD 0786632).
17. David Gapes, "Map of the Broken Hearted," *Onfilm* 15, no. 11 (1998): 22.
18. *What Becomes of the Broken Hearted?* DVD.
19. Mune, interview with author, January 21, 2002.
20. Brian McDonnell, "Saving Private Heke," *Metro* 120 (1999): 37.
21. Nicholas Reid, "Broken Warriors," *North and South* 160 (July 1999): 110.
22. See "*Came a Hot Friday*. Box Office Records," *Onfilm* 2, no. 11 (1985): 11.
23. Nic. "Came a Hot Friday," *Variety*, February 20, 1985, 23.
24. Kirsten Warner, "Living Where It's Hot," *Onfilm* 2, no. 3 (1985): 8.
25. Mune, interview with Suzette Major, September 5, 1996. My thanks to Suzette for her assistance.
26. Ibid.

27. Rick Bryant, "Dark Side of the Mune," *Metro* 188 (1997): 112.
28. See Helen Martin and Sam Edwards, *New Zealand Film, 1912–1996* (Auckland: Oxford University Press, 1997), 192.
29. *spadaNEWS* 59 (July 2000): 4.
30. Jo Smith, "Situating Cinema in/from Aotearoa/New Zealand," in *Media Studies in Aotearoa/New Zealand*, ed. Luke Goode and Nabeel Zuberi (Auckland: Pearson Longman, 2004), 94–95.
31. See Timothy W. Luke, "New World Order or Neo-World Orders: Power, Politics and Ideology in Informationalizing Glocalities," in *Global Modernities*, ed. Mike Featherstone, Scott M. Lash, and Roland Robertson (London: Sage, 1996), 101.

Ian Mune—Filmography

1968. *All That We Need* (NZ extended short film: props maker).
1971. *Pukemanu* (NZ television six-part series, 1st season: actor in the episode "A Soft Answer").
1971. *Pinocchio Travelling Circus* (NZ television drama: writer).
1971. *Gunspoof* (NZ short film incorporating found footage: actor in shots originally filmed in 1966).
1972. *Pukemanu* (NZ television six-part series, 2nd season: writer for an episode).
1972. *Section 7* (NZ television series: actor).
1973. *Rangi's Catch* (NZ eight-part children's film serial, later recut as a feature film: actor).
1974. *Derek* (NZ television drama: co-director, co-writer, actor).
1974. *Carnival Coast* (NZ drama-documentary: actor).
1974/75. *Buck House* (NZ television sit-com series: co-writer).
1975. *Matlock Police* (Australia television series: writer for the episode "First Day Out").
1975. *Homicide* (Australia television series: actor in the episode "Thou Shalt Not Want").
1975. *Taggart* (NZ television pilot for an aborted series: actor).
1975/76. *Winners and Losers* (NZ television single drama "The Woman at the Store," later followed by a further six dramas and packaged as a seven-part series: co-director, co-producer, co-writer, story adaptation, actor).
1975/77. *Moynihan* (NZ/Australia television seventeen-part series. Pilot program 1975, series 1 1976, series 2 1977: actor).
1976. *The God Boy* (NZ television film: writer).
1976. *Players to the Gallery* (Australia television three-part mini-series: actor).
1976. *Blerta* (NZ television six-part series: occasional actor).
1976. *Hunter's Gold* (NZ television thirteen-part children's series: actor).
1977. *Sleeping Dogs* (NZ feature film: co-writer, actor, co–art director).
1977. *The Bounty Mutineers* (NZ television documentary-drama in the *Castaways* series: actor).

1978. *The Mad Dog Gang Meets Rotten Fred and Ratsguts* (NZ children's drama in three parts: co-writer).
1978. *The Aunty Natal Show* (NZ short film: director, producer, graphics, interviewer).
1978. *The Postie Natal Show* (NZ short film: director, producer).
1979. *The Mad Dog Gang Spooks Wilkie, Wink, Wink, and the Wobbler* (NZ children's television drama: writer).
1980. *Little Big Man Takes a Shot at the Moon* (NZ short film: director).
1980. *Big Hearted Barney Blackfoot* (NZ short children's film: writer).
1980. *Nutcase* (NZ extended short children's film: co-writer, actor).
1980. ***Goodbye Pork Pie*** (NZ feature film: co-writer).
1981. *Dracula: Part 1* (NZ television presentation of a theater performance: director).
1981. Directed several commercials for the 1981 Labour Party election campaign.
1981. *Jocko* (NZ television series: actor in the first episode).
1982. *One of Those Blighters* (NZ television drama: actor).
1984. ***The Silent One*** (NZ feature film: writer).
1984. *Conan the Destroyer* (US feature film: co-writer for an early version of the screenplay).
1984. *The Bounty* (US/Australia/NZ/UK/Italy feature film: advisor to the director).
1985. *Porters Christmas* (NZ television drama: actor).
1985. ***Came a Hot Friday*** (NZ feature film: director, co-writer).
1985. ***Shaker Run*** (NZ feature film: actor).
1986. ***Bridge to Nowhere*** (NZ feature film: director, co-writer).
1986. ***Dangerous Orphans*** (NZ feature film: actor).
1988. *Backstage* (Australia/US feature film: actor).
1988. *Porters* (NZ television six-part series: actor).
1988. *Erebus: The Aftermath* (NZ television mini-series: actor).
1988. ***The Grasscutter*** (NZ/UK television film: director).
1989. *E Tipu E Rea* (NZ television series: actor in the drama "Thunderbox").
1990. *The Ray Bradbury Theatre* (US/France/UK/Canada/NZ television series: actor in the episode "Usher II").
1991. ***The End of the Golden Weather*** (NZ feature film: director, co-producer, co-writer).
1992. *Marlin Bay* (NZ television series: actor).
1992. *Shortland Street* (NZ television soap opera: actor).
1992. *The Ray Bradbury Theatre* (US/France/UK/Canada/NZ television series: director of the episodes "The Lonely One" and "Great Wide World Over There").
1993. *By the Light of the Mune* (NZ television documentary: featured artist).
1993. *Soldier Soldier* (UK television series: director of episode "Live Fire").
1993. *The Visitation* (NZ television drama: director).

1993. *The Piano* (Australia/NZ feature film: actor).
1994. *Fallout* (NZ television two-part mini-series: actor).
1994. *Letter to Blanchy* (NZ television sitcom series: director of the episode "A Serious Understanding").
1994. *Once Were Warriors* (NZ feature film: actor, script advisor).
1995. *Pacific Rescue* (NZ documentary: narrator).
1995. *Dead Certs* (NZ film/television drama: director, co-writer).
1995/96. *Hercules: The Legendary Journeys* (US/NZ television series: actor in the episodes "Gladiator" and "The Apple").
1996. *The Whole of the Moon* (Canada/NZ feature film: director, co-writer).
1996. *Shuriken—Prisoners of Culture* (NZ television documentary: narrator).
1997. *In the Shadow of King Lear* (NZ documentary: featured performer).
1997. *Pio* (NZ television variety show, 1st series: special guest).
1997. *Home Movie* (NZ film/television drama: actor).
1997. *Hillary: A View from the Top* (NZ television four-part series: narrator).
1997. *The Last of the Ryans* (Australia television film: actor).
1997. *Topless Women Talk about Their Lives* (NZ feature film: actor).
1999. *Metusela* (NZ television drama in the *True Life Stories* series: actor).
1999. *What Becomes of the Broken Hearted?* (NZ feature film: director, script advisor).
1999. *Nightmare Man* (Canada/NZ feature film: actor).
1999. *Savage Honeymoon* (NZ feature film: actor).
2000. *Questions* (NZ television drama: script editor).
2000. *Dark Knight* (US/NZ television series: actor in the episode "Dragon Singer").
2001. *Tarawera* (NZ documentary: narrator).
2001. *Cow* (NZ short film: actor).
2001. *Numero Bruno* (NZ television documentary: interviewee).
2001. *The Lord of the Rings: The Fellowship of the Ring* (US/NZ feature film: actor, additional second unit director).
2001. *Being Eve* (NZ television series: actor in episode "Being Grown Up").
2001/3. *Mercy Peak* (NZ television series: actor in the episodes "Basset Confidential," "Best Laid Plans," "The Making of Him," and "An Angel at My Wash House").
2002. *Mataku* (NZ television series: actor in the episode "Heirloom: Te Kura").
2003. *Lucy* (US television film: actor).
2003. *Murder on the Blade* (NZ television drama-documentary: actor).
2004. *Spooked* (NZ feature film: actor).
2004. *Ike: Countdown to D-Day* (US television film: actor).
2004. *The Making of Sleeping Dogs* (NZ documentary: interviewee).
2006. *Perfect Creature* (NZ/UK feature film: actor).
2006. *The World's Fastest Indian—The Burt Munro Story* (NZ television documentary: field director).

11

The Man Alone

BRUNO LAWRENCE'S SCREEN PERFORMANCES
OF THE KIWI BLOKE

Andrew Spicer

Bruno Lawrence is remembered by many as the driving force behind Blerta (the Bruno Lawrence Electric Revelation and Travelling Apparition), an itinerant troupe of performing artists (including Geoff Murphy) and their families, which toured New Zealand, and then later Australia, from 1971 to 1975, in a psychedelic bus giving multi-media shows that were protests against conformity and political indifference. Blerta owed more to Lawrence's energy, charisma, and musical abilities as a drummer than to his acting talents, but it led to his first feature film role in *Wild Man* (1977), directed by Geoff Murphy, an extended version of one of six Blerta sessions that had been shot for television. Lawrence never lost his status as a counter-cultural rebel, as shown by his cameo appearance in *Goodbye Pork Pie* (1980). But such rebelliousness formed part of his embodiment of the contradictions of male Pakeha (European) identity in a number of important films—most notably *Smash Palace* (1981)—through which he became arguably New Zealand's most gifted and important screen actor, if not the most celebrated. Sam Neill, in his documentary *Cinema of Unease: A Personal Journey* (1995), identifies Lawrence as the key actor of his generation, through his incarnation of the dominant Pakeha cultural archetype, that of the "man alone."[1] My aim here is not to offer a comprehensive account of Lawrence's career that extended to eighteen feature films in New Zealand as well as numerous television roles, but, through an examination of his key screen performances, to argue for his centrality to a complex process of change in cultural images of modern New Zealand masculinity.[2]

This is a shortened and revised version of the booklet *An Ambivalent Archetype: Masculinity, Performance and the New Zealand Films of Bruno Lawrence* (Nottingham: Kakapo Books, 2000).

The Pakeha Cultural Archetype: The "man alone"

The "man alone" archetype can be seen as part of an Anglo-Celtic diaspora, a "white pioneer" myth that celebrates a rugged, freedom-loving masculinity be it in North America, Australia, or New Zealand.[3] Constructed within a typical pioneer identity, Pakeha masculinity has a basically anti-authoritarian, republican temper, a belief in freedom that incarnates the wild, untamed expansiveness of the landscape itself.[4] In his authoritative history of Pakeha masculinity, Jock Phillips argues that migrants thought of New Zealand as a "man's country," far removed from the feminizing influences of polite society, where "true" manhood could be forged through a vigorous struggle to subdue the wilderness and establish democratic, egalitarian communities. In these frontier, all-male groups, emotional needs were satisfied through "mateship," the homosocial intimacy of men who depended on one another. This rough-hewn archetype gradually evolved into the settler, his endeavors shared by a supportive wife whose refining influence created a more rooted and civilized masculinity. But, as Phillips argues, these two powerful traditions, a frontier tradition of physical strength, drinking, gambling, and mateship, versus a middle-class Protestant tradition of sober, monogamous respectability, were always at odds, and it is that struggle "which more than anything else explains the peculiar character of the Pakeha male stereotype."[5]

The irreconcilable conflict between these two traditions is evident in one of the defining texts of Pakeha masculinity and New Zealand literary nationalism, John Mulgan's 1939 novel *Man Alone*. Mulgan's novel is the story of a self-reliant, taciturn drifter, Johnson, who escapes from a war-torn Europe to make a fresh start in New Zealand.[6] Johnson embodies the contradictions of the archetype: a mistrust of society, especially city life, and a preference for solitude, but the need for male companionship; suspicions about women whose motives and "nesting" instincts might curb his freedom, but a strong sexual desire; a reluctance to become angry, but a marked capacity for violence; a settled industriousness but the ability, when necessary, to return to a nomadic existence in the bush; and finally, a limited education, but the fabled ingenuity of the man who can turn his hand to anything. As Russell Campbell argues, these antithetical pulls of the itinerant, resourceful loner capable of violence and the settled, nonviolent family man, have been central to New Zealand cinema's representation of masculinity.[7] Campbell identifies Roger Donaldson's *Sleeping Dogs* (1977) as the founding film of New Zealand cinema's New Wave and paradigmatic image of modern Pakeha male identity. Here, the central character Smith (Sam Neill) is rugged and aggressive, capable of resourceful action, but also sensitive, vulnerable, and withdrawn. Soon after, Neill began working overseas and later went on to international stardom; it was then Bruno Lawrence who took over as the archetypal "man alone," becoming the New Wave's most important actor.

Lawrence the Actor and *Utu* (1983)

As noted, Lawrence made his feature film debut in *Wild Man*, but his real training as an actor came through Murphy's experimental short films such as *Dr Brunovski* (1966) and *Tank Busters* (1970), and a number of television roles, including an episode in the 1970 *Survey* series, for which he won a Best Actor award.[8] This experience, unlike the more conventional route through theater and radio drama, which still demanded that actors speak in refined "Oxford English," allowed Lawrence to retain his distinctive, "unrefined," Kiwi accent. He learned to relax in front of the camera and to have the courage to improvise, which various directors and fellow actors saw as one of his major strengths, a reaching down into his own character and experience so as to find the most authentic way of playing a scene. As in other areas of his life, Lawrence was prepared to take risks, including appearing naked if this was integral to the part he was playing. As actor-director Ian Mune recalled, "He didn't sort of capture a scene, he *created* a scene so that there was a sense when he was on camera that anything could happen."[9] Lawrence was co-screenwriter or script adviser on several of his major films, and this involvement also gave him the confidence to revise and modify his own role. He was adept at adjusting his body movements and gestures in order to give, as fellow actor Martyn Sanderson observed, "the right size of performance for camera, which very few directors in my experience can tell actors how to find."[10] Without the height, good looks, or luxuriant fullness of hair of a conventional leading man, Lawrence had a commanding presence through his powerful muscular body and resonant, bass-baritone voice; both were instruments that could project either menace or warmth. But it was his highly expressive eyes that, in particular, gave depth and complexity to his portrayal of the "man alone." Greer Robson, who played his daughter in *Smash Palace*, thought, "[t]hose brown eyes of his . . . reach out and you can feel whatever he's feeling. He seems so vulnerable and yet so blokey at the same time, and that makes people sympathize and empathize with him."[11]

This combination of menace and vulnerability was strongly evident in Geoff Murphy's quasi-western epic *Utu*, set in New Zealand in 1860 at the start of a new land war, in which Lawrence played Jonathan Williamson, the Pakeha settler-turned-avenger. A second-generation settler, Williamson has integrated, conversing happily in the vernacular with his Maori neighbor, who gives him a good-luck pendant. Williamson owns an imposing farmhouse, which his supportive wife Emily (Ilona Rodgers) has furnished with the trappings of European civilization, including the grand piano on which she plays expertly. Lawrence's subtle performance, his hesitations when he starts to speak to Emily, and his awkward gestures as if afraid that he might knock something over, capture the rugged settler's discomfort around the home and in women's company, yet also convey strong love for his wife and his pride in their aspirations toward gentility. It is this achievement that he feels he must defend, refusing to go with the other local settlers to the military stockade, determined to outface the rampaging Te Wheke (Anzac Wallace), who has vowed utu (vengeance) on the British invaders after the massacre of his village. In defending his stronghold, Williamson displays the resourceful ingenuity of the Kiwi bloke, setting fire to a cache of explosives in his outhouse so that it will not fall into Te Wheke's hands, but in the process leaving Emily vulnerable. She dies, falling from the veranda trying to escape Te Wheke.

Emily's death creates an indissoluble bond of enmity between Williamson and Te Wheke, mirror images of each other, obsessed by their need for vengeance, apparently indestructible, outsiders even among their own communities. Lawrence manages to invest an extraordinary intensity in the figure of the lone avenger, as Williamson abandons his neat suit for the full-length buttoned-up duster and broad-brimmed hat of the gunslinger, his body tense and rigid, face clenched, eyes sunken but burning with a fixed gaze. He becomes fixated on weaponry, constructing an absurd four-barreled shotgun, good for demolishing buildings and knocking him off his feet, but useless as a combat gun, serving as an index of his demented reversion to an atavistic form of manhood. However, as Martin Blythe observes, Williamson is both avenger and Holy Fool.[12] Like Tom O'Bedlam in *King Lear*, Williamson is possessed of a special wisdom that elevates him above the immediate exigencies of the conflict and allows him to question the whole purpose of colonization. And, like the traditional Fool, he has the license to flout authority, kissing Colonel Eliott (Tim Elliot) on the lips when he refuses to end the conflict, a gesture that ridicules the Colonel's status and his manhood. Williamson forms a new bond with the sagacious Maori scout Wiremu (Wi Kuki Kaa), colluding in Wiremu's "execution" of Elliot and grudgingly assenting to Wiremu's right (as his brother) to kill Te Wheke at the trial and so call a temporary end, if not a resolution, to the war.

Lawrence's performance has a range and depth that captures the shifting ambiguities of the white settler's role, the desire for civilization but the proclivity for violence, making him both hero and villain. Lawrence worked hard on this characterization, experimenting with what was, for

The pioneer pushed to extremes: Lawrence as Williamson in *Utu*. (Courtesy Ian Conrich collection of New Zealand cinema and visual culture.)

him, the rather alienating discipline of Method Acting, but still improvising in role (for instance kissing the Colonel) in order to find the most expressive gesture in a scene. Nick Roddick thought Lawrence had "an extraordinary and extremely disconcerting presence as Williamson," and judged him "the only really top class actor to emerge from the recent crop of New Zealand films."[13]

The Kiwi Bloke: Violent and Vulnerable

Roger Donaldson's *Smash Palace* (1981) charts the disintegrating marriage of the aggressive, macho, and competitive Al Shaw (Lawrence), an ex-racing driver, and his refined French wife Jacqui (Anna Jemison), the schoolteacher who longs for a more sophisticated and civilized life. Al, the ordinary Kiwi bloke with a typical mistrust of settling down, continues to chafe against what he sees as his wife's corset of gentility. As opposed to the neat order of suburban housing, Al's sprawling stronghold of Smash Palace, a wrecking yard he inherited from his father, is a male domain of machines, oily overalls, grimy hands, and half-eaten sandwiches. Al spends his spare moments restoring the veteran car his father had worked on and maintaining the racing car that he continues to compete in, rather than trying to run the yard profitably or servicing Jacqui's car. Increasingly frustrated, Jacqui feels Smash Palace is "like a graveyard," where she feels entombed among the moldering wrecks. Each has retreated into a separate world, which exaggerates their differences and removes any common ground. Their mutual hostility becomes focused on the upbringing of their seven-year-old daughter Georgie (Greer Robson). Al trains her to be like himself, teaching her which spanners to use, to ride around the yard in the miniature racer he has built, how to hunt and to shoot. Jacqui wants her to get an education, make a better match than marriage to a mechanic and escape from this world of "dead cars." Hurt and incensed by Jacqui's "hoity-toity ways," Al's only response is to take her sexually and aggressively in a scene shot with an uncompromising brutality.

When Jacqui leaves and begins seeing Ray Foley (Keith Aberdein), the local policeman, Al feels bewildered and betrayed, as Ray is his best friend who has severed the sacred bond of mateship in what seems to be the ultimate insult. Ray was the only one in whom Al could confide his doubts and fears, naturally in the context of a competitive game of snooker, that marriage is a lottery where he is emotionally out of his depth and powerless to change anything. Al makes a gesture of reconciliation, driving over to Jacqui's house with a bunch of flowers clenched in his fist all the while carefully rehearsing his lines, struggling for the right inflection of the phrase, "I know I've been totally unreasonable," only for it to come out in reverse as soon as she opens the door. About to drive off, Al spies Ray's jeep and, in a famous, partly improvised, moment that highlights Lawrence's willingness to extend the limits of himself as an actor, strips outside the front door, thrusting his clothes item by item through the letterbox, taunting Ray as he does so: "These nice, tight, poncey jeans. I hope they cut your balls off, if you've got any that is. And I'll tell you what, you'll love these: clean on today."

Humiliated by receiving a non-molestation order, Al's response is more violence. In another displaced phallic gesture, he thrusts a tow bar through Jacqui's letterbox and, pulling away in his truck, rips off the front door. Later, having been briefly jailed for violating the order, Al returns again to kidnap Georgie at gunpoint and head off to a pre-prepared hideout in the bush, the final refuge of the "man alone." Their long scene together is the most moving in the film, allowing the deep capacity for love and affection, which the Kiwi bloke often suppresses, to surface. In a desperate bid to celebrate Georgie's birthday, Al improvises, making them party hats out of newspapers, putting candles on a pie, and giving Georgie his own hunting knife as a present. "It's just like yours," she murmurs trustingly. For the first time since the snooker match with Ray, Al is able to talk freely, and it is his confused tenderness and vulnerability that make Al a more sympathetic character than would otherwise be the case. Donaldson frequently uses close-ups to emphasize Lawrence's expressive eyes, often with a sad, sunken, haunted look caught in shadow.

However, when Georgie's sickness forces him to abandon his hideout, Al becomes preoccupied with his frustrations rather than her welfare. Regaining possession of Smash Palace, he leads Ray out at gunpoint with his head in a wire hoop that Al has ingeniously attached to the shotgun. Powerless to intervene, the police are spectators as Al drives a veteran car to the nearby railway crossing, apparently into the path of an oncoming train. As it passes harmlessly along another set of tracks, Al taunts Ray, "You didn't really expect me to let that happen? . . . I mean, a beautiful car like this?" as he pulls the trigger of the unloaded shotgun and throws his head back in laughter. It is a complex climax. Knowing there is no way back for him, Al's macho masculinity has driven him, at the expense of everything else, including Jacqui's tearful protestations, into a final and futile gesture of defiance, the pleasure of humiliating Ray and the assembled police force for a final time. As the credits roll there is a prolonged close-up of Georgie's face, a concluding reminder of who is the real victim.

As script adviser, Lawrence added some key dimensions, not only to his character but also to the shape of the film as a whole. Convinced that Lawrence was essential to the success of the film, Donaldson persuaded the New Zealand Film Commission that he should play the part rather than the "established international actor" the Commission originally stipulated.[14] *Smash Palace* relies heavily on Lawrence's performance, which articulates the incipient violence and the vulnerability, the instinctive desire to be self-sufficient, and the need for love and support, that are the contradictory hallmarks of this modern "man alone." For Al, the ordinary bloke, there is no way out, recalling the anonymous driver's inexplicable car crash with which the film opens. Even overseas reviewers understood that he was perfect in this role: the *New York Times* wrote, "Lawrence is extremely effective as Shaw, capturing the ambivalence of the clumsy inarticulate character who behaves like an insensitive brute in the bedroom, but who still arouses sympathy with his paternal longings."[15] Lawrence won the Golden Eagle Award for Best Actor at the Manila Film Festival in 1982, and *Smash Palace* gained acclaim as the film in which "New Zealand cinema has decisively come of age."[16]

The Kiwi Bloke as Nurturer

In *Heart of the Stag* (1984), directed by Michael Firth, Lawrence played another loner, Peter Daley, a drifter, who takes a job on a remote farm when his pickup breaks down. But in this role he emphasizes the archetype's repressed nurturing qualities. In portraying Al Shaw, Lawrence had drawn on his native blokeishness; with Daley he uses his cosmopolitan and counter-cultural experiences. Daley is a sophisticated itinerant, sporting a trendy fawn leather jacket and flat cap and displaying a cultivated refinement in wine, the beauties of nature, and literature. His first meaningful contact with Cathy Jackson (Mary Regan), daughter of a wealthy farm owner, comes from their shared knowledge of the culminating lines of a James K. Baxter poem: "Upon the upland road ride easy strangers / Surrender to the sky your heart of anger."[17] The poem expresses the spirituality and the belief in a human capacity for change and renewal that are absent from the life of Cathy's father Robert Jackson (Terence Cooper), a fourth-generation patrician landowner (his huge estate planted with English trees) who can measure his masculinity only through conquest and possession (the numerous hunting trophies displayed on the walls). Jackson's insularity and desire to dominate takes the most brutal form: incest. His sexual abuse of his daughter is revealed, in flashback, to have started in her childhood, well before the stroke that has confined his wife Mary (Anne Flannery) to a wheelchair. Both women wish to kill Jackson but cannot.

Cathy's hope for renewal lies in her gradually developing relationship with Daley. Instead of the clenched, tense rigidity of Williamson, or the aggressive belligerence of Al Shaw, Lawrence builds the character of Daley through a very different use of his body where his movements, postures, and gestures are much looser and more expansive, his voice mellower; in place of the grimace or the haunted stare, Daley's face is much more open, the expressions softer, the big brown eyes opened much wider, as he waits for Cathy to reveal her troubles. In a lyrical, tender scene at the cottage where he is staying, away from the gloomy farmhouse, when he oversteps the mark by lifting her out of a punt and she shies away like a frightened animal, Daley's response is patience and understanding: "Hey, hey. Whatever it is that's bothering you, I'll listen." When she does confess her dark secret, the camera lingers on Daley's slowly mounting expression of anger and hatred, allowing the intensity of feeling to be created by Lawrence's stillness and eye movements as he holds her for the first time, muttering sotto voce "the bastard." That remark heralds the final confrontation between the two men as Daley persuades Cathy to leave with him and Jackson sets off in pursuit. The contest is richly symbolic: the hunter armed with his rifle against the unarmed man of nature, simpatico with the stag that gores Jackson to death as his gun jams. But, even with her father's death, Cathy is unsure whether she can trust another man, and, as Daley has been firmly established as the wanderer who distrusts rootedness, the possibility of renewal is left ambiguous.

Heart of the Stag did not have the impact of *Smash Palace* either at home or abroad. It is an altogether slighter film but notable for its determination to explore the capacity of the "man alone" for sensitivity and tenderness, his recognition of others', centrally women's, feelings, and his ability to nurture rather than destroy. It was an early attempt to sketch out the lineaments of a different type of masculinity.

The Ultimate Man Alone?

Lawrence was reunited with Geoff Murphy for *The Quiet Earth* (1985), which displays similar moral ambiguities and shifting patterns of identity to *Utu*, in what is an extended allegory about New Zealand's relationship with American nuclear dominance.[18] In the film, the American-controlled Operation Flashlight has caused a rupture of space-time fabric (the "Effect") that has seemingly wiped out humanity, leaving research scientist Zac Hobson (Lawrence) as the sole survivor, saved, ironically, by his attempted suicide from an overdose. The motif of the last man alive is a standard trope of science fiction, but its specific national resonance here is that Zac is the final "man alone." For Lawrence, who co-wrote the screenplay, the chief attraction of Craig Harrison's source novel was the opportunity to explore "the whole concept of the man alone coping with being alone and the sort of process he would go through in his own mind."[19] Murphy successfully lobbied for Lawrence to be cast in the role despite pressure from the producers for an American star, such as Jack Nicholson.

The Quiet Earth offered Lawrence his greatest challenge as an actor, having to perform alone for the first thirty-six minutes of the film. Lawrence gives a riveting study in mental breakdown, as Zac degenerates from sober rationality trying to communicate with other possible survivors, through self-indulgent sybarite engaged in an orgy of consumerism, to unshaven wild man, destroying a television set playing a recorded message about world cooperation. His identity disintegrating, Zac dresses in a petticoat, gazing at his reflection in the mirror and feeling his chest as if he could grow breasts and be his own sexual partner, before wrapping a toga over his petticoat to give a balcony address to cardboard cutouts of famous figures, past and present, as if he were a new world leader. But Zac is a leader who no longer believes in his moral right to rule, and his address turns into a confession that "the awesome forces I have helped to create have been put in the hands of madmen. I've been gagged by the taint of my own corruption." In an even more outrageous and chilling scene, he enters a church in his torn and tattered petticoat like a demented commando screaming, "If you don't come out I'll shoot the kid," as he blasts away at a statue of the crucifixion. Having "proved" that even then God will not reveal himself, Zac proclaims, "And now I am God," but his only action is a possible second suicide attempt. At the last moment he relents and is symbolically reborn through a sea baptism, after which he prepares to rectify the catastrophe.

This act heralds Al's encounter with two other survivors: a young woman, Joanne (Alison Routledge), with whom he enjoys a lyrical romance before the appearance of Api (Peter Smith), a Maori, who, like Joanne, questions the whole apparatus of white patriarchal scientific rationalism that has led only to destruction. Api and Zac compete for Joanne; as Martin Blythe observes: "She sleeps with each man once, and in a sense she could stand in for the body of New Zealand, torn between the two essentialisms, Pakeha and Maori."[20] But Zac's Pakeha identity is complex and unstable. In particular he is disconcerted by his inability to handle solitude and loneliness, wracked by a corrosive and paranoid solipsism in which he feels that Joanne and Api "have known each other a long, long time, as though I am the victim of some huge conspiracy." In a desperate act of heroism, Zac explodes a truckload of dynamite at the research station, which only precipitates the next stage of his journey. He wakes on a deserted beach, gazing out on an alien universe, now indeed the ultimate "man alone." Such a chilling conclusion may symbolize the loss of

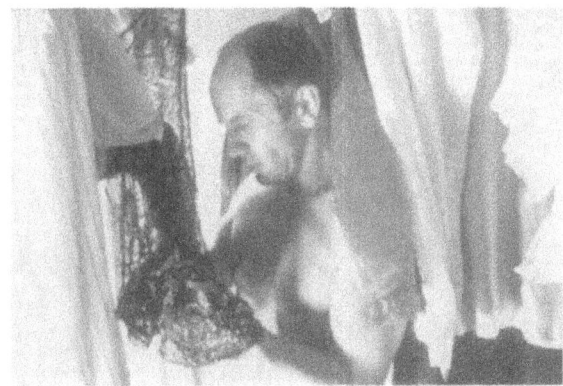

Near breakdown, Zac (Lawrence) explores the boundaries of self-identity in *The Quiet Earth*. (Courtesy New Zealand Film Commission.)

hegemony of the Pakeha male, unequipped emotionally for change and renewal.

The Quiet Earth was generally very well received, as was Lawrence's performance. The *Los Angeles Times*' reviewer enthused about Lawrence's "muscular body... brooding intelligent eyes... magnificent onstage presence... electrifying screen face."[21] Lawrence received the Best Actor award at the 1986 Rome International Fantasy Film Festival and also in the New Zealand Gofta Awards, where he shared another award for best screenplay adaptation. Differences over the film had, however, ended Lawrence's twenty-year association with Geoff Murphy, the most important creative partnership in New Zealand cinema.

Beyond the Kiwi Bloke?

After the success of *The Quiet Earth*, Lawrence had become over exposed nationally. As his biographer argues, in such a small country as New Zealand that scorns familiarity and has a tradition of knocking homegrown talent, this was an insurmountable problem that Lawrence himself acknowledged, conscious of the hostility of the "trendy media in Auckland."[22] Unwilling to go to America where his reputation meant little, Lawrence pursued his career in Australia, making eight feature films and a very successful television series, *Frontline* (1994), over the next eight years. He returned to New Zealand in 1993 to make *Jack Be Nimble*, a psychological horror-thriller, working with a gay writer-director, Garth Maxwell, and playing a role that could be identified as the SNAG (Sensitive New Age

Sensitive and caring, Teddy (Lawrence) transforms the characteristics of the New Zealand male in *Jack Be Nimble*. (Courtesy New Zealand Film Commission.)

Guy), one of the range of new male types that had developed in the space created by the declining cultural force of the "man alone" archetype. Jock Phillips argues that the archetype's cultural hegemony had been eroded by various emergent forces: increasing urbanization facilitating the growth of a more sophisticated, cosmopolitan, urban professional class, the emergence of gay cultures, increased political liberalism that was more sympathetic to Maori rights and, above all, by women's greater independence and presence in the workforce bolstered by the growth of a feminist movement hostile to the Kiwi bloke's macho aggression and domestic violence.[23] In the film industry too, as Russell Campbell notes, the hegemonic grip of the Pakeha male had weakened and that "as a normative archetype the Kiwi bloke is dead" in New Zealand cinema after the mid-1980s.[24]

Lawrence's character Teddy in *Jack Be Nimble* retains the traditional self-reliance of the "man alone" but with the SNAG's capacity to be in touch with his feelings and women's needs. Teddy, solitary, mysterious, and alternative middle class, is the lover of Dora (Sarah Smuts-Kennedy), abandoned, like her younger brother Jack (Alexis Arquette), by her natural parents but separated from him during adoption. Possessed of psychic powers, Dora and Jack form two halves of a single personality that cannot survive alone. Jack is permanently damaged through his upbringing by a heartless farming couple, who, looking for a strong, bovine male who can handle rough work and compensate them for their four daughters, attempt to crush Jack's "feminine" sensitivity through repeated humiliations and beatings. Jack's drunken, brutal stepfather (Tony Barry) is the degraded form of the Kiwi bloke, the "backblocks cockie," in his filthy balaclava. Jack eventually escapes and is reunited with Dora but sees himself as the implacable rival of Teddy for his sister's love. Teddy is instinctively hostile to his competitor, revealing an unsettling capacity for anger and potential violence, but is more concerned with nurturing Dora through to her own spiritual and emotional fulfillment. Lawrence, who insisted on creating a more compassionate character than the director had intended, saw Teddy as "the vehicle for Dora's growth and understanding of herself... the psychic force that exposes Dora to the potential of her powers."[25] After Jack's witch-like stepsisters kill both males in revenge for their parents' deaths, Dora remains ensconced in Teddy's house and pregnant with his child, but supported by her biological mother, another victim of male brutality. Dora is happy and confident about the future, assuring the unborn baby that her strength will "get him across the bridge," to achieve the self-assured manhood that her brother was denied. This is a powerful image of a new social order in which women are psychologically stronger and more capable than men, reversing traditional gender politics and leaving even the reconstructed "man alone" a marginal figure.

Jack Be Nimble was Bruno Lawrence's last New Zealand film. Returning to Australia to work on *Cosi* in early 1995, he collapsed on the set and died a few months later in New Zealand from inoperable lung cancer at the age of fifty-four. Lawrence was never an international star, and in those productions with marked foreign investment or presence—*Race for the Yankee Zephyr* (1981), *Battletruck* (1982), or *The Sinking of the Rainbow Warrior* (1992)—he played supporting roles, outranked by George Peppard, Michael Beck, and Jon Voight, or fellow countryman Sam Neill. His incarnation of the modern "man alone" was a *nationally specific* archetype rather than one composed for global consumption. But Lawrence was one of a select few stars who are genuinely iconic, who condense into their persona the varied forces that make up a particular cultural moment.[26] Lawrence was central to the development of a fledgling national cinema through his ability to represent and also to reconstruct the lineaments of the Pakeha male as it entered an era of profound, if uncertain, change.

Notes

1. For discussions of cultural archetypes as complex, mutable signifiers that evolve within specific national and historical contexts, see Graham Dawson, *Soldier Heroes: British Adventure, Empire, and the Imagining of Masculinities* (London: Routledge, 1994), and Andrew Spicer, *Typical Men: The Representation of Masculinity in Popular British Cinema* (London: I. B. Tauris, 2001).
2. For a more detailed study, see Andrew Spicer, *An Ambivalent Archetype: Masculinity, Performance, and the New Zealand Films of Bruno Lawrence* (Nottingham: Kakapo Books, 2000). See also Roger Booth, *Bruno: The Bruno Lawrence Story* (Christchurch: Canterbury University Press, 1999), and the documentary *Nu-*

mero Bruno (2000). Geoff Murphy did not appear in this documentary, but his *Blerta Revisited* was released in 2001.

3. Sally J. Morgan, "The Ghost in the Luggage: Wallace and *Braveheart,* Post-Colonial 'Pioneer' Identities," *European Journal of Cultural Studies* 2, no. 3 (1999): 375–92.

4. See Lyndsay Head, "Culture on the Fault Line," in *Pakeha: The Quest for Identity in New Zealand,* ed. Michael King (Auckland: Penguin, 1991), 22–34; Claudia Bell, *Inventing New Zealand: Everyday Myths of Pakeha Identity* (Auckland: Penguin, 1996), 28–54.

5. Jock Phillips, *A Man's Country? The Image of the Pakeha Male—A History* (Auckland: Penguin, 1996), 80.

6. John Mulgan, *Man Alone* (Harmondsworth: Penguin, 1990). Frank Sargeson's novels and short stories, very popular in the 1940s and 1950s, also perpetuated this myth.

7. Russell Campbell, "Smith & Co.: The Cinematic Redefinition of Pakeha Male Identity," *Illusions* 7 (March 1988): 19. Article revised and reprinted as "The Kiwi Bloke: The Representation of Pakeha Masculinity in New Zealand Film," in *Contemporary New Zealand Cinema,* ed. Ian Conrich and Stuart Murray (Detroit: Wayne State University Press, forthcoming).

8. Booth, *Bruno: The Bruno Lawrence Story,* 76.

9. Interview in *Numero Bruno.*

10. Quoted in Booth, *Bruno: The Bruno Lawrence Story,* 303.

11. Quoted in ibid., 301.

12. Martin Blythe, *Naming the Other: Images of the Maori in New Zealand Film and Television* (Metuchen, NJ: Scarecrow, 1994), 242.

13. Nick Roddick, "*Utu,*" *Monthly Film Bulletin* 613 (February 1985): 61.

14. Booth, *Bruno: The Bruno Lawrence Story,* 203.

15. *New York Daily News,* quoted in ibid., 212.

16. Nick Roddick, "New Zealand: Taking Off?" *Films and Filming* 333 (June 1982): 12.

17. For a discussion of Baxter, see Kai Jensen, *Whole Men: The Masculine Tradition in New Zealand Literature* (Auckland: Auckland University Press, 1996), 127–48.

18. For a discussion of these issues, see Roy Smith, "New Zealand and the Nuclear-Free Pacific: The History and the Legacy," in *New Zealand—A Pastoral Paradise?,* ed. Ian Conrich and David Woods (Nottingham: Kakapo Books, 2000), 11–30.

19. Interview by Lawrence Van Gelder, *New York Times,* March 28, 1986. British Film Institute (BFI) microfiche for Bruno Lawrence.

20. Blythe, *Naming the Other,* 201.

21. Quoted in Booth, *Bruno: The Bruno Lawrence Story,* 238.

22. Quoted in ibid., 263; see also 284.

23. See Phillips, *A Man's Country,* 267–79.

24. Russell Campbell, "Dismembering the Kiwi Bloke: Representations of Masculinity in *Braindead, Desperate Remedies,* and *The Piano,*" *Illusions* 24 (Spring 1995): 9. Article revised and reprinted as "The Kiwi Bloke: The Representation of Pakeha Masculinity in New Zealand Film," in *Contemporary New Zealand Cinema,* ed. Conrich and Murray.

25. Studio publicity, February 1994, included on the BFI microfiche for Lawrence.

26. See Will Holtzman, "Toward an Actor-Icon Theory," *Journal of Popular Film* 4, no. 1 (1975): 77–80.

Bruno Lawrence—Filmography

1966. *Dr Brunovski* (NZ short film: actor).
1966. *Ten on the Town* (Australia television series: musician).
1967. *Hurry Hurry Faster Faster* (NZ short film: co-director, actor).
1970. *Tank Busters* (NZ extended short film: actor).
1970. *Time Out* (NZ television drama in the *Survey* series: actor).
1971. *Pukemanu* (NZ television six-part series, 1st season: actor).
1974. *Von Tempsky* (NZ television drama-documentary: actor).
1974. *Percy the Policemen* (NZ television six-part children's series: actor, musician). Series not broadcast.
1974/75. *A Pig in a Poke* (Australia television series: actor).
1975. *Close to Home* (NZ television soap opera: actor).
1975. *Tully* (Australia television film: actor).
1976. ***Blerta*** (NZ television six-part series: co-producer, co-writer, actor).
1976. *Epidemic* (NZ television series: actor).
1977. *Scooby Doo* (NZ television short presentation of the Limbs Dance Company: musician).
1977. ***Wild Man*** (NZ feature film: co-producer, co-writer, actor).
1978. *Charlie Horse* (NZ extended short film: musician).
1978. *All Things Being Equal* (NZ live television sit-com: actor).
1979. *The Neville Purvis Family Show* (NZ television six-part series: actor).
1979. *The Mad Dog Gang Spooks Wilkie, Wink, Wink, and the Wobbler* (NZ children's television drama: actor).
1980. The Crocodiles: "Tears" (NZ music video: actor).
1980. *Beyond Reasonable Doubt* (NZ feature film: actor).
1980. *Goodbye Pork Pie* (NZ feature film: actor)sw.
1981. ***Smash Palace*** (NZ feature film: actor, co-writer).
1981. *Race for the Yankee Zephyr* a.k.a. *Treasure of the Yankee Zephyr* (NZ/Australia feature film: actor).
1982. *Venus Touch* (NZ television drama in the *Loose Enz* series: actor).
1982. *Battletruck* a.k.a. *Warlords of the 21st Century* (NZ feature film: actor).
1982. *Carry Me Back* (NZ feature film: actor).
1982. *A Point of View* (NZ short film: actor).
1982. *Prisoners* (NZ/US unreleased feature film: actor).
1982. *One of Those Blighters.* (NZ television drama: actor).
1982. *A Woman of Good Character* (NZ television drama extended into the 1983 feature film *It's Lizzie to Those Close* a.k.a. *Lizzie*: actor).
1983. *Return to Paradise* (NZ television children's series: actor).
1983. ***Utu*** (NZ feature film: actor).
1983. *Wild Horses* (NZ feature film: actor).
1984. *Mindout* (NZ extended short film: actor).
1984. *Pallet on the Floor* (NZ feature film: music collaborator, actor).
1984. *Death Warmed Up* (NZ feature film: actor).
1984. ***Heart of the Stag*** (NZ feature film: additional writer, actor).

1985. *The Quiet Earth* (NZ feature film: co-writer, actor).
1986. *Bridge to Nowhere* (NZ feature film: actor).
1986. *Special Squad* (Australia television series: actor in the episode "Until Death").
1986. *The Great Bookie Robbery* (Australia television three-part mini-series: actor).
1986. *Pokerface* (Australia television three-part mini-series: actor).
1986. *An Indecent Obsession* (Australia feature film: actor).
1986. *Initiation* a.k.a. *Zoomstone* (Australia feature film: actor).
1987. *As Time Goes By* (Australia feature film: actor).
1988. *Grievous Bodily Harm* a.k.a. *Bodily Harm* (Australia feature film: actor).
1988. *Rikky and Pete* (Australia feature film: actor).
1988. *O'Reilly's Luck* (NZ extended short film: actor).
1988. *The Rainbow Warrior Conspiracy* (NZ/Australia television four-part mini-series: actor).
1989. *The Delinquents* (Australia feature film: actor).
1989. *Night of the Red Hunter* (NZ television series: actor).
1990. *More Winners: Boy Soldiers* (Australia television drama: actor).
1990. *The Rogue Stallion* a.k.a. *Wildfire* (Australia/NZ television film: actor).
1991. *Spotswood* a.k.a. *The Efficiency Expert* (Australia feature film: actor).
1992. *The Sinking of the Rainbow Warrior* a.k.a. *Rainbow Warrior* (NZ/US feature film: actor).
1993. *Jack Be Nimble* (NZ feature film: actor).
1993. *The Feds* (Australia television film: actor).
1993. *Gino* (Australia feature film: actor).
1994. *Frontline* a.k.a. *Behind the Frontline* a.k.a. *Breaking News* (Australia television series: actor).
1995. *Cosi* (Australia feature film: actor—unfinished role due to illness).
2000. *Numero Bruno* (NZ television documentary).
2001. *Blerta Revisited* (compilation film of clips from the *Blerta* television series).
2004. *The Making of Smash Palace* (NZ documentary: featured actor).

12

Working in Close-Up
Jennifer Ward-Lealand, Performance, and Collaborative Film Production

Barbara Cairns

At a moment that may come to mark, with the multiple Oscar success of *The Lord of the Rings: The Return of the King* (2003), the point at which New Zealand film became successfully colonized by Hollywood, it is more important than ever to look again at the evolution of the national film industry and the forces that have shaped it. Most attempts to relate creative biographies to industrial histories have tended to focus on directors and sometimes crew,[1] but there is a strong case for shifting attention to actors as their careers often traverse a greater diversity of genres and production contexts. Given that scant attention has also been paid to women actors in surveys of the local film industry, this essay will focus on Jennifer Ward-Lealand, who has worked regularly in film for nearly twenty years, from the mid-1980s to 2004, during the New Zealand industry's most prolific phase of production.

The range of roles Ward-Lealand has been offered, and the changing circumstances under which the films she has appeared in were made, provide a particularly useful vantage point from which to chart general shifts in the industry and the problems it has encountered. Within New Zealand, Ward-Lealand is known as much for her involvement in local theater and television, but it is her cinema work that has attracted international interest for her award-winning film performances. A commanding screen presence, she is very much part of the New Wave of filmmakers who have brought the industry to the position it occupies today.

Like many other New Zealanders working in film, Ward-Lealand has been sustained for much of her career by a network of contacts, which has provided her with regular opportunities for work, and in which creative solutions have often been deployed to offset limited production budgets. However, the context of New Zealand film production has recently begun to change with a series of notable American production companies and film financiers offering local filmmakers more regular employment and enhanced opportunities to improve their technical skills. Much of this work has been on productions with high production values but little cultural relevance to New Zealand. This is especially so of Peter Jackson's *The Lord of the Rings* trilogy. Based on an allegory of "middle" England (Middle Earth), its production, budget, and financing structures have more to do with industrial processes that emanate from Hollywood than ways of working generated from within the local industry. Debates about the economic and technical benefits of a closer working relationship with Hollywood are less significant, however, than discussion of the cultural fallout of shifting conditions of production.

Gaylene Preston, in a prescient comment in the mid-1980s, foresaw the direction in which the national industry might develop and the threats that might be posed to indigenous stories:

> I don't think we have fully appreciated our superior international position. New Zealand filmmakers are still in control of their own product. That is a luxury in most other, more established film communities. It is what makes our films unique. Unfortunately, certain economic "realities" make it only a matter of time before businessmen control filmmaking in this country also. I can't help feeling that a certain cultural insecurity also contributes. I believe we should be consciously and purposefully doing our best to swim against the tide, remembering that small is beautiful.[2]

Twenty years later, New Zealand filmmakers are increasingly being forced to confront these questions of cultural significance and economic advantage in the choice of films they make and to choose between: "swim[ming] against the tide" with films firmly anchored in local experience; making only those films that can be financed offshore; or, like Ward-Lealand, looking to speak to and represent a New Zealand audience in film, while taking advantage of the opportunities offered by an increasingly globalized industry.

The New Zealand New Wave

An experienced theater actor by the time she began working in film, Ward-Lealand's first major film role, as Raewyn, in Gregor Nicholas's short, *Danny and Raewyn* (1986), came at a moment when the New Zealand film industry had re-invented itself. A group of young, male filmmakers from the Pakeha (European) community, many of them part of the country's counter culture, had successfully re-launched feature film production, after the heroic but minimal output of the 1950s and 1960s.[3] Supported by wives and friends, filmmakers such as Roger Donaldson and Geoff Murphy, described by Geoff Steven as "Cowboys of Culture" in his television documentary of the same name, had brought to the screen a collection of largely action-based movies held together by stories of men, in town and country, creating mayhem.[4] As Sam Neill comments, in his and Judy Rymer's controversial documentary account of New Zealand film history, *Cinema of Unease: A Personal Journey* (1995), they were the kinds of films "that would give the grown ups the maximum discomfort."[5]

The exuberance and energy of these films did not, however, mask either their sexism or their monocultural perspectives. Steven, in a pragmatic, unreconstructed summing up of the critical and financial success of Murphy's road movie, *Goodbye Pork Pie* (1980),[6] captures the prevailing attitude of the time: "*Pork Pie* validated hoonism.[7] It captured a Kiwi myth that we were an anti-establishment society. It sold a lot of Minis and also returned money for its investors. It was a successful film."[8]

It was some years after the establishment of the New Zealand Film Commission in 1977 before women or Maori were able to gain access to feature filmmaking resources, but two films produced in the mid-1980s, Melanie Read's *Trial Run*[9] (1984) and Gaylene Preston's *Mr Wrong* (1985),[10] drew attention to the masculine self-indulgence these "man alone" (or men alone) films had so ardently celebrated and, in turn, signaled the arrival of a New Wave of writers and directors with more diverse perspectives on New Zealand life. Both films are thrillers and, in different ways, attempted to subvert the codes of the genre. The concept of Read's film was the more daring as it focused not on the unknown, external danger to women, which the thriller uses most potently, but on threats within the family.

Preston and her producer, Robin Laing, experienced difficulty not only in financing *Mr Wrong* but also in bringing it to an audience.[11] Nonetheless, the film, together with *Trial Run*, marked a turning point in the development of New Zealand cinema. From this moment on, the centrality of the white, male hero or anti-hero and the use of "the landscape as a metaphor for a psychological interior . . . the darker heart of the menacing land" was, if not displaced, then constantly undermined.[12] It was not that the climate changed overnight. There were plenty more Boys' Own films in the can, in production and in development, but these two films set the scene for more nuanced and challenging psychological portraits of both men and women in stories set, as often as not, in towns and in cities.

Ward-Lealand's Beginnings in Film

Ward-Lealand's film career began during this period. Raised in a musical and artistic family, her interest in theater had begun early. At the age of seven, her father took her to a rehearsal for an amateur production of *Oedipus*. Sensing "something in the air" she went home announcing a desire to become an actor.[13] At the age of nineteen, working with "The Town and Country Players," she toured New Zealand undertaking a broad range of roles in clown shows, musicals, and drama: "We'd go into these small farming communities and set up in the country hall. The community would bring a potluck dinner and we'd do an evening of theater for them, which was brilliant! It gave me a certain robust approach to work. You know, you do everything yourself."[14] A more formal training at Theatre Corporate's Drama School in Auckland gave her "a very disciplined approach to work" and led to employment both in the main company and its subsidiary Theatre in Education.[15] By the time she began acting in film, when she was twenty-two, she had played a number of leading dramatic roles, including Hedda in Ibsen's *Hedda Gabler*.

The part of Raewyn in *Danny and Raewyn* offered something different. *Danny and Raewyn* was one of seven half-hour dramas, shot on film but made for television, in the 1986 *About Face* series. Produced by Bridget Ikin and John Maynard, it provided, according to Roger Horrocks, "a showcase for a new generation of filmmakers."[16] Written by Gregor Nicholas, Anne Kennedy, and Frank Stark, the film offers a sympathetic and sensitive view of a disintegrating marriage against the backdrop of working-class life in Auckland's poorest suburbs. With two small children and a limited income Danny (Peter Stevens) and Raewyn turn increasingly away from each other to pleasures outside the home: Danny to renovating a classic Plymouth Belvedere and Raewyn to netball and a part-time job as a confectionery assistant. Alienated by his menial job in a paper-pulping factory and by a lack of money, Danny spends every free moment restoring his magnificent blue car: "Original—all factory parts and American specs. Just like she rolled off the production line in Detroit." Raewyn, meanwhile, enjoys the conversation and support of the other women at work. Frustrated by Danny's unwillingness to communicate and by his obsession with the car, she finally leaves. In a frenzy of rage Danny then wrecks the car with a wrench.

In its spare script, authentic set design, and accomplished direction, the film offered an insight into themes, characters, and locations rarely portrayed on either New Zealand's small or big screens up to that point. Ward-Lealand's performance as the disappointed young wife and mother, ruefully finishing wedding cakes with icing-sugar flowers and bride-and-groom dolls, is understated and poignant. As Danny, Peter Stevens's performance is also strong, and Ward-Lealand attributes part of the success of the film to the good working relationship and dynamic the two developed in rehearsal, as well as to the ability to shoot the script in play form since the actors were not greatly familiar with film production techniques at this time.[17]

Ward-Lealand's and Stevens's next appearance together in the feature *Dangerous Orphans* (1986), directed by John Laing and written by Kevin Smith, was less successful. The performances in the film are constrained by a rambling script about revenge, drugs, and murder, in which Stevens plays the central character, O'Malley, and Ward-Lealand, Teresa Costello, a nightclub singer and pianist. Helen Martin describes the dialogue as "awkward and over-written" and the structure as problematic: "[T]oo much of the complicated plot is revealed in obviously explanatory conversations and, because the flashbacks explaining the vendetta are placed well into the narrative, the start is an overloaded blur."[18]

The main difficulty with the film is that it apes the Hollywood action genre in which the special effects and fast-moving plot require considerable financial resources. Nonetheless, *Dangerous Orphans* is notable for the skill of some of these action sequences and for the performance of Michael Hurst as Moir, one of O'Malley's two close friends. Ward-Lealand attributes her own uneven performance in the film to "lack of experience,"[19] but the character she plays is severely limited as the stereotypical girlfriend, whose relationship with O'Malley appears secondary to his need to avenge his father's murder.

New Opportunities and Networks

After this low-key feature-film debut, Ward-Lealand returned to the theater, developing her abilities as an ensemble actor in collaborations with Don McGlashan and Harry Sinclair who, in The Front Lawn, created innovative stage shows around songs and sketches linked loosely by a narrative. Ward-Lealand had known Sinclair since she was a teenager in Wellington and then had worked with him at Theatre Corporate. She had known McGlashan in the context of the Wellington music scene and had also been his next-door neighbor. When McGlashan and Sinclair were considering expanding their show's range of characters, they were keen for Ward-Lealand to join them. Quickly establishing herself within the show, she went on tour with them, throughout New Zealand, and also toured Britain, the United States, and Australia, as Glenda in *The One That Got Away*. This play with music, about a man and a woman who meet on a plane coming from Sydney, was The Front Lawn's first narrative piece.[20]

Theatrical work with The Front Lawn led to an opportunity to perform in the group's third film, *Linda's Body* (1990). The short film is a finely observed urban comedy touching lightly on the profound: in this case, death and loss. Ward-Lealand, as the central character, Linda, whose "out-of-body experience" is the subject of the film, demonstrates a growing confidence in the film medium in a delicately judged performance. The narrative revolves around Linda's metaphysical reunion with her dead lover in which she "lets him go" so as to get on with the rest of her life. Set in Auckland, the film gives the lie to clichés about alienation and menace as predominant themes in New Zealand culture. Its cyclical structure is typical of The Front Lawn's first short films, *Walk Short* (1987) and *Lounge Bar* (1988), while its sexual obsessions and satirical style look forward to Harry Sinclair's later features, *Topless Women Talk about Their Lives* (1997), *The Price of Milk* (2000), and *Toy Love* (2003).

The creative collaboration, which marked *The Front Lawn*'s stage shows and films, was a hallmark of New Zealand's small film industry at the time and in many ways characterizes the ethos of the country as a whole. Relative isolation has generated close networks of contacts and friendships in all areas of work and social life. Ward-Lealand refers to the local industry as members of "the film family":[21] "Wherever you work there's someone you've worked with before somewhere. So you can have these little families of film experience . . . and keep meeting up with them again."[22] These close relationships are what have sustained local writers, directors, and technicians and allowed them to develop their skills when they have been successful in securing further work. In some cases they have even been the inspiration for film.

Grand Designs and Small Budgets

The Director of Photography for *Linda's Body* was Leon Narbey, who at the time of the film's making had been developing his own second feature, *The Footstep Man* (1992); he had been drawn to its two main themes while working on the earlier *Illustrious Energy* (1988). Production designer Janelle Aston had interested Narby in the paintings, lithographs, and drawings of Henri Toulouse-Lautrec, while sound recordist Bob Allen had sparked his imagination in the work of the foley artist, or footstepper.[23] At the time the film was being developed, sound recording was changing from analogue to digital and Narbey conceived the film as an homage to sprocket technology.[24]

The story of *The Footstep Man* focuses on a sound recordist who works on a film about Toulouse-Lautrec and Mireille, his prostitute friend and model. Mireille wishes to escape the brothel, and Toulouse-Lautrec offers her financial help. Her hopes are dashed, however, when she discovers she has syphilis, a condition she believes she has contracted from him. Returning to work after a personal crisis, to create the effects-track for the film, the sound recordist, Sam (Steven Grives), becomes increasingly obsessed by the Mireille character. Distressed by the film's denouement, in which Mireille commits suicide, Sam pleads with the director, Vida (Rosy Jones), to change the film's ending.

As a result of their work together on *Linda's Body*, Narbey offered Ward-Lealand the dual role of Mireille and actor Sarah. Ward-Lealand loved working on the project and found the character of Mireille particularly appealing. "She is the one I really associated with."[25] As a woman fired up by the promise of freedom but seemingly betrayed by the man who offers her escape, Ward-Lealand is able to demonstrate the full range of her acting abilities. She is alternately bold, ambitious, sensitive, warm, angry, maudlin, and passionate. In the denouement, Vida allows Mireille to take her fate into her own hands by rejecting suicide despite her illness.

The Footstep Man is an ambitious project. Its original structure, based on a film-within-a-film, was more complex than any that had been attempted in local cinema to this point. However, producer John Maynard's decision, for budgetary reasons, to reduce its length by twenty minutes, just before shooting began, severely altered its intricate architecture. The role of the producer, Walter, was written out. Martin Edmond, Narbey's co-writer, comments that this undermines the role of Vida, the director character: "[Walter] would have restored Vida's character to a kind of credibility I think she lacks.... There's still the strand where Vida goes through a journey herself and realizes there's another way of finishing the film, but it's uni-dimensional because it's lost the notion of the way commercial decisions bear in on the creative process. It gives the false idea that the director has autonomy."[26]

Ward-Lealand acknowledged that "it wasn't necessarily the film we started with."[27] Because of the changes, the historical film gains greater overall significance and the final cut is strangely lopsided. The production and costume design, by Kai Hawkins and Barbara Darragh, are both impressive and remarkable given the limited budget, and Ward-Lealand herself found these elements of the film-within-the-film invaluable assistance to the actors in portraying the world of nineteenth-century bohemian Paris.[28] Despite the film's structural problems, it is also memorable for its lighting design by Allen Guilford and for the ambitious camera choreography in the "dream" sequences set in the brothel.

The problems Maynard encountered in producing *The Footstep Man* clearly highlight the fragility of the local film industry at the time and the difficulties of raising sufficient capital to sustain productions with even modest budgets. The movie was made for about NZ$2.5 million, but its structure and plot, according to Edmond, needed a sum twice this amount.[29]

Working in Close-Up

The Footstep Man confirmed Ward-Lealand's charisma as a screen actor. In part, the intensity and power of her screen presence comes from her enjoyment and command of film's technical needs and the intellectual challenges these present: "What I like about film acting is being able not only to fulfill what your character needs and what fellow actors need but the ten other things you're meant to remember: your lights, your position, your mark, making sure you're not moving too wildly so that the focus puller's having to adjust all the time, your props, your drink, all that kind of thing. Now, sometimes, it's impossible to remember all those things but it's damn fine when you can do that *and* fulfill what you want emotionally for the character."[30] This understanding of the collaborative relations involved in production and the need to serve fellow actors, crew, and director, many of whom are familiar from other projects, while fulfilling the intentions of the script, gives her relationship with the camera a particular intimacy: "There is a camera a foot away. I can hear the camera turning over. I can hear the film turning in the camera and everything is sort of heightened, heightened and delicate at the same time. That is what you don't get in the theater—the sense of those big close-ups."[31] She acknowledges that actors, crew, and director all become acutely aware when a scene is working well: "It's a really fantastic feeling when you have felt it click there in your heart and it's clicked there for everybody else. If there's a collective response from everyone within the room in which you're shooting that will hopefully have the same feeling for the audience."[32]

This ability to play to the camera and crew as if they are the audience produced a strong performance in her next film, *Desperate Remedies* (1993). Written and directed by Stewart Main and Peter Wells, it marks another departure in subject matter and style from the nationally self-conscious New Zealand films celebrated by Neill in *Cinema of Unease*. Main and Wells's two short films for the Ikin and Maynard *About Face* series—*My First Suit* (1985), about a young boy's growing acceptance of his homosexual identity, and *Jewel's Darl* (1985), a stylish and tender insight into the life of the New Zealand gay and transvestite community—had been important contributions to local film culture because they were among the first to successfully deal with these themes.

Set in a mythical frontier town sometime during New Zealand's colonial period, *Desperate Remedies* is full of delightful allusions to English literature and to some of the great cinema melodramas. The heroine, Dorothea Brook (Ward-Lealand), whose name is taken from George Eliot's *Middlemarch*, is, like Mireille in *The Footstep Man*, another woman "desperate" to control her own destiny. In the rapacious climate of the new colony everyone is either out to make their fortune or to escape their past. Dorothea wants to do both. Providing fine clothes for settler women, as a Draper of Distinction, she has acquired a small fortune. She and her lover and assistant, Anne Cooper (Lisa Chappell), wish to extricate Dorothea's sister, Rose (Kiri Mills), from a disastrous relationship with the villainous Fraser (Cliff Curtis), by whom Dorothea has once been pregnant. They offer newly arrived immigrant Lawrence Hayes (Kevin Smith) both land and gold as an incentive to marry the pregnant and drug-addicted Rose, but not before he himself falls in love with Dorothea. Believing she reciprocates his feelings, he is devastated when Dorothea marries corrupt politician William Poyser (Michael Hurst), as a cover for her own secret love. Lawrence marries Rose but she dies of typhoid. Fraser leaves for San Francisco but, returning two years later, is shot by the jealous Anne. Meanwhile, Lawrence returns for Dorothea. In a cleverly sustained denouement, Dorothea chooses Anne rather than Lawrence and the two women then sail off into the future together.

The plot is constructed around a number of different emotional entanglements. Characters conceal their intentions and feelings while trying to manipulate one another to achieve their ends. The script has all the stock elements of melodrama, including unrequited love, dark secrets, blackmail, money, and murder. At the same time, its sub-themes focus more daringly on the underbelly of colonial life, its sex, drugs, and corruption, and a dramatic operatic score underpins the whole film.

Ward-Lealand gives a striking performance as Dorothea and, despite the histrionic plot, plays the role with psychological credibility and depth. She is convincing as the character desired by all the others but who, unswervingly, follows her own heart. Commenting on her performance she says: "We never saw it as melodrama. We never saw it as anything but as real as we could be. We just entered into that world."[33] Ward-Lealand admired the performance of her equally charismatic leading man, Kevin Smith and was also impressed by the very precise and clear direction of Main and Wells in their work with the actors.[34] They allowed a lengthy rehearsal period and asked the actors to view a number of films that provide some of the stylistic and thematic reference points for the project, such as Michael Powell's and Emeric Pressberger's *The Red Shoes* (1948), William Wyler's *The Heiress* (1949), and Luchino Visconti's *Senso* (1954).

As with most New Zealand films, *Desperate Remedies* was produced on a small budget (of just over NZ$2 million) but, in this case, the directors turned the melodramatic context of the film to their advantage. A large warehouse on the Auckland waterfront became the location and, within this enclosed space, they created the artificial world of the film. The limited budget precluded expensive special effects and shot set-ups, produc-

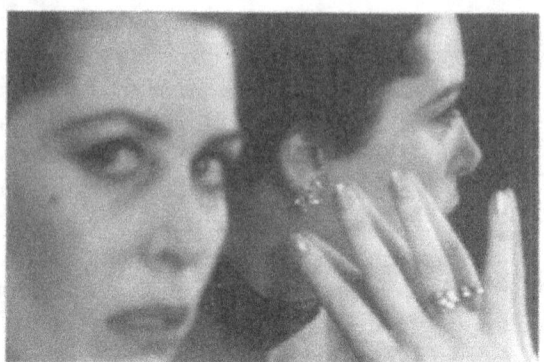

The passionate intensity of the female lead: Jennifer Ward-Lealand as Dorothea in *Desperate Remedies*. (Courtesy New Zealand Film Commission.)

ing creative solutions that drew on the general ability to improvise that characterizes New Zealand's pioneer mentality. Ward-Lealand remembers the shooting of the opening sequence in which Dorothea is required to drive a small carriage, at breakneck speed, down to the port: "There was no horse, there was no carriage. What there was was the grip, under a box, with a blanket over her head, holding the reins; people throwing leaves; a big fan and this contraption that I was standing on being rocked; Peter and Stewart yelling direction; whoever was doing the sound, playing the music really loudly; and me in this rather filthy shed in all my beautiful red finery. It was really marvellous!"[35] The film was officially selected for the Cannes Film Festival in 1993, and Ward-Lealand won an award for Best Actress at the Sitges International Film Festival.

Over the next few years Ward-Lealand played few major film roles but worked instead on a number of short films, many of which have helped nurture new film talent. Often working with quite limited or minimal material, and playing a range of neurotic or disturbed women, Ward-Lealand, nonetheless, manages to invest her characters with an intensity that marks her out as an actor of considerable talent. In one of the most accomplished of these short films, *I'm So Lonesome I Could Cry* (1994), written by Stuart Hoar and Michael Hurst, she plays tragi-comic Jane, the frustrated and unhappily married wife of beach gear salesman Bill Cottisloe, played by Mark Wright. Set on New Year's Day 1960, the first anniversary of the death of country-and-western legend Hank Williams, Bill, suffering from his own acute depression, picks up in his car a "knowing" stranger. Directed by Michael Hurst, the piece wittily evokes the New Zealand 1960s lifestyle with ironic set pieces at the beach, where Jane and Bill spend their honeymoon, and on the New Zealand Railways.

Ward-Lealand plays the cameo role of another unhappily married woman in Dorthe Scheffmann's *The Bar* (1996), and also as the scheming and murderous Lauren in *A Game with No Rules* (1994), directed by Scott Reynolds, a finely paced drama in which a couple exploit a young woman's greed in order to steal her own money. In *The Painted Lady* (1999), Ward-Lealand plays Fay, a disturbed artist, who neglects her small daughter Charlie. Despite some wooden dialogue and the labored central metaphor, which revolves around the transformation of "the Painted Lady" butterfly, from chrysalis to adult, the film is saved by Ward-Lealand's strong performance and by those of child actor Elizabeth Morris (Charlie) and Donagh Rees as her teacher, Miss Robbins.

As has often been the case in Ward-Lealand's film career, acting in one of these short films led to further opportunities. After working with Reynolds on *A Game with No Rules*, she was offered a role in his first feature, *The Ugly* (1997), playing an abusive mother whose cruelty turns her son into a serial killer. Like that of *The Silence of the Lambs* (1991), the narrative of *The Ugly* revolves around attempts by a young woman psychologist to penetrate the mind of a psychopath. After murdering his mother, Simon Cartwright (Paolo Rotondo) has undergone four years of psychiatric treatment but, on release, has committed a number of other murders. At the beginning of the film he is held in a psychiatric prison where he requests an assessment by Dr. Karen Schumaker (Rebecca Hobbs). Self-confident to the point of arrogance, she is cleverly manipulated by Simon and finally becomes one of his victims.

Performances by the principal actors, Rotondo and Hobbs, are strong, as are those by supporting actors Ward-Lealand, Sam Wallace, and Caelem Pope (as the adolescent and child Simon), and Beth Allen (as Simon's teenage friend Julie). However, the film displays a disturbing attitude toward women. The two polarities are the obsessive and crazy mother and the deluded professional woman. Ward-Lealand as Simon's mother, Evelyn, is chillingly dark, severe, and repressed. Despite the strong production design and its use of the primary colors blue and red to flag significant moments in the narrative, its early attempts at satirizing psychiatric care fall badly flat because the killing, which follows aplenty, is all too "real" even though it is presented in flashbacks, or as Simon's fantasy. Despite the limitations of the role as it is written, Ward-Lealand is, nonetheless, convincing as the "mother from hell" who creates a monster.

Controlling Interests and Cultural Relevance

Ward-Lealand's participation in two subsequent feature films once again underlines the precarious nature of the New Zealand film industry at pres-

The mother from hell: Ward-Lealand convinces as Evelyn Cartwright, the manipulative matriarch in *The Ugly*. (Courtesy New Zealand Film Commission.)

ent. Like the rest of the cast and crew of Athina Tsoulis's film *I'll Make You Happy* (1999), she worked for nothing when producer Liz Stevens was unable to raise sufficient production finance. The structure and dialogue of the film, a comedy about a young prostitute, Siggy (Jodie Rimmer), who ends up running her own business, needed further development and, unfortunately, limit the performances of the well-known cast. The film was able to secure funds for post-production but those who worked on it will not be paid until it begins to make money.

In a further sign of the financial difficulties currently facing the New Zealand industry, the film in which Ward-Lealand makes her most recent appearance, *Fracture* (2004), directed by Larry Parr and based on the novel *Crime Story* by Maurice Gee, experienced initial distribution complications following the liquidation of Parr's company, Kahukura Productions. The perennial problem of trying to raise finances in such a small economy are one of the reasons Ward-Lealand is enthusiastic about the involvement in the New Zealand industry by Renaissance Pictures, makers of the television series *Hercules: The Legendary Journeys* and *Xena: Warrior Princess,* in which she has also appeared. It is not just their financial support, however, that makes her so positive. She feels Renaissance Pictures has offered New Zealand actors, directors, and crew a training that enabled many of them to move easily into other large-scale, overseas-financed productions, such as *The Lord of the Rings*.[36]

However, at this point in the development of the national industry, the question that cannot yet be answered is whether offshore finance will still enable stories based specifically on New Zealand cultural experience to be told in a manner that does not jeopardize their uniqueness. The fear is that the movement from financial insecurity to relative stability may prove to be at the expense of the creative networks, ensemble playing, and spirit of improvisation and experiment that have, at their best, produced a body of film work that has brought to the big screen an increasingly diverse range of perspectives on contemporary New Zealand life and its historical roots. Some of the most interesting examples of New Zealand film since the mid-1980s have moved beyond the iconic figure of the "man alone" to explore the lives of women struggling to develop their own sense of self or to explore New Zealand's subcultures. Even so, taken together, this output has been quite small. Gaylene Preston comments in a telling assessment of the industry in 2004, in the context of the box-office success of *The Lord of the Rings* and the critical acclaim of Niki Caro's *Whale Rider* (2002): "It's unfortunate . . . that at the very moment when the world has finally recognized that New Zealand is a filmmaking nation par exellence . . . we haven't got a critical mass in terms of our filmmaking. What we have is excellence, but we haven't got much of it."[37]

Ward-Lealand's screen career demonstrates this very well. Her best work shows the benefits of working with New Zealand material close up, playing to the camera with a sustained intensity knowing that the immediate audience of cast and crew belong to a familiar and known community of friends and colleagues. At the same time, it demonstrates the fragility of the local industry and the scarcity of major roles for actors of her manifest talent, in stories that reflect life in New Zealand as opposed to that in "Middle Earth." The next cycle in the development of the local industry will show whether the interest among the international business community generated by Peter Jackson's Oscar and box-office success will prompt investment in specifically local stories such as *Whale Rider* as enthusiastically as they have supported the global, blockbuster ambitions of *The Lord of the Rings*.

Notes

1. See, for example, Deborah Shepard's *reframing Women: A History of New Zealand Film* (Auckland: HarperCollins, 2000).
2. See Roger Horrocks, "New Zealand Filmmakers at the Auckland City Art Gallery: Gaylene Preston," program notes, November 1, 1984.
3. See John O'Shea, "A Charmed Life: Fragments of Memory," in *Film in Aotearoa New Zealand*, ed. Jonathan Dennis and Jan Bieringa (Wellington: Victoria University Press 1992), 13–35. See also Geoff Murphy, "The End of the Beginning," in ibid., 130–49.
4. *Cowboys of Culture*, television documentary, directed by Geoff Steven, 1991.
5. *Cinema of Unease: A Personal Journey by Sam Neill*, co-directed by Sam Neill and Judy Rymer, 1995.

6. *Goodbye Pork Pie* is a comic road movie in which two men travel the length of New Zealand in a stolen Mini, pursued by the police.
7. "Hoonism" is a New Zealand colloquial expression for raffish or delinquent behavior.
8. Steven, *Cowboys of Culture*.
9. *Trail Run* is the story of a woman photographer, Rosemary Edmunds, who, while on an assignment in an isolated location, and training for a marathon, is terrorized by a mysterious stalker. The film delighted New Zealand female audiences when it was first shown because, though active in the country's vibrant sporting culture, women had never, until then, appeared as film protagonists, let alone as physically strong and capable.
10. Based on the story by Elizabeth Jane Howard, *Mr Wrong* is about a young farm girl, Meg, who has come to the city for work. Attracting the attention of a psychopath, she manages to effect her own rescue from him with the help of the ghost of a woman he has murdered. The film's humor, now a hallmark of Preston's style, challenges stereotypical perceptions of women in its use of language and symbol and offers insights into their ambivalence about love, marriage, and motherhood.
11. Robin Laing gives an account of the difficulties of raising finances for the film in Barbara Cairns and Helen Martin, *Shadows on the Wall: A Study of Seven New Zealand Feature Films* (Auckland: Longman Paul, 1994), 170. The difficulties of exhibiting the film are mentioned in Helen Martin and Sam Edwards, *New Zealand Film, 1912–1996* (Auckland: Oxford University Press, 1997), 118.
12. Neill, *Cinema of Unease: A Personal Journey*.
13. Jennifer Ward-Lealand, interview with author, December 26, 2002.
14. Ibid.
15. Ibid.
16. Roger Horrocks, "New Zealand Cinema: Cultures, Policies, Films," in *Twin Peaks: Australian and New Zealand Feature Films*, ed. Deb Verhoeven (Melbourne: Damned Publishing, 1999), 130.
17. Ward-Lealand, interview with author, December 26, 2002.
18. Martin and Edwards, *New Zealand Film, 1912–1996*, 123.
19. Ward-Lealand, interview with author, December 26, 2002.
20. The central male character of "The One That Got Away" is in therapy; the woman ends up taking him on a road trip, with love winning out. On its national New Zealand tour venues were consistently sold out.
21. Ward-Lealand, interview with author, December 26, 2002.
22. Ibid.
23. Cairns and Martin, *Shadows on the Wall*, 284–85.
24. Ibid., 288–89.
25. Ward-Lealand, interview with author, December 26, 2002.
26. Cairns and Martin, *Shadows on the Wall*, 309.
27. Ward-Lealand, interview with author, December 26, 2002.
28. Ibid.
29. Cairns and Martin, *Shadows on the Wall*, 309.
30. Ward-Lealand, interview with author, December 26, 2002.
31. Ibid.
32. Ibid.

33. Ibid.
34. Ibid.
35. Ibid.
36. Ibid.
37. Quoted in Megan Neil, "After the sequels," *Sydney Morning Herald*, February 25, 2004, 16.

Jennifer Ward-Lealand—Filmography

1972. *Gone Up North for a While* (NZ television drama-documentary: actor).
1978/80. *Close to Home* (NZ television soap opera: actor).
1986. *Seekers* (NZ television series: actor).
1986. ***Danny and Raewyn*** (NZ film/television drama for the *About-Face* series: actor).
1986. ***Dangerous Orphans*** (NZ feature film: actor).
1987. *Kaleidoscope* (NZ television series: presenter).
1990. ***Linda's Body*** (NZ extended short film: actor).
1991. *For the Love of Mike* (NZ television series: actor in episode six).
1992. ***The Footstep Man*** (NZ feature film: actor).
1992. *Open Home* (NZ television lifestyle series: presenter).
1992. *The Billy T. James Show* (NZ television series: actor in episode six).
1993. ***Desperate Remedies*** (NZ feature film: actor).
1993/94. ***Full Frontal*** (Australia television series: actor).
1994. ***I'm So Lonesome I Could Cry*** (NZ short film: actor).
1994. *A Game with No Rules* (NZ short film: actor).
1994. *Heavenly Creatures* (NZ feature film: acting coach).
1995. *Flip and Two Twisters* (NZ television documentary: narrator).
1995. *Hercules: The Legendary Journeys* (US/NZ television series: actor in the episode "All That Glitters").
1995. *Seeing Red* (NZ documentary-drama: narrator).
1995/97. *Letter to Blanchy* (NZ television sit-com series: actor in the episodes "Love Makes the World Wrong," "China Syndrome," and "Garage Sale of the Century").
1996. *The Bar* (NZ short film: actor).
1996. *The Proposal* (NZ short film: actor).
1996/98. *Shortland Street* (NZ television soap opera: actor).
1997. ***The Ugly*** (NZ feature film: actor).
1997. *Xena: Warrior Princess* (US/NZ television series: actor in the episode "The Deliverer").
1998. *Pale Blue* (NZ television drama: actor). Program never broadcast.
1998. *Duggan: Shadow of Doubt* (NZ television film: actor).
1999. *Xena: Warrior Princess* (US/NZ television series: actor in the episode "The Play's the Thing").
1999. ***I'll Make You Happy*** (NZ feature film: actor).
1999. *The Painted Lady* (NZ short film: actor).

2000. *Kiwi Buddha* (NZ television documentary: narrator).
2001. *Tarawera* (NZ documentary: acting voice-over).
2001. *Love Mussel* (NZ television drama: actor).
2001. *Early Days Yet: A Profile of the Poet Allen Curnow* (NZ film/television documentary: narrator).
2003. *Govett-Brewster Gallery* (NZ television documentary: narrator).
2004. *Fracture* (NZ feature film: actor).
2005. *Interrogation* (NZ television series: actor in the episode "True Confessions").
2006. *Elgar's Enigma: Biography of a Concerto* (NZ television documentary: narrator).
2006. *Four Wheel Drive: Danger on the Road* (NZ television documentary for *Inside NZ*: narrator).

Ward-Lealand has provided voice-overs for a number of television and cinema commercials, these include for: Healtheries (2003), BNZ (2003–5), Nescafe (2004), ACC (2004), Auckland Regional Council (2004), Orcon (2005), Ribena (2005), Handy Towels (2006), and Ambipur (2006).

13

Crisis and Conflict
THE FILMS OF JOHN LAING

Ian Conrich

Despite having made only three feature films since 1986, John Laing remains one of New Zealand's most prolific directors. His films—*Beyond Reasonable Doubt* (1980), *The Lost Tribe* (1982; released 1985), *Other Halves* (1984), *Dangerous Orphans* (1986), *Absent without Leave* (1993), *The Shirt* (1999), and *No One Can Hear You* (2001)—appear disparate, but Laing could be viewed as one of a small group of auteurs associated with the New Zealand film industry. And to view Laing as only a movie director ignores his wider screen experience and creativity. In fact, Laing has said, "I'm an editor by trade . . . I've always been aware of what you can do with construction."[1] As variously producer, director, writer, and frequently as editor, he has made in addition to the above movies more than one hundred documentaries, theatrical features, television movies, dramas, and episodes for series, while working in New Zealand, Canada, and the United Kingdom.

Such productivity has generated surprisingly little discussion, leaving Laing often unfairly marginalized within critical debates on New Zealand cinema. Here, the question as to whether Laing is an auteur has never really surfaced, partly because of the perceived lack of connection between his features, but also as a result of his critical neglect. Yet, an analysis of his films reveals strong thematic and ideological consistencies across all of the features. In interviews it is clear, however, that Laing has been largely unaware of such authorial marks within his films; moreover, he feels he has not consciously introduced any links between productions, though he accepts that he has possibly been drawn (even unconsciously) to making a movie for its continuity of a particular subject matter that was of personal interest.[2]

Laing is rarely credited on his feature films as a writer, but he did script *The Lost Tribe*, co-script *No One Can Hear You*, and has had an uncredited role on most of his films. He was also a director-for-hire, brought in once pre-production had commenced, for the films *Beyond Reasonable*

John Laing (*left*) in consultation over the script on the set of *Absent without Leave*. (Courtesy New Zealand Film Commission.)

Doubt and *Other Halves*, but *The Lost Tribe* and *Absent without Leave* were developed from Laing's own initial research and personal commitment to a story. Furthermore, *The Shirt* is an ultra-low-budget production filmed on digital video; it has an R18 (restricted) rating and has been exhibited only at select festivals, but it appears to be Laing's most treasured and heartening film experience and is arguably the central text within his oeuvre.[3] Any consideration of Laing as an auteur will see these as contradictions, though this cannot obscure the recognition that existing within his films are the recurrent themes of crisis and conflict: a depiction of the dysfunctional family, broken and in crisis; of individuals in conflict with society; and of those institutions with a responsibility for maintaining law and order failing to work within determined boundaries. True, such tensions are there in quite a number of other contemporary New Zealand films,[4] but Laing's narratives are thrillers and melodramas that are unusual within the national production context for being predominantly urban-centered. Usually within these genres the protagonists are either pursuers, or are pursued themselves in a search for truth or justice, identity and belonging, with a demonstrated desire to be either included within the dominant community or removed. Four of the productions are based on true stories, and as screen studies of hegemony and society it will be apparent that these movies, most of which were part of New Zealand's film New Wave of the late 1970s and mid-1980s, offer crucial and critical views on a developing cultural identity.

Beyond Feature Film Directing

A significant number of the New Zealand filmmakers who were to define local film production of the 1970s and 1980s were born within the immediate postwar period and within just a few years of one another: such filmmakers include Roger Donaldson (1945), Geoff Murphy (1946), John Reid (1946), Sam Pillsbury (1946), Geoff Steven (1946), Leon Narbey (1947), and Gaylene Preston (1947). Laing was born in 1948 and with his feature films of the early 1980s became part of a new film culture that was fueled by the energy and resourcefulness of a community committed to local cinematic expression. It is noticeable that many of the filmmakers of the New Zealand New Wave were young—in their early to mid-thirties—with the apparent vibrancy of this period partly a result of youth, but also due to the diversity in the different filmmakers' artistic interests and educational backgrounds.

Laing, like his contemporary Bruce Morrison, grew up in Dunedin and attended local Otago University. He graduated in 1968 with a BA in English and History, and already had a yearning for film school, of which there was no such facility in New Zealand; he liked the look of a film school in Rome but it was "a little out of my price range."[5] Laing had educated himself on world cinema, especially European and (where possible) Japanese movies, while in Dunedin, and was a regular at The State: "It was a great theater—a real fleapit, full of people in dufflecoats who'd read Dostoyevsky at half time!"[6] He joined the local newspaper, *The Evening Star*, as sub-editor, but stayed for only two months before moving to Wellington to begin work in late 1968 as a production trainee at the National Film Unit (NFU). Initially this meant a range of supporting roles, which as Laing recalls saw him employed "as an assistant grip, an assistant gaffer . . . I carried gear, I did this and that, got people cups of tea."[7] Within months, however, he was given the opportunity to direct his first film, *And Now New Zealand* (1970), a tourist documentary, in the mold of the NFU's recognized output of publicity shorts, promoting aspects of a national identity and a distinct culture. Laing describes the experience as being "thrown in at the deep end" and as a "baptism by fire."[8] He learned quickly and directed four more short documentaries in his two years at the NFU: *Kariotahi Beach* (1971), in which three Waikato men fish using innovative methods; *Picnic* (1970), which focuses on New Zealanders picnicking on the beach on a Sunday afternoon; *Bananas for Market* (1971), an educational documentary intended for Pacific Islanders, which details the processing of their bananas for exporting through New Zealand; and *Trotting* (1972), a short about equestrianism.

The NFU and Pacific Films were the two main film production houses in New Zealand, postwar and prior to the emergence of the New Wave. Both presented opportunities for film training, and it was here that filmmakers such as Preston, Barry Barclay, Pillsbury, Sam Neill, and Paul Maunder, who were to make their feature debuts in the 1970s or 1980s, had their formative years within the local industry. The two production houses were based in the Wellington area and as Laing recalls, "whenever we met in the pub there was always an element of antagonism between us."[9] Laing perhaps was based in the wrong camp, as his desire for a more overt artistic interpretation of a story would have been better appreciated at Pacific. His respect for Japanese cinema—"I love the formality . . . the simplicity and directness of the narrative, the dramatic conflicts of character"[10]—was closer to the art cinema interests of Pacific filmmakers such as John O'Shea and Roger Mirams, who were influenced by the poetry of Italian Neorealism and the modernity of 1960s Italian and French cinema. The one film that Laing directed while at the NFU, which he considered "worthwhile at the time," was the ten-minute short *Kariotahi Beach*.[11] The documentary was, compared to other NFU productions, experimental, uniquely devoid of any narration, with fishermen working mostly in silence composed in expressive shots. The film "created an absolute outrage at the Film Unit," and Laing was rebuked for making "pseudo-Japanese bullshit."[12] He realized his future was not at the NFU, and in 1972 he left for England, a destination well traveled by other aspiring New Zealand filmmakers of the time. The modernist *Kariotahi Beach* was unfortunately released locally as the first half of a bill with the British saucy comedy *Carry on up the Khyber* (1968).

Between 1972 and 1975, Laing worked for the BBC in London and Bristol editing programs such as *Collector's World*, with Arthur Negus. He also worked for companies such as Apple Films, where he edited the Ringo Starr produced documentary *Chain of the Sun* (1974), an ethnographic film set in Sulawesi, Indonesia. In 1975, he traveled to Canada, where he was employed by the National Film Board (NFB) and it was here, for the first time, that he felt support for his work. Ironically, it was *Kariotahi Beach* that secured him the post. Within a three-year period, Laing worked as an editor (and quite often writer) on ten documentaries for the NFB and on five documentaries for other Canadian producers. He was also editor and co-writer for a feature length drama, *The Rubber Gun* (1976), a film concerning a group of Montreal-based drug addicts, which Laing views as a precedent to *The Shirt*, with its Wellington-set culture of drug dealing and dependency.

The invitation to direct *Beyond Reasonable Doubt* brought Laing back to New Zealand in 1979 and to an industry that had matured. Laing was quoted as saying, "we used to talk about making features, but it had seemed impossible.... That was one reason why I had gone overseas."[13] On his return, his skills as a filmmaker, extended while in the United Kingdom and Canada, saw him working not just as a director but as an editor for the action movie *Race for the Yankee Zephyr* (1981). Later, he was to turn toward television production, directing episodes of series such as *Roche, Hercules: The Legendary Journeys, Mysterious Island, Xena: Warrior Princess, Cover Story, Jackson's Wharf, Duggan,* and *Cleopatra 2525.* He then became the producer of the highly successful television drama series *Mercy Peak,* which ran for six seasons from 2001 to 2004. Set in and around a hospital in the fictional small town of Bassett, the program focused on the personal conflicts, social tensions, community relationships, and trials and tribulations of the New Zealand family; themes that had interested Laing throughout his feature film career.

The Dysfunctional Family

A particular New Zealand cultural myth is that it is a country that offers a "great way of life," "security and equality," "good neighbors," and a "great place to bring up kids." These sentiments were perhaps strongest in the 1950s and, as Nick Perry argues, "were once part of a formally approved popular rhetoric of nationalism, understood and promulgated as cultural givens."[14] But in a transnational age of globalization and multi-culturalism, when New Zealand's national identity has extended in its complexity, diverged, and come under internal and external pressures, the myth of an estimable standard of living persists. Such utopian visions are, however, outside of Laing's screen depictions of New Zealand, where the nation is imagined and viewed as challenging and discordant and no more so than in the representation of the family.

In each of Laing's films the family unit is weakened, distant, threatened, or destroyed. These are themes Laing returns to, as he finds them "more interesting than functionality. I always feel when I'm working on a scene—even if I'm working on a piece of television and someone else has written it—as the director I always look for the conflict in the scene.... People agreeing with each other is hell for me.... If the conflict doesn't exist I will try and create it."[15] *Beyond Reasonable Doubt,* a film conceived as a documentary-thriller, is based on an infamous true crime from 1970 in the small town of Pukekawa and the subsequent murder trial; "the most baffling and controversial case in New Zealand history," the film's pressbook declares. The film opens on a darkened farmhouse, a family home that has been violently ruptured and evacuated. As the camera searches the shadowy confines of the living quarters, it reveals a washing-up bowl in a kitchen sink containing a pool of blood, and a kitchen table with half-eaten meals. The kitchen, a space associated with the cleansing and preparation of food and the gathering of the family, has become the site of severance and domestic horror, with the sink bearing the stains of an attempted purging of a crime. A baby is found in an adjacent room lying at an awkward angle in a cot. For a moment it appears that it has been murdered, but then its legs twitch; the baby's missing parents, though, have not survived and three months later are found in the Waikato River.

This is not the sole image of a shattered family within the film. The dead mother's father, Len (Martyn Sanderson), in the eyes of some shows a lack of appropriate concern for the horrific act and therefore becomes a murder suspect. Another farmer, Arthur Thomas (John Hargreaves), is soon the focus of the police investigation and is wrongfully convicted of the crime. A pardon from Prime Minister Robert Muldoon frees Thomas after nine years in prison, but he returns home to find his marriage has been ended. The uniting of the local community—at the start in the search for the missing/murdered parents and later broadened to the wider community of the nation in the fight to reverse a miscarriage of justice—demonstrates a kindred strength. However, at the heart of such a concept of community is the family, and here there can be no disguising the tarnishing of the pastoral myth of New Zealand as supposedly a country of equality and security and as an idyllic place to settle.

The utopian ideals of the rural small town are far from being exclusively associated with New Zealand, and they have been questioned more within American cinema.[16] Twenty-one years after *Beyond Reasonable Doubt*, Laing directed and co-scripted *No One Can Hear You*, a made for cable neo-slasher (a horror-whodunit following in the style of the highly successful *Scream* trilogy [1996–2000]) that is supposedly set in the Seattle-Portland region of northwest United States but clearly reveals in some shots New Zealand streets and an Auckland metropolis.[17] *No One Can Hear You* is but one of a number of American financed films shot in New Zealand and made to look like the United States.[18] Laing found that it was easy to replicate the American small town using New Zealand locations: "[I] got on the net and checked out real estates, targeted areas [in northwest America] and brought up pictures and was stunned how much they were like Auckland."[19] For some of the locations Laing returned to the Pukekawa landscape he had used in making *Beyond Reasonable Doubt*. Just a short traveling distance from that small town farming community is Pukekohe, where Laing employed the local police station for his American-set horror film. Any comparisons between these two films, made twenty-one years apart, appear more striking when the opening murder scenes are compared.

Soon after the opening credits of *No One Can Hear You*, the depth of the film's Gothic horror is revealed with the brutal murder of an entire family, one that is re-enacted on a second family soon after. An answering machine switches on to receive an incoming call and suggests that a family home is unoccupied. As the message is being recorded a pan across a range of ornaments emphasizes a personal space, but as the recording ends a hand halts the machine and challenges any perceptions of vacancy. Suddenly, Rachel (Joanna Morrison), a schoolgirl for whom the message was left, arrives and the camera placed within the home films her from a distance as she enters the front garden through an arched gateway. The camera then switches to outside and now films Rachel from behind and at a distance as she approaches her home. The accomplished technique employed by Laing impersonalizes and objectifies Rachel as she is filmed with a prowling and mobile camera, which drifts inside and outside the family space.[20] It also debases any values of home as the house is transformed into a dark and unwelcoming site. Close to her front door Rachel's figure is exaggerated in a large silhouette against the side of the house. In effect, Rachel's shadow, her dark "double," or "other" self, is the one that enters the home. Inside, the house is an uncanny space, the home rendered unfamiliar through darkness as Rachel finds the main lights are not working. Then Rachel stumbles over an unexpected object and, grasping for a working table lamp, dramatically reveals the three other members of her family gagged and strapped with duct tape to chairs. The entire scene is unsettling due to the rupturing of notions of domestic security and a functioning family. And although the actual slaughter of the family is left very much off screen, the extreme and bloody nature of this horrific intervention is made clear when the next day a police crime scene is established. Here a deputy is shown vomiting in the garden as a result of observing the crime indoors, one that Laing still refuses to detail other than through a glimpse of the vicious saw-like murder weapon, and the mentioning of facts such as decapitation. As Laing, following Fritz Lang, has said, "what is left to the imagination is far more scary, far more terrifying and thought provoking."[21]

The film's title, *No One Can Hear You*, was selected for its generic horror value. Yet a study of the film reveals the narrative centrality of communication systems, with telephones, phone booths, cell phones, and answering machines repeatedly utilized by the main characters. There are phone conversations, but there are also many unanswered calls, absent call recipients, and distinct moments where phone connections fail. Most interestingly, moments of broken telecommunication define family detachment and dysfunction. There is the young hitchhiker Robert Player (Kieren Hutchison) who could be the killer and who needs somewhere to stay while drifting through town. He phones Trish Burchall (Kelly McGillis) and claims that his parents are old friends of her late husband; unsure, Trish takes a home number for Robert's parents to seek verification but finds nobody answering her call. There is also Ben Kelly (Tom Huntington), a high-school friend of Trish's eldest daughter, Lisa (Kate Elliott), whose actions at times are suspicious. Using the Burchall's family phone he claims he is phoning his mother to let her know where he is, but he only pretends to make the call. Later, Trish, acting as local detective, phones Ben's mother, Pat (Elizabeth Hawthorne), and realizes that Ben is in fact the killer. Pat appears uncommunicative, but it is soon apparent that her son is the adopted boy that Trish has been tracking; the sole survivor and witness of his original family's slaughter, Ben is the traumatized psychotic whose rage is related to rejection and loss. By the time Trish has made this discovery, Ben and Robert are staying at her home, where she left her two daughters in the belief they were safe. Far from home on a dark country lane, Trish's car is forced off the road, where she finds in her desperation to contact her daughters that her phone has no signal. In these instances, the telephone, which could function to unite family members, serves to emphasize removal and separation.

Absent Fathers

In *No One Can Hear You* it is easy to forget that Trish is not the only absent parent in a time of family need. The Burchall home is also missing a paternal figure. Within the film there are references to a husband who had died three months earlier. A shot of Trish's workspace briefly shows a photo of an unbroken family—mother, father, and two daughters—while the film's establishing scene of the Burchall's home shows tension between mother and eldest daughter, with the mother concluding "you miss your father don't you? . . . So do I." The theme of an absent father or husband is common in Laing's work and can be observed in all of his films. In the action-comedy *Dangerous Orphans*, three young orphans form an alliance in childhood and vow to avenge the murder of one particular father.[22] *Other Halves* sees a troubled and suicidal housewife, Liz Harvey (Lisa Harrow), reject her comfortable urban existence, her wealthy husband and their son, to begin a new domestic union with a sixteen-year-old Polynesian boy, Tug (Mark Pilisi). Crucially, this cross-cultural "marriage" lacks a paternal figure. And in *Absent without Leave*, a 1942 World War II period drama set in New Zealand, Ed (Craig McLachlan), a newlywed young soldier, turns army deserter in order to accompany his sixteen-year-old wife, Daisy (Katrina Hobbs), who has recently miscarried, home to her father in Auckland. Daisy's father exists as a distant figure, living four hundred miles away from his Wellington-based daughter, and is ultimately permanently removed when he dies before she can return home. War separates the young couple and for periods emasculates or restrains the protective husband. In prison, Ed is allowed time alone with Daisy, and it is only during this stolen moment, negotiated with the authorities, and within a space of incarceration, that the new family is born; given a brief opportunity to make love, Daisy later reveals she is again pregnant. *Absent without Leave* is seen by Laing as a nostalgia film. He was born in the shadow of World War II, an event he describes as "big in my life," and as such the film is perhaps for Laing a personal journey, one that is symbolically mirrored in the long-distance journey toward home that is undertaken by the protagonists.[23] Laing's parents had died sometime before pre-production and in Daisy he was reminded of his mother. The character of Ed is based on Jim Edwards, whose true story the film is based upon, and Laing says that when he first met Jim, he "definitely reminded me of my father."[24]

Paternal identity and recognition is explored in the Kiwi Gothic film *The Lost Tribe*, where the idea is extended into a space of horror and fantasy.[25] It is by far the least urban of Laing's films and the one that can be read as his version of the enduring New Zealand myth of the "man alone," of the man abandoning domesticity, settlement, and the dominant community in favor of isolation within the harsh wilderness of the local bush. In the film, Max Scarry (John Bach) is the absent father, an anthropologist who has been away from his family while searching for the graves of a legendary lost Maori tribe. Like the character of Jack Torrance, played by Jack Nicholson, in *The Shining* (1980), the isolation of the chosen retreat unbalances Max and drives him to acts of violence. Max's daughter Katy (Emma Takle), like Danny (Danny Lloyd) in *The Shining*, is alerted to the surrounding danger through her ESP abilities. She sees her father consumed by the dark forces of the land, and in a dream sees him seated in what she describes as a "monster's cave," which is in fact the burial chamber of the lost Maori tribe. In the film, Laing returns to the theme of mistaken identities and exchanged guilt that he first explored in *Beyond Reasonable Doubt*, with Max's identical twin brother Edward (John Bach, again) blamed for Max's murder of a local prostitute. Edward is then himself murdered by Max, who assumes his brother's identity and returns to the mainland community and his waiting family.

Inspiration for the film's story, which Laing wrote, came from research he was conducting on the isolated West Coast region of New Zealand's South Island, while he was employed by the NFU. Laing discovered stories of a prospector called Wheeler, living alone in Dusky Sound, in the Fiordland region, who disappeared between supply ships: "totally vanished without trace leaving behind a completely insane diary that just got madder

Masculinity in crisis: A threatened Edward (John Bach) tries to defend himself against his murderous twin in *The Lost Tribe*. (Courtesy New Zealand Film Commission.)

and madder and madder as it went on about the spirits and the forest that were waiting for him and how he couldn't sleep at night and they came in the darkness and they were coming to kill him and take him away."[26] Laing combined this with the story of a Maori tribe, from the Dunedin region of the East Coast of the South Island, who, following a fight with another tribe, fled south and were never seen again, though a group of whalers later discovered in a remote location a cave with the bodies of a number of Maori. Finally, identical twins had been a fascination for Laing, who was drawn to "how their lives were connected.... I just wanted to explore that psychic aspect."[27] As Laing explains, "the editor in me, I suppose, slipped [the elements] together and combined them into one story."[28]

Other than at the film's end, Max is a father totally withdrawn from his family. In fact, as he is reunited with his family, just prior to the end credits rolling, there is a sense that even now he remains detached. Within the film he is replaced by the more dependable and open twin, Edward, who even sleeps with Max's wife. Katy's premonitions and ESP aside, Max is like the missing tribe, a continually lost figure. He retreats to an isolated shack on a Fiordland shore, where in an area lacking general human activity the only way of connecting with the isolated stretch of bush is via hired boat. But Max does assimilate with the locals, uniting with the discovered necropolis, the tapu (sacred) cave of the dead. Max is here overcome not just by the spirits of the dead, or the feeling of isolation, but also by the power of the land itself. In a region removed from civilization, the strength of any individual is far exceeded by the omnipotence of a land that can bewitch, bewilder, and unsettle.

The Urban Center

New Zealand's cultural, social, political, and economic identity has been to a large degree built on the country's unique land and seascape and natural diversity. As with the tourist industry, New Zealand cinema has persistently emphasized an untouched wonderland of the sublime and the extraordinary. Such is the nature myth that it frequently seems to matter little that more than 80 percent of New Zealand's population is urbanized and that this exceeds figures for countries such as Japan, the United States, and France.[29] Unlike other New Zealand filmmakers, Laing has significantly returned to images of the city and the urban center. As a filmmaker who has spent much of his time living and working in and around Auckland and Wellington it is perhaps no accident that his films are drawn to the cityscape of these major conurbations. *Other Halves* is an Auckland-centric film, with *Beyond Reasonable Doubt,* and *No One Can Hear You* employing Auckland locations. Similarly, *The Shirt* and *Dangerous Orphans* are Wellington-centric with *Absent without Leave* employing Wellington locations. To some it could be surprising that a filmmaker who grew up in Dunedin has made just one out of his seven features on the South Island, when it has a wealth of natural location possibilities.

A filmmaker who spent much of his time overseas living in cities such as London, Bristol, Toronto, and Montreal, Laing sees himself as a city man. His experiences have enabled him to see beyond the traditional use of natural locations in New Zealand film. As he states: "I suppose I've reacted against it. It's the myth, the myth that New Zealand is the rural heartland. Cities are in fact, whether we like it or not, the hub of this country now. I suppose I find stories set in cities clever and there's more opportunity for density.... It just appeals to me.... I just feel that's where life is the most concentrated and is more interesting."[30] Artistically, Laing is inspired by the paintings of the social realist Edward Hopper, who often depicted cinematic images of ordinary life in a shadowy city.[31] Laing talks passionately about Hopper as an artist "who uses darkness in contrast with light in a superb way," who could create "a kind of slightly sinister melancholy to his shadow images," and as someone who could depict the vulnerability of characters. He sees a duality and conflict in Hopper's work, a paused threat, or an environment pregnant with drama and with the potential to be unbalanced.[32] Hopper has had such a direct influence on Laing's filmmaking that a catalogue of the artist's work was handed to Simon Baumfield, the cinematographer for *No One Can Hear You*, before shooting on that production commenced.

Perhaps what attracts Laing most in these images of the city is the intensity of the social situations: "[they] tend to occur more and they're harder to escape in the city ... you can also have isolation in the city."[33] *The Shirt*, Laing's ultra-low-budget film, reflects these issues well, to the point where the intensity and excess of the situation is so great that it becomes humorous.[34] Laing is fond of *The Shirt*, a film he occasionally refers to as a "home movie." It was "enjoyable to make," "good to get back to basics," "back to straight storytelling, straight acting, good characters ... I learnt a lot from making that movie. ... I learnt more from that than just about anything else I have done."[35] The film relates the tragic (almost comic) series of events, which occur following the accidental burning of a hot iron onto a drug dealer's shirt. The dealer then abuses the heroin addict Marty (Brian Sergent), for his stupidity, who is provoked into brutally murdering the dealer with the iron. In return, contracts are put out to kill Marty, his girlfriend Gina (Kirsty King-Turner), and his mate Nick (Jeffrey Szusterman). Lawrence McDonald writes that the "rubbing out" of these "three helpless and hapless junkies ... [is] a rather redundant exercise as they're all effectively dead anyway." He also writes that *The Shirt* is "a genuine study of the crushing banality of the needle," and that "the viewer [is left] in no doubt that junkies must be strong contenders for the title of most boring people on the planet."[36] Despite a brief mention of Marty's "monomania," what McDonald undervalues is the extent to which the film is concerned with notions of power.

Marty is like Harold Shand (Bob Hoskins) in *The Long Good Friday* (1980), a mini-Napoleon who believes he is in control of his urban space but does not realize that he is surrounded by others who are, in comparison, considerably more powerful. As Laing says, "the complexity of Marty's world was far more than he realized," and "outside he is nothing at all. The world is way bigger than he is."[37] Like the figures who appear to populate Hopper's city visions, Marty is a vulnerable individual within an urban confine, yet Marty's drug-induced obsessive behavior leaves his actions distinctly immoderate. Marty is the proverbial caged animal, who similar to Max Scarry in *The Lost Tribe*, or Ben Kelly in *No One Can Hear You*, is the outsider who is removed from a wider society, but who seeks acceptance or recognition while simultaneously attempting to control a tendency for disorder or violence that inhibits community inclusion. These are characters in conflict with society, but often in Laing's films social stability leans toward a state of chaos as that stability is also threatened by institutions with a responsibility for maintaining law and order.

Within Laing's films there appears a continuous crisis in hegemony. As Laing says, he has "always been a bit of an anarchist. I've always been someone who has felt uncomfortable with authority."[38] In his films social order is threatened not just by the institution of the family appearing weakened or tainted but also by organized crime and drug rings, as in *The Shirt* and *Dangerous Orphans*.[39] Perhaps more controversially the police are often depicted as corrupt, manipulative, or racist. The negative portrayal of the police in New Zealand film is a noted recurrent, but of particular interest here is the degree to which this is articulated within Laing's narratives.[40] Whereas other New Zealand films have tended to ridicule the police, Laing has shown them to be a threatening force. Most dramatically is the police corruption in *Beyond Reasonable Doubt*, where evidence is suppressed or tampered leading to a miscarriage of justice.[41] Inspector Bruce Hutton (David Hemmings), who leads the investigation, is "an oily, ambitious career policeman who cold-bloodedly goes for a conviction at any cost," a "scheming, unpleasant and self-satisfied man far too personally involved . . . for his own good—and for justice."[42] Such was the series of negative characterizations in *Beyond Reasonable Doubt* that Laing made a point of presenting one good officer in the prison scene at the film's end to reassure the viewer that not all policemen are immoral.

With a concern for closely following original events, Laing's portrayal of the police in *Beyond Reasonable Doubt* was largely drawn from contemporary accounts; similarly, *Other Halves*, based on the autobiographical novel by Sue McCauley, and partly on fact, depicts the Auckland police as unhelpful, aggressive, destructive, sexist, and racist. Looking at Laing's other films, officer Hobbes (Marshall Napier) in *Dangerous Orphans* is corrupt, while detectives Carl Berry and Mike Hughes (Jeffrey Thomas and Marshall Napier) in *The Shirt* are prepared to work outside of the law. There is a friendly community policeman in *Absent without Leave*, but the military police are socially unaccountable, the policemen in *No One Can Hear You* make erroneous judgments, while the Maori Sergeant Swain (Don Selwyn) in *The Lost Tribe* refuses to assist as his job demands, as this is outweighed by his cultural concerns for the dead. Laing's grandfather was a policeman, something that Laing says his mother later "became ashamed of," following the police corruption during the true events on which *Beyond Reasonable Doubt* was based. Reflecting on his family, Laing says his mother "was a very feisty Scottish woman who had a healthy

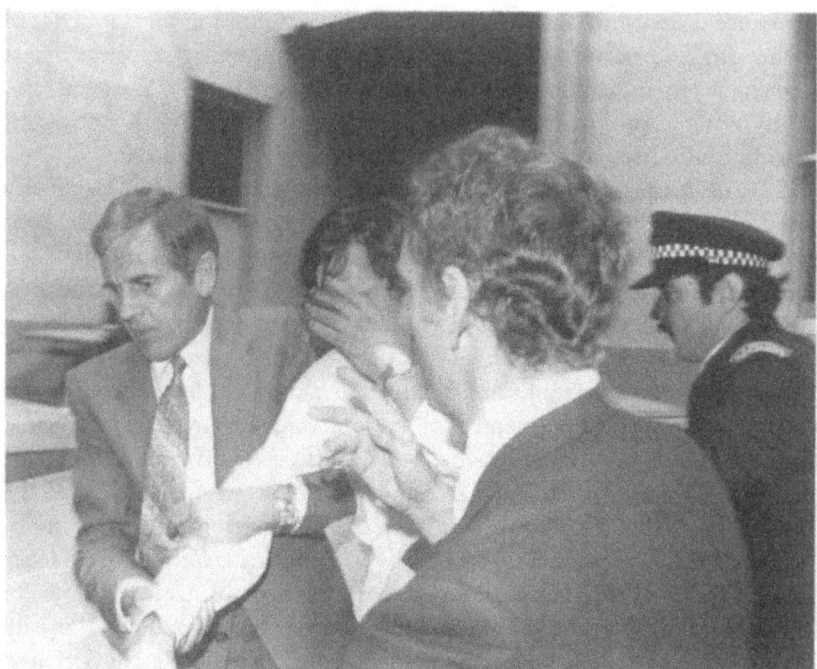

The wrong man: Farmer Arthur Thomas (John Hargreaves) is led away by police in *Beyond Reasonable Doubt*. (Courtesy Ian Conrich collection of New Zealand cinema and visual culture.)

disrespect for authority.... My father was less vehement on these feelings but he was a conscientious objector, a pacifist. I suppose that feeling of not necessarily trusting authority is something I've grown up with."[43] In fact, the effect could appear to be profound with Laing stating that he has a "fundamental distrust of [police] methods," "they are a culture unto themselves," and that they have worried him "because of their single-minded sort of blanket view of humanity." This view extends into his film characterizations, with Laing saying, "if I've got a cop I tend to look at them in that way."[44]

Laing says that his family was "seriously functional" and proposes that this "was probably the source of my fascination with the dysfunctional."[45] Images of dystopia are, however, so frequent in New Zealand films that Laing's depiction of dysfunction is not unusual. In discussing the Kiwi Gothic I have written elsewhere that "New Zealand life, for many, has appeared so normal, ordered and consummate that it became mundane and predictable," and that "the film images of horror in New Zealand . . . [are] a desire to destroy the oppressive normality."[46] Instead, within the context of New Zealand film production, it is Laing's return to a dystopian vision of the local, and his repeated locating of his films within an urban-centric narrative, that is remarkable. Laing's attraction to thrillers and melodramas where the themes of crisis and conflict are constant reveals his auterist tendencies. Certainly Laing brings to his films a series of aesthetic and ideological positions, which have been influenced by particular sociocultural developments. The social organization of the urban centers within New Zealand is crucial to understanding current issues of national identity, but such recognition is often lost beneath a desire to promote the country's natural uniqueness. Laing's visions challenge such traditional views of New Zealand as a pastoral paradise, where despite his images of conflict and crisis (some of which are based on actual events) his films represent the growth of a more secure cultural identity, one that is able to engage with alternatives to the established myths.

Notes

I would like to thank John Laing for his generosity in answering a stream of questions. I would also like to thank Mette and Niels Weisberg for their advice and suggestions.

1. John Laing, interview with author, August 17, 2001.
2. Ibid.
3. *The Shirt* was given an R18 rating largely for the excessive swearing and the detailing of the process for preparing drugs.
4. New Zealand films depicting the family in crisis include *Bad Blood* (1981), *Smash Palace* (1981), *Carry Me Back* (1982), *Heart of the Stag* (1984), *Trespasses* (1984), *Death Warmed Up* (1984), *Vigil* (1984), *Bridge to Nowhere* (1986), *Desperate Remedies* (1993), *Jack Be Nimble* (1993), *Once Were Warriors* (1994), *Heavenly Creatures* (1994), *Broken English* (1996), *Crooked Earth* (2001), *Rain* (2001), and *Whale Rider* (2002). Films depicting conflict or sociopolitical tension within a system of law and order include *Sleeping Dogs* (1977), *Nutcase* (1980), *Shaker Run* (1985), *The Grasscutter* (1988), *Never Say Die* (1988), *Chill Factor* (1988), *Zilch!* (1989), and *The Last Tattoo* (1994).
5. Laing, interview with author, August 17, 2001.
6. Roger Horrocks, "New Zealand Film Makers at the Auckland City Art Gallery: John Laing," program notes, July 4, 1985, 1.
7. Laing, interview with author, August 17, 2001.
8. Horrocks, "New Zealand Film Makers at the Auckland City Art Gallery," 1.
9. Laing, interview with author, August 17, 2001.
10. Ibid.
11. Ibid.
12. Ibid.
13. Horrocks, "New Zealand Film Makers at the Auckland City Art Gallery," 2.

14. Nick Perry, *The Dominion of Signs: Television, Advertising, and Other New Zealand Fictions* (Auckland: Auckland University Press, 1994), 47.
15. Laing, interview with author, August 17, 2001.
16. For further discussion of the New Zealand and American small town movie, see Ian Conrich, "The Space Between: The New Zealand Small Town and Its Representation on Film," *Cultures of the Commonwealth* 9 (Spring 2003): 9–24.
17. Laing says that the *Scream* films were "certainly an influence" on the making of *No One Can Hear You* (interview with author, August 17, 2001).
18. For instance, the films *Strange Behaviour* (1982), *The Frighteners* (1996), *The Climb* (1997), *Exposure* (2000), *Blood Crime* (2002), and *Boogeyman* (2004).
19. Laing, interview with author, August 17, 2001.
20. Commenting on this stylistic approach, Laing says, "I like to keep revealing things. I like sometimes starting a scene and only revealing it as it develops" (interview with author, August 17, 2001).
21. Laing, interview with author, August 17, 2001.
22. *Dangerous Orphans* is the only one of Laing's New Zealand films not to be released in New Zealand. For Laing, the film "was a complete and utter mess . . . the first assembly of it did not make any sense whatever. . . . [After] the first screening of it I was so depressed." The film was subsequently recut and restructured, but Laing still saw the final version as "a fix-up job. A *fixed* film . . . never really fixed well enough" (Laing, interview with author, August 17, 2001).
23. Laing, interview with author, August 17, 2001.
24. Ibid.
25. For more on Kiwi Gothic films, see Ian Conrich, "Kiwi Gothic: New Zealand's Cinema of a Perilous Paradise," in *Horror International*, ed. Steven Jay Schneider and Tony Williams (Detroit: Wayne State University Press, 2005), 114–27.
26. Laing, interview with author, August 17, 2001.
27. Ibid.
28. Ibid.
29. Guy M. Robinson, Robert J. Loughran, and Paul J. Tranter, *Australia and New Zealand: Economy, Society, and Environment* (London: Arnold, 2000), 168.
30. Laing, interview with author, August 17, 2001.
31. For more on Edward Hopper, see Erika L. Doss, "Edward Hopper, *Nighthawks*, and Film Noir," *Post Script* 2, no. 2 (1983): 14–36; Jean-Pierre Naugrette, "Cinémas, cinéma: Regard sur Edward Hopper," *Positif* 417 (November 1995): 55–61.
32. Laing, interview with author, August 17, 2001.
33. Ibid.
34. *The Shirt* was originally a short film made in 1998 and directed by Dunny Mulheron. Brian Sergent, the drug dealer in this short, played the protagonist and drug addict in Laing's feature.
35. Ibid.
36. Lawrence McDonald, "One from Cult Classic Pictures, Another from Gordon Productions: Shifter and the Shirt," *Illusions* 31 (Summer 2000–2001): 25.
37. Laing, interview with author, August 17, 2001.
38. Ibid.
39. Drug dealing and trafficking are themes that occur in a number of New Zealand films and are present in movies such as *Should I Be Good?* (1985), *Undercover*

(1991), *Scarfies* (1999), and *Crooked Earth* (2001).
40. See, for instance, Ian Conrich, "A State of Mild Anarchy: Lawlessness and New Zealand Film," unpublished paper presented at the Focus on Australian and New Zealand Cinema conference, Institute of Commonwealth Studies, University of London, October 4, 1997.
41. The police are not alone in perverting or hindering the course of justice with the multinational company ICI slow to assist with providing information and the court judges depicted as uncaring and ineffectual.
42. Roger Ebert, "Film Festival," *Chicago Sun-Times*, November 12, 1981; Aline Sandilands, "Few Answers, but a Hero," *Otago Daily Times*, September 1980. Both reviews from the New Zealand Film Commission's press clipping compilation for the film.
43. Laing, interview with author, August 17, 2001.
44. Ibid.
45. Ibid.
46. Conrich, "Kiwi Gothic," 122–23.

John Laing—Filmography

1970. *And Now New Zealand* (NZ documentary: director).
1970. *Kariotahi Beach* (NZ documentary: director).
1971. *Picnic* (NZ documentary: director).
1971. *Bananas for Market* (NZ documentary: director).
1972. *Trotting* (NZ documentary: director).
1972. *Mick Stimson* (NZ documentary: co-director).
1973. *Collector's World* (UK television series: editor).
1973. *The Gentleman Tramp: The Life and Times of Charles Chaplin* (US documentary: assistant editor).
1974. *Chain of the Sun* (UK television documentary: editor).
1975. *No Way They Want to Slow Down* (Canada television documentary: writer, editor).
1975. *Descent/La descente* (Canada documentary: writer, editor).
1976. *Sword of the Lord* (Canada documentary: editor).
1976. *If Brains Were Dynamite You Wouldn't Have Enough to Blow Your Nose* (Canada television documentary: writer, editor).
1976. *The Rubber Gun* (Canada feature film: co-writer, editor).
1976. *The Mackay Experiment* (Canada documentary: co-director, writer, editor).
1976. *Mother of Many Children* (Canada documentary: editor).
1977. *I Wasn't Scared* (Canada short film: editor).
1977. *The Hottest Show on Earth* (Canada documentary: editor).
1977. *Theatre for Strangers* (Canada documentary: editor).
1977. *You Never Lose until You Quit* (Canada documentary: editor).
1977. *Flash William* (Canada documentary: co-director, editor).
1977. *Three Rivers Dam* (Canada documentary: editor).

1978. *David Manzur, Bogata, Colombia* (Canada documentary: editor).
1978. *One Hundred Years* (Canada documentary: editor).
1978. *Kings and Desperate Men* a.k.a. *Kings and Desperate Men: A Hostage Incident* (Canada feature film: editor).
1980. ***Beyond Reasonable Doubt*** (NZ feature film: director).
1981. *Race for the Yankee Zephyr* a.k.a. *Treasure of the Yankee Zephyr* (NZ/Australia feature film: editor).
1982. ***The Lost Tribe*** (NZ feature film: director, co-producer, writer).
1983. *Hitchhiker* (France/Canada/US television series: director of six episodes).
1984. *Inside Straight* (NZ television series: director of the episodes "Standup Comic" and "Repossession").
1984. ***Other Halves*** (NZ feature film: director).
1985. Roche (NZ television series: director of the episodes "Sons and Fathers" and "Mates").
1986. ***Dangerous Orphans*** (NZ feature film: director).
1990. *The Ray Bradbury Theatre* (US/France/UK/Canada/NZ television series: director of the episode "Touch of Petulance").
1992. *The Ray Bradbury Theatre* (US/France/UK/Canada/NZ television series: director of the episode "The Happiness Machine").
1993. ***Absent without Leave*** (NZ feature film: director).
1993. *Bread and Roses* (NZ television four-part mini-series, also screened theatrically: actor).
1993. *Marlin Bay* (NZ television series: episode director).
1994. *Plainclothes* (NZ television series: episode director).
1994. *Cody: Bad Love* (Australia television movie: director).
1994. *Songs for a New Country* (NZ television documentary in the *Work of Art* series: director).
1995. *Singapore Sling: Road to Mandalay* a.k.a. *Asian Connection: Road to Mandalay* (Australia television movie: director).
1995. *Cover Story* (NZ television series: director of two episodes).
1995. *Mysterious Island* (Canada/NZ television series: director of the episodes "Plan and Attack," "A Pact with the Devil," and "Going, Going . . .").
1998. *Tiger Country* (NZ television film: director).
1998. *Xena: Warrior Princess* (US/NZ television series: director of the episodes "When in Rome," and "Tsunami").
1998/99. *Hercules: The Legendary Journeys* (US/NZ television series: director of the episodes "Hercules on Trial," "Render unto Caesar," "Norse by Norsevest," and "Sky High").
1999. *Greenstone* (NZ television series: director of two episodes).
1999. *Jackson's Wharf* (NZ television series: director of the two-part episode "Accusations, Illicit Love, and High Hopes," and episode 27 in series 1).

- 1999. *Duggan* (NZ television series: director of the episodes "Murder at Te Papa" and "Moving House").
- **1999.** *The Shirt* (NZ feature film: director, co-cinematographer).
- 2000. *Street Legal* (NZ television series: director of the episodes "Rest in Peace," "Maria's Trial," "The Recruit," "The Coach," and "Streetfighter").
- 2000. *Cleopatra 2525* (US/NZ television series: director of the episodes "Baby Boom" and "Reality Check").
- 2001. *Xena: Warrior Princess* (US/NZ television series: director of the episode "You are There").
- **2001.** *No One Can Hear You* (US/NZ cable television film: director, co-writer).
- **2001/4.** *Mercy Peak* (NZ television series: producer for all sixty episodes).
- 2005. *Power Rangers S.P.D.* a.k.a. *Power Rangers Space Patrol Delta* (US/NZ/Japan television series: director of the episodes "Zapped," "Reflection Part 1," "Reflection Part 2," "Robotpalooza," "Missing," "Badge," "Insomnia," and "Resurrection").
- 2005/6. *Power Rangers Mystic Force* (US/NZ/Japan television series: director of the episodes "Code Busters," "Broken Spell: Part 1," "Broken Spell: Part 2").
- 2006. *Wendy Wu: Homecoming Warrior* (US television movie: director).
- 2006. *Outrageous Fortune* (NZ television series: producer for a television movie and all sixteen episodes).

14

"Carry Me Back"

Time and Place in the Films of John Reid

Bruce Babington

Born in 1946, John Reid has directed four feature films—*Middle Age Spread* (1979), *Carry Me Back* (1982), *Leave All Fair* (1985), and *The Last Tattoo* (1994). This small but significant body of work spans much of the period of New Zealand cinema's New Wave, with Reid's first film, *Middle Age Spread*, contemporary with Roger Donaldson's *Sleeping Dogs* (1977) and Geoff Murphy's *Goodbye Pork Pie* (1980), the originating texts that kick-started the New Zealand film industry, and his latest, *The Last Tattoo*, appearing at the same time as Jane Campion's *The Piano* (1993) and Lee Tamahori's *Once Were Warriors* (1994), at a point where New Zealand cinema very definitely reached a world stage. He has also been, beyond his own films, a crucial figure in the development of the New Zealand film industry; his authorship of a 1972 report was a major factor in the setting up of the New Zealand Film Commission, though this essay restricts itself to Reid as a filmmaker rather than a facilitator of others' work.

The idea of Reid as an auteur has never taken off, understandably, since he exhibits few of the overtly recurring thematic or stylistic motifs associated with the small number of locally derived filmmakers who demand such consideration. However, his films constitute a significant body of work for reasons other than the period of time they span. For a sociology of New Zealand film, Reid may have a paradigmatic status as a director whose output has been too low key and local to promote the lure of filmic expatriatism, working as he has within the small local industry, and limited by its economic constraints to only four features. But his small cinematic oeuvre displays a surprising variety of the (often hybrid) options characterizing contemporary New Zealand cinema. Thus *Carry Me Back* and *Middle Age Spread* are, respectively, epitomes of "Old" (i.e., traditional, rural, masculinist) and "New" (i.e., contemporary, suburban/urban) comedy. *The Last Tattoo* replaces with film noir the more common horror or crime film's commentary on the darker side of New Zealand's supposed paradise, and also combines it with period reconstruction (American "occupied" Wellington in 1943–44). For its part, *Leave All Fair* crosses the biopic with the intimate, small cast kammerfilm (chamber film) and modernist memory narrative. Additionally, the four films reveal a multi-leveled play with the thematics of place and temporality characteristic of much New Zealand filmmaking, with its sense of distance; its urge to national self-assertion; its belated indebtedness to Hollywood, British, and European film models; and its (recent) self-conscious multiculturalism. These elements receive different emphases across Reid's work, though, in that the multicultural narratives common to later New Zealand cinema take second place in his features to more traditional New Zealand/American and New Zealand/British and European preoccupations (the immigrant taxi driver and George the Greek in *Carry Me Back*, and Grace and Bill Davin in *The Last Tattoo* are examples of exceptions to these preoccupations). These points notwithstanding, Reid's films embody many of the changes that have marked contemporary New Zealand cinema. One of the most important of these is dramatized in the concentration on central male characters in *Middle Age Spread* and *Carry Me Back*, a feature that is the product of a traditionally patriarchal society, and the focus on female characters in the two later films, a contrast that reflects changes in New Zealand filmmaking and society in the 1980s and 1990s. Finally, the films' meditations on place are paralleled and textually augmented by the variations of Reid's directorial career—two New Zealand–made films with all New Zealand casts, a third made in New Zealand but featuring well-known Hollywood actors alongside New Zealanders, and *Leave All Fair,* shot in France with a wholly foreign cast, so that even this most local of directors briefly shared the expatriate film experience.

Carry Me Back

Carry Me Back, as its privileging throughout this essay suggests, is Reid's most significant film. It is a minor classic of the New Zealand film renaissance, and its deceptive simplicity provides a set of thematic entries into Reid's other films—New Zealand and New Zealandness past and present; the centering on male and female subjectivities, the pastoral and the urban as well as a focus on the local and national in the face of issues of the internationalism and expatriatism his work contains. As my reading of *Carry Me Back* suggests, Reid's openness to influence, with his early films summarizing—in complex ways divided between criticism and nostalgia—older traditions of New Zealand culture, and his later features embracing changes but not without irony and critique, presupposes an ambivalent audience caught between the various polarities noted above.

The title *Carry Me Back* most obviously refers to the journey by which Arthur (Grant Tilly) and Jimmy (Kelly Johnson) illicitly return their father's body to their South Island Marlborough homestead. This is after the father, T. K. (Derek Hardwick), has died following the trio's attendance at a Ranfurly Shield rugby match in Wellington, with their actions thereby ensuring that the farm descends to them and not the local rugby union. More allusively, *Carry Me Back* invokes the famous song by James Bland (circa 1870), asking the audience to substitute T. K. and his boys for Bland's "darkey," and to replace the song's "cotton," "corn," and "tatoes" with sheep, and its beloved "Virginny" with Marlborough.[1] For viewers who know the song well there are more negative allusions as the singer imagines withering until he dies in his restored birthplace and recalls how he "labored so hard for old massa," words suggesting T. K.'s tyrannies over his sons. Even if for most viewers only the song's title and beginning have resonance, they still suggest a complex interaction with the past that links the film to other contemporaneous versions of a pastoral New Zealand, including Ian Mune's *Came a Hot Friday* (1985) and Murphy's *Goodbye Pork Pie*. But whereas *Came a Hot Friday* is placed precisely in the postwar boom of 1949, *Goodbye Pork Pie*'s epigraph is less temporally locatable: "a story . . . from an almost forgotten age . . . [when] you drove your car whenever you pleased, when petrol stations were always open and gas was less than a buck a gallon"; in other words, more a utopia of the mind than a concrete past. *Carry Me Back*'s comic/sardonic epigraph—"Back in the days when blokes were blokes, and sheilas were their mums"—though it points to the past, is equally unspecific, and the suggestion that we are to watch a retro film is quickly denied. The "old comedy" plot may spiral back temporally through its representation of the older generation, and the Donovan farm seems set in an unchanging past, but elsewhere the film's temporal location is very much the early 1980s with a Wellington of massage parlors and strip joints, and a stripper in an All Black's rugby kit gyrating to a rocked-up rendition of "God Defend New Zealand." Thus "Back" suggests less a literal historical view than a retrospective/regressive space within the present psyche. A real Ranfurly Shield rugby challenge, briefly seen in the film, marks the year of the narrative as that of the film's production, 1982, even though it reaches back into the past and gestures toward the future.

As "old comedy," *Carry Me Back* is rural, laconic, male-centered (the first female character, the stripper, does not appear until twelve minutes into the film) with the farm—the physical symbol of the older New Zealand—as its symbolic focus, but it addresses an audience more likely to consist of the suburban characters portrayed in *Middle Age Spread* than those of *Carry Me Back* itself. This point reflects the suburbanizing end result of major changes in New Zealand lifestyles due to the shrinking of the agricultural labor force from one-third in 1938 to about one-eighth in the early 1970s.[2] As Gary Hawke writes, by the later date "people ... had to accept urban life, and most preferred it."[3] For the film's audience, then, the rural world to which their surrogates Arthur and Jimmy return—if they echo Aunty Bird (Dorothy McKegg) as she says of the farm and its surroundings "It'll do me"—is a space of oblique signification, with the regaining of the farm more symbolic than actual. Such a view is implicated in Hawke's comment that "it [farming] always offered a way of living with a good deal of individual control over work. Time spent at a mid-week rugby match or on a journey to a chamber music concert (if one were accessible) had to be made up later, but at least there was no remote boss to be persuaded that it would be made up."[4] If chamber music seems unlikely for the Donovans, the other option rings true and is underlined when Arthur warns Jimmy of the consequences of losing the farm with a catalogue of the horrors of lost independence: "You wanna work for somebody else? Be a farm labourer for the rest of your life? Cut scrub for the County Council?" The element of self-conscious pastoral dream in *Carry Me Back* (though there are harsh enough elements in T. K.'s dictatorship) is clear too in the film's implicit play with the fact that the real Marlborough challenge for the Shield, the reason for the trio's journey to the capital, resulted in a 36 to 31 Wellington win, not the narrative's fantasy of rural Marlborough lifting the shield from the "city smartarses"—an extra-textual reality that underscores the actuality of metropolitan/suburban dominance.

The restoration of the farm is accompanied by hints of regeneration, thus fusing nostalgia (things are the same) and change (things will be different). The film works out this idea in miniature with regard to rugby, the provoker of the plot, and that signifier of New Zealandness that the South African Springbok tour of 1981 (the year before the film's production), with its splitting of the nation, had revealed as no longer an absolute index of a more plural and complicated national identity.[5] The narrative ends with the farm saved from the rugby union (which thus has, for a while, a quasi-villain status), with T. K.'s identification with the game seeming excessive, and Arthur's monologue to his father's corpse revealing the game's part in T. K.'s repeated characterization of his sons as "bloody hopeless." Yet, as the comically predictable funeral oration tells us, T. K. has "passed the ball" to his sons, who are clearly rugby fans, though in a less all-consuming way than their father. With the older males, T. K. and Old Mac (Frank Edwards), defunct, a reformed family is created, with Aunty Bird, who by her own account has been disinherited by T. K., representing the older generation. Arthur, the older son, is now an intergenerational figure, and Jimmy is the more flexible, but perhaps shallower, youngest, along with the unnamed Wellington waitress (Joanne Mildenhall) who chooses to stay on with him. Her presence represents a potential feminizing of the male ethos that, in the person of the corpse of its most hidebound representative, the father, T. K., "the old bastard," "the old bugger," is continually subjected to grotesque comic degradation. From the moment the corpse farts posthumously in the motel, to the disturbance T. K.'s false teeth cause at his funeral, the body is relentlessly subjected to indignity, most spectacularly in its enthronement, trousers around ankles, on the dunny (outdoor toilet) associated with the father from the film's beginning. Here, T. K. certainly suffers punishment for his patriarchal tyrannies, especially his constant claim that the boys are "sheilas."

At the same time, the film's ending, in focusing on the "odd (and old) couple" of Arthur and Aunty Bird over the vestigial new one of Jimmy and the girl, suggests the positive side of an ambivalence about the older New Zealand, which is why it is possible to speak of the return to the farm in terms warmer than an unalloyed negative critique. Arthur (for all his sexual naïveté and traumatization by his father) is more interesting than Jimmy, reflecting a feeling that, for all its faults, the old New Zealand was less superficial than the new, or at least that its mythologies had their positive as well as destructive side, though some of them have outlived their days. Here, the curious subplot involving Old Mac deserves attention. Old Mac, the escaped convict folk hero, a World War II mate of T. K.'s, has been abandoned by him postwar, presumably as his unregenerate Old New Zealandness has inflected from "man alone" into criminal. T. K., conversely, has become respectable, married (though widowed), propertied, inhabiting stasis, the converse of Old Mac's near-perpetual motion. T. K.'s sister-in-law, Aunty Bird, repays family obligation by helping Old Mac, hiding him in her house and then driving him in her van, so that his journey parallels T. K.'s, with both hidden inside identical wardrobes, T. K. finally arriving to be buried, and Old Mac to go back to jail. But if T. K.'s day is passing, Old Mac's certainly seems over, as, incongruously scrawny in contrast to his mythic status, he surrenders, remarking tiredly that it's safer inside. The Man Alone, that most pervasive myth of the male pioneer psyche, here accepts his own demise. As a compromise, fitting the film's feeling that the future must come out of, rather than wholly reject, the past, Arthur (the narrative's most sympathetic figure) remains a much-softened inflection of the archetype, the independent single rural man, but here bound into family and social sympathies.

The complicated audience positioning imagined by the film is played out in formal terms in *Carry Me Back*'s two closing sequences, containing shots of great beauty taken from a high vantage point over the Blenheim valley containing the Donovans' farm. The first shot zooms in to T. K.'s hillside funeral; the second is taken from Arthur's and Aunty Bird's position as they sit overlooking the farm, and lifts to include the whole panorama of hills and sky. Importantly, both place the observers, the audience's surrogates, at a considerable distance, formally embodying the detached, affectionate/critical response the film asks for from its contemporary audience. They are symbolically attached to, but in everyday life terms detached from, the Donovans' home and its rural world.

Middle Age Spread

Strikingly, the only non-suburban panorama in Reid's first film, his version of Roger Hall's play, *Middle Age Spread* (1977), comes when Elizabeth (Dorothy McKegg), preparing the sitting room for her dinner party, places for maximum exposure that 1960s and 1970s coffee table icon *New Zealand: Gift of the Sea*, with its cover of mountains peaking through a cloudscape, photographed from the air.[6] Ironically, everyone ignores it (attention is diverted instead to the paperback of Paul Theroux's *The Great Railway Bazaar*, which becomes the characters' symbol of escape), and it only reappears at the end when Colin (Grant Tilly) picks it up briefly but leaves it unopened. The book's cover photograph of a utopian, ahistorical, untenanted New Zealand is as far from the characters' compromised suburban existence as possible, so extreme that it cannot offer any imaginable terrain on which to enact alternatives to their present lives. Hall's play, stripped of its New Zealand references, later ran successfully in London's West End. Although this suggests that its satire of the affluent middle class is international, not nationally specific, the original play, and even more the film (with Reid increasing its local particularities) presented its audience with the masochistic pleasures of satiric self-recognition. As with Hawke's prototypes, its characters prefer their urban lives to any local rural one, but they spend most of the time lamenting their imprisonment in a suburban paradise turned sour (a critique with a long tradition in New Zealand literature, in the works of poets such as A. R. D. Fairburn and Louis Johnson). Another classic thematic of New Zealand's artistic and intellectual life has been the lure of expatriatism toward "home" or the European or American "Megalopolis" (from Katherine Mansfield's "taint of the pioneer" to Fairburn's poem "I'm Older Than You, Please Listen"), which historically may have faded as a dominant intellectual middle-class urge circa 1970, and from which Hall's/Reid's characters represent a different historical stage. Their fantasies are instead constantly turning to a form of displaced touristic life, not as citizens of anywhere else, but as spectators on the edge of somewhere else, inflecting and extending (in imagination anyway) indefinitely the young New Zealand woman's concentrated grand tour that is one of the objects of the script's wit.

Middle Age Spread is the only one of Reid's films without some major historical time shift either within the narrative or between the narrative and the original audience. The very overt structuring time shifts in *Middle Age Spread* do not deal in historical eras (the pastoral past, the World War II, the early 1980s in *Carry Me Back;* the 1920s, 1950s, and 1980s in *Leave All Fair;* the Second World War and the 1990s in *The Last Tattoo*) but with events only a few months distant that throw light on the primary action of the dinner party, the narrative's present. Although it is impossible to give one simple meaning to the time shifts in the other films, they seem to cohere in an opening up of possibilities and alternatives, which the satire of *Middle Age Spread* fails—beyond dreams of tourism—to envisage. At the same time, though, this negativity has a kind of positive energy. As well as being an exemplar of technique in converting into cinematic terms a stage original, *Middle Age Spread* is a rare example of sustained comic satiric realism in the New Zealand cinema.

Leave All Fair

Reid's third feature, *Leave All Fair,* displays a number of obvious differences from the earlier films, eschewing their comedy and following (despite its deceptive centering on a male character) twinned female protagonists. In addition, it is, in contrast to the very locally rooted worlds of *Middle Age Spread* and *Carry Me Back,* outside New Zealand. With the film set entirely in France, New Zealand, though prominent in its mental imaginary, is literally visible only in photographs of Katherine Mansfield's girlhood Wellington in the edition of her journals that plays a part in the narrative (and forms a curious link with the book cover in *Middle Age Spread*).

Like Reid's other features, *Leave All Fair* is a hybrid text, a version of the nationalist biopic (usually female, and often literary—e.g., *Iris* [1984], *Sylvia* [1985], and *An Angel at My Table* [1990]), but modulated by art film structures. At certain levels, these structures seem to run counter to its main narrative thrust, the nationalist and feminist recovery of the earliest New Zealand cultural icon, the expatriate writer Katherine Mansfield. At the film's deviant narrative center is Mansfield's husband, the English critic, John Middleton Murry (John Geilgud), who is revealed to be exploiting her reputation, disobeying her instructions to destroy her inferior work, presenting her to the world through his possessive idealizations, and crucially undervaluing the importance of New Zealand in her writing. Gielgud's portrayal of Murry combines a "masculinist" simplification of Mansfield's complex reality with a British literary establishment's

Marie enjoys a picnic with the affable Murry before discovering his past in *Leave All Fair*. (Courtesy New Zealand Film Commission.)

supposed undervaluing of her New Zealandness. In the minimalist plot, Murry, shortly before his death, visits France to meet with André (Feodor Atkine), the French publisher of an edition of Mansfield's journals some thirty years after her death. André's lover, Marie Taylor, is a young New Zealand expatriate theater designer (played by the same actress, Jane Birkin, who appears as Mansfield in both Murry's and Marie's reveries). She moves, through her meetings with Murry, her reading of Mansfield's work, and her discovery of the "leave all fair" letter Murry has not published, to the point where she sees both Murry and André as distorters of the writer's life and work. The film's written epilogue, after noting Murry's death, informs the viewer that Marie returns to New Zealand.

On a first viewing, this overtly nationalist/feminist narrative seems unconditionally validated, particularly in two scenes with high art allusions. In the first, at a rehearsal of Shakespeare's *A Winter's Tale*, Marie disagrees with the (male) producer about the presentation of (the statue of) Hermione, arguing that she should have aged, whereas the producer wants a more superficially glamorous effect. In the second, Murry and André, but not Marie, attend a performance of *La Traviata*, where Violetta's consumptive death scene is clearly inversely paralleled, in its aestheticizing glamour, to the realities of Mansfield's death from consumption; both moments foreground a (male) sentimentalizing of the heroine's predicament. However, more ambiguous elements play against this combination of nationalist and feminist assertions. One of these is extra-textual and open only to cognoscenti: the sense that even by the mid-1980s the film's (or perhaps it is Marie's) attitude to Murry seems dated, that for all his opportunism, the husband/critic was responsible for the growth of Mansfield's reputation, and that few literary critics doubt that he was right in disobeying her plea to "leave all fair" and the less ambiguous instruction expressed in her will.[7] Further, in Mansfield's brief appearances in the film, her contradictory desires for art and life, for freedom and commitment, are so extreme that, whatever Murry's faults, he could hardly be blamed for them. The question then arises—do the film's subjective memory and dream elements cohere in the straightforward, even naïve meanings that have already been suggested, or is there a more productive reading available? Here one might suggest a tension between the nationalist/feminist assertions and a more skeptical structure also based on the twin protagonists, their relatedness underscored by the near homonyms of their names (Murry and Marie), as they invent, out of the complex fluidity of Mansfield and her writing, intensely subjective, opposing but equally partial and self asserting, views of her. In Murry's case this centers on Mansfield's dependence on him, her essential Englishness/Europeanness, and the shallowness of her New Zealand connections; in Marie's case the Mansfield revealed is a mirror of herself, betrayed by her lover (there are fragmentary moments that suggest that André is having an affair with another woman), rootlessly pining for New Zealand, and fired with feminism.

Leave All Fair may well have suffered from Reid's late entry into the project as replacement director (for Stanley Harper) and from the day-to-day writing of dialogue during shooting.[8] However, its basic conceptual framework, in particular the double time scheme, seems to have been Reid's addition. The fundamental ambiguities I have suggested in the film—two views of a New Zealand icon; two competing narratives, one female, one male; nationalism and expatriatism, as well as its double, or indeed triple, time frame (i.e., 1920s, 1950s, 1980s)—relate it intricately to Reid's other films, including his most recent *The Last Tattoo*.

The Last Tattoo

The Last Tattoo revisits the past in the shape of New Zealand's "occupation" by American servicemen in 1942–44 (occasionally the material of Hollywood films, e.g., the Wellington, Masterton, and Foxton episodes of Raoul Walsh's *Battle Cry* [1955], the Paekakariki episodes of *The Sands of Iwo Jima* [1949], New Zealand films such as the television movie *Champion* [1989], and Gaylene Preston's documentary *War Stories Our Mothers Never Told Us* [1995]). Reid's reconstruction of a period enshrined in folk memory is by no means straightforward. First it is filtered through the narrative's homage to film noir; second, through reference to the crisis of New Zealand/American relations peaking in the mid-1980s; third, through allusions to the major internal political and socioeconomic changes beginning in 1984 and continuing into the 1990s; and fourth, through feminist influences of the period that, because of New Zealand's size and the concentration of its cultural institutions, exerted an extraordinarily visible pressure. The film noir homage creates a paranoid version of New Zealand history in which the Hotel Workers Union prostitutes young female workers in order to gain access, with a high-ranking American officer's connivance, to the movement of American supplies. The narrative also involves a wartime government member of Parliament being sexually blackmailed to ensure that union men are not conscripted and that New Zealand will fall under American political domination postwar. If this is fantasy, another seemingly fantastic element proves factual, with the narrative tangentially taking in the real-life 1944 mutiny of New Zealand soldiers returning on furlough, and refusing to be sent back to the war, here presented as a protest against the corrupt immunity to conscription given to union members.[9]

The film's paranoia eschews the easy option of projecting the American "other" as the source of all corruption, involving in the conspiracy immediately recognizable national types. Austen Leech (John Bach), the hard man who violently controls the girls, is a darkly hyperbolic version of local masculine insensitivity, while James Patrick Carroll, the tough, demotic smoothie (played by Tony Barry with Chamber of Commerce/Catholic businessman familiarity), is equally implicated. Of the Americans, the film's virtuous hero, and eventual partner—via various masculinist/feminist adjustments—for Kelly Towne (Kerry Fox) in the international romance is Mike Starwood (Tony Goldwyn). General Frank Zane (Rod Steiger) is a rather minatory character, seemingly uncorrupt, but harshly arrogant, or maybe comically liberating, in his unflattering view of New Zealand ("Goddamn New Zealanders! Shit, you couldn't have the crucifixion here because of the lack of nails!"). However, Conrad Dart, the Machiavellian commander (Robert Loggia), combines private greed with wider politicizing in his plan to sexually compromise Ralph Simpson (Martyn Sanderson), so that when he becomes Prime Minister, he and the Americans will control the country. Conrad, with his benign postwar-oriented rhetoric about winning the peace, but with secret plans to exert control over New Zealand, gains extra resonance as a personification of a particular flare-up of a longer term ambivalence in New Zealand–American relations caused in the mid-1980s by New Zealand's anti-nuclear stance. The film's narrative of union corruption and misdoings in the revered Labour wartime government seems less a claim to literalness than a reflection, through the use of period narrative, of an intense contemporary skepticism about the draconian policies, broken promises, and political opportunisms of both major political parties in the decade leading up to the film. (Perhaps this is most true of Labour, with its conversion to radical anti-traditional privatization and market policies that seemed a betrayal of the past to many, and that laid the ground for the intense privatizing and further diminishing of the old welfare state consensus by the succeeding 1990 National government.)

The Last Tattoo places a female, Kelly Towne, as the traditionally male investigator. Reid, researching the film, discovered references to a nurse with the wartime job of tracing venereal disease contacts.[10] Kelly's profession ingeniously inflects the new hardboiled heroines of contemporary crime fiction. Further, in finding a convincing historical rationale for a female investigator, her VD nurse, with its play on Karitane and Plunket (health care facilities) as the more usual branches of one of the main careers open to New Zealand women of the time, brings into conjunction the plot's motifs of prostitution, and military and political corruption. It allows her, like the classic private eye, to traverse the narrative world from the Simpsons' wealthy suburb to the mean streets of the union headquarters and the female workers' hostel/brothel. It also surrounds her with psychic complications: the difficulties of love where sex and disease are synonymous and where female exploitation is the norm. Kelly's idealization (beautiful in 1940s hats and big-shouldered suits, drinking Scotch, driving Mike's jeep and a fishing boat, handling a gun and throwing a punch effectively, alongside ambitions to be a doctor) makes her a fantasized 1990s woman in 1940s dress, and Reid's film part of the shift whereby female protagonists, directors, and thematics became a major presence in 1990s New Zealand cinema.

The change embodied in Kelly's centrality (via the more portentous but less lively portraits of Mansfield and Marie in *Leave All Fair*) is worth pausing over. Although Reid's earlier films are male-centered (for instance, *Middle Age Spread*'s wit is largely placed with Colin and Reg), there are intimations of the later shift. These appear not just in the Joanne Mildenhall character in *Carry Me Back*, who (though the nameless sheila of the archetypal Kiwi joke) is clearly more independent than we imagine the late Mrs. T. K. to have been, but also in the sympathies created round Judy, and eventually Isabel, and even Elizabeth in *Middle Age Spread*. Such suggestions inflect deviously in the formidable Aunty Bird of *Carry Me Back*, a carnivalesque version of Kelly. Played by Dorothy McKegg as the suburban Elizabeth's anarchic sibling, Aunty Bird is a site of multiple, often satiric-grotesque effects. The "bloody old bat" is gargoylishly unfeminine, obsessive in her family feuding, lives in a derelict property as "woman alone," is graspingly stingy, yet simultaneously is the family's historian and conscience, knows the truth about events going back to the war, and refuses to countenance T. K.'s abandonment of Old Mac. Unlike Elizabeth, she is actively mobile, outwitting the boys on the road as often

Re-creating period history for the 1990s: Kelly Towne, the female investigator, aided by Mike Starwood, in *The Last Tattoo*. (Courtesy New Zealand Film Commission.)

as they outwit her, her own illegal transportation of Old Mac paralleling the boys' illicit carrying of T. K., and managing to see off the policeman who threatens to arrest her. Finally, reconciled with her nephews, and presumably allowed her share of the farm, she ends up as the unconventional matriarch of the reformed family, replacing the two departed patriarchs. Like those "disreputable women" who feature colorfully in James Belich's writing about nineteenth-century New Zealand society (for instance the unregenerate Aucklanders Bridget Hawkey and Mary Robinson),[11] Aunty Bird is perhaps more pleasant to contemplate imaginatively than to meet with actually, but part of her meaning seems to be as an unsocialized throwback to less-constrained female pioneer energies, both positive and negative; indeed, the battered shop in which she lives, with its mildly Gothic overtones, marks her as a comic analogue to the horror film's site of the "return of the repressed." Notably, the reconstituted family has as its females Aunty Bird's pioneer throwback and Jimmy's girl's gesture to the future, but cuts out the static middle term implied by the unseen Mrs. T. K. In terms of her pioneering capability, the analogies between Aunty Bird and Kelly are clear.

As noir historical romance, with an idealized rather than comic-grotesque center of female energies, *The Last Tattoo* creates romantic and investigative resolutions, allowing Kelly and Mike to fall in love, and setting up the discovery of Conrad and the local criminals. The ending, though, can be read ambivalently. The last shot of Conrad and Carroll looking down from a high window on Kelly (just after Carroll has murdered Leech) may suggest that the conspirators will escape, and though we presume that

Kelly will leave New Zealand for the United States, the known extent of the American casualties in the fierce battle for Tarawa that the marines are heading for, may also suggest that Mike will die and that Kelly will not necessarily become an expatriate.

This ambivalent closure is characteristic of Reid's features (*Middle Age Spread* ending with Colin replying to Elizabeth's "What do we do now?" with "What we do, Elizabeth, is the dishes"; *Carry Me Back* with its unresolved backward forward movement; *Leave All Fair* with its—at least on a subtle reading—interpretative dilemmas based on Murry, Marie, and Mansfield). What is true of these closures is true of the bodies of the films as they play out the various antitheses and relationships suggested throughout this essay, in ways enabled by the filmmaker's sensitivity to historical and social currents.

Notes

1. Carry me back to old Virginny,
    There's where the cotton and the corn and 'tatoes grow,
    There's where the birds warble sweet in the Springtime,
    There's where the old darkey's heart am longed to go.
    There's where I labored so hard for old massa,
    Day after day in the fields of yellow corn,
    No place on earth do I love more sincerely
    Than old Virginny, the state where I was born.

    Carry me back to old Virginny,
    There let me live till I wither and decay.

    Available at http://www50states.com/songs/Virginia/html.
2. Gary Hawke, "Economic Trends and Economic Policy, 1938–1992," in *The Oxford History of New Zealand*, ed. Geoffrey W. Rice (Oxford: Oxford University Press, 1992), 420–21.
3. Ibid, 421.
4. Ibid.
5. See Nick Perry, "Black to the Future," in *The Dominion of Signs: Television, Advertising, and Other New Zealand Fictions* (Auckland: Auckland University Press, 1994), 88–89.
6. Brian Brake and Maurice Shadbolt, *New Zealand: Gift of the Sea* (Christchurch: Whitcombe and Tombs, 1963).
7. A review by Tom Williams, "Fair to Whom?," taking the nationalist-feminist strand as unchallenged, notes that "by reducing Murry to a sexist exploiter for financial gain [the film] simplifies the KM/Murry relationship into a cliché of our time" (*New Zealand Listener* 1 [February 1986]: 38).
8. See Helen Martin and Sam Edwards, *New Zealand Film, 1912–1996* (Auckland: Oxford University Press, 1997), 116.

9. For a short account, see James Belich, *Paradise Reforged* (Auckland: Penguin, 1996), 289–92. See also chapter 18 of F. L. W. Wood, *The New Zealand People at War: Political and External Affairs* (Christchurch: Whitcombe and Tombs), 244–60.
10. See further Teresa O'Connor, "A Nursing Premiere," *Nursing New Zealand* (December/January 1994): 45. Margaret Macnab, the prototype for Kelly, wrote a short memoir, "Girls of the Silver Dollar," in *The War Years: New Zealanders Remember, 1939–1945*, ed. Anna Rogers (Wellington: Wellington Platform, 1989), 29–42.
11. James Belich, *Making Peoples* (Auckland: Penguin, 1996), 427.

John Reid—Filmography

1967. *Something of Course* (NZ short film: director, producer, writer).
1967. *A Game for Five Players* (NZ television drama: actor).
1970. *Coming Up with the Ideas* (NZ short film: director, writer).
1971. *Arthur K Frupp 54* (NZ television drama: actor).
1972. *All That We Need* (NZ extended short film: assistant director).
1974. *One of Those People That Live in the World* (NZ television drama-documentary originally shown in two parts: actor).
1974. *The Fastest Greens in the World* (NZ documentary: writer, researcher, second unit director).
1975. *Turangi: A Town for All Seasons* (NZ documentary: narrator).
1975. *From Woe to Go* (NZ short film: director).
1976. *The Right to Know* (NZ documentary, six parts: director, writer).
1976. *From Where the Spirit Calls* (NZ documentary: director, writer).
1978. *Red Mole on the Road* (NZ documentary: co-writer).
1978/81. *Close to Home* (NZ television soap opera: frequent director of episodes).
1979. ***Middle Age Spread*** (NZ feature film: director).
1980. *Jane: The Place and Painting of Jane Evans* (NZ documentary: director, producer).
1980. *Open File* (NZ television six-part series of dramas: director of two programs).
1980. *A Question of Power: The Manapouri Debate* (NZ documentary: narrator).
1981. *Jetstream: The World Jet Boat Marathon* (NZ documentary: writer).
1981. *Seekers* (NZ television series: director of two episodes).
1982. ***Carry Me Back*** (NZ feature film: director, co-writer, actor).
1982/83. *Inside Straight* (NZ television series: director of the episodes "Horse Switch" and "Night Porter").
1983. *Hometown Boomtown* (NZ documentary: director, producer).
1984. *Iris* (NZ television feature: actor).
1985. ***Leave All Fair*** (NZ/France feature film: director, co-writer).
1992. *The Ray Bradbury Theatre* (US/France/UK/Canada/NZ television series:

director of the episode "Fee Fie Fo Fum").
1994. *The Last Tattoo* (NZ feature film: director, co-author of the original story).
1998. *The Legend of William Tell* (US/NZ television series: director of the episodes "The Labyrinth" and "Doppelganger").
1998/99. *Duggan* (NZ television series: director of the episodes "Going Overboard" and "Dog's Breakfast").
1999. *A Twist in the Tale* a.k.a. *William Shatner's A Twist in the Tale* (US/NZ television series: director of the episodes "The Duellists," "The Pirate," and "Darkness Visible").
1999/2003. *The Tribe* (UK/NZ television series: frequent director of episodes).
2001. *Dark Knight* (UK/NZ television series: director of the episode "Black Tree").
2001. *Atlantis High* (UK/NZ television series: occasional episode director).
2002. *Revelations* (UK television series: occasional episode director).
2002/3. *The Strip* (NZ television series: director of the episodes "Secrets and Guys," "All's Fair in Love and Volleyball," "Sex, Lies and Spacerocks," "Can You Handle It?," "Fish Out Of Water," "Mexican Stand Off," "Once Bitten," "Taking the Plunge," "Opening Night," "My Baby," "The Joy of Sex," and "Woof!").
2003. *Hillary on Everest* (NZ television documentary: post production consultant).
2004. *The Making of Sleeping Dogs* (NZ documentary: director).
2004. *The Making of Smash Palace* (NZ documentary: director).

3 Visionaries and Fantasists

THIS SECTION OF THE BOOK focuses on those filmmakers from New Zealand who most obviously demonstrate the idea of a film as the work of a figure committed to a particular vision or to the production of rich and striking imagery. Despite the long-standing centrality of issues surrounding collective identity in the production of New Zealand culture, the figure of the idiosyncratic and often irreverent artist has often had a key place in the national imaginary. Poet James K. Baxter and painter Colin McCahon occupy powerful positions in their respective canons within New Zealand as practitioners of a distinctly individual art, often seen as a unique product made possible only by the local circumstances under which it was made. That a culture seemingly defined by its sense of the collective can produce a tradition of individual exceptionalism is only an irony on first glance. There is a strong sense and heritage of the uniqueness of New Zealand, for example in its dramatic landscape and the quality of its light, that appears to inspire new forms in the work of the visionary or the fantasist. Because of the promise it holds or the opportunities it suggests, the country has—from Samuel Butler's creation of a remote fantasy world in his 1872 novel *Erewhon* to Peter Jackson's manufacture of Middle Earth—been subject to the imaginative manipulation of the visionary producer.

The figures discussed in this section are creators of visual worlds that carry commanding personal impressions, although these frequently take different forms. Len Lye's pioneering work in the avant-garde, the individual visual style of his direct animation, can be seen as a precursor to some of the filmmakers in this section. For a director like Vincent Ward, for example, the force of the cinematic image connects to a tradition of representation in earlier visual arts that reach out from and beyond New Zealand. His is a cinema in which the language of the image is equal to or exceeds that of the narrative in conveying stories. In a different vein, directors such as Jane Campion and Alison Maclean, although image makers in their own right, unite their films through thematic concerns to produce bodies of work that discuss the multiple positions of the contemporary, often female, subject. Their films return to the figure of the outsider, the subject not included in the hegemonic orthodoxies of the everyday. As such, they tell powerful stories of the often-precarious location of the individual. Peter Jackson and David Blyth have yet different characteristics, pushing the boundaries of film genre in order to create imaginative stories or cast sly commentaries on the nature of the social. Their films offer the opportunity to see the evolution of highly individual tales, full of (especially in Jackson's case) an increasing sophistication of cinematic method. Leon Narbey, one of New Zealand's most prominent and influential cinematographers, and a figure who went on to direct his own features, might be seen to combine a number of these positions, moving from early light and sound experiments to films driven by political commitments and interested in social commentary or with a sustained interest in the issues of form. Narbey can be seen to bring an idea of visionaries in New Zealand full circle with his contribution to *Flip and Two Twisters* (1994), the film made to celebrate the work of Lye. As with the others discussed in this section, Narbey refuses to limit the sources from which he draws inspiration, and he operates a continual return to the foundational visual nature of the screen image in his filmmaking.

It is worth noting that Jane Campion and Peter Jackson, the two New Zealand filmmakers who arguably command the most international attention, both belong to this third section. Their technical expertise, and the power of their respective visions, has captured global audiences, for all that they work increasingly within the commodified and commercialized idea of production that is characteristic of Hollywood. Such visions can be seen to have origins in ideas of space and the local in New Zealand. Because of its landscape, or because of a wider idea of it being an empty place upon which individuals might construct their stories, the country has often figured as a location in which narratives and visions of alternative worlds are played out. The contemporary forms of this—Middle Earth and Narnia—are to some degree versions that parallel earlier films, usually Australian or American, that used the country as a backdrop for events. But at the same time, these visionary or fantasy worlds are now often those made by New Zealand filmmakers themselves, and are part of a complex dynamic that links the ability to tell a cinematic story, in all its technical intricacies, to the particularities and experiences of place. Figures such as Campion and Jackson serve as reminders that it is still often the individual filmmaker, whether faced by the demands of a national audience eager to see itself on the screen or working within the complexity of the international, high-budget feature, who frequently determines the power of the specific film.

Even as their work, with its different locations, subjects, and audiences, has complicated the idea of what New Zealand film culture is, and indeed what constitutes a New Zealand filmmaker, they—and the others included in this section—continue to attest to the force of the individual cinematic vision.

15

Leon Narbey

Art, Politics, and the Personal

Helen Martin

Since he began working with film as an art student in the late 1960s, Leon Narbey's contribution to New Zealand cinema has been broad and substantial. He quickly became excited by the possibilities thrown up by his first films, the shorts *Room One* (1968) and *Room Two* (1968), made in collaboration with Elam School of Fine Arts colleagues at the University of Auckland to record his 1967 experimental light/sculpture installations; and *A Film of Real Time: A Light-Sound Environment* (1971), shot to document the five-level, interactive sound/light experience he created to celebrate the opening of New Plymouth's Govett-Brewster Art Gallery. Under the directorship of John Maynard, Narbey moved from small art films to a brief (three-year) career learning the craft of photography as a news cameraman in television. From there, he was involved in New Zealand cinema's New Wave as a key figure from its beginnings. Since 1977, his work as a freelance filmmaker has taken him across the genres of documentary and drama; short and feature length films, in collaboration with many others important in the growth of a national film culture; and in roles ranging from editor to cinematographer to writer/director, for which he has won numerous film awards. Narbey tends to avoid mainstream projects, choosing to follow his passions: assisting directors realize their vision, telling engaging stories for a thinking audience, finding the right image through meticulous research and careful use of light, exploring the dynamics of shooting and editing, and integrating landscape into the film journey. As exemplars of Narbey's work, this essay will discuss *Skin Deep* (1978; director of photography), *Bastion Point Day 507* (1980; co-director, co-producer, camera, editor), *Illustrious Energy* (1987; director, co-writer), *The Footstep Man* (1992; director; co-writer), *Desperate Remedies* (1993; director of photography), and *Flip and Two Twisters* (1995; director of photography).

In an interview, Geoff Steven noted that, "In the 1970s in New Zealand there were three groups of filmmakers all clutching around for our own sort of cinema. There were the ex-Pacific Films guys out of Wellington, who were the Acme Sausage Company/Waimarama-Blerta group with Geoff Murphy and Bruno Lawrence and others, and in Auckland Roger Donaldson's Aardvark did *Sleeping Dogs,* which was commercial and very successful mainstream cinema and across the road there was the Alternative Cinema group with a more political, more 'arty' focus."[1] Narbey associated with the artistic, political filmmakers as a natural progression from his early experimental work. When he moved in 1972 to work at the Ilam School of Fine Arts, University of Canterbury, his Auckland association with Steven was the spur to his setting up, with his partner Anita and with filmmaker Mike Glynn, Alternative Cinema Christchurch, a South Island resource center for emerging filmmakers along the lines of the cooperative Steven had been instrumental in establishing in 1972 in Auckland.[2] Narbey's move into television in 1975 was motivated by a desire to immerse himself in learning the craft of camera operation and to reach a wider audience, because "I had been doing things that were very esoteric and I realized my audience was only about half a dozen people in Christchurch."[3]

A collaboration with Steven, who shared Narbey's political and aesthetic interests, gave Narbey his first significant shoot and the opportunity to work on an independent production. With Steven as director, Philip Dadson as sound recordist, Narbey as cameraman, and Gil Scrine as assistant cameraman/editor, *Te Matakite O Aotearoa* (1975), documenting the Maori Land March from Te Hapua, Spirits Bay, to Wellington, was the first New Zealand program commissioned for an independent producer outside television. In 1976 Narbey went to Zimbabwe, Tanzania, Kenya, and Zambia as cameraman for Derek Fox on two half-hour TVNZ documentaries, *They Say We Let Them Down,* recording Black African attitudes to sporting contacts between New Zealand and South Africa, and *Countdown on Zimbabwe,* which looked at political conflicts in Rhodesia.

Narbey's first feature film opportunity, *Skin Deep,* arose out of the Land March. When the march moved through the rural town of Raetihi, Steven, looking for a feature idea that would reflect local stories and wary of the prohibitive cost of building film sets, was excited that the place, with its wide, empty, western-looking streets, "looked like a set waiting for a film to happen."[4] From this impulse, using new video technology, and an experimental, ultra-realist shooting style in the spirit of the conceptual art popular at the time, Steven produced *Aspects of a Small Town,* a three-screen installation exhibited as a New Artists project at the Auckland Art Gallery under the curatorship of John Maynard. Using the exhibition as "working notes," Steven collaborated with colleagues from the Alternative Cinema/ art scene milieu, Piers Davies (who had co-written the 1974 Australian feature *The Cars That Ate Paris*) and Roger Horrocks (who was teaching at the University of Auckland) in writing the script for *Skin Deep*, which became the first film to receive funding from the Interim Film Commission established in the wake of the success of *Sleeping Dogs* (1977).

Skin Deep is concerned with a social and capitalist dynamic and the sexual politics in a small town, at a time in New Zealand's history when "boosterism" (using expansive, expensive advertising campaigns to get noticed) was viewed by rural communities as a way of recovering their economy. Available light, actual locales rather than studios and sets, a lead actor (Deryn Cooper) who represents ordinary life rather than glamour, non-actors as extras, singers Beaver and Bunny Walters and the Country Flyers band appearing as themselves, and dialogue echoing the New Zealand voice give the film a contemporary, documentary-style realism. Unlike in Neorealist films, which are episodic and open-ended, plot construction in *Skin Deep* uses dramatic conventions, with a three-act, cause and effect, closed narrative. But Narbey's shooting style (with Paul Leach as camera operator) is very much in keeping with European films' interest in documentary-style localism and realism. Continuity shooting conveys a sense of real time, valuing the frame and the image. Takes are long and lingering (with many over twenty seconds) and slow, fluid camera movements create a contemplative rhythm. Most shots observe a documentary-style distance from their human subjects (there is only one close-up) and are held after the action to leave the viewer looking at the (often desolate) setting, emptied of life and energy. The camera is frequently an observer, with scenes like the axeman's carnival and the church service rich in documentary detail, but the way shots are composed and held offers ironic comment. Frequent high angle shots diminish characters, while tracking shots suggest uneasy relationships between people and place, giving the documentary-style observation an emotional resonance, which can be read as a naturalistic aesthetic:

> Geoff and I were very influenced by East European Czech and Polish filmmakers who were concerned with choreographing a scene so it could be obtained in one shot without the need to cut, as montage was seen as a false fabrication of truth. We were perhaps attempting a similar aesthetic in the documentary manner. One film we referenced was *Red Psalm*, a 1971 film by Hungarian director Miklos Jancso, which was shot in 10 takes. The final shot in *Skin Deep* is a homage to him. It's a 360 degree real time shot, a massive undertaking. In this shot the camera moves with a sort of determined grace that seemingly just happens to catch what's happening—the advertising

people with the local business people out in the street, the city woman's car leaving town. This choreography relates to a dance concept of space and music.[5]

While documentary-style techniques give resonance to the film's social themes, Narbey's account of the visual inspiration for the film is specific and particular: "The script came out of the place. Raetihi had all the characteristics of an American western town or a Russell Drysdale Australian town classic—wide and bare, designed for bullocks and horses and carts to turn around. Geoff and I were thinking almost like Robin White—hard-edged, straight on wide shots, framing and composition square on, almost geometric, backing off for objectivity. We liked the charm of the old cinema building, the frontal facades."[6]

Narbey's references to both the New Zealand painter Robin White and to the painter Russell Drysdale—whose depictions of Australian outback towns in works like *Moody's Pub* (1941) and *The Cricketers* (1948) are evocative narratives of the settler subject, seen as "interpretations of national identity and culture during a time of tremendous social change in Australian history"—exemplify his use of artistic imagery to inform his filmmaking vision.[7] Art historian Christopher Allen describes how Drysdale depicts the vast and barely inhabited Australian outback as "the expression of an existential state" where "the subject of the settler's confidence or anxiety is always ultimately the viability and legitimacy of his tenure on the land."[8] The isolation of the small New Zealand town, as epitomized by the fictitious Carlton (Raetihi) in *Skin Deep*, is far less severe than that, but in a similar way the New Zealand narrative successfully evokes a sense of the occupants' anxiety that borders on panic—women who fear their rural innocence is threatened, men who fear for their livelihoods and for the viability of the town itself. Disconnected from the land and afraid of continuing rural decline, the bourgeois Pakeha (European) townsfolk see that "progress" lies in aping urban commerce. While the film's dialogue and action echoes the city myth of small towns described in so much New Zealand fiction—small minded, sexist, parochial, puritanical, hypocritical, envious—Narbey's cinematography provides a strong visual complement, fanning out from specific images of character and local landmark (main street, hall, gym, motel, church) to the spaces beyond (road, field, mountain range) to show the separation and alienation of Carlton's inhabitants from the surrounding country.

In 1983, Narbey was director of photography on Phase Three Films' *Strata*, Steven's last attempt at a European-style feature. Although the disjointed, underdeveloped narrative did not appeal to local audiences, the film is visually striking. And while Geoff Steven's features did not succeed

Early experiments: Narbey's striking landscape in *Strata*. (Courtesy New Zealand Film Commission.)

in establishing the European style as a popular form in New Zealand (Paul Maunder's *Landfall,* shot in 1975 and released in 1977, was the only other New Wave feature to attempt it) they made an important contribution to the burgeoning culture of feature film production, not the least of which was in providing opportunities for Narbey to develop as a cinematographer.

Alongside feature filmmaking, Narbey had a continued interest in the value of political documentary as an instrument of change. Shot after *Skin Deep* in 1978 yet edited by Narbey in 1980, the year of its release (the delay was through lack of funding), *Bastion Point Day 507* is a political activist documentary, made by a collective to provide a partisan view of a defining moment in the history of Aotearoa New Zealand. That the protest was successful in eventually forcing the government to return the land to the people of Ngati Whatua gives viewing the film in the present day added resonance.

Focusing on collective grievance, the film records the removal, by six hundred police and the army, of land-rights protesters who had, in an unprecedented action, occupied Auckland's Takaparawha (Bastion Point) for 506 days from January 5, 1977. While often described as Merata Mita's film,[9] possibly because the project was initiated by an approach to Mita by the Bastion Point protest organizers, possibly because the sympathies of the material are determinedly Maori, the award-winning documentary was a collaboration between Mita, Narbey, and Gerd Pohlmann, with all three sharing the directing and producing credits. For Auckland's Ngati Whatua, the spur to the occupation of Bastion Point was the release of government plans, in 1976, to develop land the Crown had taken from them. The film is an eloquent narrative of resolve and action, stemming from anger about colonization and loss of Maori language and land, anger that had been honed during marae (central meeting area) visits made on the 1975 March, and which crystallized in the mid-1970s under the stewardship of a new wave of radical Maori leaders engaged in a "renegotiation of Maori identity."[10]

The shooting and editing styles, while they may have been accurately described by Mita as "a Maori approach to film making" because the viewpoint is partisan and because the lack of commentary is in keeping with the oral storytelling tradition, can also be seen to fit comfortably within Narbey's style and methods in his earlier work, such as *Te Matakite O Aotearoa*.[11] Continuity shooting and long still takes allow room for the evocation of mood and for the viewer to watch events unfold. In a radical departure from the documentary practice of the day, voice-over is used only in the prologue, and interviews are eschewed in favor of the storytelling itself through the words of protesters (in song, conversation, and rhetoric) and their evictors. The film's intercutting from points around the scene highlights the sense of clashing ideologies (the state, using force, versus the displaced indigenous people using passive resistance) and of real time; wild sound, like the throbbing of a hovering helicopter, enhances the drama of the moment. Narbey's editing gives weight to the visuals, making effective use of the freeze frame and the repetition of photographs to intensify the moment and find ironic counterpoint in the juxtaposition of images.

With no initial funding, Narbey borrowed film stock from Steven and a camera from commercials director Andy Tyler. The other eight or so cameras came from TVNZ. Funding from the QE2 (Queen Elizabeth II) Arts Council after the shoot enabled Narbey, editing on Education Department equipment, to add television news footage (from TV1 and South Pacific Television) and radio recordings (from Radio Hauraki, the only station to have kept its master quarter-inch live voice reports) and to process the actuality-enhancing black-and-white still shots provided by Robin Morrison, Bruce Foster, and the *Auckland Star* newspaper.

Bastion Point Day 507 was one of a number of political documentaries made in New Zealand in the early 1980s that, as Russell Campbell has noted, "exposed the rifts in a society structured on class and racial inequality, rifts which mainstream documentary had always plastered over."[12] The film screened on New Zealand television on May 21, 1981, adding fuel to the fires of protest gaining momentum in preparation for the South African Springbok rugby team's controversial tour of the country due to begin in July 1981. That the film's record is of continuing importance has been recognized in the use made of its footage in later accounts, such as in Morrison Grieve's 1999 *Inside New Zealand* television documentary and *Bastion Point—the Untold Story* (1999), directed by Sharon Hawke. In 2002, The Academy cinema in Auckland marked the national Waitangi Day (February 6) with a public screening of the film. Narbey regards *Bastion Point Day 507* as "one of the most important films I've worked on, and perhaps one of the most successful in content and style."[13]

In 1979, Narbey went to China as cameraman with Steven, Geoff Chapple, and Graham Morris to shoot three extraordinary documentaries—*Gung Ho: Rewi Alley of China* and *The Humble Force* were co-produced with the National Film Unit, while *China's Patriot Army* was made for TVNZ. Other political documentaries Narbey has worked on include *Man of the Trees* (1981, as director and cameraman); a portrait of ninety-two-year-old British conservationist Richard St. Barbe Baker; Gerd Pohlmann and Merata Mita's *The Bridge: A Story of Men in Dispute* (1982, as cameraman); a record of the drawn-out Mangere Bridge union strike; *Patu!* (1983, as a cameraman), which captured the protests against the Springbok rugby team's tour; *Visible Evidence* (1996, as director), where social-documentary humanist photographers discuss their work and social change; and *Punitive Damage* (1999, as director of photography), Annie Goldson's feature about a mother's attempts to bring her son's killers to justice in East Timor.

Alongside his political documentaries, Narbey has continued to follow his first love, the arts, shooting many works about artists. In this genre he has collaborated often with director/producer/writer Shirley Horrocks, on such works as *Pleasures and Dangers* (1991), *Act of Murder* (1993), *Flip and Two Twisters* (1995), *The Transformers* (1996), and *Early Days Yet: A Profile of the Poet Allen Curnow* (2001). Narbey's contribution to *Flip and Two Twisters* exemplifies how his technical and artistic skills as a cinematographer assist a director in realizing a vision. Funded by New Zealand On Air and made for television with the purpose of giving wider currency to the life and work of the celebrated New Zealand–born filmmaker/painter/sculptor/photographer Len Lye, the film contains footage from many sources: from Lye's films, from TVNZ (found footage used in a sporting montage), from the former New Zealand Broadcasting Corporation (footage shot in America and New Zealand), from hitherto unscreened film shot by an American television producer in the 1960s in New York, from film of Lye's wife Ann shot by Shirley Horrocks in 1980 in New York after Lye's death, and from stills from the Len Lye Foundation collection and from computer-generated images. The narrative of *Flip and Two Twisters* centers on Lye's sculptures being reconstructed in the present day by a team led by Evan Webb of the Len Lye Foundation (Webb calls it "keeping the works performing as he [Lye] intended them to perform"). Narbey shot the accompanying interviews and the difficult-to-achieve footage of the assembly process of the final, installed sculptures. In a sense this recalls where Narbey started out, having not at that time heard of Lye or seen his work, filming his own light/sound installations. Lye's art was kinetic, an art based on movement, what he called "figures of motion," and it was Narbey's task to capture the essence of the sculptures that Webb and team, using the latest in technology and design concepts, take from Lye's original models and recreate on a much larger scale:

> The biggest challenge in shooting Len Lye's works was eliminating unwanted reflections in the highly reflective stainless steel that was in perpetual motion. The reflections were usually those of myself, camera and lights. In lighting Len's works of stainless steel, there is always the decision as to whether you reveal it as a surface form, that is a solid, or as a transparent reflective mirror surface. *Flip and Two Twisters* was perhaps the most difficult one to film because of its sheer size. We hung up 8 meter-plus high velvet to contrast the stainless steel work and to show it as Len had wanted it to appear.[14]

As shown through Narbey's camera and lighting, the sculptures dance, glide, twist, and slither, beautiful "figures of motion," gleaming and shimmering as if with a life all of their own. Shirley Horrocks commented: "Leon has a wonderful eye and he's meticulous, a perfectionist. He loves art and he really liked working with Len's sculptures. They're very hard to shoot because of the reflective, moving surfaces and because some of the pieces are very large to light. But although lighting them was so difficult Leon will always give you the look you want. He shot Len's sculpture better than it's ever been shot before."[15] As well as screenings of *Flip and Two Twisters* on New Zealand television and the Sundance channel, there is a continuing interest in the film in education circles and on the national and international gallery and festival circuits—in 2001, for example, it was screened many times to mark the centenary of Lye's birth.

While working as a director of photography on others' productions is a challenge Narbey enjoys "because it's engaging and exciting and totally involving," he finds his own projects the most challenging.[16] Having directed four documentaries, his first dramatic feature as director (and co-writer with Martin Edmond), *Illustrious Energy* (1987), was, at 101 minutes, a considerable undertaking. Narbey's love for and fascination with landscapes was one of the springboards for setting the film on New Zealand's South Island among the schist of "heavy, dark, eroded, remote Central Otago."[17] Another was his inspirational earlier trip to northwest China. The film was initially to be a docudrama about a little-discussed part of Central Otago's history—the lives of Chinese immigrants who arrived in New Zealand during the gold rush in the 1860s—but became a drama when the original concept was refused funding. The writers were inspired by and used as source material a twenty-year collection of notes and photographs from the diary of Presbyterian minister, Reverend Alexander Don, a zealous missionary who, wanting to convert immigrants to Christianity, had set up a mission station in China and had collected data on all the Chinese in Central Otago. The diary information on an old man with dementia, Illustrious Envoy (misread by the typesetters of Don's diary as "Energy"), who was arrested and committed to Seacliff Hospital, supplied the writers with ideas for their Chinese prospector character, Chan (Shaun Bao). Other sources used in the research on lifestyles and artifacts were studies by James Ng, Charles Sedgwick, and Neville Ritchie.[18] For the film's interior night lighting, Narbey, with director of photography Alan Locke, aimed for the look of seventeenth-century baroque painter Georges de La Tour's candlelit scenes. To represent the landscape's brown and gray tones, Narbey looked at Romantic nineteenth-century painters like Caspar David Friedrich for ideas, while Janelle Aston's production design and Jan Preston's music draw richly on historical references for authenticity.

The film is set in 1895 and its main characters, Chan and his father-in-law Kim (Harry Ip), have remained living frugally in a remote Central Otago valley after the gold rush, too poor to return home. Thematically, the focus is on the plight of the immigrant who longs for home while remaining seduced by the chance of prosperity in a new land. The characters, beset by cultural dislocation, racism, and the ominous presence of surveyors old Kim calls "land butchers," are on journeys that reach into allegory. Thus the film raises questions about history, colonization, immigration, and the human condition.[19]

Shot mainly in Conroy's Gully, south of Alexandra, (with two days of the shoot at the now-flooded Cornish Point), *Illustrious Energy* is a mesmerizing film, where landscape is not a beautiful thing apart but an integral force in the film journey, a topography reflecting emotional, social, and cultural textures. With minimum dialogue, for much of the time the images and music are left to speak for themselves, a poetic effect that shows clearly in the film's beginning. While there was some argument that the filmmakers were at fault in being out of their culture,[20] *Illustrious Energy* received a positive popular and critical response on its New Zealand release and was the recipient of many awards.

Working on *Illustrious Energy* gave rise to ideas that became central to Narbey's next feature, *The Footstep Man*. While researching costumes for the prostitute scene in *Illustrious Energy*, Narbey became fascinated by brothel scenes painted by Henri de Toulouse-Lautrec. During *Illustrious Energy*'s post-production, Narbey became interested in film sound and by the process whereby film creates an illusion of space and time. From these initial ideas Narbey and co-writer Edmond developed *The Footstep Man* as an intense, psychological drama, incorporating a complex film-within-a-film narrative, and exploring themes of identity, sexual politics, love, and redemption, the relationship between art and life and between art (including film) and its audience. When his wife and child leave him, grieving Sam (Steven Grives), an obsessive footstepper (foley artist), who is working on a film about Toulouse-Lautrec, becomes fixated on the fate of Toulouse-Lautrec's prostitute lover/model Mireille (Jennifer Ward-Lealand), who is to commit suicide in the film. Mireille begins "appearing" before Sam and he loses the ability to distinguish between illusion and reality. Shot by Allen Guilford, the film is an ambitious, multi-layered work embracing many challenges: foremost, the making of a film with a number of period scenes within the NZ$2.5 million budget, then creating a production design for the French part of the story that captured the opulence, colors, and textures of the 1890s, and finding ways to link this with design elements in the contemporary story. Particular demands also existed in the construction and the organization of the narrative: the creating of a fully realized film-within-a-film depicting Toulouse-Lautrec as a complex human being, rather than "the popularized fabrication of his debauchery,"[21] while developing the characters of Mireille and her lesbian lover Marcelle (Sarah Smuts-Kennedy); writing a three-act script with transitions between the contemporary story, told chronologically, and the Parisian story, told out of sequence; marrying contemporary and historical personal stories with stories about film technologies and filmmakers—the sound for the film-within-the-film, *Monsieur Henri*, is being recorded on analogue sprocket (reel to reel recording) technology; and creating complex lighting and camera set-ups and shooting and editing scenes that were at times composites of up to five locations.

The Footstep Man is an excellent example of Narbey's meticulous research methods. In London he watched footstep artists at work; in Los Angeles he investigated sound technologies; and in Paris and Albi, Toulouse-Lautrec's birthplace, he looked at many paintings and photographs. Narbey also read written accounts to learn about the artist. Production designer Kai Hawkins and costume designer Barbara Darragh used Toulouse-Lautrec's paintings as a direct reference, while artists Ross Ritchie and Kate Lang copied many of these in the finest detail, with the addition that the faces of *The Footstep Man*'s female actors were substituted for those of Toulouse-Lautrec's prostitutes: "Getting that exactitude was important, even down to the right easel; getting the paintings to be the right proportions, the frames, the cardboard Lautrec painted on."[22] Equal attention was paid to the lighting design:

> Allen Guilford and I were searching for a reference to the period. We looked at a number of films. In the end we were looking at the paintings of Degas even though the film was about Toulouse-Lautrec, because Lautrec does not depict light/shade/shadow very well. He depicts character and the exactitude of line of the portrait of a real person but he never had a feeling for light. Degas's prints of the brothels were a great source of inspiration for us.[23]

Producer John Maynard was attracted to the project because "It was a most unusual idea for a New Zealand filmmaker; poetic, complex and brave," and while some of the local critical response to the film was quite negative, *The Footstep Man* won awards for its cinematography and editing.[24]

If each film he shoots provides Narbey with new and interesting cinematographic challenges in realizing a director's vision, the feature film *Desperate Remedies* must rate highly among his collaborations. Peter Wells, who co-directed and co-wrote the film with Stewart Main, illuminates the intent and execution of *Desperate Remedies* in his paper *Frock Attack! Wig Wars!* The aim was to create a drama where same-sex sexuality is central, with the negotiation of lesbian identity on the part of the two female leads providing the narrative drive. Dorothea (Jennifer Ward-Lealand) and Anne (Lisa Chappell), trapped in a world that legitimizes only heterosexual union, resort to elaborate deceit and subterfuge to find a triumphant way out. That the film figures a gay female rather than a gay male journey is, says Wells, because in the "dark shadow" of AIDS, "the enormity of . . . constructing a dialogue, outside of the virus itself, has been almost impossible."[25] Wells and Main chose a camp style, which Wells variously describes as "homosexual" and "elaborate and seemingly superficial"[26] for a number of reasons: to echo the black-and-white women's melodramas of the 1940s that take the viewer away from "the ordinariness of daily life";[27] as metaphor for the highly constructed nature of gender roles and cultural objects; to use wit to reveal an unspoken subtext, and to create a sense of exhilaration and energy that speaks for an intensity of pleasure. Camp, says Wells, is "a way of talking in a difficult situation."[28]

Camp in its narrative, performance, dialogue, set, props, costume, make-up, musical, shooting, and lighting styles, *Desperate Remedies* uses motifs of disguise and looking to reinforce the appearances/reality theme,

The opulence of high camp: Opium addict Rose and drug dealer Fraser in *Desperate Remedies*. (Courtesy New Zealand Film Commission.)

while heart motifs provide the key to the narrative drive. With all but one scene filmed indoors, the set, built in an Auckland wharf shed, provides bold visual cues to emotional and psychological entrapment. The opulence of the production design borrows generously from conventions of nineteenth-century theatrical melodrama.

Narbey, who had worked with Wells and Main as director of photography on their bold documentary *Napier: Newest City on the Globe* (1985), serves the film well with his cinematography. The camera highlights agitation, urgency, and unease in rapid movements and exaggerated compositions and, alternately, in claustrophobic tight shots. Dramatic use of light brings out the rich textures of costumes and furnishings and includes ingenious variations on the red/blue theme used to evoke emotional states. Shadows are prominent, creating an atmosphere of mystery and providing visual cues to the dominating idea that things are not what they seem. As Wells commented:

> Leon was an indispensable part of the chemistry of the film. You could say it was a creative partnership, with Stewart and myself pushing Leon into an unfamiliar territory of extremes, as his inclination is always toward understatement. One of the films we were most fascinated by was Orson Welles's *The Magnificent Ambersons*. The biggest challenge for us in getting the look right was realizing an essentially black and white film by translating shadow into color. We chose the highly theatrical look pioneered by, among, others, Fassbinder. I think we liked the queer analogy. Leon was a perfect DOP [director of pho-

tography] for this, as his sensitivity to color and depth has always been supreme among New Zealand DOPs... The larger picture was budgetary restrictions and the difficulty of getting a lush, visceral image on not much money. Elaborate lighting and coloring were key here, as were the sets and costumes. The intricacy of the lighting, the delicacy, the nuances and the textured look are all a product of Leon's genius and love for lighting.[29]

This discussion of examples of Narbey's work in a number of filmmaking roles and on several projects over many years demonstrates something of the significance of his contribution to New Zealand cinema as a key figure for whom artistic imperatives are paramount. Often working outside mainstream, populist tastes, he has looked for stories, both documentary and dramatic, that comment and reflect on social, political, cultural, and historical moments in New Zealand. While his work as a director of fiction features has been restricted to just two productions, both are strikingly ambitious and unique and show Narbey's ability as a visionary filmmaker. It is, however, his work as a director of photography—a position in which few others in New Zealand are held in such high regard—that reveals both his consistency as a filmmaker and a continuing demand for his expertise.

Notes

1. Geoff Steven, interview with author, August 22, 2001.
2. For an account of the film/art scene in New Zealand in the 1960s and 1970s, see Roger Horrocks's essay "Alternatives: Experimental Film Making in New Zealand," in *Film in Aotearoa New Zealand*, 2nd ed., ed. Jonathan Dennis and Jan Bieringa (Wellington: Victoria University Press, 1996), 56–88.
3. Leon Narbey, interview with author, August 13, 2001.
4. Steven, interview with author, August 22, 2001.
5. Narbey, e-mail to author, September 3, 2001.
6. Narbey, interview with author, September 22, 2000.
7. See http://www.can.net.au/projects/drysdale.htm.
8. Christopher Allen, *Art in Australia: From Colonization to Postmodernism* (London: Thames and Hudson, 1998), 140–42.
9. See Martin Blythe, *Naming the Other: Images of the Maori in New Zealand Film and Television* (Metuchen, NJ: Scarecrow, 1994), 261–62.
10. Hauraki Greenland, "Maori Ethnicity as Ideology," in *Nga Take: Ethnic Relations and Racism in Aotearoa/New Zealand*, ed. Paul Spoonley, David Pearson, and Cluny Mcpherson (Palmerston North: Dunmore Press, 1991), 97.
11. Merata Mita, "The Soul and the Image," in *Film in Aotearoa New Zealand*, ed. Jonathan Dennis and Jan Bieringa (Wellington: Victoria University Press, 1992), 46.
12. Russell Campbell, "Nine Documentaries," in *Film in Aotearoa New Zealand*,

2nd. ed., ed. Jonathan Dennis and Jan Bieringa (Wellington: Victoria University Press, 1996), 110.
13. Narbey, e-mail to author, February 17, 2002.
14. Narbey, e-mail to author, February 5, 2002.
15. Shirley Horrocks, interview with author, December 4, 2001.
16. Narbey, interview with author, August 13, 2001.
17. Narbey, interview with author, September 22, 2000.
18. See James Ng, *Windows on a Chinese Past*, 4 vols. (Dunedin: Otago Heritage Books, 1993–99); the PhD thesis by Charles Sedgwick, "The Politics of Survival: A Social History of the Chinese in New Zealand," University of Canterbury, 1982; and the PhD thesis by Neville Ritchie, "Archaeology and History of the Chinese in Southern New Zealand," University of Otago, 1986.
19. Clips from the film were used on television news bulletins in February 2002, the Chinese New Year, when the New Zealand government apologized to Chinese immigrants for forcing them to pay a poll tax on arrival (for instance 100 pounds in 1896) between 1881 and 1944.
20. See Tony Chuah, "Chan Is Missing: *Illustrious Energy*," *Illusions* 11 (July 1989): 41–43.
21. Leon Narbey quoted in Barbara Cairns and Helen Martin, *Shadows on the Wall: A Study of Seven New Zealand Feature Films* (Auckland: Longman Paul, 1994), 286.
22. Narbey quoted in Cairns and Martin, *Shadows on the Wall*, 293.
23. Narbey, interview with author, September 22, 2000.
24. Maynard Productions, Ltd, *Press Kit: The Footstep Man*, 3.
25. Peter Wells, *Frock Attack! Wig Wars! Strategic Camp in "Desperate Remedies,"* Working Papers No. 1 (Auckland: University of Auckland, 1997), 19.
26. Ibid., 6.
27. Ibid., 3.
28. Ibid., 10.
29. Peter Wells, e-mail to author, February 8, 2002.

Leon Narbey—Filmography

1968. *Room One* (NZ short film: director, editor).
1968. *Room Two* (NZ short film: director, editor).
1971. *A Film of Real Time: A Light-Sound Environment* (NZ short film: director, editor).
1972. *Earthworks* (NZ short film: assistant).
1974. *Rally... Like Little Boys in a Man Sized Sport* (NZ documentary: second unit cinematographer).
1974. *Blenheim* (NZ television documentary: cinematographer).
1974. *Focus* (NZ television documentary: cinematographer for four episodes).
1975. *The Games Affair* (NZ television six-part children's series: assistant cameraman, stills photographer).
1975. *Hanafi Hayes Looks at Queenstown* (NZ documentary, pilot for the *One Man's View* series: assistant cameraman).
1975. *Te Matakite O Aotearoa/The Maori Land March* (NZ documentary: cin-

ematographer).
1976. *Mixed Bag: Six Views of Christchurch* (NZ television documentary: director, cinematographer).
1976. *Six Rivers: The Longest Jet Boat Marathon in the World* (NZ television documentary: co-cinematographer).
1976. *Spanish Civil War* (NZ documentary: co-cinematographer).
1976. *Mike Gibson* (NZ documentary: cinematographer).
1976. *They Say We Let Them Down* (NZ television documentary: cinematographer).
1976. *Countdown on Zimbabwe* (NZ television documentary: cinematographer).
1977. *Man against the World: Pawelka* (NZ film/television documentary: assistant cameraman).
1977. *Link* (NZ documentary: cinematographer, editor).
1977. *No. 1 in Freight* (NZ training film: cinematographer, editor).
1978. **Skin Deep** (NZ feature film: cinematographer).
1979. *Gung Ho—Rewi Alley of China* (NZ television documentary in the *Lookout* series: cinematographer).
1979. *The Humble Force* (NZ television documentary in the *Lookout* series: cinematographer).
1979. *China's Patriot Army* (NZ television documentary in the *Foreign Correspondent* series: cinematographer).
1979. *Karanga Hokianga* (NZ documentary: cinematographer).
1980. **Bastion Point Day 507** (NZ documentary: co-director, co-producer, cinematographer, editor).
1980. *The Hammer and the Anvil* (NZ documentary: cinematographer).
1980. *Queen Street* (NZ film/television drama: cinematographer).
1980. *The First Step* (NZ extended short film: cinematographer).
1980. *In Joy* (NZ documentary: cinematographer).
1980. *In Spring One Plants Alone* (NZ documentary: co-cinematographer).
1980. *The Sinbad Voyage* (NZ documentary: co-cinematographer).
1981. *Man of the Trees* (NZ film/television documentary: director, cinematographer).
1981. *Stranded* (Australia documentary: co-cinematographer).
1981. *Flight 901—The Erebus Disaster* (NZ documentary: co-cinematographer).
1982. *O.K, Let's Watch* (NZ television documentary: co-cinematographer).
1982. *The Bridge: A Story of Men in Dispute* (NZ documentary: cinematographer).
1983. **Strata** (NZ feature film: cinematographer).
1983. **Patu!** (NZ documentary: co-cinematographer).
1984. **Trespasses** a.k.a. **Omen of Evil** (NZ feature film: cinematographer).
1984. **Other Halves** (NZ feature film: cinematographer).
1984. *Te Hikoi Ki Waitangi* (NZ documentary: co-cinematographer).

1984. *Thoroughbred* (NZ documentary: co-cinematographer).
1985. *Napier: Newest City on the Globe* a.k.a. *Newest City on the Globe: Art Deco Napier* (NZ film/television documentary: cinematographer).
1985. *Return Journey* (NZ extended short film: cinematographer).
1985. *A Fitting Tribute* (NZ extended short film: cinematographer).
1985. *Drum/Sing* (NZ short film: co-cinematographer).
1987. *Kai Purakau* a.k.a. *The Storyteller* (NZ/UK television documentary: cinematographer).
1988. *Illustrious Energy* (NZ feature film: director, co-writer).
1988. *Beyond Gravity* (NZ extended short film: cinematographer).
1988. *The Lounge Bar* (NZ short film: cinematographer).
1989. *Just Me and Mario* (NZ extended short film: cinematographer).
1990. *Ruby and Rata* (NZ feature film: cinematographer).
1990. *A Little Film about Tivaevae* (NZ short film: co-cinematographer).
1990. *Linda's Body* (NZ short film: cinematographer).
1991. *Red Delicious* (NZ short film: cinematographer).
1991. *Pleasures and Dangers* (NZ television documentary: cinematographer).
1992. *The Footstep Man* (NZ feature film: director, co-writer).
1993. *Bread and Roses* (NZ television four-part mini-series, also screened theatrically: camera operator).
1993. *Desperate Remedies* (NZ feature film: cinematographer).
1993. *Act of Murder* (NZ documentary: cinematographer).
1994. *Peter Peryer: Portrait of a Photographer* (NZ film/television documentary: cinematographer).
1994. *Snap* (NZ short film: cinematographer).
1994. *I'm So Lonesome I Could Cry* (NZ short film: cinematographer).
1995. *Romario: Campo Dourado* (UK television documentary: cinematographer).
1995. *Flip and Two Twisters* (NZ television documentary: cinematographer).
1995. *Putting Our Town on the Map* (NZ television documentary: cinematographer).
1995. *For Love or Money* (NZ television documentary: cinematographer).
1995. Seven television advertisements for the Nike "Just Do It" campaign (cinematographer).
1996. *The Transformers* (NZ television documentary in the *Work of Art* series: cinematographer)
1996. *Visible Evidence* (NZ television documentary in the *Work of Art* series: director).
1996. *Kiwiana—Kiwi As!* (NZ television documentary: cinematographer).
1996. *Kiwi As—Kiwiana!* (NZ television documentary sequel: cinematographer).
1997. *Coal Face* (NZ television drama: cinematographer).
1997. *Duggan: Death in Paradise* (NZ television film: cinematographer).
1997. *Blood* (NZ documentary: cinematographer).

1997. *Possum* (NZ short film: cinematographer).
1997. *Velvet Dreams* (NZ television documentary in the *Work of Art* series: cinematographer).
1998. *Flying* (NZ short film: cinematographer).
1998. *Te Kanake* (New Caledonian documentary: cinematographer).
1998. *Duggan: Sins of the Father* (NZ television film: cinematographer).
1998. *Duggan: Shadow of Doubt* (NZ television film: cinematographer).
1998. Five television advertisements for Countrywide Bank (cinematographer).
1998. Television advertisement for ALAC (cinematographer).
1999. ***Savage Honeymoon*** **(NZ feature film: cinematographer).**
1999. ***Punitive Damage*** **(NZ documentary: cinematographer).**
1999. Television advertisement for the Health Funding Authority (cinematographer).
2000. *Sticks and Stones* (NZ documentary: cinematographer).
2000. Five television advertisements for Mercury Energy (cinematographer).
2000. Television advert for the New Zealand Breast Cancer Foundation (cinematographer).
2000. *Camping with Camus* (NZ short film: cinematographer).
2000. ***The Price of Milk*** **(NZ feature film: cinematographer).**
2000. ***Jubilee*** **(NZ feature film: cinematographer).**
2001. *Clare* (NZ television film: cinematographer).
2001. Television advertisement for Toyota New Zealand's Everyday Dealers campaign (cinematographer).
2001. Television advertisement for the Ministry of Education's Te Mana (cinematographer).
2001. *Early Days Yet: A Profile of the Poet Allen Curnow* (NZ film/television documentary: cinematographer).
2002. *Tick* (NZ short film: cinematographer).
2002. Television advertisement for breast cancer screening (cinematographer).
2002. ***Whale Rider*** **(NZ/Germany feature film: cinematographer).**
2004. *Colin McCahon: I Am* (NZ film/television documentary: cinematographer).
2004. *Marti: The Passionate Eye* (NZ film/television documentary: additional cinematographer).
2004. *Kerosene Creek* (NZ short film: cinematographer).
2006. ***No. 2*** **(NZ feature film: cinematographer).**
2006. ***Perfect Creature*** **(NZ/UK feature film: cinematographer).**
2007. ***The Tattooist*** **(NZ feature film: cinematographer).**

16

Making Strange

Journeys through the Unfamiliar in the Films of Vincent Ward

Stephanie Rains

Introduction: Landscapes and Identity

In 1991, New Zealand television screened *Visual Symphonies*, a satirical travel series on towns and cities in New Zealand and Australia, presented by comedian Ginette McDonald in her well-known persona of "Lyn of Tawa." In a scene from the episode examining Christchurch, McDonald is shown gazing out across the vast and desolate Canterbury Plains. It was, she commented, "rather like a Vincent Ward movie—it looks beautiful, but there's not a lot happening."[1]

McDonald's association of a landscape as overwhelming and bleak as the Canterbury Plains with Ward's filmmaking, and her assertion of the frequent absence of a conventional narrative in his work, is a wry generalization that links Ward's artistic practice to the core issues of settlement and belonging that characterize much discussion of place within New Zealand. Prior to 2005 he had directed four major feature films, *Vigil* (1984), *The Navigator: A Mediaeval Odyssey* (1988), *Map of the Human Heart* (1993), and *What Dreams May Come* (1998). The subject matters and locations for the features range from a wind and rain lashed North Island Taranaki farm in *Vigil*, through plague-stricken fourteenth-century Cumbria and contemporary Auckland in *The Navigator*, World War II Canadian cartographers in *Map of the Human Heart*, to a highly imaginative interpretation of heaven and hell in *What Dreams May Come*. As this essay is being written, a fifth feature, *River Queen* (2005), is currently experiencing a troubled production, with filming on and around New Zealand's Whanganui River. Ward has also directed several shorter films, including an adaptation of Janet Frame's novel *A State of Siege* (1978) and the documentary *In Spring One Plants Alone* (1980), prior to making feature films. In 1992 he wrote the original screenplay for *Alien3*, with the expectation of directing the film, but left the project before production began.

Ward's early work, made on location in New Zealand, places the country's landscape, and its effects on those who inhabit it, at the heart of the films. The ideas surrounding landscape, location, and geography, as determinants of identity, also remain central to his later films, made outside New Zealand, that he directed following the international success of *The Navigator*. Equally, Ward's films frequently defy standard narrative forms, centering more on the psychological and internal developments of his characters than on external, action-driven events.

This essay will examine the insistence throughout Ward's films upon the importance of the relationship, both physical and spiritual, between the individual and a wider community. In particular, it will address the ways in which Ward uses the device of isolation and symbolic journeying in order to explore the processes by which the familiar is made strange and, eventually, the strange may be made familiar. The essay will concentrate on the ways in which Ward's use of geographical peripheries and the processes of mapping reflect the director's New Zealand identity. The essay will also include a discussion of the ways in which these films build on the tradition of Kiwi Gothic narratives through their emphasis on the convergence of physical and spiritual experience, as well as a questioning of empirical reality, and above all, a sense of the "uncanny."

Kiwi Gothic: The Familiar and Unfamiliar

With reference to Ward, the critical structure that unites the themes of the familiar and unfamiliar is that of Kiwi Gothic. While it is outside the scope of this essay to explore the Gothic tradition of New Zealand literature and film in detail, a further examination of certain aspects of Gothic narrative construction is essential to an understanding of Ward's contribution to this genre.[2] In particular, Freud's concept of the "uncanny," or *unheimlich*, is central to all of Ward's key films.[3] The concept of the uncanny develops as an experience of the strange and the unfamiliar, made particularly disturbing by its occurrence within a familiar or homely environment that should therefore be knowable and comforting. It is this combination of the unfamiliar within the familiar that was an essential component of eighteenth- and nineteenth-century European Gothic novels' evocation of the uncanny. In these novels, such as Horace Walpole's *The Castle of Otranto* (1764), William Beckford's *Vathek* (1786), or Mary Shelley's *Frankenstein* (1818), a sense of the "unhomely" was, largely speaking, induced by reference to historical differences of sensibility or belief mapped onto the contemporary landscape. Hence the reliance, in English Gothic stories, on the recurring figures of medieval Catholic monks, ruined castles, and veiled women, all of which functioned as signifiers of a repressed otherness of sensibility from the past, reoccurring to challenge and disturb the rational certainties of the modern present.[4]

In his analysis of the development of American Gothic (and later Kiwi Gothic) fiction during the nineteenth century, William J. Schafer relates its emphasis on the uncanny to a nation-building exercise in which the Gothic sensibility attempts to counter the lack of a historical-geographical continuity within settler communities such as those of the United States and New Zealand. As he argues: "To occupy a landscape comfortably, humans seem to need this chthonic feeling—'this my own, my native land'—which connects with Freud's image of the land as womb and birth canal. This connects déjà vu and chthonic feelings directly: to feel at home in a place is to feel that one has been born not just *in it* but *by it*, that the metaphorical idea of 'motherland' is in some important way literal."[5] The Gothic traditions inherent within settler communities such as New Zealand, then, can be seen as centering on the concept of the uncanny, making important use of its double nature: that of being simultaneously "homely" and "unhomely." As such, it is a reflection of the colonial and postcolonial experience of an unfamiliar home, particularly with regard to the land itself. The concept of the landscape being central to national and individual identity, and yet also hostile and profoundly unknowable, is a recurring theme in New Zealand fiction and film—and is particularly visible in Ward's films, as it is expressed through the narrative devices his films employ. Ward's frequent recourse to medieval imagery and belief systems also references the older, English Gothic style from which Kiwi Gothic, in part, drew inspiration.

In *Vigil*, the key questions surrounding the idea of "home" center on a sheep-farming family living in a remote and isolated valley. In the first few minutes of the film, husband and father Justin (Gordon Shields) falls to his death while attempting to rescue a stranded sheep. His wife Liz (Penelope Stewart) and daughter Toss (Fiona Kay), struggling to maintain the workings of the farm, are helped by a local poacher, Ethan (Frank Whitten), who is hired by Liz's father Birdie (Bill Kerr). The film combines an exploration of the difficulties of settlement with the personal and sexual tensions that come as the fragmented family is, potentially, reconstituted by the arrival of Ethan. Eventually, beaten by the multiple problems of their situation, the family leaves the land, and the final shot of the film is of Toss walking down the road that leads away from the farm.

The hostility of the landscape to the family's attempt to settle and "husband" the hill farm is clear, made most evident in Justin's fatal fall. This theme is continued throughout the film, as the valley in which the film is set is presented, in Ian Conrich's description, as "an overgrown garden, in which grow images of excess and despair."[6] While Liz shows considerable

Isolated within an inhospitable land, Toss faces an uncertain future in *Vigil*. (Courtesy New Zealand Film Commission.)

ambivalence to the farm as a home, both Toss and Birdie demonstrate a need to be "at home" on the land. However, the family's attempts to embed themselves as settlers, demonstrated by Birdie's increasingly irrational concentration on a mechanical invention designed to aid their farming, as well as by Toss's animistic shrines and rituals created around the farm landscape, are all doomed to fail, leading to the family's eventual retreat from the land. Here, the New Zealand landscape refuses familiarity to those who merely live *in it* rather than *by it*. It is Ethan, as a poacher, who does live by the land, and is thus "at home" within it, and it is impossible not to conclude that the film's portrayal of a potentially functional settler as a peripheral, isolated, illegitimate male questions the basis by which an actual society might be founded in the "new land."[7]

Ward's filmmaking also explores the concepts of historical inheritance across geographical spaces that are crucial to white settler societies such as New Zealand. If, as the narrative of *Vigil* suggests, the landscape is, for Pakeha (European) settlers, persistently threatening and potentially unknowable, then one possible solution is to reclaim the European history from which they are separated by the geography of migration as well as by the passage of time. Ward is quite explicit in his insistence that white New Zealanders have as much claim to this history and sensibility as their contemporary European counterparts, arguing that both groups are equally descended from a shared pre-colonial world: "In terms of the majority of pakehas living in this country our relationship is as direct as is an Englishman's. We may not have the same buildings here, but we are directly descended. And so therefore we have as much claim on that culture, which is inherent in our culture anyway, as anybody else does."[8]

There are clear cultural implications in such a statement, suggesting as it does a way of thinking through the complex issues of settler inheritance, but for Ward, the full force of this quote lies in the way it legitimizes his use of the technical aspects of a European art house cinematic tradition. The visual qualities of his filmmaking are perhaps the most frequently commented upon by audiences and critics alike, and all of his feature films display a cinematography that is both crafted and the product of a highly specific aesthetic. Having originally trained as a painter, Ward displays a particularly strong awareness of art history, and a distinct "painterliness" in his directorial style. In his own analyses of his films in articles and interviews, Ward has made reference to the work of artists such as Hieronymus Bosch, Albrecht Dürer, Bruegel, Matthias Grünewald, and Caspar David Friedrich as being highly influential in his own aesthetic development.[9] Certainly, the impact of all of these artists has been evident in the visual style of his films. *Vigil* and *The Navigator*, for instance, use the Flemish medievalism of artists such as Bosch and Bruegel in their depiction of miners and land-laborers in a harsh and bleak landscape, and transfer them to the fictional worlds of the films.

At the same time, much of Ward's work also makes reference to nineteenth-century Romanticism, particularly the Germanic sensibilities of painters such as Friedrich. It is also worth noting, in passing, that Ward has listed the Brothers Grimm and Sir Walter Scott as early literary influences—the fabulous nature of Grimms' Fairytales, and the Gothic Romanticism of Scott's fictions clearly reverberate in Ward's films from *Vigil* to *What Dreams May Come*.[10] The connections between Romanticism and the Gothic tradition are complex and often contradictory. However, as they have influenced the Gothic dimension to Ward's films, there is an interesting cross-fertilization between the two traditions. The nineteenth-century European Romantic movement drew considerable inspiration from a valorization of the medieval world, which was presented as having contained a spiritual completeness perceived at the time as lacking in the contemporary era. As a result, artists such as Friedrich produced considerable numbers of paintings based on the ruins of medieval constructions, typically religious buildings such as monasteries. At the same time, perhaps the strongest theme of Romantic art was that of landscape painting, as part of a greater project to emphasize the power in identity construction of nature, raw emotion, and physical sensuality over the perceived tyranny of reason and science during the era of industrialization and urbanization. As David Brett has argued, it is: "[A] system of ideas in which nations are

Gothic Romanticism: The visionary Griffin, part of Ward's adoption of traditions of medievalism and landscape painting in *The Navigator: A Mediaeval Odyssey.* (Courtesy New Zealand Film Commission.)

taken as given, have no historicity, are almost as natural as biological species. These nations have an 'essence' which in its recesses is unknowable by outsiders. It is therefore not a truly historical phenomenon at all, but a cultural inheritance of a genetic kind, that resists change. It is indeed a heritage in a quasi-biological sense."[11]

The Navigator and *What Dreams May Come* are perhaps the most obvious examples in Ward's work of his adoption of the visual imagery of nineteenth-century painting in order to explore the twentieth-century functions of the Gothic genre. In *The Navigator*, the traditional Gothic tropes of medievalism, religious mystery, and narrative uncertainty are all employed as a method of interrogating contemporary New Zealand society. In the film's complex narrative—a mix of present action and recounted dream full of poetic imagery and recurring motifs—a fourteenth-century Cumbrian mining community is threatened by the Black Death, and agrees to place its faith in the dreams of a nine-year-old boy, Griffin (Hamish McFarlane). Griffin has had a prophetic vision that the community will be spared the plague if they undertake a pilgrimage to raise a Celtic cross on a cathedral spire on the other side of the world. Under his guidance (Griffin is the "navigator" of the title), a group of men from the community tunnel through a mineshaft to arrive in late twentieth-century Auckland, where they cast the cross and succeed in raising it before dawn. However, Griffin falls from the cathedral spire as the cross is being raised (an event prefigured in his dream, only in that dream narrative the identity of the faller is unknown), and on the group's return to Cumbria, he discovers that he has the plague, passed on to him by his brother Connor (Bruce Lyons). In a concluding image highly reminiscent of Andrei Tarkovsky's *Andrei Rublev* (1966), the film ends with Griffin's coffin being floated out on a Cumbrian lake with a desolate snow-covered landscape as a backdrop.

The potential readings of the film's narrative (as a fear of nuclear capability, an AIDS allegory, modern version of a grail quest, or series of metaphors outlining settlement anxieties) are multiple, but within the context established by *Vigil* it is clear that one key element to any interpretation of *The Navigator* must be the idea of "making strange" the details of contemporary New Zealand society. As Jonathan Rayner has argued: "The highly developed sensitivities of Ward's protagonists in *Vigil* and *The Navigator* are attuned to and reflective of the individual traumas (familial and spiritual) which they experience, but the parabolic resonances of both films prompt parallel interpretations in national terms . . . and [the characters] inhabit a cinematic landscape redolent of problematic cultural history as well as of spiritual torment."[12] The effect of this maneuver is, in *The Navigator*, to emphasize the strangeness of New Zealand as a place that is emphatically not home even, or perhaps particularly, to New Zealanders themselves. The power of belief, both spiritual and communal, evident in the Cumbrian group, contrasts with the modern landscapes of urban Auckland, where community seems, on the whole, to be lost.

What Dreams May Come is based extensively on the various visual styles of Renaissance and post-Renaissance European art traditions in its explorations of the concepts of love, death, and the afterlife. Following the death of their two children in a car crash, the marriage between Chris and Annie Nielsen (Robin Williams and Annabella Sciorra) is dominated by memories of loss. Four years after the original crash, Chris is himself killed in another car crash, prompting a period of intense grief for Annie that results in her own suicide. Through the nature of their respective deaths, each journeys to a different spiritual realm—Heaven for Chris and Purgatory/Hell for Annie. The representation of both "locations" is a visual tour de force. Chris encounters a variety of Impressionistic and Romantic landscapes where he can physically touch the location *as art*, with special effects rendering the world as a tactile canvas where the paint can be felt. Annie (who is herself a painter working within nineteenth-century traditions) is trapped in a nightmarish Hell depicted in the oppressive colors and tones of religious-infused Renaissance art. As well as these explicit references, however, Ward continues, through the use of nineteenth-century paintings as landscape backgrounds, his fascination with the subject of the uncanny in the significant form of the land itself, in this case the new environment in which Chris, in particular, finds himself. For Chris, Heaven consists not only of an idealized version of his suburban home but also of physical actuations of his wife's nineteenth-century-style paintings.

The representational style of the paintings chosen is significant, as it again refers to the painterly nature of Ward's visual imagination. Referring in particular to the allusions to Friedrich's German Romanticism, Ward has stated that: "We tried to create a sense of transcendence, partly by color and partly by referencing artists who had worked with a similar intent. Friedrich had a sense of nature being more powerful than man and a feeling of aloneness that suited the narrative—Robin Williams's first vision of paradise is in fact a hell of aloneness. As for the colors, in almost all religions purple is a sacred color and it seems to evoke a sense of awe and mystery."[13] Ward also stated that he chose a painting style from an era when "they still had visions of heaven and hell," a comment that links the visual effects of the film to its explicitly redemptive narrative.[14]

Within the context of such visual style, Chris and Annie's subjective recreations of their family home—part of their experience of the afterlife in both its idealized and nightmarish forms—continue the film's reference to the wider concepts of "being at home," and to Freud's uncanny. It is a provocative reading that sees *What Dreams May Come* as a form of settlement narrative, but seen in the context of *Vigil* and *The Navigator*, and the concerns in all three films with ideas of belonging and familiarity, it is an interpretation that suggests a consistency of both aesthetic and cultural concerns.

Isolation and Abandonment: Journeys of the Imagination

One of the consistent themes of Ward's films is that of an individual who is isolated from, or abandoned by, his or her community. Writing on Ward, Michael Wilmington has commented that: "It's no accident that his central characters have included both cartographers (*Map of the Human Heart*) and visionary/guides (*The Navigator*). His movies are about isolation and his central characters are either on the edge themselves or lonely in a crowd ... heroes (or heroines) less of action than of perception."[15] In *Vigil*, for example, Toss experiences extreme feelings of loss and abandonment after the death of her father and his apparent replacement in her mother's affections by Ethan. Twelve-year-old Toss's internal journey through the experiences of bereavement and maturation is mapped out, in part, by the series of visual metaphors that represent the bleak and inhospitable landscape of the family's hill farm. As Helen Martin has commented of the film: "The bleak harshness of the landscape and the elements and the relationships of the characters to each other and to the land are conveyed through expressionistic techniques. . . . Isolated, claustrophobic and embattled by indifferent Nature, the farm is an ideal correlative for the emotional states of its inhabitants."[16] In detailing the nature of such isolation, much of the film's narrative concerns Toss's struggle to reconcile her response to her father's death with the dual process of her own and her mother's relationships to Ethan, but Liz, Ethan, and Birdie are also clearly isolated figures, especially in their varying relationships to the landscape, which creates demands on all the characters that make the forming of personal and communal bonds difficult. *The Navigator* focuses on the depiction of Griffin, also a pubescent central character who, although nominally surrounded by his community, is increasingly isolated from them by the strength of his spiritual visions. As in *Vigil*, *The Navigator* is in large part a coming-of-age narrative, in which Griffin is simultaneously inducted into, but also forever separated from, his community through his quest to save them from the Black Death. In the process, he acquires the heroic loneliness of leadership and is increasingly differentiated from his fellow travelers. *The Navigator*'s narrative conclusion, with the revelation of Connor returning to the village despite his infection with the Black Death, confirms Griffin's separation not only from his community but also from his childhood self. With the final focus on his coffin, the film ends with the figurative separation of Griffin from his community being represented literally.

The experience of isolation and abandonment as played out across actual landscapes in Ward's work is most strikingly represented in *Map of the Human Heart*. Here Ward explores more clearly than in any of his other films the themes of individual and community estrangement as well as the emotional connections between people and landscapes. The film involves a mapmaker, Walter Russell (Patrick Bergin), who while mapping unknown zones of the Canadian Arctic in the 1930s takes a local boy, Avik (Robert Joamie), back to Montreal to be cured of tuberculosis. The young Avik's traditional indigenous communal upbringing is rooted in an intimate and symbiotic relationship with the harsh landscape, and is shown in stark contrast to the rationalized and exploitative approach of the mapmakers, such as Russell, who becomes Avik's adopted father figure. While being treated in the hospital, Avik meets Albertine (Annie Galipeau), a métis girl who is half French and half Inuit, but the pair become separated. Later, and following his rejection by his own community for his Westernized ways, the adult Avik (Jason Scott Lee) sends a message, through Russell, to the adult Albertine (Anne Parillaud). Avik joins the air force as a navigator during World War II, and following its conclusion meets Albertine again. However, he rejects both Albertine and Russell and ends the film back home in northern Canada but adrift from the culture and knowledge he has known as a child.

The seduction (and abduction) of Avik by Western culture is represented in the film in a number of ways. Initially, in the Catholic hospital in Montreal where they first meet, he and Albertine attempt to plot their homelands on a large map in their schoolroom, leading Albertine to tell Avik that "you're not even on the map." Following this, Avik's later work as a navigator during World War II, in which his unusual degree of skill and survival is commented on by his fellow flyers, stresses his position as a classic postcolonial "double" subject. While his skills at map-reading project an idea of an affinity with codes of Western rationality, he is also given a dual perspective on landscape; as an indigene with a Western education, he has developed a duality of vision that Westerners themselves will never achieve. The results of such doubling on the subject himself, however, are revealed toward the end of the film. Here, Avik is involved in the rational terror of Dresden's destruction. In a series of nightmarish scenes, the fire bombing of the city functions as a kind of reverse yet also logical extreme of mapmaking, during which a "known" site is destroyed rather than surveyed. Following this experience, Avik's rejection of both his Western lifestyle and his relationships with Albertine and Russell is a traumatic product of his encounter with such excesses of modernity. When Avik ultimately returns home, the experience he has of a profound and irreversible rejection, with both he and the landscape of his childhood irreversibly altered, leave him lost between cultures and without those who were once close to him.[17]

In *What Dreams May Come,* Ward continues to explore themes of isolation and abandonment using a narrative of bereavement. For all of its visual style, the core of the film's narrative is its presentation of an adult central character experiencing the trauma of loss and grief. Indeed, it is Chris's heroic efforts to save his wife's soul after her suicide in order that they can both be reunited with their children that occupy the majority of the film; the redemptive device of true love drives Chris's journey, echoing the classical tale of Orpheus and Eurydice, though with a stock sentimental Hollywood closure. Upon his own death, when Chris is taken to Heaven, he discovers that both the form and content of the afterlife are constructed according to the individual's choices and preferences. In order to rescue his wife from purgatory, and reunite his family in paradise, Chris enlists the help of "The Tracker" (Max Von Sydow)—a character reminiscent of Griffin in *The Navigator*—as a guide through the afterlife. Here again, as with the central idea of bereavement, the process of "making strange" is key to the film's narrative of abandonment and subsequent redemption. While in Chris's personal paradise, his family home is reproduced as an ideal, in Annie's personal Hell it is shown in a nightmarish form: strange and yet strangely familiar. Discussing the redemptive thematic of the film, Ward has argued that:

It has more of a psychoanalytic point of view of paradise and particularly of hell. There's the idea of the subjective afterlife, which is the only kind that makes sense to me—why would a Native American's afterlife be the same as yours or mine? You can also view the film purely as a psychological journey, as someone coming to understand themselves and their relationships. . . . It's this odd mix—it uses nineteenth-century language to describe heaven and hell, but with a contemporary commentary.[18]

The ways in which the subjective individual is menaced by shadowy and often metaphysical forces, and must "prove" his or her virtue and courage in order to survive loss or abandonment, have Gothic and Romantic overtones. But what is more central as Ward outlines it here is the establishment of the psychological dimension inherent in solitude and isolation. All his films (and this is true of his short films as well as his features—*A State of Siege* is a masterful narrative of isolation) focus on the notion of the subject alienated within his or her surroundings, whether that be in the settlement context of *Vigil* or the familial concerns of *What Dreams May Come*. Possibly due to the Hollywood context of its production and the subsequent demands of narrative cohesion, the latter film resolves the issues of the atomized individual far more clearly that any of Ward's previous features. However, it too points to a feature key to Ward's cinema of highly stylized representation—that, for all the visual flair of his films, there is a central nagging concern that behind the images lies a portrayal of ambiguous isolation and the difficulties faced when attempting to form either personal or communal bonds.

Ward's concentration on the themes and motifs of the journey, played out in physical and psychological terms, explores both the concerns of the spiritual and the secular, and the rational and the mystical. Toss's journey from childhood and innocence to puberty and knowledge, as with Griffin's psychic journey—mirrored as it is by the physical journey undertaken by himself and his community—underscores an idea of movement that is, at heart, visionary and imaginative. As Rayner has argued in relation to *The Navigator:* "In effect, the imaginative journey encompasses a parabolic pilgrimage embarked upon by the spirit and mind rather than the body, a transmuted voyage of discovery and colonial settlement, and an interrogation of modernity, nationhood and identity linked to landscape, which builds on the debate contained in *Vigil.*"[19] In *The Navigator* the literal pilgrimage to the floodlit St. Patrick's Cathedral in Auckland's city center, object of the Cumbrian's cross-raising task, takes on the ethereal qualities of the celestial church Griffin believes it to be. This process of making strange the mundane and familiar landscapes of contemporary New Zealand, of layering the local with ideas of the spiritual and metaphysical, is here integral to Ward's notion of mobility.

Such a sense of pilgrimage is also true of the journeys of *Map of the Human Heart* and *What Dreams May Come*. In *Map of the Human Heart*, the external journeying, which takes the form of movements between communities and institutions, between indigenous, settler, and imperial locations in Canada and Europe, and between tradition and modernity, is a mask for inner loss rather than maturity. The threat to an idea of settlement signified by Avik's geographical mobility, which culminates in his stranding on an ice floe drifting out to sea (drift symbolizing perhaps the most hopeless and frightening form of human journeying), is that of the postcolonial subject confronted by the colonial and then neo-colonial machines of control and domination, and also of the individual engaged in the exploration of mind and spirit. *Map of the Human Heart* vividly portrays the intertwined interests of colonialism, in the form of Russell's cartography as well as the paternalistic Montreal hospital, with those of neo-colonialism, in the form of the oil industry's economic regime in Avik's homeland after World War II. With its focus on the crucible of the war itself, and the ways in which Avik is drawn into participating in it, as well as on the power structures that exist in the wake of conflict, the film is a narrative of identity loss in the face of hegemonic power. But it is also clearly an exploration of individual emotional development in the face of external social and cultural structures, in which Avik's psychic health is tested on numerous occasions.

What Dreams May Come's portrayal of journeying bears considerable comparison to *The Navigator* in its representation of a spiritual and psychological progression in which the apparent physical movement shown on screen is an explicit metaphor for emotional development. The experiences of Chris, as he searches for his wife to rescue her from damnation and reunite his family in paradise, invoke the narratives and structures of stories such as *Piers Plowman*, *The Pilgrim's Progress*, *Peer Gynt*, and *Orpheus in the Underworld*.[20] In all of these texts, as with many others in the Western Judeo-Christian tradition, arduous physical travel and the completion of tasks are associated with the attainment of higher spiritual understanding. Such a sense of pilgrimage is ultimately diffuse in Ward's conception, however, since the knowledge it brings may be truly enlightening, as in *The Navigator*; dystopian, as in *Map of the Human Heart*; or sentimental, as in *What Dreams May Come*. To this end, Ward is possibly best seen as a figure who is aware of the inheritance of an artistic tradition, and who uses it for disparate ends. It is however, the *form* of the journey that appears to

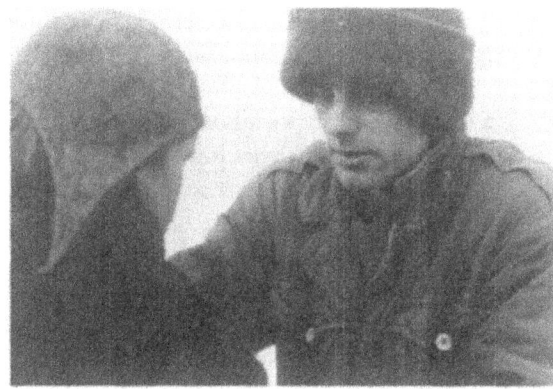

Vincent Ward directing on the set of *The Navigator: A Mediaeval Odyssey*. (Courtesy New Zealand Film Commission.)

appeal to his visual sense, with all the possibilities for the examination of the individual that this creates.

Conclusion: Making Strange

Ward's filmmaking, then, has encompassed a wide variety of subject matters and production environments. A figure from New Zealand's New Wave of filmmakers—including Geoff Murphy, Roger Donaldson, Sam Pillsbury, and David Blyth—that emerged from within the homegrown industry into the international and eventually Hollywood system, his career has reflected the influences of such production considerations. *Vigil*, his first major film, was notorious for the difficulties of its production, contained as it was within the confines of a New Zealand landscape deliberately chosen for the harshness of its setting. The locations and production values of his later films have become increasingly complex, and it is possibly this context that should be seen as shaping the kind of journeys his work explores, rather than any search for spiritual completeness his concerns with Romanticism might suggest.[21] *What Dreams May Come*, with its extensive use of costly special effects and the casting of a major Hollywood star such as Robin Williams, is a film that has production demands very different from those of *Vigil*, and each film is clearly aimed at a different audience. The technicalities that surround Ward's visual language therefore altered considerably between 1984 and 1998. Nevertheless, there has been a clear continuity of directorial vision throughout his feature filmmaking, and much of this continuity has been expressed through Ward's visual narratives: a strong emphasis on the metaphorical power of landscape, and the reflection with which landscape inflects human emotions and individual interiority.

At the end of the 1980s, when Ward's success following the reception of *The Navigator* gave him the opening for an international career, he commented on his working method: "To me what you can't see is as important as what you see. So while there might be drama enacted in front of you, I'm often interested in something on the other side of it, or in some sort of ellipsis on the edge of frame."[22] Such an observation is indicative of both a formal concern with the techniques of storytelling and a sense of depth within characters and their development. In all of his work, Ward has foregrounded internal character development rather than conventional narratives, and in particular has created highly stylized visual environments that function as metaphors of processes of psychological experience. As such, his films are the product of a visionary image maker for whom the image suggests, at its edges and through its associative potential, a depth of human experience. That this experience is one continually made strange and frequently ambiguous is, ultimately, a testament to the complexity of stories as Ward sees them.

Notes

1. Ginette McDonald, *Visual Symphonies* (TVNZ 1991). McDonald's comic persona, "Lyn of Tawa," represented a New Zealand everywoman, as demonstrated by her accent, attitudes, and origination in Tawa, a Wellington suburb in the Hutt Valley.
2. The term "Kiwi Gothic" first appeared in Ian Conrich and Sarah Davy, *Views from the Edge of the World: New Zealand Film* (London: Kakapo Books, 1997), 7. For a discussion of Kiwi Gothic film, see Conrich, "Kiwi Gothic: New Zealand's Cinema of a Perilous Paradise," in *Horror International*, ed. Steven Jay Schneider and Tony Williams (Detroit: Wayne State University Press, 2005), 114–27.
3. The uncanny, as defined by Freud in his 1919 essay of that name, is that which is disturbing or frightening, specifically within the context of places or moments that otherwise appear to be familiar or homely. Freud begins the essay with a detailed etymology of the German words *heimlich* and *unheimlich* in order to demonstrate that these apparent opposites (homely and unhomely or "uncanny," in their English translations) in fact merge with each other in their more subtle definitions, producing a fertile ambiguity of meaning. Freud explains that, "In general we are reminded that the word '*heimlich*' is not unambiguous, but belongs to two sets of ideas, which, without being contradictory, are yet very different: on the one hand it means what is familiar and agreeable, and on the other, what is concealed and kept out of sight." Sigmund Freud, "The 'Uncanny,'" in *The Standard Edition of The Complete Psychological Works of Sigmund Freud, Volume XVII (1917–1919)*, ed. James Strachey (London: Hogarth Press, 1981), 224–25.
4. This is not to suggest that classic English Gothic fiction was historically criti-

cal in its use of the returning repressed. As Allan Lloyd Smith has argued, the Gothic "is not itself historical in the sense of displaying any informed historical consciousness . . . the feudal aristocracy is not understood within its own world view but simply as an eighteenth- or nineteenth-century nightmare. . . . In this sense we can describe the Gothic as ransacking an imaginary museum of pastness, or rifling a Baedeker of 'foreignness' to deck out its touristic exoticism." Allan Lloyd Smith, "Postmodernism/Gothicism," in *Modern Gothic: A Reader*, ed. Victor Sage and Allan Lloyd Smith (Manchester: Manchester University Press, 1996), 10–11. For the primary texts listed here, see *Three Gothic Novels*, ed. Peter Fairclough (Harmondsworth: Penguin, 1968).
5. William J. Schafer, *Mapping Godzone: A Primer on New Zealand Literature and Culture* (Honolulu: University of Hawai'i Press, 1998), 143.
6. Ian Conrich, "Gothic Film," in *The Handbook to Gothic Literature*, ed. Marie Mulvey-Roberts (Basingstoke: Macmillan, 1998), 80.
7. For more on the specific dynamics of New Zealand settlement, see Stephen Turner, "Settlement as Forgetting," in *Quicksands: Foundational Histories in Australia and Aotearoa/New Zealand*, ed. Klaus Neumann et al. (Sydney: University of New South Wales Press, 1999), 20–38; and *Journal of New Zealand Literature* 20 (2002), ed. Alex Calder and Stephen Turner, a special issue on settlement studies.
8. Russell Campbell and Miro Bilbrough, "A Dialogue with Discrepancy: Vincent Ward Discusses *The Navigator*," *Illusions* 10 (March 1989): 11.
9. See Campbell and Bilbrough, "A Dialogue with Discrepancy," 13, and Kim Newman, "Never Say Die," *Sight and Sound* 8, no. 12 (1998): 18–21.
10. John Downie, *The Navigator: A Mediaeval Odyssey* (Trowbridge: Flicks, 2000), 1–2.
11. David Brett, *The Construction of Heritage* (Cork: Cork University Press, 1996), 24.
12. Jonathan Rayner, "Paradise and Pandemonium: The Landscapes of Vincent Ward," in *New Zealand—A Pastoral Paradise?* ed. Ian Conrich and David Woods (Nottingham: Kakapo Books, 2000), 47.
13. Ward, cited in Newman, "Never Say Die," 18.
14. Ibid., 19.
15. Michael Wilmington, "Firestorm and Dry Ice: The Cinema of Vincent Ward," *Film Comment* 29, no. 3 (1993): 52.
16. Helen Martin, "*Vigil*," in Helen Martin and Sam Edwards, *New Zealand Film, 1912–1996* (Oxford: Oxford University Press, 1997), 106.
17. Wilmington describes *Map of the Human Heart* as ending in "an indictment of Western politics and civilization" (Wilmington, "Firestorm and Dry Ice," 51).
18. Ward, cited in Newman, "Never Say Die," 21.
19. Rayner, "Paradise and Pandemonium," 45.
20. See John Bunyan, *The Pilgrim's Progress: From This World to That Which Is to Come* (London: Hodder and Stoughton, 1988); Henrik Ibsen, *Peer Gynt*, trans. Christopher Fry and John Fillinger (Oxford: Oxford Classics, 1998); and Ovid, *Metamorphoses*, trans. Frank Justus Miller (London: Heinemann, 1966). Downie specifically compares Ward's work—particularly *The Navigator*—to William Langland's 1370 epic quest narrative, *Piers Plowman*. See Downie, *The Navigator: A Mediaeval Odyssey*, 46.

21. Here, there are distinct similarities with the work of the German director Werner Herzog. For *Aguirre, der Zorn Gottes* (*Aguirre: The Wrath of God*) (1972), and *Fitzcarraldo* (1982), Herzog deliberately sought extreme locations for the challenging journeys that his films explore. As a figure working within the traditions of German Romanticism, Herzog has been an influence on Ward's filmmaking and has a cameo as a father figure in *What Dreams May Come*.
22. Campbell and Bilbrough, "A Dialogue with Discrepancy," 13.

Vincent Ward—Filmography

1975. *The Cave* (NZ extended short film: director, writer).
1976. *Boned* (NZ short film: director, cinematographer).
1976. *Void* (NZ short film: director, writer, actor).
1977. *Ma Olsen* (NZ documentary: director).
1977. *Samir* (NZ short film: cinematographer).
1978. *A State of Siege* (NZ extended short film: director).
1979. *Sons for the Return Home* (NZ feature film: art director).
1980. *In Spring One Plants Alone* (NZ documentary: producer, director, script research).
1984. *Vigil* (NZ feature film: director, co-writer, story).
1988. *The Navigator: A Mediaeval Odyssey* a.k.a. *The Navigator: An Odyssey across Time* (Australia/NZ feature film: director, co-writer, story).
1992: *Alien3* (US feature film: story).
1993. *Map of the Human Heart* (UK/Australia feature film: director, producer, story).
1995. *Leaving Las Vegas* (US feature film: actor).
1996. *The Shot* (US feature film: actor).
1997. *One Night Stand* (US feature film: actor).
1998. *What Dreams May Come* (US feature film: director).
2003. *The Last Samurai* a.k.a. *The Last Samurai: Bushidou* (US feature film: executive producer).
2004. *Spooked* (NZ feature film: actor).
2005. *River Queen* (NZ/UK feature film: director, co-writer, story).
2007. *The Rain of Children* (NZ documentary: director).

17

Dislocations of Home and Gender in the Films of Jane Campion

Eva Rueschmann

In a book about New Zealand national cinema and some of its most distinctive directors, Jane Campion represents a challenging case of a filmmaker who eludes easy categorization. Born and raised in New Zealand but trained and based in Australia, Campion straddles two national cinemas while receiving critical acclaim internationally as a controversial woman director concerned with feminist themes and subjects. Often identified with the global art house cinema of the 1980s and 1990s, Campion's six feature films to date dramatize the psychological tensions of women characters who feel estranged from proscribed gender and sexual roles. Frequently focusing on women's journeys into new geographical and social spaces, Campion's films reveal the instability of national identity and familial and cultural origins while tracing her heroines' struggles to redefine themselves outside conventional roles as daughters, wives, or mothers.

Jane Campion's own life and career as an expatriate filmmaker may suggest her abiding interest in women's journeys. Born on April 30, 1954, in Wellington, New Zealand, Campion comes from a family immersed in the arts; her mother is an actress and writer and her father a theater producer. Yet, Campion herself first took a degree in anthropology at Victoria University in Wellington before training as a filmmaker. Leaving New Zealand for the young antipodean's obligatory tour of Europe, Campion then settled in Sydney where she completed a bachelor's in fine arts at the Sydney College of the Arts and began her filmmaking career while at the Australian Film and Television School. Since 1979 she has been professionally located in Sydney, has worked for the Australia's Women Film Unit and Australian television, and after her notorious theatrical feature debut, *Sweetie* (1989), her film projects have been funded by various production companies in New Zealand, Australia, and the United States.

Despite her strong professional and personal attachment to Australia, two of Campion's feature films focus on subjects of particular cultural and historical significance to her country of birth: *An Angel at My Table* (1990) dramatizes the autobiography of New Zealand writer Janet Frame, and *The Piano* (1993), her best-known and most controversial film, is a fictional story of a Victorian woman's sexual self-discovery during the Anglo-Scottish colonial settlement of New Zealand in the 1850s. Of all her work, *The Piano* has garnered the greatest critical and popular attention, receiving the Palme d'Or at Cannes and an Academy Award for Best Original Screenplay. Inspired by nineteenth-century British Gothic literature, *The Piano*'s darkly ironic portrayal of European colonization of New Zealand through the story of an upper-middle-class woman's adulterous flight from patriarchal marriage conventions has sparked vigorous debate over its sexual, political, and cultural themes. However, *The Piano* reveals Campion's persistent concern with both her female characters' psychological relationship to social powerlessness and with protagonists who attempt to (re)define themselves when geographically transplanted to new cultural landscapes. Indeed, all of Campion's films, whether they are set in New Zealand, Australia, the United States, or Europe, are fundamentally concerned with her heroines' sense of displacement, their simultaneous homelessness in the world, and in the familial and social roles that psychologically estrange them from their own desires. Beginning with her early film school shorts, *Peel* (1982), *Passionless Moments* (1983), and particularly *A Girl's Own Story* (1984), through her major feature films, *Sweetie*, *An Angel at My Table*, *The Piano*, *The Portrait of a Lady* (1996), *Holy Smoke* (1999), and *In the Cut* (2003), there is a remarkable continuity in Campion's depictions of women's struggles to achieve selfhood, to find their voices as women, as artists, and as colonial and colonized subjects. Usually centering on young women, her films explore female subjectivity through dark Gothicized landscapes, which serve as symbolic correlatives for her protagonists' alienation. Critics, discussing her modern and nineteenth-century female characters' efforts to extricate themselves from both imprisoning and dangerous relationships and from their own romantic illusions, note her predilection for the Gothic and images of the grotesque and uncanny.[1] Campion's distinctive expressionistic visual style suggests the turmoil of inner experience. Her idiosyncratic framings, strange close-ups, and disorienting experiments with scale evoke the surreal world of dark fairy tales and exteriorize her characters' sense of psychological disequilibrium and social dislocation. They convey, as Freda Freiberg writes, "the edge of menace" in the quotidian world of domesticity.[2]

The journeys into the unknown taken by Campion's characters function on both a geopolitical and psychosexual level: Janet Frame's descent into mental illness and recovery in *An Angel at My Table* is followed by her travels to the mother country—England—and her later return to New Zealand as a recognized author; in *The Piano*, Ada McGrath's forced immigration to 1850s New Zealand for an arranged marriage turns into a discovery of sexual empowerment through an adulterous relationship with a man who himself rebels against traditional notions of masculinity; Isabel Archer's travels to England and Italy in *The Portrait of a Lady* end in her disastrous union with the expatriate Gilbert Osmond; and the shallow nature of Ruth Barron's escape to India in *Holy Smoke* is exposed in her subsequent journey into the Australian outback where she confronts not only the challenges of an American cult deprogrammer but also her own privilege. These various criss-crossing passages between Great Britain and its former colonies—America, New Zealand, Australia, India—are enhanced by Campion's controversial international casting choices and suggest a complicated historical and psychological web of political, sexual, and economic connections. They also highlight Campion's particular interest in what Priscilla Walton has termed the female body as "a site of imperial contestation."[3]

Campion's film version of Janet Frame's celebrated 1982–85 memoir, *An Autobiography*, displays her preoccupations with socially marginalized female characters, their struggle for identity and self-expression, and her frequent use of the trope of imperialism for male colonization of women's consciousness. Made originally as a three-part mini-series for New Zealand television and released afterward as a re-edited feature film, *An Angel at My Table* has received the least critical attention among Campion's films, despite winning the Silver Lion and Grand Jury Prize at the 1990 Venice Film Festival and a number of other awards in Europe, New Zealand, and Australia.[4] Yet, *An Angel at My Table* is a central work in Campion's oeuvre, bookended by her stylistically more flamboyant first feature *Sweetie* and the sweeping Gothic romance *The Piano*. In *An Angel at My Table*, Janet Frame's coming-of-age as a writer is marked by multiple family tragedies, including the death of two sisters and her brother's epilepsy, and Janet's own misdiagnosis as a schizophrenic, leading to her incarceration in a mental asylum and the threat of a lobotomy. In interviews Jane Campion has commented on the deep influence of Frame's autobiographical novel *Owls Do Cry* (1961) upon her own creativity during her adolescence as well as her desire to demythologize Frame's reputation as a "mad writer."[5] She also saw in this project a way to reconnect with her experiences of growing up in New Zealand, commenting that it "awakened my own memories of my childhood; her book really seemed to me to be an essay on childhood in New Zealand."[6] Indeed, it is perhaps indicative of Campion's expatriate perspective that she chose a compatriot writer for her first cinematic adaptation, one whose sense of "the adolescent homelessness of self" was compounded by her alienated relationship to New Zealand society and shame over her working-class origins and awkward femininity.[7]

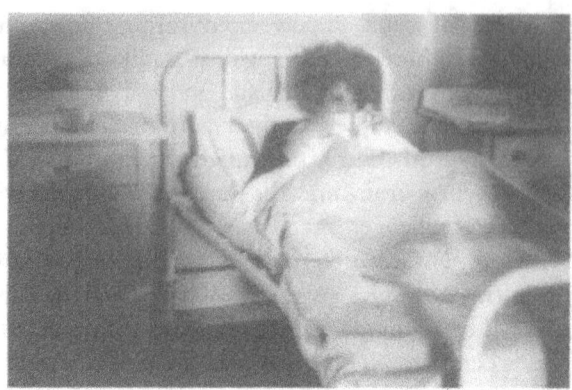

Marginalized and repressed, Kerry Fox as the adult Janet Frame in *An Angel at My Table*. (Courtesy New Zealand Film Commission.)

Campion's adaptation of *An Autobiography* follows Janet Frame's life story from an impoverished childhood as the daughter of a nomadic railway family through her troubled college years in the city of Dunedin, in New Zealand's South Island, to her odyssey as a young woman writer to Europe and back home. Although structured chronologically, Campion's film is hardly a conventional, seamless reading of the autobiographical life. Screenwriter Laura Jones, who also adapted Campion's *The Portrait of a Lady*, remains close to Frame's poetic recreation of daily experience, her elliptical structure of time, place, and incident, and her modernist mixture of remembered fact and fantasy as mirrors of the self. Thus the film mimics the work of fragmentary dreams and associative memory. It unfolds through a series of sometimes ironically juxtaposed scenes and episodes and through an interwoven chain of symbolic images that capture Frame's interior world, her imaginative response to her surroundings, her repressed sexuality in adolescence, and her lingering melancholia about the death of her vibrant, traditionally feminine sisters.[8]

Covering the period from the 1930s through to the 1950s of Frame's childhood and her young womanhood, *An Angel at My Table* poignantly reveals how cultural stereotypes of femininity initially labeled Janet Frame first as an intensely shy social misfit and later as a psychologically "disturbed" young woman. Suffering from a nervous breakdown as a consequence of her discomfort with her sexuality, shame about her own body, and her acute shyness, Frame (Kerry Fox as the adult Janet) ends up in an asylum where she is subjected to harrowing electroshock therapy. Frame's melancholia and "unnatural" poetic talent are interpreted as schizophrenia in 1940s New Zealand. Here, as in Campion's other films, female "madness" is exposed as a socially constructed category that attempts to put eccentric or nonconforming women in their places. Campion offers an ironic commentary on the "disciplining" of the female body and mind when she dramatizes a party arranged for Frame and her fellow inmates at the asylum, who are grotesquely made up to resemble "normal" middle-class women. Mirroring earlier scenes that show the childhood play-acting of Frame and her sisters masquerading as grown-ups attired in the popular feminine fashions of the era, the party at the asylum poses a central question of the film: How can women define themselves in the arena of the "symbolic," the realm of patriarchal language, which threatens to position them in predetermined roles, as wives and mothers, as sexual fantasy objects, or as "madwomen"? This is also a recurrent question in Campion's work as a whole. Furthermore, in *An Angel at My Table* the question is richly complicated by Campion's willingness to show how women sometimes comply with the roles and positions created for them in patriarchal society. As in her other films, Campion is not satisfied with merely representing women as victims of society but instead examines the psychological complexities of their responses. One of the exquisite ironies of *An Angel at My Table*—one certainly not lost on Campion—is that Janet Frame literally wrote herself out of the asylum with her short story collection *The Lagoon* (1951), receiving the prestigious Hubert Church prize. Gradually, as both Frame's own autobiography and Campion's film reveal, Frame realized she had herself used the mask of schizophrenia to seek shelter from an inhospitable world.

Campion's earlier works, *A Girl's Own Story* and *Sweetie*, had already focused on the precarious nature of female rite-of-passage, alienation, and the family as a site of psychological dysfunction and confinement. Narratively and stylistically, *Sweetie* is Campion's most transgressive feature, taking us into the uncanny, claustrophobic spaces of a suburban family. Darkly humorous and at times excruciatingly painful in its depiction of the relationship between sisters Kay (Karen Colston) and Dawn, nicknamed "Sweetie" (Genevieve Lemon), *Sweetie* shows a modern Australian family in disarray, at a complete loss at how to deal with the mental instability and excessive demands of the title character. Whimsical, absurd, and often disturbing, the film exposes the evasions, repressions, and superstitious projections that define the broken relationships among parents, children, and siblings. Eschewing narrative continuity, Campion structures her film around the central visual metaphor of trees and unruly nature that are associated with Sweetie's out-of-control behavior. The metaphor is linked in complex ways to a perverted sexuality within the family: the father's (Jon Darling) possibly incestuous relationship with Sweetie, her sister Kay's

Sweetie (*left*) and Kay, sisters yet adversaries in Campion's disturbing depiction of an Australian suburban family. (Courtesy Ian Conrich collection of New Zealand cinema and visual culture.)

neurotic fear of trees and her own sexuality, the mother's (Dorothy Barry) frustrated escape from her husband to the outback.[9] The tree imagery also obliquely suggests Campion's concern with the uprootedness of Australia's modern white urban denizens whose national identity is tenuous and unresolved. The grotesquely excessive Sweetie, the incarnation of a repressed monstrous self returned to haunt the family, dies in the end by falling from her tree house in a fit of rage against her earlier abandonment by her parents and sister, but remains an unsettling memory.

The critical concerns of *An Angel at My Table* and *Sweetie* reappear in Campion's *The Piano*. As the film opens, Ada McGrath (Holly Hunter), accompanied by her daughter Flora (Anna Paquin), is relocated from Scotland to the New Zealand frontier to fulfill an arranged marriage contract. An enigmatic heroine, Ada had stopped speaking at the age of six, communicating with the people around her only through her passionate, strange piano playing and through her impish daughter. As

Kathleen McHugh writes, Campion imagines the willful misfit Ada as a "hypothetical ancestor" for the modern Pakeha (European) New Zealanders like Campion herself, whose origins and identity are complicated by their colonial past.[10]

The Piano's cinematic recreation of New Zealand's colonial past has been debated in numerous critical essays. Its controversial representation of the Maori and its privileging of whiteness both in the mise-en-scène and in its larger vision of the nation's founding are in some cases criticized from a postcolonial standpoint.[11] But the most polarizing issue is the film's vision of women's sexuality, which is seen as either an affirmative representation of active female desire or a romanticization of rape.[12] Not surprisingly, a film that so self-consciously questions the location of female desire and sexuality invites intense spectatorial pleasure and critically addresses women's imprisonment in the voyeuristic male gaze (which is also a colonial gaze) and queries New Zealand Pakeha history through women's experience of bodily violence is bound to invite politicized readings that reveal fault lines within feminism and its relation to theories of racial and postcolonial identities. Inspired by Emily Brontë's *Wuthering Heights* (1847), Campion in fact deliberately plays upon nineteenth-century literary tropes that intertwine gender relations and colonialism: the silenced female heroine in patriarchal culture, the madwoman in the attic, femininity as Freud's dark continent, female erotic transgression that is either punished with death or disciplined through marriage in the end.

However, *The Piano*, like Campion's other films, ultimately does not lend itself to a single ideological critique of women's identity and sexuality.[13] Ann Hardy argues that *The Piano* is "unusually open in terms of the opportunities it supplies for the construction of meaning" by the spectator. "[H]er earth-bound female protagonists struggle to understand what it would be for them either to be, or to have access to, their own source of meaning."[14] The outcome of this female struggle for freedom from cultural scripts and for self-determination is not fixed in Campion's films but occurs within a complex network of power relations, often within the claustrophobic confines of the traditional nuclear family. Her exploration of this theme goes back to her early expressionistically composed film, *Peel*, in which the punishment of a boy (Ben Martin) for throwing orange peels out of a car explodes into volatile and shifting family alliances among the child, the boy's father (Tim Pye), and a female relative (Katie Pye) that leave the woman powerless and speechless with rage.

From the beginning of *The Piano*, Ada's body is a site of exchange and struggle between men and leads to her resistance and determination to claim agency: Ada's father marries her to Stewart (Sam Neill); Stewart takes her piano, which functions as Ada's primary means of artistic and emotional expression, and gives it to Baines (Harvey Keitel) in exchange for land; Ada then exchanges sexual favors with Baines to win back her piano. The entire film is centrally concerned with buying and trading—of land, objects, and bodies—a colonial ideology that sees both nature and women as possessions to be dominated and controlled. Shots of Stewart's scorched land and felled trees in the name of "cultivation" anticipate his later severing of Ada's finger to make her conform to his vision of the obedient Victorian wife. There are other deliberate correspondences between Ada and nature. Campion, her cinematographer Stuart Dryburgh, and costume designer Janet Patterson gave *The Piano*'s setting in the New Zealand bush a very distinctive look, emphasizing both its Gothic otherworldliness and oppressive intimacy. "The bush," Campion comments, "has got an enchanted, complex, even frightening quality to it, unlike anything that you see anywhere else. . . . I was after the vivid, subconscious imagery of the bush, its dark, inner world."[15] The entangling vegetation parallels the confining structures of Ada's elaborate hoops and corsets, and thus the strange landscape reflects not only Ada's fears about being displaced as a "cultured" white woman into an unknown land but also returns her psychologically to the alienation and sense of entrapment she experienced in Victorian England.[16]

Ada's final escape from her husband's sexual and emotional imprisonment, for a life with the more unconventional Baines, has been the focus of a larger critical debate about Campion's gloss on narrative images of nineteenth-century women. Ada seems to retreat to the safe, white world of Nelson, learning to use her voice again. However, on the journey across the sea to Nelson, the piano is thrown overboard as excess ballast and Ada follows it underwater before resurfacing to embrace life. *The Piano* has, in fact, a dual ending that leaves Ada suspended in an unresolved state of liminality. The final disturbing image shows Ada imagining herself silent and floating underwater, tethered to the piano that has all along functioned as a complex metaphor for the burdens and pleasures of European culture and feminine refinement. Haunting and dark, the image forces the viewer to consider the previous scene—Ada posed with Baines in a picture of domestic happiness—as ironic. Indeed, Campion's grotesque close-up of Ada's metal finger playing the piano in her new home strikes a discordant note in that otherwise domestic Victorian scene. The settling of New Zealand, Campion suggests, is predicated on death, betrayal, and dismemberment.

The themes of entrapment and displacement of female desire in nineteenth-century society are reprised in Campion's adaptation of Henry James's *The Portrait of a Lady*. As Alan Nadel astutely observes of the film, "the Victorian world becomes the gothic elsewhere of female sexuality."[17]

The film showcases Campion's supreme control over a symbolically rich mise-en-scène as it articulates Isabel Archer's (Nicole Kidman) movement from the deceptively light, open world of life's possibilities to an increasingly dark, oppressive, and menacing domestic cage devised by the parasitic Osmond (John Malkovich) and his former lover, Madame Merle (Barbara Hershey). Once again, Campion focuses on a young woman who finds herself imprisoned in the fantasies of men as the object of their controlling gaze while coming to terms with her own ambivalent sexual appetites in a repressive Victorian society that offers them no outlet. The film is filled with dramatic irony: Isabel imagines herself free to roam and choose her own destiny, especially after she has received a sizable legacy from her uncle, but the viewer realizes that her path is delimited by all her male admirers. Lord Warburton (Richard E. Grant) offers her his wealthy homes enclosed by moats; the American Caspar Goodwood (Viggo Mortenson) seeks to rescue Isabel for a conventional marriage; her consumptive, well-meaning cousin Ralph (Martin Donovan) amuses himself with "planning out a high destiny" for Isabel; and the more sinister Osmond ensnares her in the vault of his Italian residence as an item in his art collection in order to enhance his social standing among the European aristocracy.

Visually foregrounding Isabel Archer's sexual fears and desires, Campion was criticized for both reworking James's novel for a contemporary audience and including anachronistic elements into a period film.[18] It is precisely these foreign additions to James's narrative and the film's visual and emotional extravagance that mark Campion's distinct directorial touch. Furthermore, her inclusion of a black-and-white prologue that features a group of modern young Australian women in a natural setting speaking about their erotic desire for a perfect mirror self suggests the commonalities between young women across different geographical spaces and historical periods who search for their social and sexual identities, a search that places the nineteenth-century Isabel Archer in a precarious position. Another anachronism is the mock travel film, "My Journey," shot incongruously like an early home movie or moving picture album with surreal effect. Appearing after Osmond's seductive kiss, it presents back-projected scenes of Isabel voyaging across the Middle East as a tourist and veiled in Arab outfits, followed by nightmarish sexual visions involving Osmond, who has hypnotized her with her twirling parasol and nearly made her swoon. This film-within-a-film combines a kaleidoscopic array of cinematic styles and strange Freudian images such as the notorious talking beans that whisper Osmond's words, "I love you absolutely."[19] Like the Bluebeard play in *The Piano*, this cinematic interlude comments on the psychosexual themes and power relations in the larger story, in this case the relationship between travel and desire. In Priscilla Walton's words, it "imbricates [Isabel's] sexuality with her travels throughout the British Empire. ... Isabel, as an heiress, partakes of the imperial spoils, but, concomitantly, as a woman, she is also the territory to be mapped and conquered" by her various suitors.[20]

Ruth Barron (Kate Winslet), a white, privileged yet dissatisfied contemporary young woman in *Holy Smoke,* also makes her journey East (or West from Australia's perspective), this time to India. While critics associated *Holy Smoke* with *Sweetie* in its satiric portrait of a soulless, suburban Australian family, it continues Campion's exploration of displaced heroines on quests for self-fulfillment. However, Ruth, who searches for Eastern spirituality as an antidote to Australian materialism, is not looking to merge with a romantic other like Isabel Archer; it is religious conversion by an Indian guru that makes her swoon. Ruth's desire for a spiritual home is the emotional center of the film, but her orientalist fantasy is rendered parodic through Campion's psychedelic flourishes in the opening scenes in Delhi set to the retro-1970s music of Neil Diamond's "Holly Holy." Campion's ironic perspective toward Ruth's spiritual quest is characteristic of her view toward all her young female protagonists: their impulse to rebel and escape stifling social enclosures is accompanied by romantic self-delusion and their desire to lose themselves in someone or something that is ultimately no more liberating than the life they are fleeing. The psychological turning points in Campion's films occur when the heroines must confront their illusions, rejecting or succumbing to their power.

In *Holy Smoke* Ruth's struggle for self-possession takes place in the Australian desert in her battle with P. J. Waters (Harvey Keitel), the conceited American cult deprogrammer hired by Ruth's family to break down her resistance and return Ruth to her former self. However, as Sue Gillett observes, "[t]here is no homecoming in spiritual or emotional terms for Ruth."[21] Caught in the no exit space of The Halfway Hut, the headstrong Ruth meets the ultra-rationalist P. J. in a battle of wills, brains, sexual control, and power. As her newfound belief in Eastern mysticism breaks down, Ruth is the one who turns the tables, deconstructs their gender roles, and uses her sexuality to taunt P. J., make him vulnerable, and expose his carefully styled masculinity as a masquerade. In one of Campion's favored mirror shots, which function as sites of performance and doubled selves, she has Ruth humiliate P. J. by putting him in a red dress and make-up. P. J. writes on Ruth's forehead "Be kind" in reverse letters, a message Ruth can only read when she looks at herself in the mirror. Her painful realization of her sense of entitlement and lack of compassion has its comic counterpoint in P. J.'s breakdown in the desert when, in a particularly fantastic and lurid hallucination, he envisions her as a Hindu goddess. While the film develops the connections between India, Australia, and the United States through real and imaginary journeys, the ultimate impact of these moments of psychological encounter remain uncertain at the end.

In her most recent feature film, *In the Cut*, adapted from Susanna Moore's best-selling 1995 erotic thriller, Campion works within and against the well-established cinematic genre of the psychological thriller. However, there are clear stylistic and thematic continuities with her earlier work, particularly in the film's exploration of female sexuality, power relations between men and women, and the tensions between conscious choice and unconscious desire for women in a world that idealizes romance and marriage and sexualizes violence.

Set in a seedy-looking lower Manhattan neighborhood that is being terrorized by a serial killer who dismembers his victims, *In the Cut* focuses on Frannie Averey (Meg Ryan), a forty-something, single English teacher and writer who in the beginning of the film inadvertently witnesses a prostitute servicing a man in the dark basement of a bar. This scene of raw sexuality haunts her dreams and waking life, and she learns shortly thereafter from homicide detective Giovanni Malloy (Mark Ruffalo) that the man in the bar is suspected of killing the prostitute. Since Malloy wears a tattoo on his wrist similar to the one Frannie noticed on the presumed killer, she becomes increasingly suspicious of him even as they begin a passionate love affair and grow emotionally closer. When her much-loved half-sister Pauline (Jennifer Jason Leigh) becomes the serial killer's victim, a grief-stricken Frannie runs away from Malloy only to seek protection from the real murderer, Malloy's investigative partner Rodriguez (Nick Damici), whom she kills in the end with Malloy's gun.

The detective story of solving the gruesome murders is closely intertwined with Frannie's exploration of her own desires and fears. In her dreams, Frannie romanticizes her mother's whirlwind courtship with her father, even as she remembers his betrayal of her mother. The dream suggests her parents' relationship has shaped Frannie's life and view of romantic love in problematic ways, keeping her suspended between emotional vulnerability and controlled reserve. The key to the psychological core of the film are recurrent sepia-tinted sequences of Frannie's parents' romantic encounter skating on a frozen lake, shot in Campion's trademark surreal style, which form a cohesive romantic narrative but hide the true story of the philandering father's cruelty and ultimate abandonment of Frannie's mother. As Frannie confronts the darkness in her family mythology, we realize that *In the Cut* is in fact a distinctly *female* noir that traces the interior journey of its central character and makes *her* the investigator of her own story.

As an English teacher and writer, Frannie is equipped to read and interpret the nuances of language and symbolic signs, yet ironically she is blind to their meaning in the fractured urban world around her. Frannie encounters in her real and imagined cityscape a panoply of signs, which she assembles into a narrative of false clues: subway poetry, words on a t-shirt, the tattoo on the killer's wrist, the symbolic charms on a courtship bracelet that her sister gives her, and New York City slang that Frannie deciphers for its sexual and violent connotations. Misinterpretation and mistaken identities lead Frannie straight into the serial killer's arms, while her ambivalent feelings for Malloy make her suspect him of the grisly crimes.

By the film's end, Campion brings together the two stories—the detective/murder plot and the family romance plot—when Frannie faces the real killer. Rodriguez charms and woos his victims with engagement rings, flowers, and kisses before he cuts them up, and in her final confrontation with him Frannie needs to both kill him and exorcise the masochistic fantasy she inherited from her mother: the myth of her father as a romantic hero who swept her mother off her feet only to abandon her. In Campion's film universe, the physical violence is a symptom of the psychologically more dangerous cultural scripts of love and romance that hide a masculine desire for possession and control of the female body.

In the final analysis, Campion's films do not promise a particular alternative place for women—to quote Madame Merle in *The Portrait of a Lady*, "A woman, it seems to me, has no *natural* place anywhere." Campion's view of women is altogether more complicated and darker, and is perhaps linked to her own "strange history" as a Pakeha New Zealander whose relation to place and culture is uncertain and open to exploration.[22] Her heroines' journeys toward authorship and self-possession invariably involve a struggle with an other—a sister in *Sweetie* and *An Angel at My Table*, an oppressive husband in *The Piano* and *The Portrait of a Lady*, a counselor-lover-father figure in *Holy Smoke*, or *In the Cut*'s father-detective-serial killer—but their sense of autonomy and selfhood is never neatly resolved. As McHugh argues, Campion contests conventional moral frameworks, even feminist ones.[23] Her films always end provisionally: In *An Angel at My Table*, Janet Frame is left writing, living in a trailer parked at her surviving sister's house. Living close by, yet not in her sister's home, Janet moves between the external social world, dancing a few tentative steps to the twist, and the realm of the imagination where she must venture alone. In the closing shot of *Sweetie*, we see a young Sweetie singing a melancholy song in the garden after the film has ostensibly resolved Kay's sexual and spiritual crisis. The last image of Isabel Archer in *The Portrait of a Lady* shows her frozen on the threshold between the outside and interior worlds of her life after she has run away from Goodwood toward her uncle's estate. *In the Cut* offers a more tenuously positive resolution than the novel, which ends with Frannie's death: in the film, she returns to her apartment and a handcuffed Malloy after shooting the real killer. However, as the door closes upon the couple and obscures our vision, we are left with a final image as ambiguous as any in Campion's films. Is this a scene of redemption and a new beginning, or are Frannie and Malloy ironically once again trapped in a Gothic interior? In each instance, Campion refuses to situate her female protagonists in an unequivocally secure home, the very site of familial and familiar horrors that haunts all her heroines.

Notes

1. For specific readings of *The Piano* as a Gothic text, see Kirsten Moana Thompson, "The Sickness unto Death: Dislocated Gothic in a Minor Key," in *Piano Lessons: Approaches to "The Piano,"* ed. Felicity Coombs and Suzanne Gemmell (Sydney: John Libbey, 1999), 64–80; Estella Tincknell, "New Zealand Gothic? Jane Campion's *The Piano*," in *New Zealand—A Pastoral Paradise?*, ed. Ian Conrich and David Woods (Nottingham: Kakapo Books, 2000), 107–19; and Cyndy Hendershot, "(Re)Visioning the Gothic: Jane Campion's *The Piano*," *Literature/Film Quarterly* 26, no. 2 (1998): 97–108. Anneke Smelik discusses the Gothic elements in *Sweetie* in *And the Mirror Cracked: Feminist Cinema and Film Theory* (New York: St. Martin's, 1998), 139–51.
2. Freda Freiberg, "The Bizarre in the Banal: Notes on the Films of Jane Campion," in *Don't Shoot Darling! Women's Independent Filmmaking in Australia*, ed. Annette Blonski, Barbara Creed, and Freda Freiberg (Richmond, Australia: Greenhouse, 1987), 328–33.
3. Priscilla Walton, "Jane and James Go to the Movies: Postcolonial Portraits of a Lady," *Henry James Review* 18 (1997): 189. In contrast to Walton's postcolonial reading of Campion's transnational productions, Dana Polan problematizes her use of international stars and her transnational funding sources as a response to the demands of the global film market where movies such as *The Piano* and *The Portrait of a Lady* are saleable worldwide. See Polan's *Jane Campion* (London: BFI, 2001).
4. See Sue Gillett, "Angel from the Mirror City: Jane Campion's Janet Frame," www.sensesofcinema.com/contents/00/10/angel.html; Suzette Henke, "Jane Campion Frames Janet Frame: A Portrait of the Artist as a Young New Zealand Poet," *Biography* 23, no. 4 (2000): 651–69; and Eva Rueschmann, "*An Angel at My Table:* Sisters, Trauma, and the Making of an Artist as a Young Woman," in *Sisters on Screen: Siblings in Contemporary Cinema*, ed. Rueschmann (Philadelphia: Temple University Press, 2000), 36–50.
5. See interviews with Jane Campion by Lynden Barber, Michel Ciment, and Katherine Tulich in *Jane Campion: Interviews*, ed. Virginia Wright Wexman (Jackson: University Press of Mississippi, 1999).
6. Michel Ciment, "The Red Wigs of Autobiography: Interview with Jane Campion," in *Jane Campion: Interviews*, ed. Wexman, 63.
7. Janet Frame, *An Autobiography, Volumes I–III* (New York: George Braziller, 1991), 110.

8. See my more detailed analysis of the sister relationships in *An Angel at My Table*, in *Sisters on Screen*.
9. Kathleen McHugh sees trees as a genealogical metaphor, interpreting Kay's fear of roots as her anxiety about what lies behind her "family tree" ("'Sounds That Creep Inside You': Female Narration and Voiceover in the Films of Jane Campion," *Style* 35, no. 2 [2001]: 200).
10. McHugh, "Sounds That Creep Inside You," 206.
11. Felicity Coombs and Suzanne Gemmel's *Piano Lessons: Approaches to "The Piano"* (Sydney: John Libbey, 1999) offers a sampling of diverse theoretical readings of the film. See also Harriet Margolis, ed., *Jane Campion's "The Piano"* (Cambridge: Cambridge University Press, 2000). Polan provides a good overview of the controversial reception and critical debates that surround *The Piano*. For the representation of the Maori, consult Lynda Dyson, "The Return of the Repressed?: Whiteness, Femininity, and Colonialism in *The Piano*," in *Piano Lessons*, 111–21, and Mark A. Reid, "A Few Black Keys and Maori Tattoos: Re-Reading Jane Campion's *The Piano* in PostNegritude Time," *Quarterly Review of Film and Video* 17, no. 2 (2000): 107–16.
12. See "*The Piano* Debate," *Screen* 36, no. 3 (1995): 257–87.
13. For a psychoanalytic reading of the "negativity" through which *The Piano* works toward the possibility of female desire, see Suzy Gordon, "'I Clipped Your Wing, That's All': Auto-Eroticism and the Female Spectator in *The Piano* Debate," *Screen* 37, no. 2 (1996): 193–205. McHugh approaches Campion's decentering of female identity through an analysis of the complex structures of female narration and voiceover in her films ("Sounds That Creep Inside You," 193–218).
14. Ann Hardy, "The Last Patriarch," in *Jane Campion's "The Piano,"* ed. Margolis, 59 and 61.
15. Jane Campion, "The Making of *The Piano*," in *Campion's "The Piano"* (New York: Hyperion/Miramax Books, 1993), 139.
16. Stella Bruzzi offers an extended discussion of the role of costume in *The Piano*. "Tempestuous Petticoats: Costume and Desire in *The Piano*," *Screen* 36, no. 3 (1995): 257–66. See also Stella Bruzzi, *Undressing Cinema: Clothing and Identity in the Movies* (London: Routledge, 1997): 57–63.
17. Alan Nadel, "The Search for Cinematic Identity and a Good Man: Jane Campion's Appropriation of James's *Portrait*," *Henry James Review* 19 (1997): 182.
18. For a debate of these and other issues in Campion's film, see the special issue of the *Henry James Review* 18 (1997).
19. Kathleen Murphy identifies several influences: "The primitively shot and imagined silent movie—'My Journey'—that follows hard upon Osmond's seduction is equal, lurid parts *Son of the Sheik* and Hitchcock's *Spellbound*, with a little *Caligari* thrown in for good measure" ("Jane Campion's Shining: Portrait of a Director," *Film Comment* 32, no. 6 [1996]: 33). Equally relevant are visual connections to Hitchcock's *Vertigo* (1958) and Buñuel's surrealist films.
20. Walton, "Jane and James Go to the Movies," 189.
21. For *Holy Smoke*'s critique of an essentialist notion of identity and Australian nationhood, see Sue Gillett, "Never a Native: Deconstructing Home and Heart in *Holy Smoke*," www.sensesofcinema.com/contents/00/5/holy.html.
22. See Campion, "The Making of *The Piano*," 135.
23. McHugh, "Sounds That Creep Inside You," 214.

Jane Campion—Filmography

1972. *All That We Need* (NZ extended short film: actor).
1980. *Tissues* (Australia short film: director).
1981. *Mishaps: Seduction and Conquest* (Australia short video: director).
1982. *Peel* a.k.a. ***An Exercise in Discipline—Peel*** (Australia short film: director, writer, editor).
1983. *Passionless Moments* (Australia short film: director, co-producer, co-writer, cinematographer).
1984. *A Girl's Own Story* (Australia extended short film: director, writer).
1984. *After Hours* (Australia extended short film: director and writer).
1986. *Two Friends* (Australia television film: director, producer).
1986. *Dancing Daze* (Australia television six-part series: episode director)
1989. *Sweetie* (Australia feature film: director, writer, story).
1989. *The Audition* (Australia extended short film: actor).
1990. ***An Angel at My Table*** (NZ feature film, shown also as a television three-part mini-series: director).
1993. ***The Piano*** (Australia/NZ feature film: director, writer).
1996. ***The Portrait of a Lady*** (UK/US feature film: director).
1999. *Soft Fruit* (Australia/US feature film: executive producer).
1999. ***Holy Smoke*** (US/Australia feature film: director, co-writer).
2001. *Femme et cinéaste* (French television documentary: interviewee).
2003. ***In the Cut*** (UK/US feature film: director, writer).
2004. *Somersault* (Australia feature film: script advisor).
2006. *Abduction: The Megumi Yokota Story* (US documentary: producer).

18

Experiments with Desire
The Psychodynamics of Alison Maclean

Kirsten Moana Thompson

> The stories that I often think up have a certain heightened reality, or an element of the fantastic or the surreal.
>
> Alison Maclean, television interview,
> *Exposure* series, Sci-fi Channel, tx April 4, 2000.

From her first film *Taunt* (1983), Alison Maclean has been interested in what she calls "the ambiguous, contradictory side of sexual politics."[1] In her shorts, features, and music videos she examines the "unexplored territory" of women's stories from the chatty *Rud's Wife* (1986) and *Talkback* (1987) to the domestic horror in the almost wordless *Kitchen Sink* (1989).[2] Her feminist explorations into the terrain of female subjectivity and desire show the interrelationships of jealousy and revenge, threat and vulnerability. Acknowledging the influence of pioneering New Zealand feminist filmmakers Melanie Reid and Gaylene Preston, both of whom made key features in the 1980s (*Trial Run* [1984] and *Mr Wrong* [1985], respectively), Maclean is also interested in subverting the relationship of gender and genre and the heterosexual dyad in Hollywood film. From *Taunt* to *Crush* (1992), her work defamiliarizes Hollywood conventions of transparent cinematic language. From the manipulative use of point-of-view editing, to the textured layering of sound, art design, and color, Maclean's films, with their use of kitsch and irony, establish succinctly the specificities of character, location, and period. This experimentation with film form and narrative reveals a subversion of the generic conventions of Gothic horror and suspense. In the horror-sci-fi *Kitchen Sink,* a strange hairy creature is pulled free from the drainpipe of a woman's sink and becomes the object of her repulsed, yet fascinated, desire. In the Gothic *Crush,* the femme fatale Lane (Marcia Gay Harden) is the locus of desire and revenge for two women and a man. Not only does Maclean experiment with and hybridize generic and narrative structure, she often blends the aesthetics of realism with comic-surreal imagery, from the humorous kitchen-sink drama of a widow in *Rud's Wife* to the tense psychodynamics of a substitute DJ's night on the air in *Talkback*. Although her second feature *Jesus' Son* (1999), an adaptation of Denis Johnson's short stories, is a more cheerful departure in tone from her previous work, it nonetheless shares the surreal imagery and tragi-comic tenor of her earlier work.

Canadian born but moving to New Zealand when she was fourteen, Alison Maclean majored in sculpture and photography at the Elam School of Fine Arts in Auckland for her Bachelor in Fine Arts. Her first film job was as third assistant director on Geoff Steven's feature *Strata* (1983). Her career to date includes five shorts, two features, three music videos, and ten television episodes (up until *Crush*, all were New Zealand–produced and financed). Moving between Canada and New Zealand as a child and adult, and subsequently working in Australia and New York, Maclean typifies the path of New Zealand filmmakers from Roger Donaldson to Jane Campion, who through desire or necessity seek work in other national film industries. Maclean's work has always been informed by an understanding of the ways in which film language constructs the gaze, evident in her experimentation with the grammar of editing in her first short, the twenty-minute black-and-white *Taunt*.

Taunt is a self-reflexive exploration of the conventions of the thriller, and the ways in which gender is narratively central and ideologically coded. The short begins with a woman (Mary Regan) dressing on a beach who senses she is not alone—her fear embodied by a predatory, circling camera that suggests the gaze of an unknown voyeur. The woman seems to see someone and leaves, and the title sequence begins. After the credit sequence, we meet two new characters, a long-haired woman and a mustached man, who, it turns out, are both played by the same male actor (Rangi Chadwick). This performative doubling of the male stalker and female prey, together with Maclean's extensive use of shot-reverse-shot editing, foregrounds the cinematic conventions that construct suspense in the traditional Hollywood chase. It is only *through* the editing structure and agitated soundtrack, rather than through the actor's performance(s), that meaning is constructed: a suspenseful chase. Maclean plays with hair as the metonymic signifier for gender—whether in the long hair of the female character or the tied-back hair and mustache of the male pursuer—for it is only through these external distinctions that the male pursuer and female pursued signify as different characters. The film's ending deconstructs these gendered conventions when the hair is ritually shaved away and the doubling of the performer, as both subject and object of the chase and the spectatorial gaze, become evident. We understand then that the narrative pursuit is a cinematic illusion, constructed by the conventions of shot-reverse-shot cutting and a manipulated post-synch soundtrack. By using the device of the same actor portraying the pursued and the pursuer, Maclean not only foregrounds the ways in which women continue to function as objects of the gaze in Hollywood genres like the horror and the thriller but also deconstructs the classical Hollywood conventions of transparent editing that create those gendered conditions of suspense.

In *Rud's Wife*, Maclean shifts to a very different mode—a fictional kitchen-sink documentary featuring an unnamed title character (Yvonne Lawley). The film explores the differing cultural expectations and social constraints of older women's experiences in marriage and intimacy, and the limitations that their roles as wives and mothers placed on them in the 1940s and 1950s in New Zealand. Rud's wife is never named except through her familial relationships, and it is this relational inscription of identity—as mother, as wife, and as grandmother ("Nan")—that has informed and demarcated her life. Using documentary-like techniques, Maclean intercuts old photos from Nan's past that alternate with her direct address to the camera. The photos of her husband Rud are oblique ones, showing a man facing away from the camera, or obscured by a flare of light. Through the enigmatic composition of these photos and other still photography, Maclean's images work to metonymically figure the emotionally distanced and displaced figure that Rud was in his wife's life. Directly addressing the camera, Nan tells us about her dead husband and the disappointments of her marriage: "I made the best of him. It was different then . . . not like now when you can get a husband on appro and send him back if you don't like him." As she bustles over the Sunday roast she prepares for her family dinner, Nan remarks to an unseen interlocutor, "I'd never have a man around again." Maclean's observations of the rhythm and ritual of food preparation are a typical exemplar of feminist realism, in their quiet observance of domestic space and work, with the camera standing in as unseen interlocutor to the character's direct address. These initial documentary conventions then take a surreal turn, with a bizarre shot of a headless chicken that Nan drops on the floor. In keeping with this comic moment, we later see a vacuum cleaner threaten to explode, which appears in a Lucille Ball–like program that Nan's granddaughter watches on the television. Meanwhile, the cheerful period music "Maori Hula Medley," which plays on Nan's record player, heightens the absurdist tone of the image of the vacuum cleaner. The viewer will hear this melody again nondiegetically over the closing shot of Nan sitting triumphant on the deck of a cruise ship, which undercuts the tense mood of the family dinner that had preceded it. It turns out that Rud's wife has defied her disapproving son Mark (Gary Inglis)—who opposed her plan to take her first trip out of New Zealand—and has embarked on a cruise. This closing image of freedom, with Nan on the cruise, represents the escape that eluded her in her lengthy role as wife and mother.

The comic tone apparent in *Rud's Wife* is still evident in the darker psychodrama *Talkback*. Jointly financed by the New Zealand Film Commission (NZFC) and TVNZ, and co-scripted with Geoff Chapple, *Talkback* tells the story of one night on talk radio. In an emergency, DJ novice Jonah (Lucy Sheehan) must take the station helm on the graveyard shift because her boss and former lover, talk show host Roger (Alistair Douglas), has suddenly disappeared. Like *Rud's Wife* and *Jesus' Son*, the fifty-minute narrative is fascinated with idiosyncratic characters, and through its dense crosscutting and counterpointing of image and sound, links speakers and listeners in a meta-conversation of personal gossip, political debate, and social banality. The political conversations that Jonah and her callers share—from discussions of feminism, to Maori rights under the Treaty of Waitangi, to the nuclear-free zone established by the first Labour Government, which led to the banning of U.S. vessels from New Zealand waters—range across key political and cultural issues of New Zealand in the 1980s. One recurring topic for satire is the state of foreign relations between New Zealand and the United States. As Jonah cracks: "We could have been Americans. We could be all running around saying aloominum instead of al—u—minum." This fascinated concern with the figure of the American would be further developed in Maclean's later portrait of Lane, a central character and catalyst for narrative action in *Crush*.

In *Talkback*, while the narrative centers on Jonah's character, Maclean counterpoints the disembodied voices of talk radio with empty locations of Auckland after dark, and the comedic, sometimes melancholic, kitsch-filled apartments or ugly hotel rooms of the lonely callers (with striking art-designed interiors by Jackie Gilmore). In this manner, Maclean explores the gaps between caller and listener, the elements that are not visible to Jonah. Maclean's framing also withholds certain visuals from the spectatorial gaze—instead we have frames of the backs of callers, or extreme close-ups of their mouths. Here, the radio and telephone are the audio devices that connect isolated individuals, just as Maclean's editing frustrates our spectatorial expectations of the narrative intimacies opened up by sound. She plays with the aural intimacy of the telephonic voice as she cuts between a variety of interior and exterior locations, heightening the visual stillness of the city after midnight by counterpointing it with the animated buzz of the radio soundtrack. Maclean's alertness to the particularities of Auckland is evident in her exterior shots of deserted streets and wharves and well-known local spaces like the White Lady (a portable diner in Queen Street), Rendalls' store, and Uncle's Bar

Suburban Gothic: The transformation of a domestic space invaded by a stranger in *Kitchen Sink*. (Courtesy New Zealand Film Commission.)

on Karangahape Road. These images magnify the insubstantiality of the soundtrack's voices that permeate the city after midnight—many loosely modeled on real individuals (Waitangi Joe is modeled on Waitangi Bill, and well-known tradesman and personality The Mad Butcher also has a cameo). Fascinated by the political and sociological dimensions of talk show popularity, Maclean conducted research at Radio Pacific: "it's like a voice for middle New Zealand in a way. It's called redneck radio, and often it is, but on the other hand you get other kinds of minority voices, people who are lonely or isolated, and interesting non-conformist views as well."[3] Peter Tait (who would also star in Maclean's short *Kitchen Sink*) plays Jim, an ex-convict who repeatedly calls in and seems obsessed with Jonah, adding the threat of a potential stalker to the stress of Jonah's night. As with *Taunt* and *Talkback,* Maclean's work often returns to a sense of danger that lies at the center of gender relationships. The unpredictable terrain that Maclean explores through the cacophony of talk takes a surreal direction in the unsettling, near silent tale, *Kitchen Sink,* which would be her next film.

Kitchen Sink is a compelling blend of horror and domesticity, with its mise-en-scène of a mundane home interior—a kitchen plughole, table, bath, and bed. Like Hitchcock's *Psycho*, which it invokes, the film foregrounds the loneliness and pathology of domestic space, but unlike Hitchcock, Maclean is concerned with the psychic desires of her female protagonist. As Maclean notes, the genesis of the film developed from a simple domestic observation: "The story came to me in much the same way as events unfold for the woman in the film. I could see this hair sticking out of the plughole and on closer inspection, the story began to emerge and to transform itself in quite a surprising way."[4] After washing the dishes, a woman (Theresa Healey) finds a hair in her kitchen sink plughole, which she pulls to find it attached to a strange hairy embryonic creature. At first repelled, she places the small alien object in the trash, but later, after further thought, she places it in running water in the bath. While an interruption (phone call) prolongs this suspense, the woman returns to find a full-grown hairy man (Peter Tait) in the bath. After shaving and dressing him, into a more human-like form in, to use Maclean's words, a "reverse Pygmalion effect,"[5] he becomes her object of desire; she places him in her bed and goes to sleep next to him. However, when she wakes up next to him, he remains corpse-like and so she places him in a garbage bag. The film builds suspense through repeated zoom-ins from behind the woman, first as she reads a book and later as she sits in the bath. Each time, the camera's gaze seems to embody a presence, constructing a spectatorial fear about the creature. In a frightening moment, the creature comes alive in the garbage bag, and the woman cuts him free, as if from an amniotic sack. Then as the creature-man and the woman kiss, she discovers a single hair on the back of his neck, with the horror enhanced by the canted framing of a close-up of Healey's widened eye, peering over the man's shoulder. Maclean cuts to her point of view of a close-up of the single hair at monumental scale (with special effects designed by Andrew Turney).[6] Stuart Dryburgh's stark black-and-white photography heightens the abstract qualities of the single hair, which in close-up looks like a thick trunk embedded in elephantine-like skin. In this way, Maclean's imagery, influenced by Hiroshi Teshigahara's *Woman of the Dunes* (1964), shows a fascination for the surreal texture of surfaces, from the repulsive hairy creature in its first appearance to this defamiliarizing final shot of the shaft of hair. Like a perfectionist Pygmalion, the woman cannot resist pulling the single hair out, with a cataclysmic result for the creature—yet as it screams, Maclean frustrates our spectatorial expectation that we will see what happens. Instead, the film concludes with a cryptic iris-out. The woman ends up destroying the creature that she had discovered and shaped, for as Maclean explains: "It was also like he wasn't quite perfect—she'd missed something."[7]

Sponsored by the NZFC's Bonsai Epic Short Films program, and produced by Hibiscus Films, the fourteen-minute *Kitchen Sink* had a $NZ100,000 budget. Following its selection for competition in Cannes it screened at both the Sundance and Toronto film festivals. Winner of eight international awards and the *Listener* Best Short Film of the Year, it has been described as "a dark and tender love story from the bowels of the plumbing system."[8] Critical and popular reception situated the film as a horror/sci-fi hybrid, and it has been aired on science fiction and art house cable channels in the United States and the United Kingdom. *Kitchen Sink* plays with spectatorial repulsion, constructing and manipulating our suspense, through a near wordless visual storytelling. Interested in the intense erotic attraction and repulsion between woman and monster, *Kitchen Sink* inverts the traditional gendered power relationships in a Hollywood film like *King Kong* (alluded to through a poster on the kitchen wall). The hairy monster, which was literally born of the domestic space, becomes an intensely private love object for the woman. Accentuating the eerie non-diegetic score by the cult New Zealand band The Headless Chickens are abrupt diegetic noises—running water in the bathtub, the unbearable scrape of a single-edge razor on skin, and the desperate rasp of the creature struggling for breath in a plastic trash bag. As Roger Horrocks notes, four visual leitmotifs recur—hair, eye, razor, water—that remind one of Luis Buñuel's *Un chien andalou* (1929).[9] Maclean shares with Buñuel strategies that shock and disgust. She does this through extended long takes and painful close-ups of the woman's single-edge razor shaving off the creature's hair (and at one point accidentally cutting him), coupled with a visceral use of sound. In this way, the spectator is placed in uncomfortably close spatial and aural proximity to the alien body, which is at once both grotesque and vulnerable. Defamiliarized and uncanny, the surrealist dimension to Maclean's imagery also permeates the Gothic eeriness of *Crush*, with its tourist kitsch, uncanny mannequins, and otherworldly mud pools.

It is in *Crush*, Maclean's first feature, that experimentation in generic convention and spectatorial expectation are at their most developed. Here she blends an interrogational mode of the Gothic with a wry citation of Maori culture as tourist commodity within the iconic space of New Zealand's principal tourist location, Rotorua, and the geothermal region of Whakarewarewa. The script for *Crush*, co-written with Anne Kennedy, had its development in the Sundance Institute's 1991 screenwriting workshop, which Maclean notes encouraged the "idiosyncratic and regional elements in the script to emerge more strongly."[10] Location shooting took eight weeks in Rotorua and Auckland. The story is a quartet of desire centered on a mysterious American femme fatale, Lane (Marcia Gay Harden) who disrupts the lives of three people; Angela Iseman (Caitlin Bossley); her father Colin Iseman (William Zappa); and Lane's friend, Christina (Donogh Rees). Maclean develops the thematics of obsession and desire through the conflicting desires and jealousies of these three characters for Lane: "I could almost see *Crush* as being a more complex variation on *Kitchen Sink*'s story, although spread out between four people instead of just two."[11]

The film explores the metaphoric ambiguity of its title "Crush" from both its analysis of emotional infatuation and growing obsession, and the physical wounds of a terrible car accident that opens the narrative. Christina is severely brain damaged by the accident and abandoned at the scene by Lane. As Christina recuperates in the hospital, Angela, appalled by Lane's action, visits Christina, and takes an increasing interest in her recovery. After the car accident, Lane appropriates Christina's professional identity as a writer and critic, and then proceeds to seduce both the teenage Angela and Colin. Angela, jealous of Lane's sexual relationship with her father, focuses her rage through Christina. Her hatred and resentment, developed as she slowly nurses Christina back to a state of partial recovery, finally redounds on Lane, when at the film's climax, the crippled Christina pushes her off the top of a waterfall to her death.

The credits for *Crush* open with shots of boiling mud at Hell's Gate in Rotorua, foreshadowing the tense emotional undercurrents among the three women that the narrative will soon reveal, tensions that ultimately lead to the Jacobean revenge tragedy that ensues. Two women are on a road trip. On the road, Lane looks at the sheep-studded green hills from the car window, observing "everything is so empty," to which Christina replies "McCahon said it's a landscape with too few lovers, but you'll fix that, won't you Lane?"[12] Invoking a key modernist trope in New Zealand literary and artistic criticism, that of the "empty landscape" assumed by the colonialist imaginary, Maclean explores the relationship between Maori and Pakeha (European) through the absent presence of Maori culture in the film's ersatz tourist topography. Christina, who appears as a literary critic (author of *Godzone Frontier* and articles in the New Zealand literary journal *Landfall*), is traveling with Lane to interview Colin Iseman, novelist and recent winner of the Booker Prize. Ever the critic, Christina babbles literary clichés: "No predators, no poisonous spiders, no snakes. New Zealand's this totally benign, paradisial, pre-lapsarian world ... and we're very uneasy about it. It's like what I said about Colin. There's this obsession to uncover the germ of evil, to search for the snake. That's the New Zealand psyche—looking for serpents. I guess we have a streak of perversity!" Understandably infuriated by Christina's pompousness, and momentarily distracted at the wheel while speeding (a surreal female man-

Emerging from the upturned car, and abandoning her companion in the wreck, a callous Lane checks her appearance in a wing mirror in *Crush*. (Courtesy Ian Conrich collection of New Zealand cinema and visual culture.)

nequin is glimpsed at the side of the road), Lane loses control, crashing the car. The violence of the car crash recalls a similar unexpected eruption in the opening of Roger Donaldson's *Smash Palace* (1981), for there too the car crash is a marker of impending doom.

Lane is the cultural outsider in this quartet, her American identity central to her seductive and mysterious appeal. As Maclean notes, "Lane was an American from the beginning. Her brashness, confidence, and sexiness were part of the attraction. That is part of being an American, I suppose."[13] Maclean suggests the powerful valence of desire across Pakeha, Maori, and American registers. Notwithstanding the sociopathic dimensions of Lane's callousness and manipulation, Marcia Gay Harden's nuanced performance also offers an emotional complexity to Lane's character, for she is a compelling vector of desire for three people. Like the gender reversal in the Pygmalion myth that structured the earlier *Kitchen Sink*, Lane seduces and remakes the tomboy Angela with dress and makeup, and gives Colin a haircut as a prelude to his own seduction. She blithely notes, "The less I know about a place the more I like it," as she playfully twirls poi, in a dance of seduction of both Angela and her father.[14]

Crush is a darkly comic film whose mise-en-scène of New Zealand tourist kitsch and carefully placed graffiti ("Land of the Wrong White Crowd,"[15]) figures the topography of settlement's aftermath and the postcolonial present. The tacky 1970s decor of the Rotorua geothermal region, with its cheap motels (Goldie reproductions on the walls) and tourist culture, is a color scheme of washed-out browns, reds, and sulfurous yellows. Angela observes of Pohutu Geyser, "it used to be much bigger," to which Lane comically scolds, "This country's obsessed with size," one of the more successful condensations of the ways in which gender and national identities intersect in the film. A postcolonial response to the "empty landscape" anxieties articulated by Pakeha modernist artists like McCahon, rehearsed earlier by Christina, is figured through other instantiations of Pakeha appropriation—the haka of the All Blacks national rugby team playing on a television screen in the background, and the mannequin of a Maori woman in traditional dress on a deserted Rotorua street.[16] Here, Maori culture figures as reified tourist iconography—the metonymic figures for the historical appropriations and mediations of Pakeha settler culture.

Crush then shifts in tone from comic bathos to Gothic revenge. Suffering brain damage and memory loss, Christina initially appears to be Angela's puppet. Angela begins by caring for Christina, then correcting her speech, and ultimately directing a tale of crime and punishment. Holding up a tiny cut-out photo of Lane's head that she has brought to the hospital, Angela instructs Christina, "This is the person who did this to you." Maclean's construction of a key scene underscores Donogh Rees's performance as the increasingly malevolent Christina, who rises from the near dead to confront and finally kill Lane for her misdeeds. A series of shot-reverse-shots encapsulates the guilt and rage between the two, when Christina meets Lane again for the first time since the accident. Her sudden appearance in an ominously scored slow motion sequence, from the point of view of Lane, Angela, and Colin, is of Christina glaring like the Grim Reaper from the back seat of her taxi. Shot-reverse-shot cutting, a dramatic score, and abrupt zoom-ins all underscore Lane's unease at Christina's damaged appearance and speech. Despite Lane's later expression of regret, it comes too late, moments before Christina pushes her to her death. The film explores the unforeseen repercussions that Lane's actions have for Angela, Christina, and Colin, and the permeable boundary between desire and hate that the femme fatale often triggers.

In the seven years between *Crush* and her next feature film, *Jesus' Son*, Maclean underwent what she acknowledges as a difficult period: "I spent most of the time writing, writing my own scripts, and then going through a lot of frustration and not being able to finance them."[17] Her first work during this time was contributing the "Greed" section of the Australian compilation feature *Seven Deadly Sins* in 1993. After Jonathan Demme saw *Kitchen Sink,* he invited Maclean to contribute a segment, "Honey-Getter," for the 1997 Home Box Office feature *SUBWAY Stories: Tales from the Underground,* which tells the story of a young woman's (Surita Choudhury) revenge on a subway harasser. Between 1997 and 1998, Maclean worked on three music videos for Australian singer Natalie Imbruglia (including the Grammy nominated "Torn"), a *Homicide* television episode, and two shows in the first season of Emmy winner *Sex and the City*—"Models and Mortals" and "Valley of the Twenty-Something Guys." In speaking of her work in *Sex and the City,* Maclean noted the different aesthetic strategies necessitated by the turnaround of television schedules:

> I think they were interested in me because they wanted a film director, they wanted it to have a more cinematic look, they wanted it to be unusual television—but I think that at a certain point that wasn't particularly economic. It's time consuming to shoot that way with that kind of care. They quickly told us we were being a little too extravagant and we had to kind of make it simple. I think they said shoot it like *Seinfeld,* just link it with the comedy work. Comedy is very technical; it is so much about timing. That got me thinking about those things in ways that were perhaps helpful for the more comic parts of *Jesus' Son.* It also gets you used to a slightly faster pace of working and having to rehearse on the day on set which is not ideal but that was pretty much the way we shot *Jesus' Son* too.[18]

Through her American television and music video work, Maclean's increased prominence in the United States led to Elizabeth Cuthrell and David Urrutia of Evenstar Films approaching her to direct an adaptation of Denis Johnson's *Jesus' Son.* Maclean, Cuthrell, Urrutia, and Oren Moverman wrote the screenplay, but its counter-culture subject matter and unconventional narrative structure failed to obtain Hollywood financing. Consequently, outsider investors Lion's Gate and Alliance funded *Jesus' Son.* Armed with a mere U.S. $2.5 million budget, and prominent actors like Dennis Hopper, Holly Hunter, and Denis Leary working for scale, the film was shot in a compressed thirty-four days on locations in Philadelphia and South Jersey that stood in for the film's Midwest settings. *Jesus' Son* is an elliptical film following the memories and anecdotes of a petty thief and junkie known only as Fuckhead or FH (Billy Crudup) and the large cast of junkies, weirdos, and misfits whom he meets, and whose random untimely deaths he often witnesses. The film's title refers to a line from Lou Reed's song "Heroin," written for the Velvet Underground, "When the smack begins to flow / And I feel like Jesus' son." As Maclean explains, "It's this provocative, poetic, absurd title that suggests he is a Christ-like figure, that there is something special about him, the fact that he constantly has these premonitions and hallucinations and that he experiences without judging."[19]

With a richly textured 1970s soundtrack, and the surreal visual imagery that has become Maclean's trademark, *Jesus' Son* is a secular story, which nonetheless frequently calls upon Catholic iconography. When FH looks through a diner's window, the reverse angle reveals an artfully composed framing of his face, with a laurel crown produced by the window's lettering—a kind of accidental beatitude. This image is accompanied by the portentous words "you—you're the one," which are then comically undercut—the speaker is a waitress who has recognized FH as a customer that stiffed her for a previous bill. Beginning in 1971, FH's story is a picaresque road trip wandering through five years of his life and a succession of Midwest cities, and loosely linked through his encounters with lovers Michelle (Samantha Morton)[20] and Mira (Holly Hunter). Maclean's episodic rendition of the bizarre life of Fuckhead is an intriguing visualization of retrospective memory, with all the circumlocutions, lacunae, and incoherencies of FH's often drug-addled perspective. FH's memory controls the narrative direction, "but wait, I forgot to tell you," as the narrative jumps backward and forward in time, or overlaps with itself, with title sequences signaling temporal transitions: "Three Years Earlier 1971," "Holiday." Each sequence has its unique visual style, color palette, and camera style, from the unsettling handheld camera and harsh neon lighting of "Emergency," to the warm brown and yellow earth tones of "Beverly Home." The hallucinations, non sequiturs, and dreamlike imagery that permeate the story suggest the surreal experiential quality of FH's memories, with images like a naked woman paragliding or a man with a knife in his eye (Dennis Johnson in a cameo), and are heightened by the atmospheric lighting effects of cinematographer Adam Kimmel, in the grimy mise-en-scène of laundromats and subway cars. Fuckhead perceives the world as a collective hallucination, or at least as a kind of privileged entry into others' psychic spaces: "As nearly as I could tell, I'd wandered into some kind of a dream that Wayne was having about his wife and his house." The hallucinatory and surreal quality to FH's subjective experience are exemplified in his scenes with his pill-popping lunatic friend Georgie (Jack Black), whose manic behavior is both comical and threatening, and exemplary of Maclean's hybridization of tone and genre. Wandering with Georgie, FH misrecognizes a deserted drive-in for a cemetery, which, as Maclean lights the drive-in listening posts to highlight their resemblance to graveyard crosses, aligns the viewer's gaze with FH's experiential disorientation in a world that surrounds him with death.

Whereas in Maclean's earlier films *Crush* and *Kitchen Sink*, the monstrosity of desire leads to death, in *Jesus' Son*, death itself becomes random and absurd, oxymoronically gaining a comical pathos. This pathos is underscored through FH's encounters with four characters who die: the Oldsmobile driver, McInnes, Wayne, and Michelle. Like *Crush*, *Jesus' Son* opens with a car crash, but this time the crash is visually oblique, a poeticized blur of slow motion and red lights. FH, who was given a lift in the car that crashes, sits in the emergency room as we hear the muted background screams of the woman who lost her husband in the crash. For FH, death becomes a thing of beauty: "she shrieked as I imagined an eagle would shriek. It felt wonderful to be alive to hear it. I've gone looking for that feeling everywhere." In Mira, FH meets someone who like him is a death magnet—"almost every man I've ever loved ended up getting killed." Mira's portrait is comical in its absurd details ("my first husband fell through a thousand evergreen branches up in the mountains ... he was a tree surgeon and he crushed his head") and the sheer excess of her lovers' deaths (at least six) that mirror the comic absurdity of Fuckhead's own brushes with mortality. Maclean's use of split-screen demonstrates Fuckhead's bizarre luck as he and Wayne simultaneously, yet separately, shoot up with some bad junk one afternoon. In the split-screen, we see Wayne die from an overdose at the same time that Michelle's serendipitous arrival saves FH. In a later echo, this time with a tragic turn, Michelle's halfhearted suicide by overdose succeeds, because FH does not see her suicide note in time "to wake me up if you want me." Unlike the earlier cold shower that saved FH from his overdose, FH's similar attempts to revive Michelle are in vain. Fuckhead ultimately finds redemption at the Beverly Center in Arizona, looking after the sick and old, some of whom "couldn't be allowed out on the streets with their impossible deformities," with Maclean's comic tone wryly observing, "they made God look like a senseless maniac." The film ends with a Brechtian sequence in which FH walks with the hospital patients who perform their daily exercise by circling the hospital reception booth. In a ritualized theatrical gesture, the characters freeze, then change direction, FH now joyful in his discovery of empathy: "I had never known, I had never even imagined for a heartbeat that there might be a place in the world for people like us." To the words of a Mennonite singer, "we'll understand it all by and by," FH finds redemption, walking off down the road to a new encounter. Like the characters in Maclean's earlier work, her portrait of FH is that of an outsider whose subjective world expresses the themes of alienation and loneliness to which the director repeatedly returns.

In her concern for the contradictory, ambiguous, and conflicted elements of passion and desire, Maclean uses hybridized techniques mixing tone, genre, and a subversion of the spectatorial expectations constructed by Hollywood narrative. By realigning the relationship between the camera's gaze and dominant gender relationships, she explores an alternative articulation of subjectivity, and one that is most often female. Her eye for the comedic and the kitsch, most often expressed through her mise-en-scène, adds a heightened, if not surreal, quality to the psychic spaces of her characters. From her subversive investigations of genre in *Taunt* and *Crush* to her analyses of desire and repulsion in *Kitchen Sink* and of the subcultures in *Jesus' Son*, Maclean shows an original and acerbic eye for narratives about idiosyncratic outsiders, lonely wanderers, and comic saints.

Notes

1. Alison Maclean interviewed in Shirley Horrocks's documentary *Pleasures and Dangers* (1991), and further cited in Roger Horrocks, "Alternatives: Experimental Film Making in New Zealand," in *Film in Aotearoa New Zealand*, 2nd ed., ed. Jonathan Dennis and Jan Bieringa (Wellington: Victoria University Press, 1996), 78.
2. Miro Bilbrough, "Interview," in *Pleasures and Dangers*, ed. Trish Clark and Wystan Curnow (Auckland: Longman Paul, 1991), 63–68.
3. "Alison Maclean Talks Back," *Bi Film* (June 1988). NZFC pressbook on *Talkback*, 18.
4. Interview with Maclean, New Zealand Film Commission Presspack, *Kitchen Sink* (Wellington, 1989), 3.
5. Bilbrough, "Interview," 64.
6. Ibid., 67.
7. Ibid., 64.
8. Jonathan Dowling, "NZ Front Runner," *New Zealand Herald*, May 24, 1989.
9. Horrocks, "Alternatives: Experimental Film Making in New Zealand," 78.
10. New Zealand Film Commission Presspack, *Crush* (Wellington, 1992), 3.
11. Maclean, quoted in Bernard D. McDonald, "Coming Clean," *Stamp* (March 1993): 13.
12. Colin McCahon (1919–87) is New Zealand's most influential modernist painter for whom the landscape was a recurrent subject in his paintings. Works include *I Paul to You at Ngatimote* (1946), *King of the Jews* (1947), *Towards Auckland* series (1953–54), *I am* (1954), *Northland Panels* (1958), *Gate* series (1961–62) and *Victory over Death 2* (1970).
13. Lawrence Chua, "Crush Groove," *Village Voice*, September 28, 1993, 68.
14. Poi are colored straw balls on long strings that are twirled in elaborate choreographed movements as part of traditional Maori waiata (song) and dance.
15. This graffiti is an ironic retort to the traditional Maori name for New Zealand, Aotearoa, or the "Land of the Long White Cloud."

16. The haka was a traditional Maori war dance/action song meant to intimidate opponents before battle. Warriors would chant the haka and gesticulate, bulge their eyes, and stick out their tongues as part of a strategy to terrify. The All Blacks have appropriated this warrior tradition and perform the haka before each rugby game.
17. Anthony Kaufman, "ND/NF Interview: Alison Maclean's Acclaimed Second Coming," *Indiewire*, April 6, 2000, http://www.indiewire.com/onthescene/fes_00NDNF_000406_Ma_2A0E1.html.
18. David Edwards, "Q and A with Alison Maclean," http://www.filmfestivals.com/int/overviews/2000/brisbane_maclean_00.htm, Brisbane Film Festival, July 27–August 6, 2000.
19. A. G. Basoli, "Alison Maclean's Second Coming," *Moviemaker* 39 (March 2002), formerly available at http://www.moviemaker.com/issues/39/maclean.html.
20. In contrast to Johnson's stories, the screenplay expanded the role of Michelle and used her as an emotional anchor point for FH, as well as a continuity device in the episodic narrative.

Alison Maclean—Filmography

1983. *Taunt* (NZ short film: director, writer).
1983. *Strata* (NZ feature film: 3rd assistant director)
1984. *Vigil* (NZ feature film: production assistant).
1985. *Jewel's Darl* (NZ film/television drama: continuity).
1985. *Drum/Sing* (NZ extended short film: production co-manager).
1986. *Rud's Wife* (NZ extended short film: director, co-writer).
1987. *Talkback* (NZ extended short film: director, co-writer).
1988. *The Rainbow Warrior Conspiracy* (NZ/Australia television four-part mini-series: script supervisor).
1989. *Kitchen Sink* (NZ short film: director, writer).
1991. *Pleasures and Dangers* (NZ television documentary: featured artist and interviewee).
1992. *Crush* (NZ feature film: director, co-writer).
1993. *Seven Deadly Sins* (Australia television seven-part mini-series: director of the episode "Greed").
1996. *The Adventures of Pete & Pete* (US television series: director of the episode "Dance Fever").
1997. *SUBWAY Stories: Tales from the Underground* a.k.a. *Subway* (US television series: director of the episode "Honey Getter").
1997. *Homicide: Life on the Street* (US television series: director of the episode "Birthday").
1997/98. Three music videos for Natalie Imbruglia (director for "Torn," "Big Mistake," and "Wishing I Was There").
1998. *Sex and the City* (US television series: director of the episodes "Models and Mortals" and "Valley of the Twenty-Something Guys").
1999. *Jesus' Son* (US/Canada feature film: director).
2001. Three commercials for The Legal Society of New York (director for

"Shoe," "Wallet," and "Trophy").
2003. *Carnivale* (US television series: director of the episode "The River").
2003. *Hollywood High* (US television documentary: interviewee).
2004. *Persons of Interest* (US documentary: co-director).
2004. *The L-Word* (US television series: director of the episode "Loyal").
2006. *Intolerable* (US extended short film: director).
2006. *The Tudors* (US television series: director of two episodes).

Maclean has directed a number of commercials, those for Legal Aid, PSA (2001), Verizon (2001), Partnership for a Drug Free America (2002), Harvard Pilgrim Healthcare (2002), Quaker Oats (2003), Dunkin Donuts (2003), FX Network (2004), Rice Krispies (2004), Starz Network (2004), Sony Dreams (2004), Fruit Wise (2005), Post Cereals (2005), Liberty Mutual (2005), and Women's Health (2005).

19

Bringing It All Back Home
THE FILMS OF PETER JACKSON

Barry Keith Grant

Having directed nine movies to date, Peter Jackson has assumed a unique and particularly important place in New Zealand cinema, both locally and around the world. Jackson has been more important than anyone else in New Zealand film in putting the nation's cinema on the international map. The only New Zealand filmmaker to have attained international recognition who has not been lured away by the temptations of Hollywood, he has steadfastly refused to work abroad, instead making the mountain come to Mohammed. *The Frighteners* (1996), *The Lord of the Rings* trilogy (*LOTR*, 2001–3), and *King King* (2005) were funded by major Hollywood studios but filmed in New Zealand. Financed by the American company New Line Cinema with a budget of NZ$264 million/U.S. $130 million, the *LOTR* trilogy was touted in the press as "the biggest cinema production ever undertaken in the Southern Hemisphere," and its success has confirmed Jackson's international celebrity status.[1] Jackson has met the challenge of Hollywood on a practical level by creating his own studio and production company, WingNut Films, and special-effects facility, WETA (WingNut Effects & Technological Allusions Ltd.), which provides state-of-the-art work less expensively than major American companies such as Industrial Light & Magic. Initially created to allow Jackson to do his own post-production work on *The Frighteners* (1996), WETA has since provided special effects (FX) for such movies as Robert Zemeckis's *Contact* (1997).

In his own films, Jackson adeptly mobilizes and exploits different genres to make films that will have commercial appeal while addressing and referencing both Kiwi culture and his own position as a filmmaker within a country whose sense of cinema, as for so many other countries,

---

This is a significantly revised and updated version of the booklet *A Cultural Assault: The New Zealand Films of Peter Jackson* (Nottingham: Kakapo Books, 1999).

Body horror on a budget: Jackson directs himself as victim in *Bad Taste*. (Courtesy New Zealand Film Commission.)

has been largely determined by Hollywood. A producer, director, writer, and actor, Jackson's visual imagination was apparent with his first feature length movie, *Bad Taste* (1988), although its adolescent gross-out content, which carried over into his next two films, *Meet the Feebles* (1989) and *Braindead* (1992), caused him to be dismissed prematurely by many serious critics. But the subsequent breakthrough of "the Kaiser of Kiwi ketchup" to art cinema auteur with *Heavenly Creatures* (1994) was no surprise to perceptive viewers who saw Jackson's style through the splatter.[2]

Jackson has expressed the hope that his own example will help reverse the trend of Hollywood immigration by showing that "you can actually stay in your country and make really good top-quality films."[3] For New Zealand, as for so many other countries, this inevitably means confronting Hollywood, which dominates international cinema, on an aesthetic as well as practical level—that is, by working simultaneously with and through Hollywood genres. Brazilian political filmmaker Glauber Rocha once remarked that any discussion of national cinema must necessarily begin with Hollywood, and this is certainly true of New Zealand, a country that, lacking the problem of a language barrier, enthusiastically embraced American films from the beginning. The overwhelming majority of movies screened in New Zealand in any given year are American, with the presence of Hollywood so pervasive in Kiwi culture that, for Geoff Lealand, "the mythologies of Hollywood became 'naturalised' in the absence of any more powerful propositions, integral to the ways of 'reading' the world for New Zealanders."[4]

Hollywood and Hollywood-style movies are mostly genre films, and in the history of film many national movements (e.g., the Australian New Wave) and generic styles (e.g., spaghetti westerns) have reworked Hollywood genres to their own cultural sensibility. New Zealand, unsurprisingly, has produced many films, both significant (*Sleeping Dogs* [1977], *Goodbye Pork Pie* [1980]) and superficial (*Battletruck* [1982]), that play on American film genres. According to Peter Jackson, New Zealand cinema has no particular generic tradition, just a loose bunch of filmmakers who, merely making what is of interest to them, "end up muddying the genres."[5] But Jackson himself, as Lawrence McDonald notes, is the most successful New Zealand filmmaker to explore a single genre with any consistency. McDonald places Jackson generically within comedy, although the director's sensibility is rooted at least as much within horror and fantasy film traditions.[6] British film critic Kim Newman saw *Bad Taste*, along with Geoff Murphy's *The Quiet Earth* (1985) and Vincent Ward's *The Navigator: A Mediaeval Odyssey* (1988), as establishing a distinct tradition of Kiwi *cinéfantastique*, and many other New Zealand films do fall within this category.[7] However, while many of them are imitations of American movies, Jackson's approach to genre is to problematize the easy reception characteristic of classic genre films by mixing them in unsettling ways.

Bad Taste, for example, about a government team that combats aliens who have packaged the residents of Kaihoro (population 75) for their new intergalactic fast food franchise, blends the iconography and conventions of horror (the proverbial old dark house, bodily violation), science fiction (aliens, space travel), and slapstick comedy. Jackson's generic hybrid was so original that when it was shown in Wellington at the Fringe Film Festival, *Bad Taste* received an award for the creation of a new genre in New Zealand filmmaking—comedy splatter. *Heavenly Creatures*, Jackson's breakthrough film based on the Pauline Parker–Juliet Hulme murder case that rocked New Zealand in 1954, is at once a teen exploitation movie and art film, simultaneously lowbrow and high culture. Its subject is a notorious murder case (contemporary headlines screamed of "the crime of the century" committed by lesbian teenage mother-killers), but because the film refrains from making easy judgments by keeping us within the girls' perspective, it embraces that sense of ambiguity that David Bordwell argues is a central quality of the art film as genre.[8]

Meet the Feebles, Jackson's second feature, overlays a bawdy, scatological, and adult sensibility onto a Jim Henson family-type Muppet movie. Immediately dubbed a "spluppet creature feature," it was conceived with musings about the sexual life of Miss Piggy and Kermit the Frog and ended up as a riposte to all those family movies that present their cuddly puppets sans genitalia.[9] The film's parodic references include *Casablanca*

(1942), *The Godfather* (1972), *The Deer Hunter* (1978), *Platoon* (1986), and, of course, Henson's television series, *The Muppet Show*. A postmodern pastiche of classic musicals, *Meet the Feebles* plays off traditional backstage musicals such as *42nd Street* (1933) and *Gold Diggers of 1933* (1933) by failing to depict the successful mounting of the show through communal effort. Jackson subverts all the genre's conventions, as the show turns into a disaster culminating with the insanely jealous hippo chanteuse, Heidi, machine-gunning everyone in the cast.

Like American genre directors George A. Romero, Sam Raimi, Stuart Gordon, and Frank Henenlotter, Jackson has explored the unlikely combination of horror and comedy known as "splatstick" (Raimi is reported to have described *Braindead* as "splatstick's *Intolerance*").[10] *The Frighteners*, Jackson's first film for a Hollywood studio, confused many viewers precisely because of the way it combined comedy and horror and juggled several narratives simultaneously. Jackson described the film as a "thrillomedy" ("*Caspar* [sic] meets *The Silence of the Lambs*"), and unlike most other horror/comedy hybrids, the supernatural forces in *The Frighteners* are both reassuringly benign and gruesomely malevolent.[11] For Brian McDonnell, *The Frighteners* "is actually two different films in one, with both parts fighting for our attention." The film, he says, "seems unsure what genre it is," so that "audience expectations never get a chance to settle down."[12] The film did not do particularly well in its primary North American market, and Jackson has suggested that is because *The Frighteners* requires an active spectator rather than the passive viewing model, encouraged by the comfort of clear generic boundaries, preferred by American audiences.[13]

Jackson locates the site of horror in the body, cheerfully embracing images of abjection—blood, pus, piss, shit, vomit, guts—and so his films have been cited as exemplars of bad taste, but they are more accurately a frontal attack on traditional cultural and aesthetic values, a carnivalesque slap in the face of bourgeois culture. The title of Jackson's first feature, *Bad Taste*, directly acknowledges the politics of aesthetics and suggests a deliberate attempt to attack accepted norms.[14] If in *Las hurdes* (*Land without Bread*, 1933) Luis Buñuel and Salvador Dalí wanted to provoke the bourgeoisie by, as they put it, stabbing them with an Iberian dagger, Jackson in *Braindead* bludgeons us with a hover mower, that proud icon of bourgeois Kiwi culture, as it plows through a room of zombies. The iconic presence of the hover mower, like the sheep that explodes from an errant bazooka blast in *Bad Taste*, suggests that Jackson's uncompromising approach is itself an attack on the whole tradition of "'quality' New Zealand cinema" and ultimately an assault on the timorous decorum of New Zealand culture as inherited from England.[15]

Certainly Jackson's horror movies are vivid examples of what Robin Wood and others have seen as the genre's characteristic "return of the repressed," the revisiting of primal horrors, yet at the same time they refer to their national context.[16] Not unlike David Cronenberg in Canada (who also emphasizes images of bodily abjection), Jackson has found a way to make genre movies that appeal to an international audience while at the same time inflecting them with issues of national culture and identity. *Braindead*'s most terrible mother and gory "rebirthing" scene, when the hapless hero Lionel (Timothy Balme) cuts his way out of his monstrous mother's womb, not only recalls Derek (played by Jackson himself) chainsawing his way through Lord Crumb's (Doug Wren) body in the climax of *Bad Taste* but also addresses New Zealand culture's past emphasis on the cult of domesticity and motherhood,[17] a theme that is central to *Heavenly Creatures*. Tellingly, both *Braindead* and *Bad Taste* begin with images of the Queen before proceeding to their gruesome horror shows. *Braindead* opens with an image of the New Zealand flag and the sound of the national anthem, followed by a portrait of the youthful Queen Elizabeth II. This references local cinema-going of the past, when audiences stood patriotically to the Queen and the national anthem at the start of each film program, but it also suggests a connection between the terrible mother and the mother country.

Forgotten Silver (1995), Jackson's made-for-television mockumentary about a non-existent New Zealand film pioneer, addresses another aspect of New Zealand national culture—the acceptance of traditional news broadcasts and documentary film, and the philosophical and ethnocentric assumptions those traditional styles imply. Revealing Jackson's ability to appropriate documentary codes and conventions as well as those of fictional genres, *Forgotten Silver* was immediately controversial because of its mix of a comic, at times absurd, fictional narrative with what Bill Nichols calls documentary's characteristic "discourse of sobriety."[18] Indeed, its understanding of documentary rhetoric and techniques was so exact that the film became "New Zealand's biggest-ever hoax."[19]

The subject of Jackson's apparent biography is the hapless but heroic early New Zealand filmmaker Colin McKenzie, whose "lost" films Jackson claims to have "discovered" in an old chest belonging to McKenzie's widow, a neighbor of Jackson's mother. According to the film, among his numerous innovations McKenzie invented the first process for color film (unfortunately, he was arrested for smut after his film was confiscated for containing images of topless Tahitian women) and the first synchronized sound feature (a commercial disaster because McKenzie neglected to translate the dialogue of his Chinese actors into English). The initial broadcast of *Forgotten Silver* was preceded by coverage in the reputable

Listener magazine that similarly presented the story as fact. And when it was shown on prime-time television as the season's finale of TVNZ's quality series, *Montana Sunday Theatre* on October 29, 1995, many of the estimated 400,000 New Zealanders who watched it fell for the deception.[20] When the hoax was subsequently revealed the next day, viewer response was decidedly mixed, but most seemed resentful at being duped and many considered the whole affair further evidence of exceptional "bad taste" on Jackson's part.

However, one letter to the *Listener* did identify a more serious issue raised in *Forgotten Silver* by pointing out that the filmmakers have "done us all a service by showing how easy it is to hoodwink a viewing public that has been conditioned to believe that anything labelled 'documentary' is necessarily the truth."[21] Indeed, *Forgotten Silver* mocks the willingness of viewers anywhere to believe anything told in documentary style, no matter how absurd, and it shows how documentary signifiers of "truth" and "reality" are merely a matter of generic convention. But at the same time, the film's satire is also aimed specifically at New Zealand culture: Jane Roscoe and Craig Hight suggest that *Forgotten Silver* may be seen as a challenge to the foundational assumptions of Kiwi television viewers who embrace TVNZ's tradition as "a BBC-styled public broadcasting service."[22] The film also spoke to New Zealanders' strong desire for a sense of national identity and cultural heroes, as Ian Conrich and Roy Smith have noted, by exploiting the national myth of "Kiwi ingenuity."[23]

Bad Taste also exploits the nation's emphasis on male self-reliance in the bush as well as the concept of mateship (there are no women in the film), another important aspect of the ideology of masculinity in New Zealand. Battling the aliens, one of The Boys, as the government team is known, kicks a decapitated extraterrestrial head through the window, observing that "the old magic is still there"—a joke heartily appreciated in rugby-crazed New Zealand. Among those aspects of national life debunked in the film, one reviewer noted sheep meat processing, government bureaucracy, and "the New Zealand cult of the chainsaw."[24] The film's most well-known moment, the accidental blowing up of a sheep with a bazooka, is an iconographic image that consciously bends horror convention to New Zealand content. *Bad Taste*'s vision of the invasion of New Zealand by fast food franchises refers to the Americanization of eating habits in the country that was fully underway while the film was being made. It is no mere coincidence that the aliens all wear denim jeans and shirts; their pot bellies and large buttocks, bursting through their clothes, testifies to an idea of conspicuous consumption characteristic of American culture.[25]

Braindead's "explanation" of how people become zombies—the result of initially being bitten by a Sumatran rat monkey—is merely a pretext for

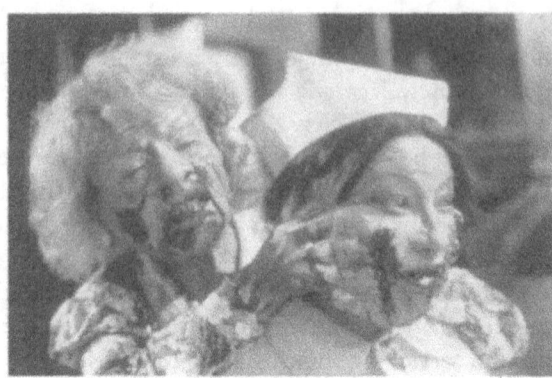

Horror as carnivalesque: Nurse McTavish as the body violated by the possessed Mum in *Braindead*. (Courtesy New Zealand Film Commission.)

an exercise in splatstick, beginning with a parody of Spielbergian adventure in the opening scene: "I'm a New Zealand zoo official. And this monkey is going to Newtown." A deft synthesis of comedy and splatter, *Braindead* ingeniously uses the violated bodies of the "meat movie" as props for gags and situations with a Kiwi accent. So Nurse McTavish (Brenda Kendall) ends up with a porcelain wall duck ornament—an international image of conservative suburbia but also, according to McDonald, a notable item of Kiwiana—in her forehead that, as the resourceful Lionel discovers, serves as a convenient handle to open and close her slit throat for feeding purposes.[26] In the kitchen a zombie is partially puréed in the blender, a nod to one of the gags in Joe Dante's *Gremlins* (1984), but the joke is given a particularly national inflection when Lionel wields his all-important hover mower as the iconic Leatherface does his chainsaw in *The Texas Chain Saw Massacre* (1974). One of the film's funniest sight gags has Lionel taking a zombie baby (the instant progeny of the zombie priest and zombie nurse) out for a walk in a pram: initially we cannot see inside, but after the creature within has tossed out a shredded stuffed animal, Lionel responds by sealing the pram's opening with a makeshift grating of number 8 fencing wire, a tool of talismanic importance for New Zealand masculinity.[27]

Several critics praised both *Braindead* and *Heavenly Creatures* for their attention to local detail. The latter was described as paying "meticulous attention" to the historical details of 1950s Christchurch, commonly considered the most "English" of New Zealand cities.[28] The Hulmes's actual house in Ilam was used in the film, as was the classroom at the Christchurch Girls' High School, restored to look as it did forty years earlier.

Actual entries from Pauline's copious diaries, written at the time, are used periodically as voice-over commentary to help in telling the story from the girls' point of view. This emphasis on historical verisimilitude in the context of a story of fantastic proportions allows *Heavenly Creatures* to comment, as did *Braindead,* on the repressive orderliness of Pakeha (European) New Zealand culture. The theme is immediately invoked by the 1950s travelogue, with its relatively static camera, which opens the film. Recalling the openings of both *Bad Taste* and *Braindead,* the travelogue conveys the bourgeois orderliness and prosperity of postwar Christchurch. Its montage of official images of social order is, however, abruptly offset by the following shots of the girls (Kate Winslet and Melanie Lynskey) frantically running from the murder scene, covered with blood, pursued by a handheld camera. The sudden violence that intrudes upon the peaceful world of the opening inaugurates the exploration of the murder as an eruption of extreme emotion and madness that constitutes a challenge to polite Christchurch society even more horrific than the possibility that the girls were involved in a lesbian relationship.

In contrast, the discourse around *LOTR* has mostly been around the difficulties of translating J. R. R. Tolkien's epic three-volume fantasy to the screen or assessing the films as adaptations, with little attention devoted to the films from an auteurist perspective.[29] As Graham Fuller flatly stated about the first film of the series, *The Fellowship of the Ring,* "Certainly it is not an auteur's film, since Jackson . . . has made nothing comparable and there is nothing in the movie that reveals a shaping personality, for all that it's a massive feat."[30] Yet the trilogy may also be read for its New Zealand subtext even though conceived as an international blockbuster "movie event," it would seem to be Jackson's most impersonal work.

Tolkien's trilogy has accommodated a variety of interpretations, among them as a Christian parable, an allegory of Nazism and World War II, or nuclear Armageddon, and has been analyzed for its Jungian archetypes (which exhorts readers to know their "inner Gollum").[31] The novels can accommodate such divergent readings and approaches because, as Ishay Landa has noted, while Tolkien's grand themes of "'power struggles' may be automatically summoned to explain *every war,* it in fact explains no war at all."[32] The *LOTR* films have also been read in interestingly divergent ways—as, for example, a tale about terrorism, with Christopher Lee's Saruman said to resemble Osama bin Laden and the orc army expressing "the fearful din and bedlam of advancing self-hypnotized hordes of darker-hued races beyond civilized control."[33] In relation to these readings, before *The Two Towers,* the second film of the trilogy, was released in December 2002, a petition was widely distributed over the Internet calling for Jackson and New Line to change the title of the film, which for some was too evocative of al-Qaeda's destruction of the World Trade Center just over a year before.

But if they are about anything material, anything other than a variation of the threat of "the dark side of the force," then the *LOTR* films are a celebration of New Zealand, the place where, as everyone now knows, the films were made. The trilogy is populated with fantastic creations, some of them digital, but the production design emphasizes above all else the materiality of Middle Earth, recalling the bodily emphasis of Jackson's horror films (one critic views *The Fellowship of the Ring* as an action movie that sacrifices Tolkien's emphasis on character for "more of the usual Jackson grotesquerie").[34] Elves and dwarves, hobbits and orcs, men and wizards alike have hair matted with sweat and dirt beneath their fingernails. Jackson consistently emphasizes the heft and weight of swords, and the One Ring resounds with a thud when Bilbo Baggins (Ian Holm) reluctantly drops it. The fantasy world of Middle Earth is given palpable detail, like Borovnia in *Heavenly Creatures*.

Jackson claimed that his goal was to make Middle Earth look like it was shot on location, and in the films the hobbit houses of the Shire suggest the myth of so many New Zealand communities with their houses dotting the picturesque and pastoral landscape.[35] The hobbits, like New Zealanders, live in a new world order that can no longer be cozily isolated from the political machinations of the outside world. In The Shire, their self-contained—"island"—community within Middle Earth, hobbits are stunted by a collective cultural cringe not unlike that commonly regarded as characteristic of New Zealanders. As if to drive the point home, many New Zealand actors and filmmakers—Harry Sinclair, Grant Tilly, Ian Mune—appear in hobbit cameos.

Much was made in the publicity for and reviews of the *LOTR* films that they were shot entirely in New Zealand, a country frequently promoted as having the widest range of topographical features for its size in the world. Stan Jones, exploring the importance of New Zealand as the location for *LOTR*, remarks that the films present a vision of New Zealand that the Tourist Board and the Government itself "are trying to sell to tourists, and, most importantly, through Filmnz [*sic*] to filmmakers as a desirable place to realize your fictions."[36] In October 2002, the *New York Times* reported that, after a brief decline as a result of September 11, tourism in New Zealand was up 3.8 percent (compared to a 5.5 percent decline in the same period in Australia), which was attributed to New Zealand's hold on the America's Cup yachting race and to *LOTR*.[37]

Given the films' emphasis on their local quality it may not be stretching too much to see this epic tale, in Jackson's hands, as also being about Jackson's own position as a filmmaker who chooses to stay in New Zealand. Just as the Fellowship is corrupted by the power of the Ring, so were Jackson's fellow New Zealand directors lured by the glamour and wealth of Hollywood. The evil of the One Ring from faraway Mordor, which threatens to decimate the Shire and enslave the hobbits, is not only an allegory of fascism, World War II, the cold war, and the contemporary threat of terrorism but also a fantasy expression of American cultural influence in the era of globalization.

Certainly Jackson's other films have similar autobiographical or self-reflexive elements to them. In *Heavenly Creatures* the beguiling, appealing atmosphere of the girls' private Xanadu is perfectly understandable in the context of an otherwise rather dull world of fishmongers, unwelcome boarders, and boring school lessons but also may be read as something of an aesthetic manifesto on the part of the filmmaker. For like the madness of Pauline and Juliet, Jackson's images—whether the repellent gore of body horror or the seductive beauty of Borovnia—go against respectability and social decorum. *Heavenly Creatures* itself is a kind of private delirium, its style and story perfectly matched, the girls' fantasies, like Jackson's, a shock to sensibility. The girls' imaginary narratives, like Jackson's films, are rooted in the traditions of pulp fiction—in their case, romantic melodrama (the films and songs of Mario Lanza) rather than horror and science fiction—so that *Heavenly Creatures,* as Michael Atkinson perceptively noted, "can be read as autobio, New Zealand punk style."[38]

In *The Frighteners,* Frank Bannister (Michael J. Fox) is a con man who cheats homeowners by pretending to exorcise poltergeists and other spirits. The irony is that he does have extrasensory ability and works with a trio of co-con-spirit-tors who create ghostly manifestations in people's homes in order to convince them to hire Bannister to drive the spirits out. Like a director, Bannister rehearses his spectral cast and choreographs their "special effects." As part of his "investigation" of a client's house, he checks out the scene through his special "viewfinder." Of course, as a horror filmmaker Jackson is himself a "frightener," and one who might be said to be possessed by his visions, haunted by them just as Bannister is haunted by his ghosts.

Similarly, the imaginary biography of filmmaker Colin McKenzie in *Forgotten Silver* invokes the backyard inventor myth of New Zealand culture. In a sense, Colin McKenzie embodies the historical character of New Zealand cinema itself, which, as Jim and Mary Barr assert, "has always had a direct, hands-on quality."[39] Jackson himself worked this way early in his career, filming in his own backyard, ingeniously creating special effects just as McKenzie supposedly used a bicycle to power his projector. The legendary production history of *Bad Taste* attests to Jackson's Kiwi-esque spirit, with Jackson serving simultaneously as writer, producer, director,

On the boundaries of social acceptability: Pauline and Juliet are watched by Juliet's father, Henry, in *Heavenly Creatures*. (Courtesy New Zealand Film Commission.)

photographer, special-effects technician, and actor (playing the roles of Derek and the alien Robert). Production on the film began in October 1983 and was completed four years later, in October 1987, partly because Jackson's cast and crew were friends who were holding down full-time jobs and were available only on Sundays. After a year of shooting, Jackson rented a cheap editing machine from the National Film Unit and edited an hour-long rough cut on his parents' dining room table. Given this, the film's continuity is itself an impressive feat—"the ultimate filmic expression of New Zealand's Jerry-build number 8 fencing wire ethic," as Laurence Simmons puts it.[40] No wonder Jackson said that in the career of his imaginary director McKenzie, "I recognize my own passions."[41]

So it can be seen that, just as Frodo Baggins (Elijah Wood) successfully journeys to the heart of Mordor to destroy the ring, so with *LOTR* Peter Jackson (the popular press often referring to the short and hirsute filmmaker as "hobbit-like") has successfully incorporated the Hollywoodized transnational blockbuster into his own distinctive Kiwi kind of filmmaking. Kristin Thompson has persuasively shown how *LOTR* successfully combined conventions of other action and martial arts movies with Tolkien's fantasy narrative to produce films with broad international appeal, and how the films have been cannily marketed in DVD and VHS formats, collectibles, and computer games, making *LOTR* emblematic of New Hollywood synergy.[42]

At the time of writing, Jackson has recently finished a second remake of *King Kong* (1933, remade in 1976), a locus classicus of Hollywood and the movie he has often cited as his favorite, the one that inspired him to try his hand at special effects and filmmaking.[43] In the movie, the giant ape Kong climbs to the very top, the mooring mast, of the Empire State Building, towering above the urban jungle of New York City only briefly before being brought down to size, as it were. The first two *LOTR* films garnered nineteen Oscar nominations, winning six, while part three equaled a record of eleven Oscars won. Combined, the films have become the most commercially successful film series since *Star Wars*. *Fellowship* alone has become one of the ten highest-grossing movies in U.S. history. But only time will tell if Jackson is able to keep riding high with American and international audiences.

Yet already Jackson's work has been crucial to the recent history of New Zealand cinema, a period of maturation in which a number of filmmakers have attained international recognition. Not only has Jackson provided the practical resources for filmmaking, including postproduction facilities in New Zealand, but his films have also made New Zealanders cognizant of their own culture and cinema by having them look through what Raymond Durgnat has called the crazy mirror of comedy.[44] Just as New Zealand struggles with its colonial past, Jackson's films embrace and incorporate elements of Hollywood film, which has colonized the nation's cinematic imagination, appropriating its discursive forms to make films that are at once commercially appealing and personal expressions.[45] In his films, Jackson has addressed New Zealand culture and his own position within New Zealand national cinema even as his films employ the commercial requirements of genre. For these reasons, if national cinemas are, as Tom O'Regan writes, "simultaneously an aesthetic and production movement, a critical technology, a civic project of state, an industrial strategy and an international project formed in response to the dominant international cinemas (particularly but not exclusively Hollywood cinema),"[46] then Peter Jackson is without question New Zealand's most important filmmaker.

Notes

Thanks to Olga Klimova, my graduate research assistant, for her research help on material related to *The Lord of the Rings*.

1. Simon Beattie, "Jackson Lands $264m Film Deal," *Evening Post*, August 25, 1998, 1.
2. Alan Jones, "Braindead," *Midwest* 10 (1996): 18.
3. Tiffany Bakker, "Frightening," *TNT* 701 (1997): 9.
4. Geoff Lealand, *A Foreign Egg in Our Nest?: American Popular Culture in New Zealand* (Wellington: Victoria University Press, 1988), 90. For details on the American dominance of film exhibition in New Zealand, see chapter 4.
5. Jim Barr and Mary Barr, "NZFX: The Films of Peter Jackson and Fran Walsh," in *Film in Aotearoa New Zealand*, 2nd. ed., ed. Jonathan Dennis and Jan Bieringa (Wellington: Victoria University Press, 1996), 156.
6. Lawrence McDonald, "A Critique of the Judgment of Bad Taste or beyond Braindead Criticism," *Illusions* 21–22 (Winter 1993): 11.
7. Kim Newman, "Bad Taste," *Monthly Film Bulletin* 56, no. 668 (1989): 267–68. For a comprehensive account, see Ian Conrich, "Kiwi Gothic: New Zealand's Cinema of a Perilous Paradise," *Horror International*, ed. Steven Jay Schneider and Tony Williams (Detroit: Wayne State University Press, 2005), 114–27.
8. David Bordwell, "The Art Cinema as a Mode of Film Practice," *Film Criticism* 4, no. 1 (1979): 56–64.
9. Helen Martin and Sam Edwards, *New Zealand Film, 1912–1996* (Auckland: Oxford University Press, 1997), 146.
10. Michael Atkinson, "Earthy Creatures," *Film Comment* 31, no. 3 (1995): 33.
11. Martin and Edwards, *New Zealand Film*, 190.
12. Brian McDonnell, *Pavement* 20 (December–January 1996): 113.
13. Ibid.
14. Jackson's films flaunt the subversive notion that there is a good taste of bad taste, as Susan Sontag says of camp, a sensibility with which Jackson's work has some affinity. See Sontag, "Notes on Camp," in *Against Interpretation and Other Essays* (New York: Dell, 1966), 290. For a discussion of abjection and its relation to the horror film, see Barbara Creed, *The Monstrous-Feminine: Film, Feminism, Psychoanalysis* (New York and London: Routledge, 1993).
15. McDonald, "Critique," 12.
16. Robin Wood, "An Introduction to the American Horror Film," in *American Nightmare: Essays on the Horror Film*, ed. Robin Wood and Richard Lippe (Toronto: Festival of Festivals, 1979), 7–28. Barbara Creed reads Jackson's horror films in a similar way, as instances of colonial island culture giving birth to the terrible otherness it had repressed. See Creed, "*Bad Taste* and Antipodal Inversion: Peter Jackson's Colonial Suburbs," *Postcolonial Studies* 3, no. 1 (2000): 61–68.
17. McDonald, "Critique," p. 15 refers to the work of Jock Phillips, who argues that "the excessive mothering of New Zealand boys left them permanently dependent on women." Phillips, "Mummy's Boys: Pakeha Men and Male Culture in New Zealand," in *Women in New Zealand Society*, ed. Phillida Bunkle and Beryl Hughes (Auckland: George Allen and Unwin, 1980), 239.
18. Bill Nichols, *Representing Reality: Issues and Concepts in Documentary* (Blooming-

ton: Indiana University Press, 1991), 3–4.
19. Geoff Chapple, "Gone, Not Forgotten," *Listener,* November 25, 1995, 26.
20. Denis Welch, "Heavenly Features," *Listener,* October 28, 1995, 31–32. For details on the reception of *Forgotten Silver,* see Ian Conrich and Roy Smith, "Fool's Gold: New Zealand's *Forgotten Silver,* Myth and National Identity," *British Review of New Zealand Studies* 11 (1998): 57–65.
21. "Letters," *Listener,* November 25, 1995, 12.
22. Jane Roscoe and Craig Hight, "Mocking Silver: Re-Inventing the Documentary Project (or, Grierson Lies Bleeding)," *Continuum* 11, no. 1 (1997): 75.
23. Conrich and Smith, "Fool's Gold," 60.
24. John Parker, "The Joy of Exploding Entrails," *Metro* (September 1988): 202.
25. On the domination of American popular culture in New Zealand, see Lealand, *A Foreign Egg in Our Nest?*
26. McDonald, "Critique," 14.
27. New Zealanders joke about the versatility of number 8 wire the way North Americans do about duct tape, although for Kiwis it involves overtones of national character, masculinity, and mythology. In Elizabeth Orsman and Harry Orsman, *The New Zealand Dictionary,* 2nd. ed. (Auckland: New House, 1995), 184, number 8 wire (also No. 8) is defined as "the standard number 8 gauge (4 mm), smooth fencing wire, especially when used inventively for other than fencing purposes, for example, for making repairs to farm machinery."
28. Martin and Edwards, *New Zealand Film,* 177.
29. See, for example, Jane Chance, "Is There a Text in This Hobbit? Peter Jackson's *Fellowship of the Ring,*" *Literature/Film Quarterly* 30, no. 2 (2002): 79–85, who sees the films as "reductive literalism" (85) of Tolkien's books.
30. Graham Fuller, "Trimming Tolkien," *Sight and Sound* 12, no. 2 (2002): 20.
31. Roger Kaufman, "*Lord of the Rings* Tapes a Gay Archetype," *Gay and Lesbian Review Worldwide* 10, no. 4 (2003): 31.
32. Ishay Landa, "Slaves of the Ring: Tolkien's Political Unconscious," *Historical Materialism* 10, no. 4 (2002), 116.
33. John Downie, "Frodo's Face, State of the Art, and the Axis of Evil," *Illusions* 35 (Winter 2003): 6.
34. Chance, "Is There a Text in This Hobbit?," 84.
35. See Warren Barton, "Lord of the Fantasy," *The Dominion,* August 29, 1998, 23.
36. Stan Jones, "Middle-Earthly Creatures: Some Local Comments on the Cinematic Ring-Cycle So Far," *Metro* 136 (Spring 2003): 63.
37. James Brooke, "New Zealand Finds Isolation Is an Asset," *New York Times,* October 6, 2002, section 5, 3.
38. Atkinson, "Earthy Creatures," 33.
39. Barr and Barr, "NZFX," 150.
40. Costa Botes, "Bad Taste," *Midwest* 10 (1996): 14.
41. Welch, "Heavenly Features," 32.
42. Kristin Thompson, "Fantasy, Franchises, and Frodo Baggins: *The Lord of the Rings* and Modern Hollywood," *The Velvet Light Trap* 52 (Fall 2003): 45–63.
43. Jackson had already been planning a remake of *King Kong* before committing himself to *LOTR,* but the project fell through reportedly because Universal was concerned that it would have to compete against the scheduled mid-1998 release dates of both *Godzilla* and *Mighty Joe Young.*

44. See Raymond Durgnat, *The Crazy Mirror: Hollywood Comedy and the American Image* (New York: Dell, 1970).
45. Rebecca Robinson discusses this approach to *The Frighteners* in "Authenticity, Mimicry, Industry: *The Frighteners* as Cultural Palimpsest," *Illusions* 28 (Autumn 1999): 2–9.
46. Tom O'Regan, *Australian National Cinema* (New York: Routledge, 1996), 45.

Peter Jackson—Filmography

1971. *The Dwarf Patrol* (8 mm amateur short).
1973. *World War Two* (8 mm amateur short).
1978. *The Valley* (8 mm amateur short).
1979. *Coldfinger* (8 mm amateur short).
1982. *The Curse of the Grave Walker* (abandoned 8 mm amateur film).
1987. *Wurzel Gummidge Down Under* (NZ television series: special effects).
1987. *Stalin's Sickle* (NZ short film: special effects).
1988. *Bad Taste* (NZ feature film: director, producer, writer, cinematographer, co-editor, special effects, actor).
1988. *The Lounge Bar* (NZ short film: special effects).
1988. *The Quick Window* (NZ short film: second unit camera).
1988. *Good Taste Made Bad Taste* (NZ short documentary: interviewee).
1989. *Meet the Feebles* a.k.a. ***Just the Feebles*** (NZ feature film: director, co-producer, co-writer).
1989. *Sex, Drugs, and Soft Toys* (NZ short documentary: interviewee).
1991. *Freddy's Dead: The Final Nightmare* (US feature film: writer for an unused early screenplay).
1992. *Braindead* a.k.a. ***Dead Alive*** (NZ feature film: director, co-writer).
1992. *Valley of the Stereos* (NZ short film: executive producer, story).
1994. *Heavenly Creatures* (NZ feature film: director, co-writer).
1994. *Hercules and the Circle of Fire* (US/NZ television movie: creature, prosthetic and digital effects project manager).
1994. *Hercules and the Lost Kingdom* (US/NZ television movie: creature and prosthetic effects project co-manager).
1994. *Hercules in the Maze of the Minotaur* (US/NZ television movie: creature and prosthetic effects project co-manager).
1994. *Hercules in the Underworld* (US/NZ television movie: creature and prosthetic effects operations co-manager).
1994. *Jack Brown, Genius* (NZ feature film: co-executive producer, co-writer, second unit director).
1995. *Forgotten Silver* (NZ television drama: co-director, co-writer, actor).
1995. *Dirty Creature* (NZ short film: executive producer).
1996. *The Frighteners* (US/NZ feature film: director, co-producer, co-writer).
1997. *Contact* (US feature film: additional visual effects).
2000. *Behind the Bull* (NZ short documentary: interviewee).

2001. *The Lord of the Rings: The Fellowship of the Ring* (US/NZ feature film: director, co-producer, co-writer).
2002. *The Lord of the Rings: The Two Towers* (US/NZ feature film: director, co-producer, co-writer).
2003. *The Lord of the Rings: The Return of the King* (US/NZ feature film: director, co-producer, co-writer).
2003. *The Long and Short of It* (US short film: producer, cameo appearance).
2005. *King Kong* (US/NZ feature film: director, co-producer, co-writer).

20

The Nightmare within the Everyday
THE HORRIFIC VISIONS OF DAVID BLYTH

Stacey Abbott

In 1978 a film was released that caused much controversy for the recently formed New Zealand Film Commission (NZFC). *Angel Mine* (directed by David Blyth, then a relatively unknown filmmaker, having only made the experimental short films *Cancelled* [1975] and *Circadian Rhythms* [1976] while at Auckland University) was a low budget experimental film that was criticized for its disturbing and explicit depictions of sex and violence. Moral campaigners felt that it was not appropriate for the NZFC and the QE2 (Queen Elizabeth II) Arts Council to invest in this kind of production, while censors were compelled to introduce a new rating, R18, that warned audiences that the film "CONTAINS PUNK CULT MATERIAL." Today Blyth is still seeking to undermine the conventional image of New Zealand, this time with his digital video documentary *Bound for Pleasure* (2001), about the thriving dominatrix circuit in Auckland. Composed of interviews with the dominatrices and their clients, the film is a sympathetic look at a previously invisible subculture. Blyth has largely self-funded this project, with some international support, as he felt the government funding bodies would never agree to a film containing such subject matter. In making *Bound for Pleasure*, he sought to "illuminate taboo areas of the human condition, stuff that's never acknowledged but freely practised."[1] These two films at either end of his career thus far demonstrate that rather than promoting the image of a pastoral and idyllic New Zealand, Blyth prefers to explore life on the margins of acceptable society while offering a severe critique of mainstream culture.

Blyth's career between *Angel Mine* and *Bound for Pleasure* has been a roller coaster ride of success and frustration. Having gained attention with *Angel Mine*, his aggressive and experimental style was perceived as a risk to investors, and as a result he did not direct a feature film again until he received NZFC funding to make the B-movie horror film *Death Warmed Up*, in 1984. In the interim, he received a grant to travel to London where he worked as a director's assistant on Jim Sharman's *Shock Treatment* (1980).

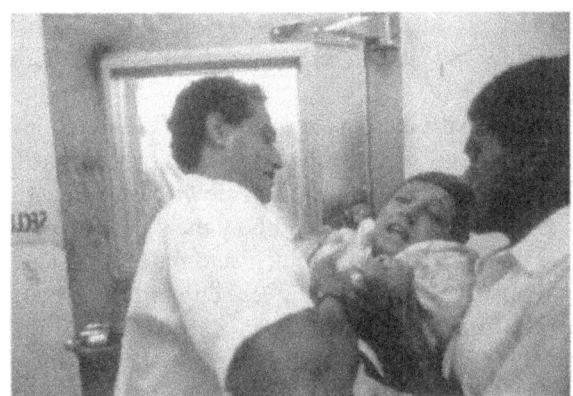

In the confines of an asylum Michael is physically restrained in the confrontational *Death Warmed Up*. (Courtesy New Zealand Film Commission.)

Upon his return, he directed videos and commercials as well as twelve episodes of the New Zealand drama *Close to Home* (1982). He also directed the award-winning television drama *A Woman of Good Character* (1983).

It was with *Death Warmed Up* that Blyth once again gained attention as a feature filmmaker of shocking and confrontational material, with the film described by *Variety* as "surreal-art deco punk, with dollops of action and blood."[2] The film was not well received by the critics in New Zealand. According to Roger Horrocks, the film's "B-movie style was interpreted by reviewers as a rejection of seriousness and local 'relevance,'" and it did not do well at the box office.[3] The film was more successful internationally, playing at the London Film Festival and winning the Grand Prix at the 1984 Paris International Science Fiction and Fantasy Film Festival. Due to its international success Blyth decided to leave New Zealand and go to Los Angeles. This experience was both positive and negative. Blyth spent a great deal of time developing film projects and, as in New Zealand, he continued to supplement his film work with jobs directing for television. In 1992, Blyth returned to New Zealand to make the successful children's film *Moonrise* and spent some time shuttling back and forth between the United States, Canada, and New Zealand. During this time he established a productive relationship with Canadian producer Nicholas Stiliardis, with whom he developed and directed two horror films for Home Box Office Television, *Red Blooded American Girl* (1990) and *Red Blooded American Girl II* (1997). Blyth, however, has now settled back home. While still developing feature film projects, difficulty in receiving funding has led him to digital video documentary production with *Bound for Pleasure* and his personal documentary, *Our Oldest Soldier* (2002), about his grandfather's experiences in World War I.

As a result of a career that has taken many turns, Blyth's filmography spans a range of genres including thrillers, period dramas, action films, and documentaries. Regardless of genre, Blyth's films are preoccupied with the perception of normality and abnormality and how these concepts are often at times interchangeable. With this in mind, it is to the horror genre that he has consistently returned, as he sees it as enabling him to express his interest in social satire and black comedy.[4] Even *Angel Mine* and the shot-in-New Zealand, U.S.-funded television thriller *Exposure* (2000) are flavored with the style and visual flourishes of his horror films. At the time Blyth began making films there was no established horror film tradition in New Zealand. With the success of Peter Jackson's *Braindead* (1992), as well as films such as *Jack Be Nimble* (1993) and *The Ugly* (1997), New Zealand has become increasingly known for its production of horror. Geoffrey Macnab points out this development in the New Zealand film industry in his review of *Jack Be Nimble* when he claims, "New Zealand, judging by the way it has depicted itself in recent films, must be a daunting place. Peter Jackson's *Braindead* suggested a land full of murderous zombies; Alison Maclean's *Crush* showed a soggy, grey country, with dark emotions simmering away."[5] Ian Conrich describes this trend as Kiwi Gothic:

> New Zealand, a country which is isolated and on the "perimeter" of the world, is known for its natural beauty. In this Eden there would appear, however, to exist an overgrown garden, in which grow images of excess and despair. The films present culturally deprived, remote communities, where industrialism is absent. Here characters struggle against a frightening, powerful and enchanted landscape in which they are trapped and suffocated. Individuals find it difficult to communicate and can be physically or mentally disadvantaged, making their isolation even greater. A stranger or outsider, often viewed with suspicion and fear, can break the isolation and disrupt the community.[6]

As a key director in the development of Kiwi Gothic cinema, Blyth's films explore many of the dark undercurrents of this idyllic landscape. His earliest films, *Angel Mine*, *It's Lizzie to Those Close,* and *Death Warmed Up*, deliberately undermine the traditional representation of the nation's pastoral heritage. The tag line on the poster for *Angel Mine* reads "New Zealand's own erotic fantasy that's far too close to home!"[7] and in his defense of the Arts Council contribution to the production, Hamish Keith described it as a "black comedy cut from the cloth of New Zealand suburban life ... rather than some moving myth about the land."[8] *Angel Mine* begins with a dreamlike montage of spectacular waves crashing onto the shore in slow motion intercut with a long shot of a nude woman (Jennifer Redford) sitting on a toilet on the beach looking out to sea. A man in a sailor's uniform (Derek Ward) emerges from the water and slowly approaches the woman. He pulls a bottle of tablets from his uniform and feeds one to the woman before holding the bottle up to the camera as the title *Angel Mine* appears on the screen. As the man dresses the woman there is the sudden introduction of a voice-over advertising a new pharmaceutical product, Angel Mine, designed to cure marital problems. In this opening the presentation of the landscape is transformed from a dreamlike beauty to an empty advertising image. The film then withdraws from this familiar rural landscape as Blyth relocates his film firmly within the modern suburbs of Auckland. *Angel Mine* is primarily a surreal foray into the blurred distinction between dream and reality, confirming that Blyth's main filmmaking influences were not classic horror films but rather the surreal visions of Luis Buñuel and David Lynch.[9] In *Angel Mine*, Blyth seeks to find the nightmare within the everyday.

While *Angel Mine* mocks images of the country's natural landscape, *It's Lizzie to Those Close* deliberately draws on New Zealand's spectacular landscape as a backdrop for its story of a nineteenth-century English woman, Lizzie (Sarah Peirse), arriving in New Zealand to work as domestic help. While not a horror film, the harsh life that awaits Lizzie in this wondrous but lonely setting evokes, more than any other film by Blyth, the themes of Kiwi Gothic cinema as described by Conrich. While overwhelmed by the beauty of her surroundings on the long journey to her new home, Lizzie's romantic fantasies are dashed when she arrives at the dilapidated cabin inhabited by three uncommunicative and uncaring men. Lizzie finds herself trapped between a father (Derek Hardwick) and son (Jeremy Stephens) who have not spoken to each other in years while her only companion is the second son (Bruno Lawrence) whose cognitive impairment alienates him from the other men. The violence of her new surroundings is brought home to her when she arrives at her new house only to have one of the men shoot her dog because it began to chase the sheep grazing nearby. Horrified by this act of cruelty and disregard for her feelings, she threatens to leave only to realize that it is a week's journey to town and that she is unable to find her own way. Suddenly the rolling hills that recently seemed so inviting are revealed to be the walls of her prison. The isolation of this beautiful but formidable landscape, matched by the coldness of the men and the claustrophobia of the cabin interior, causes

Lizzie to descend into the loneliness and despair that is so characteristic of Kiwi Gothic. Only the death of the father and disappearance of the eldest son, leaving her ownership of the land and a responsibility for the second son, allows for a reinterpretation of this setting. The last image of Lizzie, standing pregnant and alone, overlooking the land while remembering her romantic expectations of New Zealand, is ambiguous. It remains an image of isolation, but her gaze and stature within the environment suggest an acceptance of this setting as home.

Death Warmed Up, Blyth's first true horror film, offers a contrast between the idyllic natural landscape and the concrete constructs of modern medical institutions. The film opens with a teenage boy, Michael Tucker (Michael Hurst), running through a forest looking up through the trees at the blue sky. He is late for an appointment at a large, brick multi-story hospital. The film cuts to a series of low angle shots of the hospital's looming towers followed by a bird's-eye-view shot of Michael running through the parking lot, dwarfed by the vastness of the surrounding buildings. Once inside the hospital, Michael becomes trapped within its labyrinthine corridors, a setting made all the more unsettling by the film's consistent use of Steadicam and the dominance of red lighting. The mise-en-scène of this man-made location presents science as a monolithic institution, alien, empty and unwelcoming, that has grown away from the service of humanity to its exploitation. This is supported by the fact that the image of Michael figuratively trapped within the maze of the hospital becomes literal when Dr. Archer Howell (Gary Day), the villain of the film, abducts Michael in order to experiment on him.

Later in the film the contrast between the natural landscape and the man-made medical institution is taken further when Michael takes his friends to a summer resort island that has actually been transformed into a psychiatric convalescence hospital in which monstrous experiments are performed. While they begin by indulging in the natural pleasures of the island, sunning themselves on the ferry, driving through the hills and then frolicking on the beach, they are unable to escape the presence of the hospital, which becomes increasingly threatening in its domination of the scenery. The spectacular views are blocked by large billboards advertising the psychiatric institution; the group hears an unnatural industrial humming noise throbbing through the hills and is chased along the road by two of the hospital's more unstable inmates. Later, they decide to explore the island's extensive tunnel system that leads them to the hospital. The tunnels show the rankness beneath the surface beauty of the island. Bodies from failed experiments are strewn below, the group becomes lost within the underground maze, and they are chased on motorcycle by the guardians of the hospital's underworld, the same two monstrous men who chased them through the countryside. Through Blyth's distinctive visual style these spaces are also attributed with their own aesthetic appeal as they are lit in spectacular primary colors, the movements through the tunnels being the most visually dynamic of the film. The picturesque natural landscape in this film is presented as a facade that conceals the darker world beneath, one resplendent with its own horrors.

In tandem with the exploration of the dark underside of the surface beauty of New Zealand, Blyth's films also offer a critique of mainstream society and its dominant institutions by unleashing monstrous alternatives. Through his films, Blyth seeks to overturn traditional concepts of acceptable and unacceptable behavior. For instance, *Angel Mine* is the story of an alienated middle-class couple being stalked and eventually murdered by their youthful punk mirror images, played by the same actors. The film is an angry critique of the numbing effect of successful suburban life and unchecked consumption. Blyth describes this film as an attack on the "New Zealand dream" of material success.[10] As in so many of Blyth's films, the disenfranchised punk couple are a vibrant and refreshing alternative to their more respectable counterparts. This is primarily conveyed through the graphic representation of sexuality that the moral campaigners found so unsettling. The middle-class couple's clumsy fumblings in the bedroom are directly contrasted with the punk couple's more voracious sexual appetites. When the wife attempts to seduce her husband away from the television with kisses and caresses, he returns her affection without looking away from the screen and alternates between kisses and eating his chips. Furthermore, the Angel Mine of the title is a prescription drug designed to aid couples in finding the much-needed spark in their sexual relationship. The punk couple, however, is consistently presented as embodying unchecked desire, requiring no chemical supplements. In the cinema, husband and wife look on in increasing discomfort as their punk counterparts make love in front of them. This voracious sexual appetite is made literal when they break into the married couple's suburban house, going through their fridge and devouring all of their food before enthusiastically murdering them and then having sex in the main entrance to the house. In this sequence their blood lust is intrinsically linked to their sexual and carnivorous desires. Through murdering their middle-class alter egos, the punk couple expunges sexual repression, demonstrating their ultimate liberation. They are truly the return of the repressed.

This film's critique of the repression inherent within respectable society foreshadows a similar critique in Blyth's more mainstream road movie *Red Blooded American Girl II*. Blyth claims that this film was based on his own concept rather than operating as a director for hire as he did on his other North American projects.[11] In this film, Trent (Kristoffer Ryan

Jennifer Redford and Derek Ward as the unnamed couple, exemplars of sexual and social transgression in *Angel Mine*. (Courtesy New Zealand Film Commission.)

Winters), a college student, helps a prostitute, Miya (Kari Salin), escape from two men trying to murder her. As a result, Miya takes Trent on a wild trip through the American landscape in which he sheds his middle-class values along with his virginity. Like the punk couple in *Angel Mine* and the dominatrices in *Bound for Pleasure*, Miya embodies an alternative lifestyle that offers a release from the restraining conventions of polite society. While Miya's behavior and choice of profession is linked to familial trauma—she is the victim of long-term sexual abuse—it increasingly becomes clear that her specialization in S&M prostitution has enabled her to regain the control of her body that was taken by her father. This is the type of control she attempts to exert on the road. While she seems manic and destructive, her actions, which include armed robbery, shooting a police officer during a high speed chase, and recklessly climbing onto the front of her father's truck in order to force him off the road, are actually a part of her attempt to release herself from her past with her father (Burt Young), and Trent from his own repression. She wants to give Trent the power that she has found for herself. This is reinforced by her murder of her abusive father and her near murder of Trent's father (David Keith), which suggests that for Miya patricide is the only way to escape the normal social hierarchy that privileges the will of the father over the child. While Trent is unable to go through with the murder of his father and is forced to destroy Miya instead, her loss is felt more strongly than any relief at the rescue of the father, who is portrayed as overbearing and fundamentally hypocritical. Miya's actions are not condoned, but her death is presented as a violent attempt to curtail the energies that she unleashed. If *Angel Mine* celebrates the release of the repressed, then *Red Blooded American Girl II* mourns its containment.

The theme of patricide appears in Blyth's earlier film *Death Warmed Up* and links his films to other New Zealand horror movies, *Strange Behaviour* (1982), *The Ugly,* and *Jack Be Nimble*. *Red Blooded American Girl II*, *The Ugly,* and *Jack Be Nimble* present the murder of a parent as a response to abuse, leaving the children on the margins of society attempting to detach themselves from their past and reinvent themselves anew. *Strange Behaviour* and *Death Warmed Up*, however, present patricide as a result of external mind control exerted by scientists protecting their research. In both cases scientists use the subjects of their brainwashing experiments to silence their detractors. The fact that the sons are forced to murder their fathers is an added irony and a cruel touch. In *Death Warmed Up*, Blyth is concerned with critiquing the ambition and inhumanity of medical science rather than the repression of the bourgeois home and family, the destruction of which in this case is the result of science gone mad. The story begins as Michael Tucker, having finally made it to the hospital, overhears an argument between his father (David Weatherly) and his partner Howell about the ethics of Howell's experiments in longevity. Aware that Michael has been eavesdropping, Howell decides to brutally attack and drug the boy, programming him to shoot his father. The horror of his actions leaves Michael locked within a padded cell for seven years until released with a determination for revenge.

Blyth's image of science out of control extends to Howell's experiments in brainwashing and also to his research into cryogenics. Howell's experiments do not simply prolong the lives of his patients; they prohibit them from dying despite the fact that their bodies are virtually decaying while still alive. As a result they are transformed into mindless, tortured zombies. Through Howell's experiments and the manner in which his patients are presented as grotesque monstrosities, the film expresses skepticism about medical science, not as a result of its insane ambitions but more through the lack of humanity expressed by the medical establishment. The hospitals are cold and alienated, the hospital staff on Howell's island seems uncaring and indifferent, while Howell's own surgical practices are brutal in the extreme. These images of brutality in the scientific and medical establishment are echoed in other New Zealand horror films such as the violent and violating experiments performed in *Strange Behaviour* and the cruelty of the orderlies and doctors in the psychiatric institute in *The Ugly*. In *Death Warmed Up*, the scene of Howell beginning his operation on the cranium by using an electric drill is a particularly disturbing image, demonstrating that the desire for progress that fuels scientific advancement is fundamentally undermined by the antiquated practices that are perceived here to be used by the medical establishment. Science is presented in this film as both ambitious and barbaric. The film's climax as the patients overrun the hospital and destroy its staff is as ferocious an attack on science as *Angel Mine* is an attack on material consumption. Both films end on an apocalyptic note as the dark underside of familiar, mainstream culture erupts and is no longer containable.

In a 1985 interview, Blyth suggested that each of his films represent different levels of his own emotional state.[12] So if *Angel Mine* and *Death Warmed Up* capture his youthful anger and aggression, through *Moonrise* we see a mature director who has let go of his anger but not his thematic preoccupations. While *Moonrise* is essentially an innocent children's film, it shares with *Angel Mine* and *Death Warmed Up* an inherent criticism of middle-class values and, with *Bound for Pleasure*, the support of marginal cultures of society, in this case children and the elderly. To achieve this the film offers a re-working of the vampire myth. Often portrayed in the cinema as a metaphor for repressed sexuality or the decadence of unchecked consumption, in Blyth's film the vampire becomes a metaphor for the innocence and wonder of childhood. The idea of reinterpreting the vampire film was not unprecedented for Blyth, as his film *Red Blooded American Girl* also attempted to reinvent the genre. In *Red Blooded American Girl* vampirism is no longer a Gothic monster from the past but rather a contagious disease that infects the bloodstream. The association of vampirism with a blood disease is of course not new. The manner in which vampirism is linked with sexuality in Bram Stoker's *Dracula* (1897), along with the emphasis on its spread among the youthful women in the novel, can be seen as capturing the nineteenth-century fear of a sexually transmitted disease.[13] In 1980s North America, with the rise of AIDS awareness and the increasing fear of contagion, it is no surprise that the vampire became infused with those biological fears once more.[14] *Red Blooded American Girl* is, among many such films, one that attempts to present the vampire imagery clinically as a disease that should and must be cured. Other examples include *The Hunger* (1983), *Lifeforce* (1985), and *Near Dark* (1987), a film that shares with *Red Blooded American Girl* the introduction of a cure for vampirism. What Blyth's film has to offer that is new is the suggestion that vampirism is not only something that can be cured by science but is actually a product of modern science trying to find a cure for AIDS and as a result producing and unleashing something much worse. The villainous vampires of the film are the scientists themselves, both seeking a cure and infecting others along the way.

Moonrise, however, is a much more subtle and innovative reworking of the genre. Written by Michael Heath and based on a successful radio play, Blyth was attracted to the project because it "turned the conventions upside down and it was a plea for children to be allowed to keep and develop their imaginations."[15] I would add that it is also a plea for the elderly to be free from the restraints of expected social standing in order to explore the pleasures of uninhibited behavior. The story is of a young American boy, Lonny (Justin Gocke), who has traveled to New Zealand to spend the summer with this Aunt Leah (Pat Evison) and ailing grandfather Cooger (Al Lewis). Cooger dies soon after, but the normality of the situation is overturned when he returns as a vampire. On one level, the film addresses the horrors of death and the process of working through the trauma of loss. Throughout the film, Lonny must deal with his grandfather's illness and death and later try to save Cooger from Leah's boyfriend, Ernie (Noel Appleby), as he attempts to hammer a stake through the vampire's heart. Finally, Lonny must accept the loss of his beloved grandfather when Cooger decides that he has lived among humanity too long and must return to his vampire-kind. This time Lonny is able to say goodbye to his grandfather and emotionally move on.

On another level, the film's reworking of the vampire genre is equally preoccupied with presenting vampirism as a release from enforced social behavior. Even before Cooger is revealed as a vampire, he is presented as being different. Cooger is a free spirit who is first introduced in the film gleefully flying through the air before returning to the ground and resuming his normal appearance for the benefit of his daughter and her belligerent boyfriend. The earthbound Cooger, however, maintains his free spirit as he sneaks into the back of a fairground horror train in order to scare the participants. Unfortunately, the ride's patrons and manager do not appreciate his apparently immature behavior and he is thrown out. At this point he has the first of his attacks that cause him to be confined to bed and become trapped within the role deemed socially acceptable for a man of his age. His daughter seems both saddened and relieved by his pending death.

Through the presence of Lonny, along with his New Zealand friend Kanziora (Milan Borich), Cooger regains his youthful spirit and energy. Each time they enter his room, he comes alive with movement and laughter, even dancing around the room. Furthermore, unlike Leah and Ernie, Lonny and Kanziora accept and are drawn to Cooger's eccentricity rather than preferring him to act his age. Even as Kanziora realizes that Cooger does not appear in photographs and both boys spot Cooger's fanged dentures soaking in a glass, causing them to suspect that his eccentricity maybe more ominous than simple whimsy, they are never threatened by him but rather are increasingly intrigued. He becomes all the more worthy of saving from the social pressures imposed by Leah and Ernie. Most importantly, the youthful music and games played by the boys after the wake, brings Cooger back to life. After his return from the dead, Cooger and the boys become increasingly bound together in opposition to the adults

David Blyth (*left*) and Al Lewis on the set of *Moonrise*. (Courtesy New Zealand Film Commission.)

who surround them. They share adventures as Cooger takes the boys flying through the air, and later the boys work together to hide him from Leah and Kanziora's parents. For the boys, Cooger's vampirism offers an alternative to the other grown-ups they encounter. Kanziora's parents are blind to the activities of their son. At the wake the boys are surrounded by strange and scary adults who mock and tease them for their youthfulness, and traditional authority figures like the priest and the police officer who are presented as frightening and bumbling, respectively.

The trio particularly stands in opposition to Leah and Ernie, who take on the generic roles of vampire hunters and killers, no longer heroes but villains attempting to destroy Cooger because of their narrow-minded views of the world. He is an embarrassing old man who does not know and respect his place: when you are dead, you stay dead. While the film ends with the boys forced to say goodbye to Cooger who is planning to rejoin his vampire-kind, their final wish to stay young forever enforces their complete resistance to what the mainstream adult has to offer in favor of the wonders of youthful spirit and imagination.

While *Moonrise* is a more gentle engagement with the horror genre, it encapsulates many of the themes of Blyth's other work. The manner in which the film reinterprets the vampire genre enables Blyth to appropriate the image of the vampire to represent traditionally underrepresented cultures—youth and the elderly. Blyth's emphasis upon life on the margins in all of his films serves as a critique of middle-class values that act as repressive and oppressive forces rather than offering any form of liberation or self-expression. In his films, Blyth is searching for a different kind of truth, not bound by hypocrisy, but one that exists on the margins of society, challenging the entire concept of normality.[16]

Notes

1. David Blyth, e-mail to author, May 21, 2002.
2. "Death Warmed Up," *Variety*, September 5, 1984.
3. Roger Horrocks, "New Zealand Film Makers at the Auckland City Art Gallery: David Blyth," program notes, June 6, 1985, 2.
4. See Caroline Vié and Claude Scasso, "*Death Warmed Up:* Entretien avec David Blyth," *Ecran Fantastique* 52 (January 1985): 76.
5. Geoffrey Macnab, "*Jack Be Nimble*," *Sight and Sound* 4, no. 2 (1994): 54.
6. Ian Conrich, "Gothic Film," in *The Handbook to Gothic Literature*, ed. Marie Mulvey-Roberts (London: Macmillan, 1998), 80.
7. Horrocks, "New Zealand Film Makers at the Auckland City Art Gallery: David Blyth," 2.
8. Hamish Keith, "Where Angel Treads," *The Listener*, December 2, 1978, 28–29, cited in Horrocks, "New Zealand Film Makers at Auckland City Art Gallery: David Blyth," 2.
9. Blyth, e-mail to author, May 21, 2002.
10. Vié and Scasso, "*Death Warmed Up:* Entretien avec David Blyth," 53.
11. Blyth, e-mail to author, May 5, 2002.
12. Vié and Scasso, "*Death Warmed Up:* Entretien avec David Blyth," 76.
13. See Christopher Craft, "'Kiss Me with Those Red Lips': Gender and Inversion in Bram Stoker's *Dracula*," *Representations* 8 (1984): 107–33; Anne Cranny-Francis, "Sexual Politics and Political Repressions in Bram Stoker's *Dracula*," in *Nineteenth Century Suspense: From Poe to Conan Doyle*, ed. Clive Bloom, Brian Docherty, Jane Gibb, and Keith Shand (Basingstoke: Macmillan, 1988), 64–79.
14. See Edward Guerrero, "AIDS as Monster in Science Fiction and Horror Cinema," *Journal of Popular Film and Television* 18, no. 3 (1990): 86–93.
15. Blyth, e-mail to author, May 21, 2002.
16. Ibid.

David Blyth—Filmography

1975. *Cancelled* (NZ short film: cinematographer, editor).
1976. *Circadian Rhythms* (NZ short film: director, cinematographer, co-editor).
1977. *Solo* (NZ feature film: third assistant director).
1978. *Angel Mine* (NZ feature film: director, co-producer, writer).
1980. *Shock Treatment* (US feature film: director's assistant).
1982. *Close to Home* (NZ television soap opera: director for twelve episodes).
1982. *A Woman of Good Character* (NZ television drama extended into the 1983 feature film *It's Lizzie to Those Close* a.k.a. *Lizzie*: director).
1984. *Death Warmed Up* (NZ feature film: director, co-writer).
1984. *Heroes* (NZ television series: director for two episodes).

1987. *Nasty Hero* (US feature film: director for the main stages of production).
1989. *The Horror Show* a.k.a. *House III* a.k.a. *Horror House* (US feature film: director for the initial stages of production).
1990. Red Blooded American Girl (Canada feature film: director).
1992. Moonrise a.k.a. **Grampire** a.k.a. **My Grandad's a Vampire** a.k.a. **My Grandpa is a Vampire** (NZ feature film: director).
1993. *White Fang* (Canada/France television series: director of the episodes "Burnt River," "The Mine," and "Fangs for the Memories," and writer for the episodes "Blair's Glory [Arrow River]" and "Fangs for the Memories").
1993. *Mighty Morphin' Power Rangers* (US/Japan television series: director of the episodes "I, Eye Guy," "Power Ranger Punks," "The Trouble with Shellshock," and "The Spit Flower").
1993. *Kahu & Maia* (NZ television drama: director).
1994. Music video for Andrew Fagan (co-director for "Now You Know").
1995. *Tala Pasifika* (NZ television series of six short films: supervising director).
1995. *The Call Up* (NZ film/television drama: director).
1997. Red Blooded American Girl II a.k.a. **Hit and Run** a.k.a. **Hot Blooded** a.k.a. **Red Blooded II** (US television film for HBO: director).
1997/98. *The Drum* (NZ television entertainment show: director for four episodes).
1998. *Fresh Up in the Deep End* (NZ television series: director of the episodes "Private Eyes" and "Braveheart").
2000. *Exposure* (US/Germany/NZ feature film: director).
2001. Bound for Pleasure (NZ documentary: director, producer, writer).
2002. Our Oldest Soldier (NZ television documentary: director, writer).
2003. *Fish Tank Telly* (NZ "tranquility" DVD: director, producer).
2005. *Age of Aquariums* (NZ television documentary: director, producer).
2007. *Transfigured Nights* (NZ documentary: director, producer, cinematographer, sound).

Contributors

STACEY ABBOTT is Senior Lecturer in Film Studies at Roehampton University. She is the author of *Celluloid Vampires* (2007) and *Angel* (forthcoming) for the TV Milestones series of books. She is the editor of *Reading Angel: The TV Spin-Off with a Soul* (2005), co-editor of *Investigating Alias: Secrets and Spies* (forthcoming), and has contributed to *The Horror Film: Creating and Marketing Fear* (2005), *Vampires: Myths and Metaphors of Enduring Evil* (2006), and *Horror Zone: The Cultural Experience of Contemporary Horror Cinema* (2007).

BRUCE BABINGTON is Professor of Film at the University of Newcastle, co-author of *Blue Skies and Silver Linings: Aspects of the Hollywood Musical* (1985), *Affairs to Remember: Hollywood Comedy of the Sexes* (1989), *Biblical Epics: Sacred Narrative in the Hollywood Cinema* (1993), and the forthcoming *Carmen: A Cultural History on Film*. He is the author of *Launder and Gilliat* (2002) and the forthcoming *Staunch As: A History of the New Zealand Feature Film*, editor of *British Stars and Stardom: From Alma Taylor to Sean Connery* (2001), and co-editor of *The Trouble with Men: Masculinities in European and Hollywood Cinema* (2004).

TERENCE BAYLER, born in 1930 in Wanganui, was educated at the local Technical College. After playing the male lead in *Broken Barrier* (1952), he studied in Britain on a government bursary and in 1953 gained drama diplomas from the University of London and RADA. He toured with Richard Campion's NZ Players throughout 1957, and in 1981 featured in Michael Black's film *Pictures*, produced by John O'Shea. In 1991 he appeared in the television mini-series *The Other Side of Paradise*, co-produced by South Pacific Pictures. His film roles in Britain include Macduff in Roman Polanski's *Macbeth* (1972) and Gregory in *Monty Python's Life of Brian* (1979).

BARBARA CAIRNS teaches film and television production at the University of Lincoln, in the United Kingdom, where she is head of the Media Production department. She is a member of the Executive Committee of the Association of Media Practice Educators, and is co-author of *Shadows on the Wall: A Study of Seven New Zealand Feature Films* (1994) and *Shortland Street: Production, Text and Audience* (1996). A documentary filmmaker, she is director of *Ruia Taitea: The World Is Where We Are* (1991).

JAMES CHAPMAN is Professor of Film at the University of Leicester. He is the author of *The British at War: Cinema, State and Propaganda, 1939–1945* (1998), *Licence to Thrill: A Cultural History of the James Bond Films* (1999), *Saints and Avengers: British Adventure Series of the 1960s* (2002), *Cinemas of the World: Film and Society from 1895 to the Present* (2004), *Past and Present: National Identity and the British Historical Film* (2005), and *Inside the Tardis: The Worlds of Doctor Who—A Cultural History* (2006). He is co-editor of *Windows on the Sixties: Exploring Key Texts of Media and Culture* (2000), and his articles have appeared in the *Historical Journal of Film, Radio and Television*, *Journal of Popular British Cinema*, and *Visual Culture in Britain*.

IAN CONRICH is Director of the Centre for New Zealand Studies, Birkbeck, University of London, and Chair of the New Zealand Studies Association. He is an editor of *Journal of British Cinema and Television*, an associate editor of *Film and Philosophy*, an advisory board member of *Interactive Media*, *Journal of Horror Studies*, *Studies in Australasian Cinema*, and *British Review of New Zealand Studies*, and a guest editor of *Asian Cinema* (for a special issue on Sri Lankan cinema) and *Post Script* (for a special issue on Australian and New Zealand Cinema). He is the author of *New Zealand Cinema* (2007) and editor or co-editor of eleven books, including *New Zealand—A Pastoral Paradise?* (2000), *The Cinema of John Carpenter: The Technique of Terror* (2004), *Film's Musical Moments* (2006), *New Zealand Fictions: Literature and Film* (2007), and *Horror Zone: The Cultural Experience of Contemporary Horror Cinema* (2007). He has also contributed to more than forty-five books and journals.

SAM EDWARDS was, until his retirement, Associate Professor in the Department of Screen and Media Studies at the University of Waikato. He is the author of *Film and Television in the Classroom* (1984) and *Reading the Pictures: Activities with Film and Television in the Classroom* (1996) and the co-author of *New Zealand Film, 1912–1996* (1997). He has also written articles on New Zealand Film for *Illusions*, the *New Zealand Journal of Media Studies*, and the *New Zealand Journal of Social Studies*. He is the weekly film columnist for the *Waikato Times*.

DAVID GERSTNER is Associate Professor of Cinema Studies at the City University of New York, College of Staten Island. Previously he served as lecturer for two years at the University of Otago. He is the author of *Manly Arts: Masculinity and Nation in Early Cinema* (2006) and is the co-editor of *Authorship and Film* (2003). He has written on New Zealand cinema for *CineAction* and *Interdisciplinary Literary Studies* and contributed to *Film Quarterly*, *The Stanford Humanities Review*, *The Velvet Light Trap*, *Wide Angle*, and *Cultural Critique*.

Contributors

BARRY KEITH GRANT is Professor of Film Studies and Popular Culture at Brock University in Ontario, Canada. He is the author, co-author, or editor of numerous books, including *Film Genre: Theory and Criticism* (1977), *Planks of Reason: Essays on the Horror Film* (1984/2004), *Film Genre Reader* (1986), *Voyages of Discovery: The Cinema of Frederick Wiseman* (1992), *The Dread of Difference: Gender and the Horror Film* (1996), *Documenting the Documentary: Close Readings of Documentary Film and Video* (1998), *A Cultural Assault: The New Zealand Films of Peter Jackson* (1999), *The Film Studies Dictionary* (2001), *John Ford's Stagecoach* (2002), and *Five Films by Frederick Wiseman* (2006).

ROGER HORROCKS is Emeritus Professor in the Department of Film, Television, and Media Studies at the University of Auckland. He is author of *Composing Motion: Len Lye and Experimental Film-Making* (1991), and *Len Lye: A Biography* (2002), and co-editor of *Figures of Motion: Len Lye/Selected Writings* (1984), *Len Lye* (2000), *Len Lye: Happy Moments, Texts and Images* (2002), and *Television in New Zealand: Programming the Nation* (2004). He has contributed articles on New Zealand cinema to journals such as *Illusions, Alternative Cinema,* and *Islands*.

STAN JONES is Senior Lecturer in Screen and Media Studies at the University of Waikato. He has special interests in teaching and researching German/European cinema (particularly the work of directors Wim Wenders and Marcel Ophüls) and the reception of New Zealand filmmaking in Germany. He is the author of *Projecting a Nation: New Zealand Film and Its Reception in Germany* (1999), and he has contributed to *European Identity in Cinema* (1996), *Screening the Past: Film and the Representation of History* (1998), *Twin Peeks: Australian and New Zealand Feature Films* (1999), and *Fifty Contemporary Filmmakers* (2002).

HELEN MARTIN is Academic Advisor at UNITEC, Auckland. She spent six years as film critic for the New Zealand *Listener* and is the author of *Critical Media Studies: A Teachers' Handbook* (1991) and the co-author of *Shadows on the Wall: A Study of Seven New Zealand Feature Films* (1994), *Shortland Street: Production, Text, and Audience* (1996), *New Zealand Film, 1912–1996* (1997), and *It's All Done with Mirrors: About Television* (2001). She has contributed articles to *Alternative Cinema, Illusions, Onfilm, Script, New Zealand Journal of Media Studies,* and *The Big Picture* and has written study guides on New Zealand films for Learning Media and Communicado.

STUART MURRAY is Senior Lecturer in Postcolonial Literatures at the University of Leeds. He is the editor of *Not on Any Map: Essays on Postcoloniality and Cultural Nationalism* (1997) and the author of *Never a Soul at Home: New Zealand Literary Nationalism and the 1930s* (1998). He has been the guest editor of special issues of the *Journal of New Zealand Literature* and *Moving Worlds* and has published articles on the literature and cultural history of New Zealand, Australia, Canada, the Caribbean, West Africa, and Ireland. His current research is divided between work on issues of postcolonial encounter and settlement, especially in New Zealand, the Pacific, and Australia, and cultural representations of disability, particularly autism. He is working on a contemporary cultural history of autism and a study of filmmaker Barry Barclay.

GERALDENE PETERS has recently completed a PhD on political documentary in New Zealand and is currently an independent researcher, writer, and filmmaker. She has contributed to the *Encyclopedia of Documentary Film* (2006) and written for *Onfilm, Illusions, The Big Picture, Pacific Journalism Review, Red and Green: A Journal of Left Alternatives*, as well as writing study guides for ATOM and the Auckland Documentary Collective. She has co-organized a series of documentary conferences for the University of Auckland and worked on a number of local and international documentary productions ranging from small format community video to high production value international documentaries.

STEPHANIE RAINS is a lecturer in Media Studies at the University of Manooth. Her book, *The Irish-American in Popular Culture, 1945–2000*, was published by Irish Academic Press in 2007.

JONATHAN RAYNER is Senior Lecturer in Literature and Film at the University of Sheffield. He is the author of *The Films of Peter Weir* (1998/2003), *Cinema Journeys of the Man Alone: The New Zealand and American Films of Geoff Murphy* (1999), *Contemporary Australian Cinema* (2000), and *The Naval War Film: Genre, History, and National Cinema* (2006).

EVA RUESCHMANN is Associate Professor of Cultural Studies at Hampshire College, Amherst, Massachusetts. She is the author of *Sisters on Screen: Siblings in Contemporary Cinema* (2000) and the editor of *Moving Pictures, Migrating Identities* (2003). Her current book project focuses on the meanings of landscapes and space in films by Australian and New Zealand women directors.

LAURENCE SIMMONS is Associate Professor in the Department of Film, Television, and Media Studies at the University of Auckland. He has written extensively on critical theory as well as contemporary New Zealand art and film. In the field of New Zealand film studies he has published on John O'Shea in *Landfall, Interstices*, and *New Zealand Music*, on Gaylene Preston and Gregor Nicholas in *Illusions*, on Lee Tamahori in *Southern Review*, Peter Jackson in *Mid-West*, and Jane Campion in *Piano Lessons: Approaches to* The Piano (1999). He is the author of *The Image Always Has the Last Word: On Contemporary New Zealand Painting and Photography* (2003), and the co-editor of *Derrida Dow-*

nunder (2000), *Baudrillard West of the Dateline* (2003), and *From Z to A: Žižek at the Antipodes* (2005).

ANDREW SPICER is Reader in Cultural History at the Bristol School of Art, Media, and Design, University of the West of England. He is the author of *Typical Men: The Representation of Masculinity in Popular British Cinema* (2001), *Film Noir* (2002), and *Sydney Box* (2006) and the editor of *European Film Noir* (2007). He has contributed to many collections and written for numerous journals including *Journal of British Cinema and Television, Journal of Contemporary History,* and *Film Criticism.*

KIRSTEN MOANA THOMPSON is Associate Professor of Film Studies at Wayne State University in Detroit. She is the author of *Apocalyptic Dread: American Cinema at the Turn of the Century* (2006) and *Crime Films: Murder Most Foul* (2007), and co-editor of *Perspectives on German Cinema* (1996). She has contributed discussions on New Zealand cinema to *Piano Lessons: Approaches to The Piano* (1999), *Movie Blockbusters* (2003), and *From Hobbits to Hollywood: Essays on Peter Jackson's Lord of the Rings* (2006).

ESTELLA TINCKNELL is Head of the School of Cultural Studies at the University of the West of England. She is the joint author of *The Practice of Cultural Studies* (2004) and author of *Mediating the Family: Gender, Culture, and Representation* (2005). She has contributed to *p.o.v., Feminist Media Studies, Gender and Education, Journal of Sociology of Education, Journal of European Cultural Studies, Journal of Popular Film and Television* and is on the editorial board of *Body and Society.* She is the co-editor of *Film's Musical Moments* (2006) and *New Zealand Fictions: Literature and Film* (2007), and has contributed to *New Zealand—A Pastoral Paradise?* (2000), *Lost Highways: The Road Movie Book* (2000), and *Reality Television: A Reader* (2003).

Index

Aardvark Films, 257
Abbott, Stacey, 9, 336–48
Aberdein, Keith, 143, 190
Aboriginal, 21, 91
About Face, 204, 208
Absent without Leave, 217–18, 224–25, 227, 229
Academy, The (movie theater), 262
Academy Awards, 1, 143, 201, 213, 290, 331
Accented Cinema, An (book), 180
Ackerman, Chantal, 78
Acme Sausage Company, 257
Act of Murder, 262
advertisements, 19–20, 64, 89, 127, 130n5, 157, 170, 337–38
African, 27
Aguirre, der Zorn Gottes (*Aguirre: The Wrath of God*), 288n21
AIDS, 125, 132n19, 266, 279, 344
Air New Zealand, 170
Aku Mahi Whatu Maori/My Art of Maori Weaving, 90
Albania, 38, 47
Albi, 265
Alien3, 273
All Blacks (rugby), 9, 124, 238, 313, 318n16
Allen, Beth, 211
Allen, Bob, 206
Allen, Christopher, 259
Allen, Tom, 139
Alliance Atlantis, 314
All Soul's Carnival, 31
All the Way up There, 73
al-Qaeda, 328
Alternative Cinema Christchurch, 257
Altman, Robert, 140

American Fleet, 37
America's Cup, 328
And Now New Zealand, 209
Andrei Rublev, 279
Andrews, E. Stanhope, 65
Angel at My Table, An, 242, 289–94, 300
Angel Mine, 6, 9, 336, 338–39, 342, 344
Angel of the Anunciation (painting), 67n17
animation, 13n7, 15, 20, 23, 26, 62
Antarctic, 170
anthropology, 58, 289
Antonioni, Michelangelo, 60
ANZUS Treaty, 160
Appleby, Noel, 345
Apple Films, 220
Arab, 297
Arab-Israeli War, 142
Arahanga, Julian, 174
Arizona, 316
Arquette, Alexis, 196
Art Deco, 126
Arts of Maori Children, The, 38
Ashby, Hal, 140
Asia, 60
Asia-Pacific, 180
Aspects of a Small Town, 257
Aspects of Utu, 166n11
Associated TV, 48
Aston, Janelle, 206, 264
Atha, John, 61
Atkine, Feodor, 243
Atkinson, Michael, 329
Attenborough, Richard, 146
Auckland, 20, 37, 60–61, 79, 103, 109, 117n24, 121, 124, 126, 149n3, 179, 195, 204, 206, 209, 222, 224, 227, 229, 247, 257, 260, 262, 267, 273, 278–79, 283, 305, 307, 310, 336

Auckland Art Gallery, 257
Auckland Film Festival, 103
Auckland Star (newspaper), 261
Auntie Hope (Tumanako Rewiti), 110
Austen, Dale, 44
Australia/Australian, 10, 19–21, 36–37, 48, 90, 92, 135, 137–40, 152, 185–86, 195, 197, 205, 254, 259, 289, 291, 293–94, 297–98, 305, 313–14, 322, 328
Australian Film and Television School, 289
Autobiography, An (book), 291
avant-garde, 15, 19–22, 25–26, 123

Babington, Bruce, 6, 236–50
Bach, John, 225, 245
Bad Blood, 231n4
Bad Taste, 10–11, 321, 323–25, 327, 329
Baker, Richard St. Barbe, 262
Baldwin, Alec, 139, 147
Ballarat, 138
ballet, 26
Balme, Timothy, 324
Bananas for Market, 219
Bao, Shaun, 264
Bar, The, 211
Barclay, Barry, 4, 8–9, 12, 16, 55, 66, 88–102, 117n36, 220
Barnett, John, 88–89
Barr, Jim, 329
Barr, Mary, 329
Barry, Dorothy, 294
Barry, Tony, 154, 196, 245
Basinger, Kim, 139, 147
Bastion Point. *See* Takaparawha
Bastion Point Day 507, 8, 103–4, 107–8, 110–11, 256, 260–62
Bastion Point—the Untold Story, 262
Battle Cry, 244
Battletruck, 197, 322
Baumfield, Simon, 228
Bayler, Terence, ix–x, 58, 67n11
Bay of Plenty, 38, 42, 116n1
Baxendale, Jack, 45
Baxter, James K., 192
BBC (British Broadcasting Corporation), 38, 48, 75, 220, 325

Beck, Michael, 197
Beckford, William, 274
Belfast, 179
Belich, James, 247
Bergin, Patrick, 281
Beresford, Bruce, 137
Berlin, 95–96
Berresford Street Primary School, 73
Beth, Stephanie, 67n25
Betrayer, The, 36
Beyer, Georgina, 121, 130n2
Beyond Reasonable Doubt, 6, 217, 220–22, 225, 227, 229
Big Brother, Little Sister, 174, 176
Big Clock, The, 147
Biko, Steve, 109
bin Laden, Osama, 327
biopic, 237, 242
Birkin, Jane, 243
Birth of New Zealand, The, 20, 37
Black, Jack, 315
Black Death, 278, 281
Blake, Rachael, 83
Blakeston, Oswell, 22
Bland, James, 238
Bland, Peter, 177
Blenheim, 240
Blerta, 152, 185, 257
Bligh, Captain, 145
Blind Side, 153, 161, 163–64
Bloke from Freeman's Bay, The, 38
Bloody Chamber, The (short stories), 81
Bloomsbury, 22
blues, 27
Blyth, David, 2, 5–6, 9, 254, 285, 336–48
Blythe, Martin, 188, 194
Bodle, Frank, 42
Boer War, 44
Bogdanovich, Peter, 140
Bolivian, 91
Bollinger, Alun, 152
Bolt, Robert, 145–46
Bolton, Heather, 80
Bond, James, 148, 163
Bonsai Epic Short Films, 310
Booker Prize, 311
Bordwell, David, 322
Borich, Milan, 345

Bosch, Hieronymous, 277
Bossley, Caitlin, 311
Bound for Pleasure, 336, 338, 342, 344
Bounty, The, 138, 144–46
Braindead, 11, 321, 323–27, 338
Brakhage, Stan, 28
Brando, Marlon, 145
Brasch, Alan, 100n1
Brazilian, 321
Bread and Roses, 73
Brecht, Bertolt, 317
Brennan, Barry, 139
Brescians, 36
Brett, David, 277
Bridge: A Story of Men in Dispute, The, 106, 111, 262
Bridge to Nowhere, 178–79, 231n4
Bristol, 220, 227
Bristowe, Tania, 155
British Airways, 26
British School of Art Therapists, 72
Brixton, 73
Brixton College of Further Education, 73–74
Broadbank, 144
Broadley, Colin, 60
Broken Barrier, ix, 4–5, 54–60, 62
Broken English, 231n4
Brontë, Emily, 295
Brosnan, Pierce, 139, 148
Brothers Grimm, 81, 277
Brown, Nancy, 174
Bruegel, Pieter, 277
Brussels, 25
Brussels World Fair, 27
Bryant, Rick, 179
Buñuel, Luis, 302n19, 310, 323, 339
Burgess, Bruce, 73
Bush Cinderella, The, 44–45
Butler, Samuel, 253

Cadillac Man, 147
Cairns, Barbara, 10, 201–16
Callen, John, 98
Caltex, 63–64
Cambridge (UK), 72, 74–75
Came a Hot Friday, 176–77, 238
Cameramen at War, 26

Cameron, Gen. Duncan, 41
Cammell, Donald, 75
camp, 266–67, 332n14
Campbell, Gordon, 38
Campbell, Russell, 186, 196, 261
Campion, Jane, 2, 10–12, 82–83, 85, 165, 236, 253–54, 289–303, 305
Canada/Canadian, 179, 217, 220–21, 273, 281, 284, 305, 324, 337
Canby, Vincent, 139
Cancelled, 336
Cannes, 94, 180, 210, 290, 310
Canterbury Plains, 273
Cape Fear, 147
Captain Bligh and Mr. Christian (book), 145
Caro, Niki, 12, 13n7, 88, 213
Carry Me Back, 6, 231n4, 236–42, 246, 248
"Carry Me Back to Old Virginny" (song), 248n1
Carry on up the Khyber, 220
Cars That Ate Paris, The, 258
Carter, Angela, 81, 83
Carter, Carey, 100n1
Casablanca, 322
Casseli, Nola, 41
Castle of Otranto, The (novel), 274
Catholic, 55, 106, 170, 245, 274, 282, 315
Cavalcanti, Alberto, 25–26
Cavani, Liliana, 142
Cell Barnes Hospital, St. Albans, 72
censorship, 55, 336
Central America, 90
Cézanne, Paul, 19
Chadwick, Rangi, 305
Chain of the Sun, 220
Champion, 244
Channelling Baby, 13n7
Chapman, James, 6
Chappell, Lisa, 128, 209, 269
Chapple, Geoff, 262, 307
Chatham (ship), 96
Chatham Islands, 96–97
chien andalou, Un, 310
Children of China, 48
Chill Factor, 231n4

China/Chinese, 38, 47–48, 262–64, 269n19, 324
China's Patriot Army, 262
Choudhury, Surita, 314
Christchurch, 18, 55, 82, 110, 257, 273, 326–27
Christian, Fletcher, 145
Christianity, 43, 131n13, 327
Churchill Cigarettes, 26
cine-magazine, 54
Cinema of Unease: A Personal Journey, 185, 208
cinema verité, 26
Circadian Rhythms, 336
Clark, Justine, 132n23
classical music, 24, 64
Cleopatra 2525, 221
Close to Home, 337
"C'mon" (song), 63
Cocktail, 146–47
Collector's World, 220
Collins, Annie, 109, 114
Color Cry, 27
Colour Box, A, 4, 23–25, 32n27
Colour Flight, 29
Colston, Karen, 293
comedy/comic, 38, 44–45, 77–78, 83, 157, 161–62, 175–77, 205, 212, 220, 236, 238, 242, 313–14, 322–23, 326, 338
commercials. *See* advertisements
community comedies, 38, 44
Conrich, Ian, 1–13, 139, 217–35, 275, 325, 338–39
Contact, 320
Cooper, Deryn, 258
Cooper, Terence, 192
Coppola, Francis Ford, 140
Cormack, Danielle, 12, 13n7
Corra, Bruno, 25
Cosi, 197
Costner, Kevin, 139, 146, 148
Cottrell, Anna, 76
Countdown on Zimbabwe, 257
Country Flyers, 258
Cover Story, 221
Cowan, James, 41–42
Creed, Barbara, 332n16

Crével, René, 124
Cricketeers, The (painting), 259
Crime Story (novel), 212
Cronenberg, David, 324
Crooked Earth, 13n7, 231n4, 233n39
Cross, Ian, 170
Crudup, Billy, 314
Cruise, Tom, 139, 146
Crump, Barry, 60, 170
Crush, 11, 304–5, 307, 310–13, 316–17, 338
Cuban Missile Crisis, 148
cubist, 19–20
Cumbria/Cumbrian, 273, 278–79, 283
Curtis, Cliff, 12, 128, 209
Curtis, David, 24
Cuthrell, Elizabeth, 314
Czech, 258

Dadson, Philip, 257
Dafoe, Willem, 147
Dalí, Salvador, 323
Damici, Nick, 299
dance, 23, 26, 259
Dances of the South Pacific, 58
Daniels, Piripi, 99
Dangerous Orphans, 205, 217, 224, 227, 232n22
Danny and Raewyn, 202
Dante, Joe, 326
Dante's Peak, 11, 148, 164
Dargaville, 117n24
Darling, Jon, 293
Darragh, Barbara, 207, 265
Davies, Piers, 257
Davies, Sonja, 73
Davy, Sarah, 139
Day, Gary, 340
Death in the Family, A, 125
Death Warmed Up, 9, 231n4, 336–38, 343–44
de Certeau, Michel, 78, 123
Deer Hunter, The, 323
Degas, Edgar, 266
Delamere, Rangimarie, 113
de La Tour, Georges, 264
de Laurentiis, Dino, 144–46
Delhi, 298

de Malmanche, Alan, 97
Demme, Jonathan, 314
Dennis, Jonathan, 29, 110
Department of Education, 170
Departure of the Second Contingent for the Boer War, The, 15
Depression, the, 22, 45, 55
Derek, 170
Derrida, Jacques, 60
de Sade, Marquis, 81
Desperate Remedies, 9–10, 126–29, 131n13, 132n25, 208–10, 231n4, 256, 266–68
Diamond, Neil, 298
Dingle, Graeme, 73
disability, 72–74
Disney, Walt, 23
documentary, 8–10, 15, 19, 25–26, 38, 48, 54–59, 62, 64–66, 72–77, 88–91, 96, 103–4, 106–12, 114–16, 117n36, 126, 130n2, 185, 202, 217, 219–21, 244, 256, 258, 260–63, 267–68, 306, 324–25, 336, 338
Doll's House, The, 38
Don, Alexander, 264
Donaldson, Melissa, 149n3
Donaldson, Roger, 2, 5–7, 9, 11–12, 135–51, 164–65, 169–70, 186, 190–91, 202, 219, 241, 285, 305, 312
Don Baretto and his Cuban Orchestra, 24
Donizetti, 131n9
Donovan, Martin, 297
Don't Let It Get You, ix, 4, 54, 62–64
Doone, Robert, 26
Dostoyevsky, Fyodor, 219
Douglas, Alistair, 307
Downstage Theatre Company, 169
Dracula (novel), 344
Dr Brunovski, 187
Dresden, 282
Dryburgh, Stuart, 296, 309
Drysdale, Russell, 259
Duff, Alan, 97, 172
Duggan, 221
Duncan, Carmen, 64
Dunedin, 48, 131n17, 219, 226–27, 292
Duration of a Kiss, The (short stories), 121

Dürer, Albrecht, 277
Durgnat, Raymond, 331
Dusky Sound, 225
Dutch, 91

E.T.: The Extra-Terrestrial, 141
Ealing comedies, x
Early Days Yet: A Profile of the Poet Allen Curnow, 262
East Timor, 73, 262
Easy Rider, 140
Ebert, Roger, 139
Edison Kinetograph, 15
Edmond, Martin, 207, 263, 265
Edwards, Frank, 239
Edwards, Sam, 3, 35–53
EEC (European Economic Community). *See* EU
Eel History Was a Mystery, 38
Eilbacher, Lisa, 162
Elam School of Fine Arts, 256, 305
Eliot, George, 208
Elizabeth II (queen), 121, 124, 324
Elliot, Tim, 156, 188
Elliott, Kate, 224
Ellitt, Jack, 20, 24–25
Elsaesser, Thomas, 140
Empire State Building, 331
End of the Golden Weather, The, 171–73
End of the Golden Weather, The (play), 172
Erebus, Mount, 170
Erewhon (novel), 253
Eruera, Clint, 174
ethnography, 58, 115
EU (European Union), 61, 67n19
Europe/European, 3–4, 6, 19, 21–22, 25, 32n27, 38, 60, 90–91, 95, 100, 140, 237, 274, 276–77, 279, 284, 289–90, 292, 296–97
European Common Market. *See* EU
Eurydice, 282
Evening Star (newspaper), 219
Evenstar Films, 314
Evison, Pat, 345
Exposure, 338

Fairburn, A. R. D., 241
fairy tale, 80–83, 277, 290

Falconer, Alun, 4, 54
Fallout, 170
family, 6, 36, 38, 44–45, 75, 142–43, 218, 221–27, 229–30, 239, 247, 275–76, 280, 282, 291, 293, 295, 299–301, 306, 322, 342
Family Fare Productions, 149n3
Family Life, 75
Fassbinder, Rainer Werner, 124, 127, 267
Fatal Attraction, 84
Feathers of Peace, The, 8, 88–89, 96–100
femininity/feminism, 2, 9–11, 38, 66, 72–85, 105, 113–14, 196, 242, 245, 289–301, 304, 306–7
Filmads, 19
Film Art (magazine), 22
Film Industry Working Party, 135
film noir, 164, 236, 244–45, 247, 299
Film of Real Time: A Light-Sound Environment, A, 256
Films in Review (magazine), 139
Finney, Edmund, 41
Fiordland, 225
Firth, Michael, 192
Firth, Tony, 44
Fischinger, Oskar, 24
Fisher, Toby, 179
Fitzcarraldo, 288n21
Five Easy Pieces, 140
Flaherty, Robert, 20
Flaming Creatures, 126
Flannery, Anne, 192
Fletcher, Norman, 94
Flip and Two Twisters, 254, 256, 262–63
flipbook, 19
Food for Thought, 62
Foolish Things, 9, 123, 126
Footstep Man, The, 10, 207–8, 256, 264–66
Forgotten Silver, 324–25, 329, 333n20
42nd Street, 323
forza del destino, La (opera), 128
Foster, Bruce, 261
Fourth Cinema, 90, 94
Fox, Derek, 257
Fox, Kerry, 245, 292
Fox, Michael J., 329
Foxton, 244

Fracture, 212
Frame, Janet, 6, 273, 289–90, 292–93, 300
France/French, 67n19, 220, 227, 237, 243, 265, 281
Francis, Alton, 48
Francis, Diane, 48
Frankenstein (novel), 274
Franz Josef glacier, 62
Freejack, 153, 162–63
Free Radicals, 27–28
Freiberg, Freda, 290
French Family in New Caledonia, A, 48
Friedrich, Caspar David, 264, 277, 280
Friendly Road, The (radio), 45
Freud, Sigmund, 19, 274–75, 280, 286n3, 295, 297
Frighteners, The, 320, 323, 329
Frock Attack! Wig Wars! Strategic Camp in Desperate Remedies (booklet), 269
Front Lawn, The, 205–6
Frontline, 195
Fry, Roger, 22
Fulbourn Hospital, 72
Fulford, Stephen, 172
Fuller, Graham, 327
futurist 19, 25

Gable, Clark, 145
Galipeau, Annie, 281
Game with No Rules, A, 211
Gandhi, 146
Gate (paintings), 317n12
Gauguin, Paul, 19
Gee, Maurice, 212
Geilgud, John, 242
Georgie Girl, 130n2
Germany/German/Germanic, 23–24, 56, 94–95, 156, 277, 280, 286n3, 287–88n21
Gerstner, David, 9, 121–33
Getaway, The, 147
Get Carter, 142
Getting to Our Place, 76
Gibson, Mel, 142, 145
Gillett, Sue, 298
Gilmore, Jackie, 307
Gilmour, Ian, 171

Ginna, Arnaldo 25
Girl's Own Story, A, 290, 293
Girven, Ross, 92
Gisborne, 110
Gluck, Sophie, 132n20
Glynn, Mike, 257
Gocke, Justin, 345
Godard, Jean-Luc, 60
God Boy, The, 170, 172
Godfather, The, 323
"God Defend New Zealand" (anthem), 110
Godzilla, 333n43
Gold Diggers of 1933, 323
Goldie, C. F., 313
Goldson, Annie, 66, 73, 130n2, 262
Goldwyn, Tony, 245
Gone Up North for a While, 67n25
Goodbye Pork Pie, 6, 123, 141, 152–57, 161–63, 172–73, 185, 202–3, 214n6, 236, 238, 322
Good Intentions (a.k.a. *Postcard from New Zealand*), 124
Goodwin, Neville, 45
Goodwin Sands, The, 48
Gordon, Phillip, 177, 178
Gordon, Stuart, 323
Gossage, Star, 98
Got a Moment, 64
Gothic, 9, 77, 223, 225, 230, 247, 274–75, 277–78, 286n2, 286n4, 290–91, 296, 301, 304, 310–13, 336, 339–40, 344
Govett-Brewster Art Gallery, 28, 256
GPO [General Post Office] film unit, 25–26, 32n32
Grace, Patricia, 90
Grant, Anaru, 174
Grant, Barry Keith, 11, 320–35
Grant, Richard E., 297
Grasscutter, The, 178–79, 231n4
Graur, Shirley, 154
Graves, Robert, 22
Great Day, A, 170
Great Railway Bazaar, The (novel), 241
Greek tragedy, 26
Green Dolphin Street, 128
Greenwich Village, 27

Gremlins, 326
Grey, George, 97
Greymouth, 72
Greystoke: The Legend of Tarzan, Lord of the Apes, 146
Grierson, John, 4, 25–26, 65
Grieve, Morrison, 261
Griffith, D. W., 18, 22, 44
Grives, Steven, 206, 265
Grünewald, Matthias, 277
Guardian (newspaper), 60
Guilford, Allen, 207, 265–66
Gung Ho: Rewi Alley of China, 262

Hall, Roger, 241
Hamilton, Linda, 148
Hamilton Talks, 45
Happy Moments, 27, 29
Harden, Marcia Gay, 304, 310, 312
Hardwick, Derek, 238, 339
Hardy, Ann, 78–80, 295
Hardy, Thomas, 124
Hargreaves, John, 222
Harper, Stanley, 244
Harrison, Craig, 193
Harrow, Lisa, 224
Harvest of Sunshine, 59
Hauraki Gulf, 180
"Have You Ever (Seen A Letterbox)" (song), 63
Hawai'i/Hawaiian, 58, 103
Hawke, Gary, 239, 241
Hawke, Joanne, 110, 117n32
Hawke, Joe, 110
Hawke, Piupiu, 110
Hawke, Sharon, 262
Hawkes Bay, 101n10
Hawkey, Bridget, 247
Hawkins, Kai, 207, 265
Hawthorne, Elizabeth, 224
Hayward, Hilda, 43
Hayward, Ramai Te Miha. *See* Ramai Te Miha
Hayward, Rudall, 3, 5–6, 15, 35–53
Headless Chickens, The, 310
Healey, Theresa, 309
Heart of the Stag, 10, 192–93, 231n4
Heath, Michael, 344

Heavenly Creatures, 11, 82, 231n4, 321–22, 324, 326, 328–329
Hedda Gabler (play), 204
Heiress, The, 209
Hell's Gate, 311
Hemmings, David, 229
Henenlotter, Frank, 323
Henson, Jim, 322–23
Hepworth, Barbara, 20
Herangi, Princess Te Puea, 104, 113–14, 116
Hercules: The Legendary Journeys, 212, 221
"Heroin" (song), 315
Hershey, Barbara, 297
Herzog, Werner, 287–88n21
Heyward, James, 112
Hibiscus Films, 310
Hight, Craig, 325
Hindle, Ann, 32n36
Hiroa, Te Rangi, 104
Hitchcock, Alfred, 131n13, 302n19, 309
Hoar, Stuart, 210
Hobbs, Katrina, 224
Hobbs, Rebecca, 211
Hodges, Mike, 142
Hoffman, Dustin, 143
Hokianga, 38, 60, 106
Holden, Stephen, 131n9
Holder, Philip, 177
Hold Up, 73
Hollywood, 2–3, 6, 11–12, 15, 44, 47, 100, 121, 126–27, 129, 136–41, 144–48, 164–65, 176, 201–2, 205, 237, 244, 254, 282–83, 285, 304–6, 310, 314, 317, 320–23, 329, 331
"Holly Holy" (song), 298
Holm, Ian, 328
Holy Smoke, 290–91, 298, 300
Homicide, 314
Hopkins, Anthony, 145
Hopkins and Weir, 20
Hopper, Dennis, 140, 314
Hopper, Edward, 227–28
Horrocks, Roger, 18–34, 106, 204, 258, 310, 337
Horrocks, Shirley, 262–63
horror, 9, 147, 222–23, 225, 230, 236, 247, 304, 306, 309–10, 321–26, 328–29, 332n16, 336, 338–40, 343–46
Hoskins, Bob, 228
Hotene, Tipene, 42
Hotere, 104, 115–16
Hotere, Ralph, 115–16
Hough, Richard, 145
Howard, Elizabeth Jane, 214n10
Howard, Trevor, 147
Hubert Church prize, 293
Hudson, Hugh, 146
Hulme, Juliet, 322
Hulme family, 326
Humble Force, The, 262
Hungarian, 258
Hunger, The, 344
Hunt, Tina, 42
Hunter, Holly, 11, 294, 314–15
Hunter, Matthew, 179
Huntington, Tom, 224
hurdes, Las (*Land without Bread*), 323
Hurley, Frank, 19
Hurrell, John, 29
Hurst, Michael, 128, 205, 209–10, 340
Hutchison, Kieren, 223

Ibsen, Henrik, 204
Ihimaera, Witi, 174
Ikin, Bridget, 204, 208
Ilam, 326
Ilam School of Fine Arts, 72, 257
I'll Make You Happy, 212
Illustrious Energy, 10, 172, 206, 256, 263–65
Imagine, 73, 75
Imbruglia, Natalie, 314
Imperial Airways, 26
I'm So Lonesome I Could Cry, 210
India, 291, 298
Indonesia, 73, 220
Industrial Light & Magic, 320
Inglis, Gary, 306
Inside New Zealand, 261
Inside Red China, 48
In Spring One Plants Alone, 273
International Cinema Festival, 25
In the Cut, 290, 299–300
Intolerance, 323

Inuit, 281
Invercargill, 154, 157
Ip, Harry, 264
I Paul to You at Ngatimote (painting), 317n12
Iris, 242
Irish, ix, 55, 58
Irwin, Kathie, 105
Italian Neorealism, 57, 220
Italy/Italian 25, 55, 57, 77, 220, 291, 297
It's Lizzie to Those Close, 9, 338–39
I Want to Be Joan, 67n25

Jack Be Nimble, 195–97, 231n4, 338, 343
Jackson, Peter, 1, 10–11, 82, 165, 180, 202, 213, 253–54, 320–35, 338
Jackson, Syd, 105
James, Henry, 296
James, Billy T., 177
Jancso, Miklos, 258
Japan/Japanese, 219–20, 227
Jarman, Derek, 124
jazz, 24
Jeanne Dielman, 23 Quai du Commerce, 1080 Bruxelles, 78
Jeffs, Christine, 12, 13n7, 169
Jemison, Anna, 142, 190
Jesson, Bruce, 106
Jesus' Son, 11, 304, 307, 313–17
Jesus' Son (short stories), 314
Jewel's Darl, 125, 208
JFK, 148
Joamie, Robert, 281
Johnson, Denis, 304, 314–15, 318n20
Johnson, Kelly, 154–55, 238
Johnson, Louis, 241
Johnston, Sheila, 143–44
Jones, Laura, 292
Jones, Oliver, 92
Jones, Rosy, 207
Jones, Stan, 169–84, 328
Jung, Carl, 327

Kaa, Canon Hone, 110
Kaa, Peter, 95
Kaa, Wi Kuki, 92, 156, 188
Kahukura Productions, 212
Kaingaroa State Forest, 57

Kaitaia, 157
Ka Mate! Ka Mate! 101n10
kammerfilm, 237
Karangahape Road, Auckland, 308
Karanga Hokianga, 103, 106
Kariotahi Beach, 219–20
Karitane, 246
Kavka, Misha, 130n9
Kay, Fiona, 275
Keitel, Harvey, 11, 296, 298
Keith, David, 342
Keith, Hamish, 339
Kemp, Philip, 172
Kennedy, Anne, 204, 310
Kennedy, John F., 148
Kenya, 257
Kerr, Bill, 275
Keskidee-Aroha, 106
Kidman, Nicole, 297
Kill or Be Killed, 26
Kimmel, Adam, 315
King, Michael, 66, 89, 96
King, Noel, 82
King Kong (1933), 310
King Kong (2005), 320, 331, 333n43
King Lear (play), 188
King Movement, 89
King of the Jews (painting), 317n12
King-Turner, Kirsty, 228
Kinleith 1981, 106
Kirikiri, Sonny, 98
Kitchen Sink, 304, 308–12
"kitchen sink" realism, 72, 304, 306
Knight, Stanley, 45
Koha, 117n9
Korean, 175
Kramer vs. Kramer, 143

Labour Party (NZ), 45, 170, 245–46, 307
Lagoon, The (short stories), 293
Laing, John, 4, 6–7, 204, 217–35
Laing, R. D., 75
Laing, Robin, 203, 214n11
Landa, Ishay, 327
Landfall, 260
Landfall (journal), 311
Lang, Fritz, 223
Lang, Kate, 265

Index

Langland, William, 287n20
Lanza, Mario, 329
Larsen, Erna, 177
Last Tattoo, The, 231n4, 236–37, 242, 244–48
Laughton, Charles, 145
Lawley, Yvonne, 78, 306
Lawrence, Bruno, 10, 135, 142–43, 152, 155, 157, 159, 163, 178–79, 185–200, 257, 339
Lawrence, Michael, 177
Lawrence of Arabia, 145
Leach, Paul, 258
Lealand, Geoff, 321
Lean, David, 145–46
Learning Fast, 73
Leary, Denis, 314
Leary, Leonard, 49n8
Leatherface, 326
Leave All Fair, 236–37, 242–44, 246, 248
Lee, Christopher, 327
Lee, Jason Scott, 281
LeGrice, Malcolm, 23
Leigh, Jennifer Jason, 299
Lemon, Genevieve, 293
Len Lye Foundation, 28, 262
Letch, David, 80
Lévi-Strauss, Claude, 58
Lewis, Al, 345
Life and Times of Rosie the Riveter, The, 77
Lifeforce, 344
Linda's Body, 205–7
Lion's Gate, 314
Listener, The (magazine), 310, 325
Little Queen, 121, 125
Little Shepherdesses, The, 48
Lloyd, Danny, 225
Lloyd, Frank, 145
Loach, Ken, 75–76
Locals, The, 13n7
Locke, Alan, 264
Loggia, Robert, 245
London, ix–x, 3, 20, 22, 67n11, 73–74, 85, 106, 220, 227, 241, 265, 336
London Film Festival, 337
London Film Society, 20–21
London Women's Film Group, 74

Longford, Raymond, 20, 36
Long Goodbye, The, 140
Long Good Friday, The, 228
Long Loop Home (memoir), 131n12
Lord of the Rings, The (trilogy), 1, 11, 82, 169, 180, 202, 212–13, 320, 327–29, 330–31
Lord of the Rings: The Fellowship of the Ring, The, 169, 327–28, 331
Lord of the Rings: The Return of the King, The, 1, 201
Lord of the Rings: The Two Towers, The, 327–28
Los Angeles, 1, 138, 265, 337
Los Angeles Times, 195
Lost Tribe, The, 217–18, 225–29
Louis, Joe, 48
Lounge Bar, 206
Lucas, George, 141
Lye, Len, 3–4, 15, 18–34, 253–54, 262–63
Lye, Phillip, 22, 28
Lymposs, Richard, 179
Lynch, David, 339
Lynskey, Melanie, 327
Lyons, Bruce, 278

Mack, Al, 44
Mackay, Yvonne, 10
Mackie, John, 45
Maclean, Alison, 2, 11, 85, 253–54, 304–19, 338
Macnab, Geoffrey, 338
Madama Butterfly (opera), 84
Mad Butcher, The, 308
Mad Max, 141
Mad Max II, 141–42, 144
Magnificent Ambersons, The, 267
Magnificent Seven, The, 164
Mahia Peninsula, ix, 56, 58
Main, Stewart, 9, 126–27, 129, 132n20, 208–10, 266–67
Maketu, 105
Makoare, Lawrence, 12, 13n7, 174
Malkovich, John, 297
Man Alone (novel), 60, 186–87
man alone, 60, 174, 185–200, 203, 213, 225, 240. *See also* masculinity

Mana Waka, 103–4, 106, 108, 114–16
Mangere Bridge, 111
Manila Film Festival, 192
Manley, R. G. H. (Jim), 113–15
Man of the Trees, 262
Man Ray, 25, 27
Mansfield, Katherine, 38, 241–44, 246
Maori, ix, 3, 5, 8, 18, 22, 35–36, 38–43, 45, 47–49, 55–58, 60, 62–63, 76, 78, 88–100, 101n17, 103, 120, 127, 142, 153, 155–56, 159, 174–76, 180, 187–88, 194, 196, 225–26, 229, 260, 295, 310–13, 317n15, 318n16
Maori art, 19, 21, 64
Maori filmmaking, 2, 8–9, 88–102, 103–20, 203, 261
"Maori Hula Medley" (song), 306
Maori Land March, 257
Maori language, 162, 261
Maori Maid's Love, A, 36
Maori politics, 261, 307
Map of the Human Heart, 273, 280–81, 284
March of Time, The, 26
Marie, 146
Marlborough, 238–39
Married, 75, 78
Martin, Ben, 295
Martin, Helen, 10, 101n10, 205, 256–72, 280
Marx, Karl, 19
masculinity, 6–7, 9–10, 15, 39, 44, 121–24, 131n10, 136, 142–43, 145, 153–56, 161–63, 174–75, 185, 188, 191–93, 196, 197n1, 203, 236, 242, 245, 298, 325–26
Mason, Bruce, 171
Masterton, 244
Matthews, John, 28
Maunder, Paul, 66, 67n25, 220, 260
Mauri, 8, 103–4, 108, 111, 113
Maxwell, Garth, 126, 195
Maynard, John, 204, 207–8, 257, 266
Mazursky, Paul, 140
McCabe and Mrs. Miller, 140
McCahon, Colin, 60, 67n17, 253, 311, 313, 317n12
McCarron, Deidre, 60

McCarten, Deidre, 67n25
McCauley, Sue, 229
McDermott, Thomas, 42
McDonald, Ginette, 273, 286n1
McDonald, Lawrence, 228, 322, 326
McDonnell, Brian, 176, 323
McFarlane, Hamish, 278
McGillis, Kelly, 224
McGlashan, Don, 205
McGraw, Ali, 147
McHugh, Kathleen, 295, 300
McKegg, Dorothy, 239, 241, 246
McKenzie, Midge, 74
McLachlan, Craig, 224
McLaren, Norman, 25, 32n30
McQueen, Steve, 147
Meet the Feebles, 11, 321–23
Meisner, Gunter, 95
Melbourne, Hirini, 113, 116
melodrama, 9–10, 20, 38–41, 44, 47, 77, 83, 126–27, 174, 176, 178–79, 208–9, 218, 231, 266–67
Memory and Desire, 13n7
Merchant Ivory Productions, 129
Mercy Peak, 221
MerGer Productions, 108
Merito, Gerry, 63
Merleau-Ponty, Maurice, 126
Mete-Kingi, Lee 78
Metro (magazine), 179
Mexico, 164, 175, 177
Meyerhold Theater, 19
MGM (Metro-Goldwyn-Mayer), 128, 145
Middle Age Spread, 6, 73, 236–37, 241–42, 246, 248
Middle Age Spread (play), 241
Middle East, 297
Middlemarch (novel), 124, 208
Mighty Civic, The, 67n25, 126
Mighty Joe Young, 333n43
Mildenhall, Joanne, 240, 246
Milestone, Lewis, 145
Miller, George, 141
Miller, Toby, 82
Mills, Kiri, 128, 209
Mindout, 73
Ministry of Information (UK), 26

Miracle of the Pine: An Epic of Industry, The, 38
Mirams, Gordon, 55–56
Mirams, Roger, ix, 4, 54–59, 220
Miró, Joan, 23
miscegenation, 41–42
Mita, Merata, 8–9, 12, 16, 90, 103–20, 156, 260–62
Moana, 20
modernism/modernist, 19–20, 22–23, 123–24, 132n23, 220, 237, 292, 311, 313
Monk, Claire, 131n13
Montana Sunday Theatre, 325
Montreal, 220, 227, 281–82, 284
Monty Python, 177
Moody's Pub (painting), 259
Moonrise, 337, 344–46
Moore, Henry, 20
Moore, Susanna, 299
Morehu, Warwick, 174
Moren, Armitage, 45
Moriori, 96–100
Moriori: A People Rediscovered, 96
Morrieson, Ronald Hugh, 176
Morris, Elizabeth, 211
Morris, Graham, 262
Morrison, Bruce, 219
Morrison, Howard, 62
Morrison, Joanna, 223
Morrison, Robin, 261
Morrison, Temuera, 12, 162, 172, 175–76
Mortensen, Viggo, 297
Morton, Samantha, 315
Moscow, 19
Mount Eden, 110
Moverman, Oren, 314
Movietone News, 56
Moynihan, 170
Mr Wrong, 9, 72–73, 80–81, 203, 214n10, 304
Muldoon, Robert, 222
Mulgan, John, 60, 186
Mulheron, Danny, 232n34
Mune, Ian, 7, 12, 142, 149n3, 169–84, 187, 238, 328
Munz, Peter, 55

Muppet Show, The, 323
Murphy, Geoff, 2, 5–7, 9, 12, 112, 135–36, 138, 141, 149n3, 152–68, 172, 185, 187, 193–95, 198n2, 203, 219, 236, 238, 257, 285, 322
Murray, Scott, 138, 147
Murray, Stuart, 1–13, 8, 35–53, 88–102
Museum of Modern Art, The (US), 31, 139
Museum of New Zealand Te Papa Tongarewa, 76
music, 24, 28, 205, 239, 259
musicals, 23, 62–63, 204, 323
music video, 13n7, 24, 73, 304, 314
Mutch, Karl, 106–7
Mutiny of the Bounty, The, 36
Mutiny on the Bounty, The, 145
My First Suit, 208
My Lady of the Cave, 5, 20, 39, 41, 44
Mysterious Island, 221

N. or N.W., 32n32
Nadel, Alan, 296
Naficy, Hamid, 180
Napier, 37, 72, 126, 132n18
Napier, Marshall, 177, 229
Napier: Newest City on the Globe, 67n25, 126, 267
Narbey, Leon, 10, 108, 206–7, 219, 254, 256–72
National Film Board (Canada), 25, 220
National Film Theatre (UK), 85
National Film Unit (NFU), 4, 15, 48, 55, 65, 85, 219–20, 225, 262, 330
National Party (NZ), 246
Native American, 27, 158
naturalism, 129
Naughty Little Peeptoe, 126
Navigator: A Mediaeval Odyssey, The, 169, 273–74, 277–84, 286, 322
Nazism, 25, 327
Near Dark, 344
Neglected Miracle, The, 88, 90–91
Negus, Arthur, 220
Neill, Sam, 12, 55, 83, 142, 185–87, 197, 203, 208, 220, 295
Nelson, 296
Nelson Golf Club, 67n17

neorealism, 258
Never Say Die, 152–53, 161–63, 231n4
Newey, Murray, 179
New Frontier: The Story of Kawerau, 57
New Line Cinema, 320, 327
Newman, Kim, 322
New Plymouth, 28, 55
news/newsreels, 15, 26, 37, 48, 57, 77
Newspaper Train, 26
New York, 26–29, 31, 262, 299–300, 305, 331
New York Times, 139, 192, 328
New Zealand Academy of Fine Arts, 19
New Zealand Broadcasting Company, 170
New Zealand Film Archive (NZFA), 29, 94, 113
New Zealand Film Commission (NZFC), 1, 6, 8, 28, 123, 135–36, 138, 179–80, 191, 203, 236, 307, 310, 336
New Zealand Film Guild, 48n8
New Zealand: Gift of the Sea, 242
New Zealand Gofta Awards, 195
New Zealand House (UK), 85
New Zealand On Air, 262
New Zealand Railways, 210
New Zealand Wars, 35, 41, 126, 155, 158–59
New Zealand Wars, The, 41
Ng, James, 264
Ngarimu, Katy (Kay), ix, 58
Ngaruawahia, 114
Ngata, Apirana, 104
Nga Tamatoa, 8, 88, 105
Ngati, 8, 88–89, 91–94, 96–97, 99, 101n10
Ngati Apa, 8
Ngati Mutunga, 96–98
Ngati Pikiao, 116n1
Ngati Porou, 88, 93–94, 104
Ngati Tama, 96–99
Ngati Whatua, 8, 107, 260
Nicaragua, 91
Nicholas, Gregor, 202, 204
Nichols, Bill, 54, 107, 324
Nichols, Mike, 146
Nicholson, Ben, 20

Nicholson, Jack, 194, 225
Night Mail, 26
Night Porter, The, 142
No One Can Hear You, 217, 222–24, 227–28, 232n17
Normal Love, 126
Norma Rae, 146
North and South (magazine), 176
Northern Ireland, 179
Northland Panels (painting), 317n12
No Trouble, 22
No Way Out, 146–47
Noyce, Phillip, 137
Nunuku's law, 98
Nutcase, 149n3, 231n4

Oates, Warren, 142
Oberman, Claire, 154
Oedipus (play), 122, 204
O'Gorman, Dean, 12, 13n7
Once Were Warriors, 11, 97, 171, 173–74, 231n4
One That Got Away, The (play), 205, 214n20
Onfilm (trade journal), 88
On the Friendly Road, 45
OPEC (Organization of Petroleum Exporting Countries), 142
opera, 64, 84, 126–28, 130n8
Opera House, Auckland, 15
Opo: The Amazing Dolphin of Opononi, 38, 48
Orakau, 41, 47
O'Regan, Tom, 331
Orlando, 82
Ormond, Tom, 56
Orpheus, 282
Orpheus in the Underworld (opera), 284
Orwell, George, 73
Oscars. *See* Academy Awards
O'Shea, John, ix, 4–5, 15, 35, 54–71, 73, 89, 220
Otago, 263–64
Other Halves, 6, 217–18, 224, 227, 229
Our Oldest Soldier, 338
Owen, Rena, 12
Owls Do Cry (novel), 291

Pacific/Pacific Islanders, 19, 23, 29, 55, 57, 73, 103, 106, 140, 219
Pacific Films, 4–5, 8, 54–55, 64, 73, 89, 220, 257
Paekakariki, 244
Page, Greg, 12, 13n7
Painted Lady, The, 211
Pakula, Alan, 140
Pal, George, 23
Palmerston North, 55
Pangaru, 106
Pansy, 131n12
Papps, Stephen, 172
Papua New Guinea, 19
Paquin, Anna, 294
Paratene, Rawiri, 174–76
Parillaud, Anne, 281
Paris, 21, 56, 207, 265
Paris Exposition, 32n27
Paris International Science Fiction and Fantasy Film Festival, 337
Parker, Bill 56
Parker, Christine, 13n7
Parker, Dean, 176
Parker, Pauline, 322
Parr, Larry, 212
Particles in Space, 28
Passionless Moments, 290
Patterson, Janet, 296
Patu! 8, 103–4, 106–11, 262
Paul, Susan Ramiri, 112
Peanut Vendor, a.k.a. *Experimental Animation*, 23
Pearls and Savages, 19
Peckinpah, Sam, 147
Peel, 290, 295
Peer Gynt (opera), 284
Peirse, Sarah, 339
Peppard, George, 197
Perfect Creature, 13n7
Perfect Strangers, 12, 13n7, 73–74, 78, 81–84
Performance, 75
Perrault, Charles, 81
Perry, Nick, 221
Peru, 91
Peters, Geraldene, 8, 103–20
Pewhairangi, Connie, 92

Phase Three Films, 259
Philadelphia, 314
Phillips, Jock, 44, 186, 196, 332n17
Piano, The, 11, 82–83, 236, 290–91, 294–97, 300
Picnic, 219
Picnic at Hanging Rock, 129
Picture Palace, Auckland, 126
Piercy, Perry, 80
Piers Plowman (novel), 287n20
Piers Plowman (poem), 284
Pilcher, Leo, 47
Pilgrim's Progress, The (prose allegory), 284
Pilisi, Mark, 224
Pillsbury, Sam, 219–20, 285
Platoon, 323
Playing Safe in Small Boats, 48
Pleasures and Dangers, 262
Plunket, 246
Poata, Tama, 92
Pohlmann, Gerd, 108, 260, 262
Pohutu Geyser, 313
Point Chevalier, 121
Polan, Dana, 301n3
Poland/Polish, 258
police (NZ), 190–91, 222–23, 229–30, 233n41, 247, 260, 342, 345
Polynesia, 3, 57–58, 179
Ponsonby, 73
Pope, Caelem, 211
Portrait of a Lady, The, 290–92, 296–98, 300
Potter, Sally, 82
Pound, Ezra, 19
Powell, Michael, 209
Practice of Everyday Life, The, 78
Pressberger, Emeric
Preston, Gaylene, 4, 9–12, 16, 55, 72–87, 166n11, 202–3, 213, 214n10, 219–20, 244, 264, 304
Pretty Mary, 64
Price of Milk, The, 13n7, 206
Protestant, 186
Proust, Marcel, 123–24, 132n18
Pryme, Lew, 63
Psycho, 309
public information films, 54

Puccini, Giacomo, 84
Pukekawa, 221–22
Pukekohe, 222
Pukemanu, 170
Punitive Damage, 73, 262
puppetry, 23
Pye, Katie, 295
Pye, Tim 295

Quebec, 179
Queenstown, 179
Queen Street, Auckland, 307
queer cinema, 2, 9, 121–33, 195, 208, 266–67
Quiet Earth, The, 10, 111, 152–53, 159–64, 193–95, 322

Race for the Yankee Zephyr, 197, 221
radio, 45, 107, 187, 307–8, 344
Radio Hauraki, 261
Radio Pacific, 308
Raetihi, 257, 259
Rafelson, Bob, 140
Raiders of the Lost Ark, 141
Raimi, Sam, 323
Rain, 13n7, 169, 231n4
Rainbow Dance, 26, 29
Rains, Stephanie, 6, 273–88
Rambo, 163
Rambo, John, 163
Rameka, Roger, 108
Ranfurly Shield, 238
Rare, Vanessa, 78
Rayner, Jonathan, 6, 152–68, 279, 283
Read, Melanie, 10, 203
realism/realist, 57, 62, 73, 75, 78, 81, 112, 123, 132n23, 142, 176, 227, 257–58, 304, 306
Realist Film Unit, 26
Recruit, The, 12
Red Blooded American Girl, 337, 344
Red Blooded American Girl II, 337, 341–43
Redford, Jennifer, 339
Red Psalm, 258
Red Shoes, The, 209
Red Skirts on Clydeside, 77
Reed, Lou, 314–15

Rees, Donogh, 211, 311, 313
Regan, Mary, 192, 305
Regin, Nadja, 61
Reid, John, 6–7, 55, 73, 219, 236–50
Reid, Melanie, 304
Reid, Nicholas, 176
Rekohu. *See* Chatham Islands
Renaissance Pictures, 212
Resnais, Alain, 60
Reuben, Faenza, 158
Rewi's Last Stand (1925), 41–42, 45
Rewi's Last Stand (1940), 41, 47–48
Reynolds, Harrington, 20, 36–37
Reynolds, Scott, 211
Rhodesia, 257
Richter, Hans, 22
Rickard, Eva, 111–13
Ricordi! (play), 130
Riding, Laura, 22
Riff-Raff, 75
Rimmer, Jodie, 212
Ritchie, Neville, 264
Ritchie, Ross, 265
Ritt, Martin, 146
River Queen, 273
road movie, 140, 154, 164, 172, 341
road safety films, 55
Road Warrior, The. See Mad Max II
Robbins, Tim, 147
Roberts, Julia, 179
Robinson, David, 177
Robinson, Helen, 131n10
Robinson, Mary, 247
Robson, Greer, 142, 187, 190
Rocha, Glauber, 321
Roche, 221
Roddick, Nick, 139, 143, 190
Rodgers, Ilona, 156, 188
Roeg, Nicholas, 75
Romanticism/Romantic, 277, 279–80, 283, 285, 288n21
Rome, 219
Rome International Fantasy Film Festival, 195
Romero, George A., 323
Room One, 256
Room Two, 256
Roosevelt, Eleanor, 48

Roscoe, Jane, 325
Rossellini, Roberto, 57
Rossini, Gioacchino, 64
Rotondo, Paolo, 211
Rotorua, 42, 62–64, 310–11, 313
Routledge, Alison, 159, 194
Rowe, Nevan, 149n3
Rowlands, Gena, 74
Royal Academy of Dramatic Art, 67n11
Royal Albert Hall (Auckland), 36
Royal Shakespeare Company, 170
Ruapehu, Mount, 73
Rubber Gun, The, 220
Ruby and Rata, 9, 75, 78–79
Rudall Hayward Award, 180
Rudd's New Selection, 36
Rud's Wife, 304–7
Rueschmann, Eva, 11, 289–303
Ruffalo, Mark, 299
Runaway, 4–5, 54, 60–61
Russell, Ken, 124, 127
Russian Revolution, 19
Ryan, Meg, 299
Rymer, Judy, 203

Salin, Kari, 342
Samoa, 19–20, 22
Sanderson, Martyn, 152, 187, 222, 245
Sands of Iwo Jima, The, 244
San Francisco, 209
Santa Barbara, 126
Sargeson, Frank, 170, 198n6
Sayle, Jane, 80
Scarfies, 233n39
Schafer, William J., 275
Scheffmann, Dorthe, 211
Schembri, Jim, 146
Schrader, Paul, 140
Schwieters, Brett, 175
science fiction, 147, 159, 164, 193–94, 310, 322
Sciorra, Annabella, 279
Scorsese, Martin, 140, 147
Scotland/Scottish, 229, 294
Scott, Cecil, 44
Scott, Sir Walter, 277
Scream (trilogy), 222, 232n17
Scrimgeour, Reverend Colin, 45

Scrine, Gil, 257
sculpture, 21, 27–28, 115, 262–63, 305
Seacliffe Hospital, 264
Seattle, 222
2nd New Zealand Division, 55
Sedgwick, Charles, 264
Seeing Red, 66
Seinfeld, 314
Seizin Press, 22
Self, David, 148
Selwyn, Don, 177, 229
Senso, 209
Seresin, Michael, 55
Sergent, Brian, 228, 232n34
Seven and Five Society, 20
Seven Deadly Sins, 314
Sex and the City, 314
Shaker Run, 231n4
Shakespeare, William, 243
Sharman, Jim, 336
Sharpeville, 109
Shaw, George Bernard, 37
Sheehan, Lucy, 307
Shelley, Mary, 274
Shell Oil, 26
Shelton, Lindsay, 138
Shields, Gordon, 275
Shining, The, 225
Shining with the Shiner, 177
Shirt, The (1998), 232n34
Shirt, The (1999), 217–18, 220, 227–29, 231n3
Shock Treatment, 336
Shoreline, 73
short films, 9–11, 13n7, 15–16, 38–39, 44, 73, 88, 121, 123–24, 187, 205–6, 208, 210, 219–20, 232n34, 256, 273, 283, 304–5, 336
Should I Be Good? 232n39
siapo, 19, 29, 31n6. *See also* tapa
Sight and Sound (magazine), 26, 148
Silence of the Lambs, The, 211, 323
Silent One, The, 111
Silkwood, 146
Silver, Ron, 161
Simmons, Laurence, 4, 54–71, 330
Sinclair, Harry, 12, 13n7, 205–6, 328
Singin' in the Rain, ix

Sinking of the Rainbow Warrior, The, 197
Sitges International Film Festival, 210
Si'ulepa, Nikki, 197
Skin Deep, 256, 257–60
Sleeping Dogs, 6, 123, 138–39, 141–44, 149n3, 154, 169–70, 186, 231n4, 236, 257–58, 322
Smash Palace, 6, 10, 123, 138–47, 149n3, 163, 185, 187, 190–93, 312, 231n4
Smith, Allan Lloyd, 287n4
Smith, Beaumont, 36
Smith, Jack, 126
Smith, Jo, 180
Smith, Kevin, 128, 205, 209
Smith, Patrick, 131n13
Smith, Peter, 159, 174–75, 194
Smith, Roy, 325
Smuts-Kennedy, Sarah, 196, 265
Snakeskin, 13n7
Some of My Best Friends Are Women, 67n25
Son of the Sheik, 302n19
Sontag, Susan, 332n14
Sotheran, Cheryll, 77
South Africa, 8, 108–9, 239, 257, 261
South America, 90–91
Southern Alps, 62, 179
South Pacific Pictures, 88
South Pacific Television, 261
Soweto, 109
Species, 147
Spellbound, 302n19
Spicer, Andrew, 10, 185–200
Spielberg, Steven, 141, 326
Spooked, 12
Springbok rugby tour, 108–10, 239, 261–62
Squeeze, 131n9
St. Albans School of Art, 72
Standring, Glenn, 12, 13n7
Stark, Frank, 204
Starr, Ringo, 220
Star Wars, 141, 331
Star Wars: The Phantom Menace, 173
State, The, Dunedin (movie theater), 219
State of Siege, A, 273, 283
State of Siege, A (novel), 6
Steiger, Rod, 245

Stephens, Jeremy, 339
Steven, Geoff, 203, 219, 256–57, 259–60, 261–62, 305
Stevens, Liz, 212
Stevens, Peter, 204–5
Stewart, Penelope, 275
Stiliardis, Nicholas, 337
Stoker, Bram, 344
Stoltenberg, Hans, 25
Stone, Oliver, 148
Storck, Henri, 25
Strange Behaviour, 343
Strata, 259–60, 305
Studio des Ursulines, 21
suburban/suburbia, 78–79, 82, 238, 279, 293, 326, 339, 341
SUBWAY Stories: Tales from the Underground, 314
Sumatran, 325
Sundance (television channel), 262
Sundance Film Festival, 310
Sundance Institute, 310
surreal/surrealism, 72, 81–82, 290, 297, 299, 304–6, 308–11, 315, 317, 337, 339
Survey, 187
Sweetie, 10, 82, 85, 289–91, 293–94, 298, 300
Sydney, 10, 19–20, 23, 64, 124, 131n13, 289
Sydney College of the Arts, 289
Sylvia, 13n7
Szusterman, Jeffrey, 228

Tahitian, 96, 145–46, 324
Tainui, 106, 113, 115
Tait, Peter, 308–9
Takaparawha (Bastion Point), 8, 107–8, 111, 260
Takapuna Scandal, A, 44
Takle, Emma, 225
Talkback, 304–5
Tamahori, Lee, 11–12, 97, 173, 236
Tamati, Tuta Ngarimu, 94
Tangata Whenua, 8, 66, 89–90, 99
Tank Busters, 187
Tanzania, 257
tapa, 23, 29, 31n6. See also *siapo*

Index

Taranaki, 96–97, 273
Tarawa, 248
Tarkovsky, Andrei, 279
Tarzan, 146
Taste of Kiwi, A, 124
Taunt, 304–6, 317
Te Arawa, 8, 105, 116n1
Te Atairangikaahu, Maori Queen Te Arikinui, 113
Te Awa Marama, 101n10
Te Awamutu, 41
Technicolor, 26
Te Hapua, 257
Te Iwi, 47
Te Kanawa, Kiri, 62, 64
Te Kooti, 110
Te Kooti Trail, The, 5, 42–43, 45
television, ix, 8, 11, 27, 54, 66, 73, 75–76, 85n7, 88–89, 105–6, 121, 124, 130n3, 143, 164, 170, 173–74, 177, 179, 185, 187, 194, 201, 203–4, 212, 217, 221, 244, 256–57, 261, 262–63, 289, 291, 305–6, 313–14, 323–24, 338
Te Makakite O Aotearoa, 257, 261
Temara, Hema, 113
Te Miha, Ramai, 37–38, 47–48, 117n3
Tennessee Parole Board, 146
Te Pahu, 113
Te Poho o Rawiri, 110
Te Rangi, Te Pairi Tu, 42
Terminator, The, 148
terrorism, 327, 329
Terry, Sonny, 27
Te Rua, 8, 88–89, 94–97, 101n17
Teshigahara, Hiroshi, 309
Te Ua, 110
Te Urewera, 90–91
Te Wheke, 188
Te Whiti, 110
Texas Chainsaw Massacre, The, 326
Thatcher, Margaret, 75
theater, 111, 121, 124, 130n1, 187, 201–5, 208, 289
Theatre Corporate Drama School, 204–5
Theatre in Education, 204
Theroux, Paul, 241
They Say We Let Them Down, 257

3rd New Zealand Division, 55
Thirteen Days, 148
This Valley, 59
Thomas, Arthur, 222
Thomas, Jeffrey, 229
Thompson, Jane, 32
Thompson, Kirsten Moana, 11, 304–19
Thompson, Kristin, 331
Thomson, David, 140
thriller, 77, 179, 203, 218, 221, 231, 299, 305–6, 338
Tibble, Michael, 94
Tilly, Grant, 238, 241, 328
Timber for All Time, 57
Times (London newspaper), 177
Tina, Miss, 41
Tincknell, Estella, 9, 72–87
Tobeck, Joel, 12, 13n7, 83
Todd, Helen, 73
Tolkien, J. R. R., 327–28, 331
To Love a Maori, 6, 48–49, 117n3
Tonga, 58
Toomath, William, 132n23
Topless Women Talk about Their Lives, 13n7, 206
"Torn" (song), 314
Toronto, 227
Toronto Film Festival, 310
Toulouse-Lautrec, Henri de, 206, 265–66
tourist/tourism, 45, 62, 219, 227, 241–42, 310–11, 313, 328
Towards Auckland (painting), 317n12
Town and Country Players, The, 204
Toy Love, 206
Trade Tattoo, 26
Transformers, The, 262
Traviata, La (opera), 243
Treaty of Rarotonga, 160
Treaty of Waitangi, 113–14, 307
Trespasses, 231n4
Trial Run, 203, 214n9, 304
Tristes tropiques, 58
Trotting, 219
Tsoulis, Athina, 212
tuberculosis, 281
Turner, Lana, 124, 128
Turner, Stephen, 99
Turney, Andrew, 309

Tusalava, 4, 20–24, 29
Tuteao, Calvin, 99
TVNZ (Television New Zealand), 257, 261–62, 307, 325
Tyler, Andy, 261

U.S. Cavalry, 158
Ugly, The, 211, 338, 343
Undercover, 232n39
Under Siege 2, 153, 163
UNESCO, 55, 67n13
United Kingdom, x, 15, 18, 27, 35, 37, 41, 47–48, 58, 60–62, 65, 67n19, 72, 85, 96–98, 121, 124, 156, 159, 179–80, 205, 217, 220, 237, 291, 310
United States, 3, 11, 18, 26–28, 35, 58, 62, 91, 103, 121, 127, 137–42, 144, 146, 153–54, 159–65, 177, 180, 193, 201, 205, 222, 227, 236–37, 241, 244–46, 248, 254, 259, 262, 275, 289, 291, 297–98, 307, 310, 312, 314, 320–23, 325, 329, 331, 332n4, 333n25, 337–38
Universal Pictures, 333n43
University of Auckland, 256, 258, 336
University of Canterbury, 72, 257
University of Otago, 219
Urban, Karl, 12
Urrutia, David, 314
Utu, 111, 152–53, 155–59, 161–64, 166n11, 187–90, 193

Valley of Dry Bones, The (painting), 67n17
Vanguard Films, 108
Variety (trade paper), 139, 147, 177, 337
Vathek (novel), 274
Velvet Underground, The, 315
Vemiere, James, 130n9
venereal disease, 246
Venice Film Festival, 25, 291
Verdi, Giuseppi, 124, 128, 131n9
Vertigo, 302n19
Victorian, 19, 290, 296–97
Victoria University, Wellington, 55, 289
Victoria University College, 55
Victory over Death 2 (painting), 317n12
video, 23, 54, 179, 257, 337–38
Vietnam, 139

Vigil, 6, 93, 101n12, 169, 231n4, 273, 275–77, 279–81, 283, 285
Visconti, Luchino, 124, 209
Visible Evidence, 262
Visual Symphonies, 273
Voight, Jon, 197
Von Sydow, Max, 282
Von Tempsky, Gustavus, 47

Waihirere, 110
Waikato, 47, 115, 219, 89
Waikato (river), 222
Waimarama, 152, 257
Waipiro Bay, 94
Waitangi Bill, 308
Wakatipu, Lake, 179
Wake, 66
Walk Short, 206
Walker, Paul, 132n23
Wallace, Anzac, 111–12, 155, 188
Wallace, Sam, 211
Walpole, Horace, 274
Walsh, Raoul, 244
Walters, Bunny, 258
Walton, Priscilla, 291, 297
Wanda, 74
Wanganui, 55, 157
Wanganui Technical College, 55
Ward, Derek, 339
Ward, Vincent, 2, 5–6, 93, 169, 253, 273–88, 322
Ward-Lealand, Jennifer, 10, 127–28, 201–16, 265–66
War Game, The, 75
War Stories Our Mothers Never Told Us, 9, 73, 76–77, 244
Warhol, Andy, 75, 124
Warner Bros., 48
Watkin, Ian, 149n3
Watkins, Peter, 75
Weatherly, David, 343
Webb, Evan, 262–63
Weekly Review (NFU), 65
Weir, Peter, 137, 140
Welles, Orson, 267
Wellington, x, 28, 55–56, 59, 67n11, 76, 89, 108, 128, 157, 169, 205, 219–20, 225, 227, 236, 238–39, 240, 242,

Wellington (*continued*)
  244, 257, 289, 322
Wellington Film Society, 55
Wellington Film Society Bulletin, 55
Wellington Fringe Film Festival, 322
Wellington Hospital, 58
Wellington Technical College, 19
Wells, Peter, 9, 16, 66, 67n25, 107, 121–
  33, 208–10, 266–67
Wells, Russell, 132n19
Welsh Theatre Company, 169
West, Helen, 39
West, T. J., 36
western, 43, 157–59, 162–65, 177, 187,
  322
West Indies, 117n8
WETA (WingNut Effects &
  Technological Allusions Ltd.), 320
Whakarewarewa, 62, 310
Whakatane Films, 43
Whale Rider, 13n7, 88, 176, 213, 231n4
Whanganui (river), 273
What Becomes of the Broken Hearted?
  13n7, 171, 173–76
What Dreams May Come, 273, 277–80,
  282–85
When the Pie Was Opened, 26
White, Robin, 259
White House (US), 148
Whitehouse, A. H., 15
White Sands, 147
Whitten, Frank, 275
Whole of the Moon, The, 178, 180
Whose School? 73
Who Will Be a Statistic? 64
Wilde, Oscar, 124
Wild Man, 6, 152–53, 157, 162, 185, 187
Williams, Hank, 210
Williams, Mark, 7
Williams, Robin, 147, 279, 285
Williams, Tony, 55
Wilmington, Michael, 280

Wilton, Caren, 163
WingNut Films, 320
Winners and Losers, 170, 174, 177
Winslet, Kate, 298, 327
Winters, Kristoffer Ryan, 341–42
Winter's Tale, A (play), 243
Witheford, Hubert, 55
With the Headhunters in Papua, 31n4
Wolverhampton, 36
Woman of Good Character, A, 337
Woman of the Dunes, 309
Wonders of China, 48
Wood, Elijah, 330
Wood, Helena, 98
Wood, Robin, 324
Work Party, 26
*World Is Turning (Towards the Coloured
  People), The*, 48
World's Fastest Indian, The, 12, 148
World Trade Center, 328
World War I, 338
World War II, 57, 77, 121, 224–25, 240,
  242, 281–82, 284, 327, 329
Wren, Doug, 324
Wright, Mark, 210
Wuthering Heights (novel), 295
Wyler, William

Xena: Warrior Princess, 212, 221

You Are the Jury, 64
Young Albanians, The, 38
Young, Burt, 342
Young Guns II, 153, 164
Youth at the Wheel, 64

Zambia, 257
Zappa, William, 311
Zemeckis, Robert, 320
Zilch! 231n4
Zimbabwe, 257
Zorro, 177

www.ingramcontent.com/pod-product-compliance
Lightning Source LLC
Chambersburg PA
CBHW070232240426
43673CB00044B/1762